W9-BZB-655

BLINDSIDE

BLINDSIDE

Why Japan Is Still on Track to
Overtake the U.S. by the Year 2000

Eamonn Fingleton

HOUGHTON MIFFLIN COMPANY
BOSTON • NEW YORK

For information about permission to reproduce
selections from this book, write to Permissions,
Houghton Mifflin Company, 215 Park Avenue South,
New York, New York 10003.

Library of Congress Cataloging-in-Publication Data
Fingleton, Eamonn.
    Blindside: why Japan is still on track to overtake
the U.S. by the year 2000 / Eamonn Fingleton.
        p.   cm.
    Includes bibliographical references and index.
    ISBN 0-395-63316-8 ᵬ⟁ 27.50|14.96 5|96
        1. Japan — Economic conditions — 1989–
2. Economic forecasting — Japan. 3. Industries —
Japan. 4. United States — Economic conditions —
1981–   5. Economic forecasting — United States.
6. Industries — United States.   I. Title.
HC462.95.F56 1995
330.952 — dc20   94-44958   CIP

Printed in the United States of America

MP 10 9 8 7 6 5 4 3 2

Book design by Robert Overholtzer

Contents

A Note on the Japanese Language

To facilitate the pronunciation of the Japanese words mentioned in this book, here are some basic rules for pronouncing the Japanese language.

a as in c*a*r
e as in t*e*n
i as in sk*i*
o as in m*o*re
u as in R*u*mania
ai as in *ai*sle
au as in b*au*h*au*s (or as ow in c*ow*)
ei as in r*ei*ndeer
ou as in th*ou*gh
ch as in *Ch*ina
g as in *g*o
s as in *s*ee
y as in *y*oung

Other letters are pronounced as in English.

It is important to remember that, whereas English is written in letters, the basic unit of written Japanese is the syllable. Generally each syllable is given approximately equal weight in pronunciation. Take, for instance, *konnichiwa*, which means hello. The pronunciation is kon-ni-chi-wa. Similarly *sayonara*, meaning good-bye, is pronounced sa-yo-na-ra. In general every syllable is sounded. The Japanese rice wine *sake*, for instance, is pronounced sa-ke.

For English speakers, one of the many peculiarities of Japanese is that it does not generally have separately designated plurals. Thus the plural of *samurai* is *samurai*. In this book I treat important terms of Japanese business life as English words and give them English plurals. Thus the plural of *keiretsu* will be rendered *keiretsus*.

Like other East Asian languages, Japanese usually places people's given names after their family names. In accordance with the practice of the Western press, however, I present these Japanese names in Western order, given name first.

BLINDSIDE

1

Sayonara, Capitalism

Anyone who looks at the record notices a striking pattern: the West always seems to underestimate Japan. Some systematic flaw in Western psychology leads Westerners, and particularly Americans, to exaggerate Japan's weaknesses and belittle its strengths.

Few Americans other than historians of Japanese economics realize quite how consistent this pattern is. Although anecdotes about American corporations being caught off-guard by fast-moving Japanese competitors are part of American corporate folklore, Americans have tended to blame such disasters not on flaws in American psychology but on the exceptional incompetence of a few supposed "dinosaurs" of American business. The truth is that such experiences are the rule rather than the exception in America's many-faceted relationship with Japan. America's most influential newspapers and policy think tanks have, if anything, an even more embarrassing record than American business of underestimating Japan.

This pattern goes back to Japan's emergence as an industrial power in the last century. It has become even more noticeable in the five decades since the United States defeated Japan in World War II.

General Douglas MacArthur set the tone in an interview with the *New York Times* in September 1945, just a month after Japan surrendered. Speaking in his capacity as head of America's program to democratize the defeated Japanese, he flatly declared: "Japan will never again become a world power." Less than two decades later, Japan's postwar economic miracle had already proved MacArthur wrong. By 1964, the year he died, Japan ranked as the world's third-largest manufacturing power, after the United States and the Soviet Union.

Over the years almost every diplomat, writer, and policymaker who has tried to assess Japan has erred similarly on the downside. Here are some examples:

• In 1950, MacArthur's American economic experts advised that the Japanese economy's best course in the postwar era would be to make "knickknacks" — their word — for underdeveloped countries. Japanese exporters aimed a bit higher. By 1987 the American military had become so dependent on Japanese electronic "knickknacks" that the Pentagon launched the $1 billion Sematech program to revive the beleaguered American electronics industry.

• In 1957, Columbia Pictures released *The Bridge on the River Kwai,* a World War II epic that painted Japan's military engineers as incompetent oafs. Today the joke is on Columbia Pictures, which has been owned by Tokyo-based Sony Corporation since 1989. For Sony chairman Akio Morita, this represents one of the great last laughs in history: he started his career in the early 1940s as a Japanese military engineer.

• In 1972, the American foreign policy analyst Zbigniew Brzezinski published *The Fragile Blossom: Crisis and Change in Japan*, in which he publicized various overblown "crises" that seemed at the time to be undermining Japan's social contract. Less than two years later, in facing a real crisis in the form of the Arab oil embargo, Japan reacted less like a fragile blossom than a mountain cat. In the teeth of widespread predictions in the West that Japanese industry would collapse, Japan adapted so quickly that it was able to surpass the United States in several crucial oil-related industries by 1980.

• In 1989 Bill Emmott, editor in chief of the influential London magazine the *Economist,* wrote a book arguing Japan's savings rate would soon fall and this would eliminate Japan's trade surpluses. Instead of falling, the savings rate actually rose — with the result that in the next four years the current account surplus more than doubled!

Why do top Western observers continue to misread Japan? Several factors are at work. These include:

1. *Cultural misunderstandings*. The Japanese consider it a form of politeness to engage in ritualized understatement of themselves and their institutions. Sometimes they take this modesty to ludicrous ex-

tremes. In the presence of a non-family member, for instance, a polite Japanese father may even pour ritualized scorn on his own family. He may refer to his son as "gusoku," a characteristic idiom that literally means "my stupid son." The son involved may be a brilliant overachiever — but that is the point. The intent of the father's modesty is to spare the blushes of his hearer whose children may not be as gifted.

2. *Japanese public relations strategy.* Japanese officials and business leaders have found that it is good strategy to play down Japan's economic strengths. They are practiced hands at acting out pantomimes of exaggerated anxiety that serve not only to spur Japanese workers to ever greater efforts but to foster complacency among foreign rivals.

3. *Western hubris.* The Western mind has a powerful subconscious wish to look askance at Japanese economic ideas. This wish is so strong that Westerners time and again suppress the hard evidence of their senses and even invent fictitious "facts" in an effort to preserve their condescending view of Japan.

The Japanese economic system has often tended to understate the profitability of its corporations, the productivity of many of its workers, the living standards of its consumers, and even the strength of its financial system. The Western press, eager to criticize Japanese economics, generally takes the self-deprecatory comments of Japanese economic leaders at face value.

The result is that even the most sophisticated Westerners are hopelessly in the dark about the reality of Japan in the mid-1990s. In particular, they are blind to one of the most consequential events of the twentieth century: the emergence in Japan of a revolutionary new system of economic thought that is now visibly overturning many supposedly universal theories that shape Western economic behavior.

Not only have the West's economists failed to understand this new system but, with almost no effort to study the underlying facts, they continue to condemn Japanese economics as a backward, almost irrational system that trails far behind the West in economic evolution. True, a few noted Western economists such as Lester Thurow and Michael E. Porter have come to admire certain features of Japan, notably the rigor of its educational system and the long-term mindset of its big banks. But even such observers have failed to grasp the full picture. They see Japanese economics merely as a "new paradigm" of

Western capitalism. The truth is, though many aspects of Japanese economics look like capitalism, the Japanese system is not capitalism at all but a new formulation that is as sharp and portentous a break from capitalism as capitalism was from feudalism.

In essence, the Japanese have discovered that the basic assumptions underlying the West's economic thinking have been undermined by a sea change in the way wealth is created in advanced countries. Japanese government and business leaders spotted this sea change as early as the 1930s and, on the strength of radical economic experiments carried out by the Japanese military in Japan's then colony of Manchuria, they devised a new economic system better able to create growth in modern conditions than capitalism. This system was sketched out in a historic government manifesto in 1940 and was substantially implemented by the late 1940s. Labeled in English the Economic New Structure, this system quickly proved an extraordinary advantage in Japan's effort to catch up with the West. And today it is a bigger advantage than ever. Precisely because this system is so effective, Japanese leaders have shied away from discussing it frankly with Western policymakers and economists — and even with the Japanese people. But in the mid-1990s the outlines of this new system are fully visible to those who can shed their Western hubris and evaluate it on its merits.

The Japanese collapse that never was

The West's tendency to underestimate Japan was rarely more evident than in the way Western observers misinterpreted Japan's economic performance in the early 1990s. Virtually without exception, commentators in the West maintained that Japan was going through an economic agony as terrible as the wrenching recessions in the United States and Britain. As reported by the American press, Japan entered a "slump" after the Tokyo stock market peaked at the end of December 1989 and was still supposedly floundering four years later.

Language-blocked American correspondents simply assumed that because the Tokyo stock market had collapsed, the Japanese economy must also be in terrible shape. As we will see in Chapter Ten, this was a classic case of applying inappropriate Western logic to Japan: given Japan's very differently structured financial system, stock market turbulence did not constitute a threat to the extraordinary efficiency of the advanced industries at the heart of the Japanese economic miracle.

The remarkable thing about the early 1990s in Japan was how well the economy was doing in the face of the worst global recession since the 1930s. Here are some facts that the American press's prophets of doom overlooked in the early 1990s:

• Measured by current exchange rates, Japan surpassed the United States in 1993 to become the world's largest manufacturing economy.

• Japan jumped from sixth to second in per capita income between 1989 and 1993.

• In 1992, Hitachi passed IBM, America's largest high-technology company, in sales.

• Japan's net national savings totaled $819 billion in 1993. As calculated by the Paris-based OECD, this represented 56 percent of the entire industrial world's savings. By contrast, the United States' savings came to just $75 billion, or only 5 percent of the industrial world's total.

• Japanese employers consistently invested two to three times as much per worker as American employers.

Underlying all this was a stunning performance by the yen, which soared 27 percent in the first four years of the 1990s to finish 1993 at ¥112 to the American dollar. As the yen rose, the reaction in the West was disbelief. Western commentators did what they have always done when the yen rises: they predicted that Japan's exports would soon be priced out of world markets and major Japanese exporters would be forced out of business. Nothing of the sort happened. Instead of falling, Japan's export revenues rose even in yen terms and soared in dollar terms. We will look at the reasons later. For now let us just look at the numbers: exports reached $362 billion in 1993, a rise of 32 percent since 1989. With exports booming, not a single significant employer collapsed, and as of 1994 unemployment stood at less than 3.5 percent. Certainly, if the stock market crash threw people out of work, this was not apparent in Japan's total work force, which rose by about 1 million a year even as stock prices slumped.

The bottom line on the early 1990s is this: powered by the strong yen, Japan ended 1993 with an economy 68 percent the size of America's. By contrast, four years earlier when the Tokyo stock market was riding high, Japan was just 55 percent of America's economic size. In other words, Japan remained triumphantly on track toward its reputed goal of passing the United States to become the world's largest economy by the year 2000.

Seeing things as they are

American economists and business publications use a host of devices that systematically obscure the truth about Japan's strength.

In particular, in making U.S.-Japan comparisons, they value the yen at 30 to 50 percent less than the market rate. This reflects the use of the so-called purchasing power parity method of currency translation. Advocates of this method regard the yen as grossly overvalued at recent exchange market rates. Thus, unbeknownst to the American public, they "correct" Japan's economic numbers downward by valuing the yen at the low levels of a decade ago. As a result, Japanese incomes are often stated as if they are considerably lower than American incomes, when in fact they are more than 30 percent higher.

The purchasing power parity method therefore deflects attention away from one of the most important questions of the 1990s: How can high-wage Japan outexport America in virtually every category of manufactured product — and do so with just half of America's work force?

American economists justify the purchasing power parity method on the basis that, thanks to high retail prices in Japan, Japanese consumers get less for their money than income numbers translated at market exchange rates would imply. But, as we will see, purchasing power parity calculations are highly misleading because of a host of cultural factors overlooked by Western observers. In any case, anyone who measures Japan's economic performance by the Japanese people's standard of living misses the point: Japanese leaders do not share the Western view that the economy should be primarily run to provide citizens with a good life. Rather, they see the Japanese economy mainly as an instrument of power. And the mighty yen, which has trebled against the dollar since the early 1970s, is one of the principal levers of that power.

Nowhere is the changing balance of power more apparent than in corporate rivalry. Driven by the high yen, Japanese corporations are now the sales leaders in most industrial sectors. Even in high technology, as we have seen, IBM has had to make way for Hitachi. Skeptics wonder whether this matters. Actually, it does. Other things being equal, a company with larger sales can afford to invest more heavily in developing new manufacturing technologies. This is amply evident in the case of Hitachi: powered by a trebling in its sales, Hitachi's capital spending as measured by Value Line shot from $1,695 million in 1983 to $5,763 million in 1993. In other words, Hitachi's capital spending is now 182 percent of IBM's, up from just 34 percent a decade ago. As Hitachi and IBM pay the same prices for high-technology manufacturing equipment, Hitachi's success translates directly into a real advantage on the factory floor.

Moreover, Japanese corporations are now better placed than ever to innovate. Thanks to the high yen, they can comfortably pay top dollar to engage more and more of the West's best scientists, industrial designers, inventors, and software writers in creating the products of tomorrow. We will be seeing the fruits of this effort on Main Street in the second half of the 1990s.

And the high yen enables the Japanese economic system to make friends everywhere money talks. Corporate Japan can now wield vast public relations budgets to influence Western scholars, authors, editors, publishers, lawyers, management consultants, and investment bankers. Japan now outspends the United States in foreign aid in many countries, including parts of the former Soviet bloc. In this sense, the prominent Japan scholar Chalmers Johnson is right to say that it was Japan, not the United States, which won the cold war. Certainly foreign aid is a key lever of global politics, and it ensures that when the chips are down many nations in the Second and Third Worlds generally side with Japan in international disputes. And as the dollar declines, Japan can buy political favors in foreign capitals with the same ease with which corporate America did in the great days of American leadership in the 1950s.

Even more troubling for Americans, every increase in the yen brings nearer the day when Japan will surpass America to become the world's largest economy. And if Japan passes America, it will soon take over the leadership role America has long enjoyed in setting global rules on trade and other economic matters.

The dollar's decline dramatically raises the price of America's imports of manufacturing equipment — a crucial point given that American industry is now highly dependent on Japan, and to a lesser extent Germany, for the advanced machines needed to boost America's manufacturing productivity.

Seen from a Tokyo vantage point, the degree of self-delusion prominent Americans displayed in underestimating Japan's strength in the early 1990s was clear evidence that the United States is incapable of taking even the first step toward restoring its ability to compete with Japan. That first step is to remove the blinders and see things as they really are.

Japanese economics — the mystery

Japan's growth in the last half-century is unsurpassed in the history of economics. The numbers are more remarkable than even many economists realize. In 1950, Japan was only 3 percent the size of the American economy; in 1960, it had moved to 8 percent; in 1970 to 20 percent; and in 1980 to 39 percent. Japan's success since 1980 has now taken it to 68 percent of the United States. The speed with which Japan passed the United States in per capita income in the Reagan-Bush era was unprecedented in world economic history. By comparison, as the British economic historian Nicholas Crafts pointed out, the United States took more than a century to achieve a similar income gain against Britain in a time of stable exchange rates.

Japan's growth since 1980 has been all the more surprising because by the late 1970s Japan had already drawn level with or surpassed the United States in many advanced industries. Thus fifteen years ago Western economists already believed that Japan's era of economic overachievement had ended. Given that Japan is regarded as the economy that "breaks all the rules of good economics," why has it been so successful?

None of the conventional explanations comes close to solving the mystery. Japan's work ethic, for instance, explains almost nothing. The Japanese today work 228 fewer hours annually than they did twenty years ago. Meanwhile, as the Harvard economist Juliet B. Schor explained in *The Overworked American* in 1992, Americans have actually increased their hours by 160 hours in the same period. Thus, had the work ethic been the pivotal factor, America should have noticeably outperformed Japan in recent years, not the other way around.

Many in the West regard Japan's high-quality products and skilled work force as key factors in Japan's success. But the world's currency markets are supposed to realign currencies automatically to adjust for such differences in national performance. In this case, this would have meant that a higher yen should long ago have weakened Japan's export prowess.

Reaganite commentators in the United States have attributed Japan's success to low tax rates — but this is a classic example of how influential Americans misinterpret the facts of Japanese economics to suit their own theories. The truth is that Japan's tax rates are higher than America's — not only for corporate profits and executive salaries but for most investment gains.

Another explanation often advanced by American economists is that Japan's trade surpluses are caused by Japan's high savings rate. This begs the question of why the Japanese save. Economists unfamiliar with Japan are content to ascribe the pattern to "culture." Yet economic historians know that the Japanese people have no deep-seated tradition of frugality. Japan's super-high savings rate emerged only after the American occupation of the country ended in 1952. In the subsequent eight years the rate of total net savings nearly doubled, rising from 10.2 to 18.2 percent. Why? In truth, this is one of the most significant untold stories of Japan's miracle economy.

The Yale historian Paul Kennedy has argued that Japan has been "free riding" under America's defense umbrella and thus has been able to outspend America in industrial investment. At best, this provides only a small part of the story. For one thing, Japan's defense spending is not as low as it seems: official international comparisons understate Japan's true defense burden by leaving out such notable items as military pensions. In any case, Kennedy's theory is contradicted by the evidence of Korea and Taiwan. They both spend massively on defense — proportionately, far more than the United States — yet, using Japanese-style economic policies, they too have consistently boomed.

A related theory holds that American defense spending has weakened America by diverting too many of America's brightest scientific and engineering brains away from consumer manufacturing. But this views the problem in too narrow a focus. There is no absolute shortage of bright Americans — only a shortage of incentives for them to pursue careers in consumer manufacturing. By comparison, the incentives are greater not only in the defense industry but in myriad service activities such as law and finance. Japanese students are twice as likely as their American counterparts to study science or engineering because, unlike in the United States, these disciplines put young Japanese on the fast track to the boardroom. As Americans contemplate Japan's surging technological exports, the mystery to ponder is why America's free market system persistently underrewards industrial scientists and engineers.

Some people say Japan is doing well not so much on its own merits but because America is mismanaging itself. This can hardly be the key factor because countries such as Germany and Switzerland are now finding it almost as difficult as America to compete with Japan — yet they are largely untroubled by low savings, poor schools, and the other tribulations of late-twentieth-century America.

One of the most amazing things about the Japan story is that it has been almost completely ignored by conventional Western economists. In fact, top Western economists seem instinctively to shrink from Japan — as if they recognize that Japan poses a fatal threat to their deepest beliefs. Despite Japan's record of growth, no student of Japanese economics has come away with any insights that might merit the Nobel Prize. In fact there have been practically no insights that merit even a footnote in standard American college textbooks.

Public comments by American economists on Japan are often embarrassingly ill-informed. In the 1970s, for instance, Nobel Prize–winner Milton Friedman attributed Japan's success to the supposed especially *free* nature of markets in Japan!

Although hundreds of scholarly books on Japanese economics are published each year, most consist of narrowly focused essays, each written by a different essayist who has typically spent just a few weeks in Japan as a guest of the Japanese authorities. Such books are full of unresolved internal contradictions. The sum total of the American economics profession's work on Japan is a Tower of Babel.

The West's most influential economic publications have hardly been a beacon of light either. They keep contradicting themselves about many of the basic facts of Japan. Is Japan an unfair trader? After thirty years of mulling the evidence, the *Wall Street Journal* is still scratching its head. Sometimes it accuses Japan of a massively coordinated effort to dump products in foreign markets. Sometimes it says no such campaign exists and anyone who thinks otherwise is a despicable conspiracy theorist!

The *Economist*'s coverage of Japan has also been perplexing. All through the 1970s and 1980s, the *Economist* argued that Japan's market-defying economic policies were "bad economics." Recently it has quietly shifted its ground. It now argues that Japan's "bad economics" was probably effective in the past but is somehow no longer effective today. But what has changed? The magazine's embarrassed editors have never frankly addressed this question. The truth is, as we will see, Japan's controversial economic policies have always been highly effective. And once one understands why they work, one sees that in the future they will be even more effective than ever.

Japan's many trade barriers are the best-known example of its "bad economics." Then there are the *keiretsus*, Japan's groups of financially interlinked companies that trade in cliquish ways. Other examples abound: Japan's lifetime employment system, its strict seniority promotion system for corporate employees, its cartels, its ubiquitous government interference in the economy, its strange land policies that artificially restrict people's living space, and its tight financial regulation. All are, in the language of Western economics, "rigidities." They interfere with the workings of the market and are therefore condemned by Western economists as hindrances to economic efficiency.

Some conventional economists have concluded that Japan's peculiar economic arrangements are cultural hangovers from the days of the shoguns, the military dictators who ruled Japan until 1868. But for these "feudal dysfunctions," they have argued, Japan would have been even more successful. This was always an unlikely theory and it has become untenable in recent years as Taiwan and South Korea succeeded spectacularly in emulating Japan's growth soon after they copied many of the "rigidities" of the Japanese economic system. Clearly East Asians know something Westerners don't. But what?

To solve the mystery, we must start by reevaluating the basic principles of Western economics.

Sayonara, capitalism

Economics is an evolutionary science. Economic ideas are not sacred principles carved in stone, as economists like to suggest, but merely inferences drawn from observing man's constantly evolving efforts to create wealth. Thus economic ideas need to be re-evaluated whenever the pattern of man's economic activities undergoes significant change.

The last great sea change in man's economic behavior originated in Europe in the fifteenth and sixteenth centuries, as feudalism began to give way to early capitalism. The trend was driven mainly by breakthroughs in transportation; mariners began to make longer voyages thanks to innovations such as the rudder, the compass, the three-masted caravel, and accurate mapmaking. Roadmaking, a lost art since the decline of the Roman Empire, was revived first in France and later in England.

Cheaper and faster transport fostered trade. This spurred specialization and the development of factory production, which was pioneered in the English woolen industry in the sixteenth century. The rise of industry eventually brought a shift in power as Europe's landowners were pushed aside by an emerging class of city-based entrepreneurs. In the process, capital emerged as a crucial dynamic. In the Middle Ages, society had invested its excess energies — otherwise known as capital — in building cathedrals and castles; now entrepreneurs were applying their surplus to building ships and spinning machines, which generated good profits and thus created the wherewithal to build still more ships and spinning machines.

Eighteenth-century philosophers and writers who understood how the world was changing — and where the changes were leading — evolved the collection of interlinked ideas we now call capitalism. Much of the earliest thinking originated in Paris, capital of Europe's then largest economy. In the 1730s the banker Richard Cantillon wrote *Essai sur la Nature du Commerce en Général*, which provided the groundwork for capitalist theories of prices and trade. Meanwhile the Marquis d'Argenson propounded the principle of laissez faire. And after meeting such leading French economic thinkers as François Quesnay and A. R. J. Turgot on an extended trip to France in the 1760s, the Scottish philosopher Adam Smith systematized the French ideas. Smith published *The Wealth of Nations* in 1776, thus definitively outlining what was for his first readers a startlingly new way of looking at the creation of wealth.

Two centuries later, capitalism has proved so successful that we tend to assume it will go on forever. But just as feudalism was eventually swept aside by breakthroughs in transportation, capitalism is now under threat from new economic forces at work in late-twentieth-century society. These forces are driven mainly by technological change, and in particular by information's emergence as a critical source of wealth.

The Berkeley economist Paul Romer, a noted prophet of the information-age revolution, has said that information is a new kind of economic force whose properties are fundamentally different from those of the traditional factors of production (labor, capital, and land). The information age's magic is seen at its simplest if you consider a vineyard. Suppose the owner of the vineyard shares his grapes with his neighbors. The more he gives away, the less he has for himself — a mathematical relationship so obvious we assume it is the basic building block of all economics. But if the vineyard owner discovers a more productive way of propagating the vines, he can share this valuable *information* with other vineyard owners without taking away a single grape from his own harvest. A good idea is never depleted or worn out — it works tirelessly to increase the world's total production of goods. "Knowledge doesn't face diminishing returns," says the Geneva-based scholar Richard Baldwin. "It is an expanding universe."

Thus knowledge is an exception to the iron law of finiteness that has always governed the traditional factors of production. This law is at the core of capitalist thought. The fact that it is no longer universally valid calls into question capitalism's claims as the most effective system for creating wealth.

At this stage two consequences of the information age in particular merit special mention. The first is a phenomenon best designated the Cost Structure Revolution. Industry's cost structure is being joltingly transformed in the information era. So-called fixed costs are accounting for a much greater proportion of manufacturers' total costs, while variable costs are a declining element in the total. Fixed costs are the up-front costs a producer incurs before he starts production. Variable costs include payments for wages and raw materials.

The swing to fixed costs has been particularly marked in some of Japan's advanced manufacturing industries, where fixed costs now sometimes exceed 90 percent of total costs. By contrast, in Adam Smith's time, fixed costs represented considerably less than 20 percent of the total. As we will see, a key reason for the swing to fixed costs is the rise of information as an economic force.

The second major economic consequence of the information age is best termed Global Natural Monopoly. This refers to an observed tendency in advanced manufacturing for strong manufacturers to grow ever stronger and weak ones to grow weaker.

The Cost Structure Revolution and Global Natural Monopoly are interlinked in complex ways; working with other economic forces unleashed by technical change, they are relentlessly undermining the rules of capitalism. The Japanese have been the first to understand this, and in the characteristic manner of the nation that gave the world jujitsu, they have turned what at first seemed to be a problem into an opportunity. Having discovered that capitalism faced new difficulties in modern conditions, they set out to invent a better way.

The Cost Structure Revolution

A key factor driving the swing to fixed costs is that industry is deploying more and more sophisticated production equipment which rapidly becomes obsolete. Depreciation charges have therefore been soaring in advanced industries. Certain machines used in making semiconductors, for instance, have a useful life of only two years; computers must be replaced every five or six years. By contrast, the simple tools in the famous pin "manufactory" described in Adam Smith's *The Wealth of Nations* might have been expected to last a lifetime.

The amount of capital equipment required to create new jobs in advanced manufacturing is now extraordinary. The Tokyo-based Sharp Corporation announced in 1994 that a new factory is expected to cost more than $470 million to create four hundred new jobs. Each job will therefore cost about $1.2 million. And at the Yamazaki company's new factory, the investment cost per job is $1.5 million. Just ten years ago, numbers like these would have been considered incredible. Now, in Japan at least, they are routine.

Much of the cost of capital equipment represents "congealed" information — an accumulation of know-how acquired over years or even decades. And the speed with which capital equipment becomes obsolete is also driven by information — in this case the discovery of more efficient production techniques.

Besides investing in congealed information in the form of production equipment, manufacturers also participate directly in the information revolution through heavy research and development spending. Though conventional economists consider it a "sunk cost" and accountants consider it a current cost, research and development is a fixed cost for the purposes of this book because, in suitably amortized form, it constitutes an up-front cost that managers recover in pricing products. Various other forms of overhead such as worker training and executive education — information again — also represent fixed costs in this sense.

The Cost Structure Revolution has powerful implications for the core objective of economic policymaking, the maximization of output of useful goods and services. In Adam Smith's time, nations achieved greatest efficiency by leaving everything to free markets. If the owner of the pin factory had mistakenly overestimated demand, he could instantly reduce his costs by letting some of his people go. In a simple economy where skills hardly mattered, those workers were then released to find useful alternative employment immediately in any one of several small businesses nearby. In a simple economy, the free market was the most efficient mechanism for maximizing the deployment of labor, the key factor of production in that time.

Look at the situation today. Because machines have superseded muscles as the largest item in industry's cost mix, an industry downturn or an overoptimistic projection of future demand by corporate planners results in serious waste in the form of idled investment. Particularly in industries where technical progress is fast and production facilities become obsolete quickly, lost production can never be recovered.

In essence, it has become much more difficult for modern entrepreneurs to achieve orderly growth in production. If entrepreneurs expand their operations without coordination, they risk creating periodic excess capacity. Then they compete desperately with each other to sell their products and the result is something that the Japanese call *kato kyoso,* excess competition. Kato kyoso is inherently a waste of human effort, and Japanese economics is designed to minimize it.

Thanks to various innovative economic policies, the Japanese have consistently achieved superb capacity utilization rates over the years, but this fact has been obscured from the West by Japan's ultraconservative measurement methods (many Japanese corporations consider that they are working at full capacity only if they operating around the clock). Erroneous and exaggerated reports of overcapacity problems are a perennial feature of Western press coverage of Japan. For instance, in 1978 *Time* magazine reported that Toyota Motor would have to cut back capacity dramatically. In the event, Toyota more than doubled its capacity in the next fifteen years.

Judging by independent evidence based on Japanese industry's break-even levels, Japan's capacity utilization as calculated by American yardsticks was probably more than 85 percent even in the recession year of 1993 — way above the world average of just 70 percent at the time. Thus even in this worst recession since the 1930s, policies based on an understanding of the Cost Structure Revolution enabled Japanese industries to achieve notably greater efficiency than their Western competitors.

Another development that has been fostered by the Cost Structure Revolution is the extraordinary growth of strategic pricing in recent years. A classic example of strategic pricing is the practice by many companies of selling abroad at much lower prices than at home. For the American economy this is a problem — and for the Japanese it is an opportunity. Although selling at cut prices abroad breaks the rules of capitalism, it is often the best way for a corporation to maximize its revenues and is certainly quite rational so long as the export prices at least cover variable costs. The result is that international price discrepancies can be enormous: in a recent dumping investigation, one major Japanese corporation was found guilty of selling photographic paper in America at *one-quarter* of its prices in Japan.

Corporate Japan's penchant for strategic pricing in the world's advanced manufacturing industries is a hidden factor behind the often criticized shortsightedness of American corporations. Take, for example, the downsizing trend in American industry. Many downsizing American corporations choose to shut their aging American component factories rather than invest in the latest production technology. Then they outsource components from overseas suppliers, typically the Japanese. The rationale seems compelling because Japanese suppliers often quote very low initial prices to get the American business. They can afford to do so thanks to the Cost Structure Revolution, which allows them to gear their prices to low variable costs. Once the Americans can no longer make the components concerned, the Japanese raise their prices to take account of their full costs, fixed as well as variable. In the meantime, thousands of Americans have lost good jobs that the United States will have great difficulty replacing.

The real blame here lies with American business schools that urge American managers to focus singlemindedly on minimizing immediate costs. This so-called by the numbers management style overlooks the possibility that Japanese suppliers might be using strategic pricing that will work to the Americans' disadvantage in the long run. Basing their theories on how the world worked before the Cost Structure Revolution, the business schools just assume that the Japanese use the same short-term profit maximizing strategies as American corporations.

The Cost Structure Revolution has touched off an explosive increase in transaction costs. Transaction costs consist of the time and other resources we must expend on the act of buying or selling something. Stated like this, transaction costs do not seem a very serious concern, but in fact they are a heavy — and largely hidden — business expense in many industries. Corporate procurement executives, for instance, often have to do extensive studies to check on quality and prices. And if the goods delivered do not measure up to vendors' promises, buyers may have to engage in costly lawsuits.

The transaction cost explosion is in large measure a result of pricing instability triggered by the rising proportion of fixed costs in producers' cost mixes. By contrast, in Adam Smith's time, producers had little difficulty calculating prices. The proprietor of the pin factory, for instance, looked at the cost of wages and raw materials and then added a little for himself. The result was his price. But in today's conditions, where fixed costs overshadow variable costs, determining the "correct" price for, say, a new type of semiconductor is a problem to challenge a Nobel Prize–winner. Whereas variable costs are easy to allocate accurately, the allocation of fixed costs is largely a matter of guesswork. For a producer pricing a new product, this guesswork includes estimating (a) the size of the total potential market, (b) what share competing suppliers will take and, most important, (c) what share *they think* they will take (this determines the guesswork on which they base their pricing). In trying to make rational pricing decisions in an advanced free market economy, therefore, talented executives are spending an ever-increasing amount of time gathering market information and laboring over spreadsheets.

In sum, burgeoning transaction costs combined with unstable capacity utilization and the growth of predatory pricing have created major problems for Adam Smith's model of a market economy. Thus the Cost Structure Revolution has seriously undermined the case for free markets. But as we will see in the next section, this is only the beginning of capitalism's problems in modern conditions.

Global Natural Monopoly

When economists talk of natural monopolies, they usually mean regulated utilities such as telephone and electric power companies. In the era of the Cost Structure Revolution, however, the concept has broken out of the utility area and is now, almost unnoticed, transforming the world's most advanced manufacturing industries — and, by extension, the whole science of economics.

In the language of economics, natural monopoly appears when an industry's long-run average cost curve continues to fall *indefinitely* as production increases. In traditional manufacturing, a natural monopoly was an extreme rarity because, above a certain level of output, a manufacturer's costs almost invariably started rising sharply. This concept is intuitively obvious if you take the history of a nineteenth-century industry like steel: although in the 1860s Britain accounted for fully 70 percent of world steel production, the British steelmakers could never have hoped to establish a global natural monopoly. In trying to serve more and more customers, the British would eventually have needed to supplement their local supplies of iron ore and coal with imports from faraway mines in, say, North America. Then their costs would suddenly jump to the point where they could no longer be efficient producers.

By contrast, in today's leading industries, the cost of procuring and transporting basic material inputs is minuscule. This has created truly global markets in many sophisticated components and capital goods. One nation, or even just one manufacturer, can now obtain a global lock on an industry.

As with the Cost Structure Revolution, a crucial factor powering the rise of Global Natural Monopoly is research and development. Generally, research and development must be organized on an exceptionally large scale to be reasonably efficient. In the United States, for instance, about 90 percent of all research and development is conducted by just two hundred major corporations. Advanced laboratories get their results from conducting enormous numbers of highly repetitive experiments involving small variations in mixes of ingredients and different sequences of actions.

Take a typical problem in electronics: achieving the highest purity in raw materials (up to 99.99999999 percent pure is the norm in many cases these days). Let us assume, hypothetically, that there are ten separate processes involved in treating a particular raw material and these processes can be conducted in any order. The industry will want to know which sequence of processes yields the best results. Often there is no substitute for testing each sequence individually. If each competitor conducts testing on its own, the industry's duplication of effort on losing gambits will be enormous — the total number of possible sequences is 3,628,800! To eliminate duplication, competitors need to cooperate in a joint research operation that tries each losing gambit only once.

By organizing huge industrywide research projects and by taking other steps to eliminate duplicating research, Japanese cartels dramatically reduce overall research costs. These cartels now enjoy such an efficiency edge that American laboratories, competing individually, are finding they suffer a critical cost disadvantage. Particularly in research fields where the Japanese are known to be active, the Americans are in retreat and sometimes do not contest the field at all.

One of the most obvious consequences of the rise of Global Natural Monopoly is that it casts a pall over the future of free trade. The case for free trade was conclusively argued in 1817 by the British banker David Ricardo in his famous theory of comparative advantage. Ricardo's point was that even if Nation A's industries are more efficient than Nation B's right across the board, the two nations can still benefit from trading with each other: they maximize their joint output if Nation A concentrates on making those products where its edge over Nation B is widest while buying from Nation B those products where Nation A's edge over Nation B is narrowest. But, as Ricardo noted in small print, this conclusion is correct only if neither nation can achieve a natural monopoly. This was a reasonable assumption in 1817, but it no longer holds today. Thus Ricardo's theory, still regarded by American policymakers as a cornerstone of the case for American capitalism, has foundered.

Gregory Clark, a veteran Japan-watcher who teaches at Tokyo's Sophia University, cites semiconductors as a prime case where free trade no longer works. He comments: "Efficiencies gained as a result of large volume production can allow unit costs to fall by as much as 90 percent. So the more Company A or Nation A makes and exports semiconductors, the lower its unit costs. The lower its unit costs, the more it can export. In all logic, one country, and maybe even one company, should end up dominating all world production. Rival companies have to be alert twenty-four hours a day to make sure that competitors do not steal a march on them. Anyone who gains the slightest technological or market advantage can expand production and wipe out rivals."

In a world of manufacturing natural monopolies, if a country achieves leadership in a cluster of important industries it inevitably starts drawing further and further ahead of other nations. Strength in electronics, for instance, helps Japan extend its lead in the car industry, and vice versa. Industry leadership gives a country the big profit margins that enable it to invest in more and more sophisticated equipment and in new research and development, thus generating even more profits. As they gain leadership in world markets, corporations can gradually raise their profit margins in export markets to recover more and more of their fixed costs from the world's consumers.

Viewed from Main Street, the new monopolies are almost invisible. For consumers, the range of brand names available has, if anything, been widening. In computers, for instance, young companies such as Compaq and Dell are now contesting the market with established companies such as IBM and Digital Equipment. But what consumers do not see is that the new entrants are mere assemblers and merchandisers who rely heavily on a few highly oligopolistic suppliers for vital components. Moreover, established companies such as IBM and Digital also rely on these same suppliers, many of whom are Japanese.

Perhaps the most startling example of the monopolistic tendency in components is the deceptively simple-looking screens used in laptop computers. Virtually all are made in Japan. Sharp Corporation alone is believed to have nearly half the world market. These screens can cost as much as $1,200 each, making them by far the most expensive component in a typical laptop, more expensive than Intel's advanced microprocessors.

As we will see in Chapter Two, it is a similar story in the case of many other components and parts. The process of natural monopoly has gone even further in a crucial category of goods that few consumers ever see — manufacturing equipment. In many categories of manufacturing equipment, the world is already down to just one or two suppliers, and typically such suppliers are Japanese. "Steppers," lithographic machines that perform some of the most sophisticated work in the semiconductor manufacturing industry, provide a good example.

Decades ago economists sensed the seriousness of the threat that natural monopoly posed to traditional theory, but most remained silent in the evident hope that the problem would go away. Only a few of the more farsighted ones publicly drew attention to the problem. The most notable was John Kenneth Galbraith, who pointed out as far back as the 1940s that oligopolistic industries such as automaking and steel could not be reconciled with conventional theory. More recently, the iconoclastic Stanford economist W. Brian Arthur has taken up the cause. In a challenge to his peers that is Copernican in its boldness, he has pointed out that the modern economy is full of "positive feedbacks" — Arthur's word for the snowballing profit patterns associated with natural monopolies. He went on to argue that America may be making a big mistake in persisting with free trade in an era of Japanese industrial targeting.

It is a measure of the hostility with which the American economics profession greets efforts to update economic theories that Arthur was rebuffed repeatedly in trying to get his ideas published in American scholarly journals. In the end he gave up on the United States and published the first version of his ideas in a British journal. He later published a paper in the United States, and, significantly, not in an economic journal but in *Scientific American.*

Conventional economists believe that, equipped with tough antitrust laws, regulators can not only quell natural monopoly but strengthen the economy as well. But recent evidence indicates this belief is not only misguided but has contributed significantly to America's decline. Evidence mounts that tough antitrust action in the United States has driven natural monopoly offshore, particularly to Japan, where regulators are much kinder to natural monopolies.

American regulators have in effect handed leadership of several key industries to Japan on a silver salver. Perhaps the most notable example is the Justice Department's 1982 breakup of AT&T. Most American observers feel that the breakup has enhanced the American telecommunications industry's efficiency. Perhaps — but the international trade figures tell a disconcerting story. In the first four years of the 1990s alone, America's telecommunications imports from Japan shot from $3.2 billion to $4.4 billion, while America's exports to Japan fell from $800,000 to $700,000. Japanese suppliers have been using the strategic pricing possibilities opened up by the Cost Structure Revolution to increase dramatically their share of the American telecommunications equipment market, to the point where AT&T itself has tacitly admitted that it is now dependent on Japanese monopolies for telecommunications parts.

Even so, many American economists have hailed corporate America's "downsizing" as heartening evidence that free markets will eventually topple the strongest manufacturing monopolies. In this view, downsizing is a welcome wave of "creative destruction" that makes America more efficient. Yet no similar wave of "creative destruction" has taken hold in Japan. The contrast is particularly startling in the electronics industry. While American companies such as Zenith and RCA started downsizing more than two decades ago, their Japanese counterparts have not had to resort to layoffs (not even in the recession of the 1990s — press reports of the supposed collapse of lifetime employment in Japan were a hoax). In most cases, the Japanese have increased their employment numbers over the years. Corporate America's downsizing represents adjustment by American losers to a new breed of winners — companies such as Hitachi, Toshiba, and Matsushita. These winners are now clearly pulling ahead: Hitachi has increased its work force by 5,000 since the mid-1980s. In the same period IBM has cut its work force by 150,000. Meanwhile Fujitsu, a specialist computer company that was only one-fiftieth IBM's size two decades ago, now probably contributes more added value to the Japanese economy than IBM does to the American economy.

The American press has recently taken to deriding IBM as a bloated bureaucracy that deserved to fail. This view says more about the American press's amnesia than about IBM's efficiency: the press has forgotten that it fell over itself to hail IBM as the ultimate "excellent" company in the mid-1980s, just at the time IBM made various mistakes that are now alleged to have led to its downfall. A measure of bureaucratic muddle is a necessary evil in any large organization, American or Japanese, and it cannot be regarded as the fundamental reason why, one after another, America's largest and proudest companies are disappearing.

The fact that companies like IBM are firing American workers while becoming ever more dependent on Japanese rivals for components is a function less of their internal weaknesses than of the systemic inability of the American economy to compete with Japan's.

Faced with the problems and opportunities of the age of natural monopoly, the Japanese have invented a more efficient approach to corporate competition. They have invented an economic concept that is best labeled the Good Cartel. To that surprising new entity we now turn.

The Good Cartel

Cartels are among the least studied aspects of Japanese economics, yet they are the cornerstone of Japan's solution to the problems raised by Global Natural Monopoly. Cartels get bad press in the West because they are seen to push the narrow interests of top executives and shareholders at the expense of consumers and workers. Japan's Good Cartel, however, is a subtly different structure that deliberately sets limits to the acquisitiveness of top executives and shareholders and instead puts the interests of the nation and of labor first.

To the Japanese, cartels have something in common with the *fugu* fish. The fugu is a prized delicacy of Japanese cuisine despite the fact that its liver contains a deadly poison. Just as the fugu must be prepared by an officially licensed chef who knows how to remove the offending liver, the cartel must be regulated to eliminate the antisocial side effects of concentrated ownership. But once this is done, the Good Cartel is a formidable weapon of global competition. As we will see, Japan's cartels help achieve efficient results in training and in standard-setting. More important, they cut the cost of developing new manufacturing technologies by avoiding the wasteful duplication that ensues when corporations compete individually in research and development.

Of course, in Western eyes, the great drawback of cartels is that they conspire against the consumer. Japan's cartels do indeed appear to exploit Japanese consumers by charging high prices. But far from fostering inefficiency, as Western theorists maintain, these high prices represent one of the great secrets of Japan's success. Cartels provide Japanese corporations with rich profits that are plowed back into improving manufacturing technology and subsidizing efforts to build new markets.

In fact, many of Japan's most cartelized industries enjoy labor productivity rates startlingly higher than their American equivalents.

As we will see in Chapter Two, this applies even in domestic-oriented industries such as banking and tobacco, which have been characterized as inefficient in superficial Western studies.

Japan is constantly investing around 30 percent of its GNP in new production equipment and processes, and much of this is paid for by the unwitting Japanese consumer who has to bear a hidden "cartel surcharge" built into most retail prices in Japan. This surcharge represents roughly 15 to 20 percent of retail prices. Focusing narrowly on this surcharge, the West's free market economists are appalled. Japanese policymakers, however, look at growth. Japan's living standards continue to double every ten to fifteen years, thanks in large measure to the reinvestment of cartel profits.

Westerners imagine that the cartels suppress competition among Japanese corporations. The truth is more complicated. The cartels have a dual effect: on the one hand, they tend to suppress undesirable forms of competition that spawn disproportionate transaction costs. On the other hand, they tend to stimulate desirable forms of competition. Members of Japanese cartels compete fiercely on product designs and on service to customers. More important, they compete on quality: cartels are a key reason why Japanese goods are generally superior in quality. The pricing umbrella under which Japanese companies operate in the home market encourages them to find inexpensive ways to add a surprising degree of extra quality to their products. The Japanese consumer pays for the setup costs for these additional touches. Thus, as far as export pricing is concerned, the quality comes gratis.

Western economists are blinded to the Good Cartel's efficiency advantages because they look at it in the static terms of conventional economic theory. In reality the Good Cartel is a dynamic instrument designed for an era of technological change.

A Western economist looking at the Good Cartel is a bit like a hot-air balloonist watching Wilbur and Orville Wright roll out their first plane at Kitty Hawk. The balloonist naturally doubts whether the Wright brothers' contraption, which "breaks all the rules" of lighter-than-air flight, will ever get off the ground.

Just as the propeller is the innovative dynamic that lifted the Wright brothers' plane, the mechanism of lifetime employment is the prime force for efficiency in Japanese cartels. Japan's lifetime employment system powerfully concentrates executives' minds on maximizing their company's *long-term* growth prospects, thereby assuring their own future prosperity and that of the thousands of younger colleagues whose careers are entrusted to their care. Thus, even when corporations enjoy rich cartel pricing, they are under great pressure to operate efficiently. They need to generate the highest possible profits to provide capital to invest heavily in the next generation of production technology, thus enhancing everyone's long-term job security. Moreover, they also typically need big profits to expand into new lines of business outside the purview of the existing cartel.

To make sure that cartel profits are not diverted to shareholders or to top executives, Japan's industrial regulators "guide" the level of both corporate dividends and top executives' compensation. At a stroke the cartel has been transformed from a device that in the Western system furtively lines the pockets of tycoons and top executives to a powerful machine for enhancing the quality of everyone's job.

The limits of freedom

Adam Smith argued that a nation maximizes its prosperity if it gives each citizen full freedom to pursue his economic interests in his own way. The central theme of *Blindside* is that, for better or worse, this proposition no longer holds: in today's world of high technology and instantaneous communications, a nation *can* improve its economic performance by setting judicious limits to its citizens' economic freedom.

Japan has amply demonstrated the validity of this principle, yet the idea that authority can do us a favor by restricting us seems a troubling, even alien, observation. It is actually less strange than it seems. You have only to consider a local bus route to see the principle at work. The chances are you live a few minutes' walk from the nearest bus stop, even if the buses pass your door. Suppose the city transit authority decided, in the name of fairness and "the right to choose," to allow any commuter to stop the bus anywhere along the route. You could now stop the bus right outside your door, saving yourself a walk each morning. But everyone else would have the same idea and the result would be counterproductive, with the bus jerking to a halt every few yards.

This illustrates the importance of Japanese group logic. Much of Japan's success is a function of the fact that Japanese leaders seek to create structures that maximize group welfare even if this means infringing on the freedom of individuals.

Overlooked by most Western economists, there are many situations in a modern economy where if each individual follows Adam Smith's logic and attempts to maximize his own position, the group ends up with a result that satisfies no one. The world of international trade provides a good example of how economic officials can benefit society by moderating or even overruling our conflicting economic tendencies as individuals. If we all function as "right to choose" consumers in a world of textbook free trade, we create patterns of wildly fluctuating capacity utilization and general instability. Instability is wasteful and expensive in today's conditions of high fixed costs, and someone has to pay for it. Although as consumers we may sometimes pick up bargains due to, for example, dumping by foreign suppliers, we pay the bill in other ways. For one thing, instability creates shortages as well as gluts of goods — so prices can fluctuate upward as well as downward. More important, we pay the bill in high transaction costs in the labor market, as workers are often terminated due to dumping by foreign suppliers. Perhaps most seriously of all, instability leads to underused investments in plant and machinery. We are therefore all affected as investors via insurance policies, pension programs, and mutual funds.

If society can control imports in a system like well-planned bus stops, it might be able to achieve more efficient capacity utilization. The point is not certain in every industry or under every political system, but the Japanese have created political and economic mechanisms that enable them to benefit from restricting trade. Even so, this seems a strange time for economic planners to emerge as the wave of the future. After all, many of the world's socialist countries have recently rejected their economic planners. The truth is that Japan approaches planning in a revolutionary manner that in many ways sharpens rather than suppresses economic competition.

To a Westerner, all this raises a serious question: Should a society seek economic success by sacrificing individual freedom? As our task here is merely to describe how the Japanese economy works and not to make philosophical judgments, the larger question of whether Japanese economics is better than the West's in its overall contribution to human happiness is beyond our border. We must merely note that if economics is the science of maximizing the output of useful goods and services, the Japanese have invented a better way.

Konnichiwa, Big Logic

The economist Lester Thurow has described the Japanese system as "communitarian capitalism." The Tokyo-based business executive Douglas Moore Kenrick has called it "competitive communism."

Such designations make the point that the Japanese system is in some ways most easily understood as a blend of capitalism and socialism. In truth, however, the Japanese system is so different from both capitalism and socialism that it really must be thought of as a genuine third way.

The socialist streak in the Japanese system is apparent not only in the powerful economic management role accorded to Japan's elite bureaucrats but in the Japanese employment system, whose egalitarianism is startling even compared to Eastern Europe in the communist era. But the Japanese system differs sharply from socialism in its vastly superior ability to adjust to technological change. In the words of the noted British Japanologist Ronald Dore, Japan's economic system is characterized by "flexible rigidities."

The important point is that the Japanese system cannot be considered capitalism in the normal sense of the word. To be sure, capital plays a crucial role in the Japanese system. But then it does so also in communism — so much so that the economically successful Stalinist version of communism, with its huge investments in infrastructure and heavy industry, was sometimes known as "state capitalism."

In truth, however, the Japanese system is almost as antithetical to American capitalism as the Stalinist system was. These are some of the key distinctions.

1. Whereas capitalism pursues growth by empowering the individual, the Japanese system works by the opposite principle of suppressing the individual. Perhaps the most important manifestation of this distinction is how Japan's huge capital flows are channeled into industry. The Japanese system rejects the central capitalist idea that individuals (and freely associating groups of individuals) should in

principle control the disposition of the nation's savings. Instead the nation's capital is regarded as a national resource to be harnessed collectively in furtherance of national economic goals. This principle was one of the key proposals in the Economic New Structure manifesto of 1940. Although Japan's plutocratic *zaibatsu* families blocked the proposal at the time, they won only a temporary reprieve. In the confusion after World War II, the idea was promptly resurrected by financial bureaucrats, who created a cartelized financial system that was government-owned in all but name. This has cleared the way for a dramatically different approach to finance. In a strategy similar to "mass" in warfare, the Japanese economic system has concentrated its capital in an effort to establish overwhelming superiority in a limited number of "targeted" industries. This contrasts with the tendency of a free market financial system, which is to give a country a noncontrolling presence in a much wider range of industries.

2. The Japanese system diverges fundamentally from capitalism in its labor economics. In a temporary market turndown, for instance, American companies sacrifice jobs to protect profits whereas Japanese companies sacrifice profits to protect jobs. The Japanese response stems not from "paternalism" but from a basic difference in the logic built into the Japanese system. Not only do Japanese and other East Asian employers generally not lay off labor in a global recession, they continue to export, and thus they force Western producers to adjust by reflexively firing labor in a pattern that ultimately proves fatal. Although the Japanese labor system's group dynamics seem irrational to Western theorists, we will see that it is a highly rational tool of growth in the information age.

3. The Japanese system also diverges from capitalism in its method of harnessing the productive instincts of the human psyche. Our psyche equips us not only to compete but to cooperate, and both instincts have played an important role in human progress. With the rise of capitalism, however, the urge to compete has been emphasized almost to the exclusion of cooperation. Now the Japanese system seeks to harness both instincts. Particularly in such cartelized activities as research and development, the instinct to cooperate is given full play in the Japanese system.

Seen from an American point of view, the Japanese system is perhaps best designated Big Logic Economics. The new system's salient feature is that it is a national approach to economics that is guided pragmatically by a closely knit group of administrators in the bureaucracy and in banking. By contrast, Western capitalism can be seen as Small Logic Economics because the economy is driven by myriad separate — and often conflicting — decisions by millions of individual savers, bankers, entrepreneurs, workers, consumers, and government officials.

The fact that Big Logic Economics has superseded Small Logic Economics does not mean the free market is obsolete in Japan. Just as people didn't stop walking when the automobile was invented, they have not ceased to trade in markets just because Big Logic Economics has come along. The market remains as a tool in the toolbox of the Big Logic system and is in fact widely used at all levels in Japan, particularly small neighborhood enterprises. But the Big Logic system provides more complex enterprises with new tools to improve efficiency. Generally, this system is applied in its purest form to the biggest companies in the most advanced industries and in those product lines furthest from the consumer, such as steel, basic electronic components, and production machinery.

The power of minimalism

Many skeptics say that any attempt from above to impose a Japanese-style industrial policy on an economy will result inevitably in muddle and misallocation of resources. So how can a handful of Japanese public administrators and bankers efficiently guide the workings of the world's second-largest economy?

Actually, the skeptics set up a straw man. They imply that Japan's leaders try to control *everything*. In reality, so little is controlled in Japan that most ordinary citizens are hardly aware of any control at all. The country's leaders set a few key policies such as promoting industrial investment, providing a job for every willing worker, minimizing foreign corporations' strategic pricing in the Japanese market, establishing systems of long-term accountability in government and industry, and making sure that executives in cartelized industries are reasonably honest. Such policies are conceptually obvious and are structured so that they virtually administer themselves.

Japan's auto industry's success provides a good example of how

Japanese economic minimalism can profoundly affect the economy. As many commentators have noted, government officials have had little influence over the day-to-day management of the auto industry. But this does not mean that their contribution has been insignificant. Far from it. In his authoritative study of the Japanese auto industry, the Harvard Business School scholar Michael A. Cusumano concluded that one simple government policy proved crucial to the auto industry's success — the protection of the Japanese home market against imports. Up to the late 1970s, the bureaucrats made it virtually impossible for foreign automakers to sell more than a token number of cars in Japan. As a result, Japanese companies enjoyed huge home-market profits that they were able to invest in ever more prolific production techniques, raising the industry's yearly output from just 32,000 units in 1950 to about 11 million in 1980.

Because many of the keiretsus are hierarchies of companies, Japanese industry is easier to administer than the atomistic societies of the West. The keiretsu system tends to discourage imports — thus maximizing Japan's capacity utilization — because each member of a keiretsu automatically looks to fellow members before it looks abroad for components and other supplies. The cartel system works similarly to minimize imports because cartel members police each other to ensure they all comply with the national effort to protect the Japanese market from disruptive foreign competition.

Simple policies and logical organizational structures explain much of Japan's minimalism — but its greatest advantage is its strong system of government, to which we now turn.

The pinnacle

How does power work in Japan? The answer to this question constitutes one of the major contributions this book will make to the story of Japan.

To a Western eye, the evidence is bafflingly contradictory. At one level, Japan appears to be an amazingly well-run country. Japan's streets, for instance, are famously safe. On dozens of other obvious tests of the quality of government, Japan also scores well.

But at another level Japan seems almost anarchic. Foreigners who live in Japan for a long time become jaded by endless political scandals that have been a recurring feature of Japanese public life for a century. And there are factional battles among various agencies of the bureaucracy, not to mention jousting between the bureaucrats and industry. Many foreigners conclude that while specific agencies like the police are well run, Japan lacks machinery to coordinate the various interests in working together in the national interest.

But this "ungovernable Japan" is hardly the whole story. Japan has long been considered "ungovernable," yet the Japanese have always somehow been able to work with superb coordination in pursuit of national goals.

The myth of Japan's ungovernability goes back to before World War II. In prewar days, Japan's military-dominated government was seen by Westerners as hopelessly deadlocked by feuds — and in particular a feud between a pro-war faction in the army and a pro-peace faction in the navy. American observers in Tokyo in the last days of peace in 1941 were told that Japan's course was being charted by "unofficial conferences of shifting little groups." Understandably many Americans came to believe Japan was in a state of near-anarchy. But they were soon to stand rudely corrected when in December 1941 Japanese navy fliers launched the Pearl Harbor attack. Simultaneously, hundreds of thousands of Japanese troops appeared as if from nowhere to take dozens of Allied strongholds sprawled across eight of the world's time zones. In its epic scale and stopwatch coordination, the Pearl Harbor offensive probably ranks as military history's ultimate masterpiece of planning. Certainly, it was not the work of "shifting little groups."

In retrospect we can see that although prewar Americans were not wrong to perceive divisions in Tokyo, they made a mistake in assuming that Tokyo lacked the means to resolve disputes and get people to work together. Similarly, those who today suggest that Japan's economic policy is anarchically pushed hither and thither by "shifting little groups" are victims of a cultural mirage. If you look beyond the headlines to what Japan's economic leaders actually do, they are revealed as having an impressive delicacy of touch in crafting and implementing complex policies demanding cooperation, and even self-sacrifice, from various competing interest groups.

The truth is that, as in other "strong government" nations of East Asia, Japan's destiny is determined in top-down fashion by a powerful and well-organized civil service. Despite much theatrical buck-passing and disavowing of responsibility for controversial policies, Japan is the ultimate example of the strong-state syndrome that pervades the Confucian world.

At the center of the mystery of Japanese power is an agency called the Ministry of Finance. Virtually unknown outside Japan, the Ministry of Finance enjoys unsuspected authority that not only pervades the entire economic system but extends into the world of electoral politics. The Ministry of Finance is thus the ultimate pinnacle of Japan's extremely hierarchical economy.

The Ministry of Finance (MOF) is not to be confused with the better-known Ministry of International Trade and Industry (MITI). The MITI occupies an important place in the Japanese economy and is rightly credited by the scholar Chalmers Johnson with inventing many of the ideas that underlie Japan's modern economic system. But it is subordinate to the MOF and it has lost power relative to the MOF in the last two decades. Where industrial policy is concerned, the MITI proposes and the MOF disposes. The MOF has the last word because it controls the allocation of Japan's vast financial flows and much else besides. Operating from a barracks-like building two blocks from Emperor Akihito's moated palace in central Tokyo, the MOF is quite literally the most powerful economic organization on earth.

By comparison, Japan's elected representatives are of little consequence. Thus the much publicized change of government in 1993 which ousted the Liberal Democratic Party from office after nearly forty years in government was far less significant than it seemed. Although the new government talked bravely about restoring parliament's authority, few who know Tokyo expected to see a substantial reduction in the MOF's power.

The MOF combines under one roof a degree of concentrated power unheard of in the West. Subject only to token supervision by the Japanese parliament, the MOF writes Japan's tax laws, collects tax revenues, controls the national budget, supervises the savings system, allocates the foreign aid budget, and even, via some adroit backseat driving, steers Japan's military policy. In other words, it controls the three basic functions of government — taxing, spending, and national security.

Many Western observers are blind to the reality of Japanese power because they have difficulty making the psychological leap necessary to see things from a Japanese point of view. They believe that for the MOF even to attempt to control functions that in the West are the prerogative of elected representatives would represent a dastardly "hijacking of democracy." In taking such a judgmental view, Westerners forget that for millennia East Asians have been governed by pyramidical bureaucratic power systems — and usually governed well. Westerners do not see the special respect that is accorded high officials in East Asia and thus fail to understand how effective this respect is in attracting Japan's most capable young men to work for the MOF. Unaware that the muddle of American bureaucracy is attributable to checks and balances that are conspicuously weak in the Japanese power system, they assume that a bureaucrat-dominated Japan is a recipe for gridlock. In reality, the Japanese consider it only natural that power-holders should arrogate to themselves the necessary power to get things done efficiently. In that endeavor, Japanese bureaucrats do not shrink from using coercive and manipulative strategies that would not be tolerated by the courts or the press in a Western country.

Economic theorists have added to Westerners' comprehension problems by preaching that Japan's economic policies are "dysfunctional." Westerners naturally conclude that if Japanese economics is dysfunctional, then Japanese government also must be at least equally dysfunctional.

If the MOF is so powerful, why have we heard so little from it up to now? Because East Asian rulers have long believed that the more unobtrusive power is, the more effective it can be. The MOF's near invisibility automatically shields it from all sorts of domestic and overseas pressures for changes in Japan's controversial economic policies. The MOF acts in such indirect ways that not one in a thousand ordinary citizens recognizes the MOF's hand in Japan's most important policies. As we will see, there are few examples as instructive of the MOF's unobtrusive hand at work as Japan's savings system.

Forced saving

The MOF's single biggest contribution to Japanese success has been its brilliantly counterintuitive system for promoting savings.

In the early 1950s, the MOF realized that Japanese corporations desperately needed to invest in new production technology if they were to catch up with the West. But where would the money come from?

The MOF decided literally to *force* people to save. Instead of merely passively accepting the decisions of ordinary savers about how much they would save, the MOF set out from above to *impose* a high savings rate on the nation. This is an apparent impossibility but it is easy to see when you remember that, for an economist, a high savings rate is another way of saying a low consumption rate. As we will see in Chapter Six, Tokyo set out comprehensively to suppress consumption. Historically, Japan's main tools in this endeavor have been trade barriers (especially against Western luxuries), curbs on Japanese citizens taking foreign vacations, and tight zoning laws that artificially constrain the Japanese people's living and shopping space.

Even today, after various liberalization measures over a period of three decades, the suppressed consumption policy still ensures that Japan consumes significantly less than the free market economies of the West. The result is that Japan now accounts for fully half of all the world's new savings each year.

This fact alone gives Japan enormous power to shape the world's economic destiny — but there is more to Japan's position than this. Much more.

Monopolistic Supergrowth

The lengths to which Tokyo has gone to suppress the Japanese people's consumption represents an extraordinary effort to establish Japan as the world's economic leader.

But Japan is a small country whose 123 million citizens account for only 2 percent of the world's population. The key to the Japanese economic system's strategy for global leadership is to dominate certain high-growth industries where monopolistic tendencies are particularly strong. By pumping its huge savings single-mindedly into a narrow range of high-growth monopolistic industries, Japan's economic leaders can realistically aim to control the world's economic future.

For an industry to be targeted by Japanese economic leaders, it should ideally have several important characteristics:

1. *High entry barriers.* Corporate Japan likes industries where new competitors must spend heavily to acquire expertise, buy expensive machinery, train workers, and build a strong reputation. Example: Japan prefers making supercomputers to hand-knit sweaters.

2. *Powerful economies of scale.* The Japanese would rather make electronic-grade silicon than high-quality silk because the silicon business is a capital-intensive one entailing large-scale economies. By contrast, the silk industry, a traditional industry from which the Japanese withdrew thirty years ago, offers virtually no scale economies and is therefore unattractive to Japan's modern economic leaders.

3. *Good export prospects.* Japan invests in industries making high-value, lightweight goods because the freight costs in exporting such goods are a negligible component of the total cost to the consumer. This strengthens the prospects of establishing a global monopoly. Japan thus sees greater economic advantage in making carbon fiber than beer or concrete blocks.

4. *Opportunities for research and development.* A desire to exploit their cartel-based comparative advantage in research and development has led many Japanese corporations to transform their product range in recent years. Many ceramics companies, for instance, have stopped making traditional products such as teacups and have moved into research-intensive activities such as making heat-resistant ceramic parts for jet engines.

5. *Elastic demand.* As people's incomes rise, their spending patterns change; for example, their demand for entertainment typically increases much more rapidly than their demand for food. In its search for elastic demand patterns, corporate Japan prefers making compact disk players and multimedia machines to cookies or corn flakes.

Once a Japanese cartel has leapfrogged over the Americans and Europeans in a targeted industry, its lead becomes almost impregnable: using the combination of cartel discipline and the logic of the Cost Structure Revolution, the Japanese create a fortress around each industry. Their chief weapon is strategic pricing. Japanese cartels enjoy enormous discretion to cut their prices to drive out existing competitors or scare away would-be challengers. As long as their low prices cover their marginal costs, they do not suffer greatly. By successfully eliminating competition now, they hope to recoup lost profits through improved pricing later.

In sum, in today's conditions, Forced Saving in combination with Global Natural Monopoly has created a phenomenon best designated Monopolistic Supergrowth. This is a self-feeding syndrome allowing Japan to claim an ever-larger share of the world's future growth. Through comprehensive regulation, the MOF channels the nation's savings to strategic industries that strengthen the country's monopolistic grip over the world economy. Once Japanese cartels have established price control in an industry, they can readily raise their prices to pay for their ever-expanding research and development programs. These programs in turn propel Japanese cartels ever further ahead of rivals in the United States and Europe. As Japan grows rich from its Monopolistic Supergrowth strategy, its workers prosper, enabling the financial system to "harvest" an ever-larger amount of personal savings from them. Thus Japanese industries garner yet more capital to launch leadership bids in yet more industries.

Manufacturing: the fortress

If you are to believe Western economists, Japan lags behind America in the sophistication of its service industries. This is a classic example of Western blindness to Japan's strategy. The truth is that Japanese leaders have deliberately avoided building a large American-style service economy. Why? Because service industries generally aren't promising candidates for the Monopolistic Supergrowth strategy. Remember the five items that the Japanese look for in a targeted industry — high entry barriers, major economies of scale, good export prospects, large research and development opportunities, and elastic demand patterns. Service industries rarely score well on these criteria: few service industries feature high entry barriers, for instance. And not only are most service industries easy to enter, but service expertise generally spreads quickly to competitors around the world. Thus, with few exceptions, service industries offer little prospect of establishing a monopolistic lead.

By contrast, many areas of advanced manufacturing measure up well on all five of Japan's targeting criteria. Thus the Japanese economic system has focused single-mindedly on developing its manufacturing prowess.

Japan's manufacturing focus has been somewhat obscured in recent years by much ill-informed talk suggesting the Japanese have been "trying to get into services." Corporate Japan's acquisitions of service corporations in the West have appeared to confirm this talk. But such acquisitions generally do not represent any attempt to expand in services per se. Sony and Matsushita, for instance, have acquired American movie studios not out of any intrinsic desire to make movies but rather because they see control of Hollywood movie libraries as a lever that enables them to set global standards for future generations of entertainment hardware. They discovered the importance of movie libraries in the late 1970s when a threatened boycott by Hollywood almost aborted their fledgling videocassette recorder operations.

That said, Japan's dogged concern to promote manufacturing seems anachronistic to Westerners. After all, a basic tenet of Reaganomics (and even more so of Thatcherism) has been that the future of the world's most advanced economies lies in services. But the truth is that the Reagan/Thatcher case for services was always flawed.

For a start, most service jobs are conspicuously badly paid. Take tourism. The Florida tourism industry goes head to head with cheaper destinations such as Spain, Mexico, and even Thailand in attracting European tourists. Florida cannot aim to establish a significant productivity edge because making beds and waiting on tables are not notably less labor-intensive in Florida than anywhere else.

Even in better-paid service industries such as finance, the prospects have been exaggerated. Such services promise few jobs for ordinary workers who, by contrast, as the Japanese experience shows, can be highly productive in capital-intensive manufacturing. In any case, as Stephen S. Cohen and John Zysman authoritatively explained in *Manufacturing Matters: The Myth of the Post-Industrial Society,* some of the apparent growth in America's financial services exports in the early 1980s was traceable to optimistic bookkeeping in the American banking industry. Many American banks used controversial accounting techniques to credit themselves with growing amounts of nonexistent "interest income" on loans to bankrupt Third World countries.

For the foreseeable future, America's hopes of building a strong international financial services industry are constrained by deeply entrenched protectionism in many overseas markets. East Asia's fast-growing nations, for instance, pay lip service to the need for globalism in financial services but put obstacles in the way of their savers investing abroad. Their attitude is understandable: by forcing savers to invest at home, a government can exercise a firmer hand in taxing its citizens, particularly the wealthy. Moreover, many governments are reluctant to internationalize their financial systems for fear of weakening the effectiveness of domestic financial policies in fine-tuning domestic demand and maintaining a stable level of employment.

In any case, Americans have been crucially misled on America's competitiveness in finance. Startlingly, as we will see in Chapter Two, American financial services are actually quite inefficient in labor productivity. That many Americans think otherwise is a reflection of Wall Street's aptitude for public relations.

Another problem with international financial services is that, in common with most other service activities, competition from lower-wage countries is increasing. New York often finishes second best in competition with London and, thanks to low-cost communications, London's financial job base is now under pressure as back-office functions migrate to areas where labor is even cheaper.

The story is similarly disappointing in other sophisticated service activities. America's inventiveness, for instance, is no economic panacea. As Britain long ago learned to its cost, unless a creative nation can manufacture its inventions, it rapidly loses control of them to efficient manufacturers overseas. Nor is software a panacea. Much of America's optimism about software is based on the misleading success of Microsoft. In reality, Microsoft is unique in that it enjoys a global monopoly by virtue of a catastrophic mistake by IBM.

The ultimate test of an industry's potential for the United States is how much it contributes to America's pool of well-paid jobs. Increasingly America's software workers are pitted in head-to-head wage competition with workers in other countries. British workers, for example, write much of the software for IBM's big computers. Recently American software work has been migrating to small job-shops in Singapore, Israel, and Hong Kong. Shanghai is also becoming an important software development center, and such leading companies as Intel and IBM have already set up offices there. Now India, with a per capita income of $313 per year, has targeted software and has multiplied its software exports more than sixfold in the last six years.

India's Tata Consulting alone employs 3,600 software workers and recently completed a complex stock exchange software system for Switzerland.

Advocates of America's services strategy have wrongly claimed that Japanese companies "cannot make software." In reality, the Japanese are noted for high-quality software: a Japanese camcorder alone contains as much software as a classic IBM 360 mainframe computer. True, in recent years Japan has become a major importer of software, but that is only to be expected because labor costs are now so much lower abroad. When a few years ago Hitachi wanted to develop supercomputer software, it went to Ireland. Other Japanese companies have begun sourcing software from small software job shops in India and China. Corporate Japan's very act of sourcing abroad is itself the strongest possible hint that the Japanese see little prospect that any country can establish a monopolistic lead in software. Software know-how migrates quickly around the world via textbooks and journals, not to mention the reverse engineering of innovative products. Virtually the only thing needed to create software is brainwork. And these days brainwork is a commodity that can be sourced anywhere there are modems and telephone lines. In fact, the Indians got their start in software because plummeting telecommunications rates enabled them to do software maintenance during the American night on corporate America's computer systems via international telephone lines.

Postindustrialists also hold out high hopes for a prosperous American future in activities such as systems integration (creating things using sophisticated components and materials supplied by others) and designing electronic chips. Here again the prospects have been exaggerated. Such activities are somewhat analogous to architectural design. Although they require sophisticated brainwork, most of the special expertise necessary migrates rapidly around the world. In essence, many of the best new ideas can be reverse-engineered so there are few opportunities to create a monopolistic national lead. Here again, a harbinger of things to come is apparent in India, where engineers in Bangalore have been working via satellite to design field-programmable gate arrays for Texas Instruments.

America's service strategy contains an even more troubling flaw than low-wage foreign competition: many American service industries have become parasitic because they promote unnecessary activity that saps an economy's vitality. Perhaps the most obvious example is legal services, but dozens of other service industries such as finance, advertising, direct mail, government, and insurance are also similarly debilitating for an economy (even if the waste is usually less egregious than in legal services). This tendency for an economy to develop wasteful services will be referred to in this book as service-ization.

The trend toward service-ization is largely a function of perverse incentive systems and does not reflect any moral failing on the part of those providing the service. The fee structure of the American legal profession, for instance, encourages dubious class actions. The commission system in stockbroking fosters "churning" of clients' portfolios. Problems with such incentive systems have in many cases been exacerbated by the transaction cost explosion unleashed by the Cost Structure Revolution.

As we will see in Chapter Two, Japanese leaders use officially supervised cartels to control the rise of the service economy and in particular to nip parasitical services in the bud. Their objective is clear: to channel as many of Japan's best brains as possible into sophisticated manufacturing and thus keep Japan on the fast track to global leadership.

Winner take all

Conventional economists hold that the increasing "globalization" of the world economy will derail the Japanese planners' supergrowth ambitions. In this view, Japanese corporations have no choice but to move more and more high-grade jobs to the United States and Europe to escape the high yen. This will improve Westerners' incomes and simultaneously curb the rise in Japanese incomes. Thus with Japanese incomes supposedly staying roughly in line with those in the West in the long run, the United States will remain the leading economy because its population is twice Japan's.

Championed by such prominent scholars as Robert Reich and Michael E. Porter, this view has been espoused by virtually the entire American establishment. In particular it is taken for granted in much of what the American press says about U.S.-Japan economic relations. Unfortunately, this is an example of the tendency for Western commentators to see no one's point of view but their own. From a Japanese point of view, things look quite different.

Remember that the key to Japan's superior output in advanced manufacturing is vast investment in capital equipment. In many cases, this equipment accounts for most of a Japanese corporation's in-house manufacturing costs. Production workers' wages are by comparison a tiny outlay, as low as 10 percent of total costs and getting proportionately smaller all the time. From a Japanese corporation's point of view, therefore, the saving in wages from sending capital-intensive activities offshore is minimal. And there are many persuasive advantages to locating in Japan. For a start, this automatically shields a Japanese corporation from expropriation or nationalization by fickle foreign governments. (Even in the United States political risk is not insignificant given that history shows that few Great Power governments remain friends forever.) Locating their most expensive plants in Japan also minimizes Japanese corporations' vulnerability to foreign strikes and other forms of labor disruption (Japanese company unions are, of course, in a league of their own in their reliability and responsibility). Finally, locating in Japan helps a Japanese corporation keep its technological secrets from Western competitors.

This last advantage is the clincher. As we will see in Chapter Eleven, Japan's cartelized system of research and development has a hidden but powerful tendency to persuade corporate Japan to keep the best technology at home. By contrast, Western capitalism contains a hidden tendency to diffuse technology abroad.

Implicit in the globalists' argument is the idea that capital now flows freely around the world. Thus Japanese corporations are supposedly losing their traditional advantage of low capital costs. But capital does not flow in the way the globalists imagine — and it probably never will. The question of how free the world's capital flows truly are cannot be answered merely by looking at the policies of the United States and Britain, the only countries the globalists know well. The United States and Britain strongly favor the globalization of capital flows, and for good reason: they depend on constant infusions of foreign capital to keep going.

The real test of globalism is how it plays in such capital-surplus countries as Japan and Taiwan. Governments in such countries have no intention of implementing real liberalization: their control of their savings systems not only gives them powerful leverage over domestic corporations but provides increasing influence over debtor governments such as those of the United States and Britain.

This is not to say that capital-exporting countries do not see advantages in *appearing* to liberalize their capital markets. Japan in particular has ostensibly been easing its financial controls for decades. But the evidence is that, rather as with trade liberalization, this often consists of peeling off one layer merely to reveal another. That the flow of Japanese savings to industry is controlled by government-guided financial cartels is one of the most significant — and most often denied — facts of Japanese economics. Will Japan's cartelized banks provide financial backing to American industry to go into head-to-head competition with members of their own keiretsus? To state the question is to answer it.

The story of flat panel displays provides a compelling insight into how immobile Japanese technology is. Flat panels form the screens in laptop computers but they are critical components also for defense and aerospace contractors (because they boast a major weight advantage over traditional instrument displays). Virtually all the world's flat panels are made in Japan, a fact so troubling to American defense chiefs that the Clinton administration in 1994 felt moved to create an American flat panel industry from scratch. At first sight the administration's decision seemed odd because IBM owns a half-share in a highly sophisticated $750 million Japanese flat panel factory. Why can't IBM solve America's security problem by setting up a similar flat panel factory in the United States? Good question, and one that the Clinton administration evidently investigated before committing more than $500 million of taxpayers' money to try to reinvent IBM's half-owned technology. Even when the Americans own a half-share of a key Japanese technology, Japan has ways of making sure that that technology stays at home. Technology is a one-way street for corporate Japan, which gets to keep its own technology yet simultaneously enjoys easy access to the technological riches of the West's open societies.

Japan's combination of almost limitless capital plus the ability to maintain a firm proprietary lock on its advanced technologies is a phenomenon the world has never seen before.

Too many goods?

Many Western observers maintain that Japanese industry's very productiveness is the country's Achilles' heel. Japan, they say, will soon choke on a disastrous glut of productive capacity.

Yet in a world of scarcity, the idea that producers can ever produce "too much" is one of the oldest canards in economics. All the evidence of both history and logic is that, given reasonably stable demand-management policies in major economies, a country that produces a steadily rising output of desirable goods will find buyers for them. There may be temporary gluts in particular industries but, taking the world economy as a whole, exchange rates will adjust automatically to ensure "market clearing." This is, after all, what exchange rates are for.

The debate over who will buy Japan's exports has been rumbling on in the West since the Great Depression. Despite being shut out of many Western markets, Japanese industry geared up in the 1930s to produce vast exports of cotton cloth and light bulbs. To the dismay of Western skeptics, Japan made its own economic luck by selling to East Asian countries, and its economy positively boomed.

In today's conditions, Japan's exports increasingly enjoy a monopolistic edge that makes it difficult for Western nations to shut them out. The distress for consumers and for business users of Japanese equipment and components would be just too great. In any case, precisely because Japan's exports are increasingly monopolistic, there are few remaining powerful interest groups in Western nations that feel disadvantaged by corporate Japan's economic expansionism.

Thanks to the Cost Structure Revolution and to the risk-sharing possibilities inherent in the keiretsu system, Japanese corporations have enormous flexibility to cut prices. They can even maintain their prices at little more than raw-material costs for extended periods to nurse markets along. Moreover, miniaturization has reduced materials costs to almost nothing in many industries. Take the electronic calculator. The first versions launched by Sharp Corporation in 1964 weighed around 55 pounds (25 kilos). Today's one-ounce credit card versions have achieved a weight reduction of 99.9 percent. This represents an enormous reduction in claims on the earth's material and energy resources that has resulted in a concomitant reduction in retail prices from $2,400 down to $15.

In effect, the Japanese are now bearing the torch of abundance originally raised by Henry Ford more than eighty years ago. The lesson Ford taught was that if you can keep producing more and more cars, you can keep reducing their price. So demand will increase to the point where almost everyone can afford one. Miniaturization has given Japan the possibility of rolling out economic abundance on a scale never even dreamt of by Henry Ford.

In all the discussion about future markets for Japanese goods, Westerners have overlooked Japan's biggest advantage — its neighbors in East Asia. In fact, until recently Americans had considered East Asia America's "secret weapon" in winning any tussle with Japan for leadership of the world economy. In the mid-1990s, Americans are beginning to realize something that has been obvious in Tokyo for years: East Asia is *Japan's* secret weapon. In the short run, East Asia's greatest significance is that it provides Japan with enormous cover against efforts by the West to force Japan to play by Western trade rules. This is because more and more of Japan's exports of components and high-technology materials are being shipped to offshore assembly plants in East Asia that assemble products for the American market. Thus if America wants to get tough with Japan over trade, it must also risk alienating some of the twenty-first century's biggest consumer economies. Already, judging by their actions as opposed to their words, most East Asian nations are firmly in Japan's camp in the looming battle for leadership of the world economy.

Japan now finds itself in an enviable position: the opportunities to pursue its growth strategy seem to extend as far as the eye can see.

Has the balance been tipped?

In the light of what we've learned about Japan's economic strategy, it's worth again looking at Japan's "slump" of the early 1990s.

What we find is that, in contradiction to most of the reporting in the American press, the true story of the early 1990s was that America's leverage over Japan suddenly declined precipitously. America's ability to talk back to Tokyo weakened dramatically at almost every level of U.S.-Japan relations. Although in 1993 a new president came to office dedicated to putting America's interests first, he inherited a bargaining position much weaker than he had realized.

Japan has created a wonderful self-fulfilling prophecy that can be summed up like this: the greater Japan's current account surpluses, the more money the Japanese system has to invest abroad. And the more money the system invests abroad, the more leverage it enjoys over debtor governments, particularly the United States. The more leverage Japan has over the United States, the weaker the United States' position is in trying to rein in Japan's account surpluses.

The mystery of why Japan's trade surpluses soared as the yen rose is now apparent. At the time, Americans got the story backward: they said that Japanese mercantilism was driving the yen higher. But actually mercantilism per se had no impact on the currency; even if Japan does not import, it nonetheless fully recycles its foreign exchange receipts by buying American bonds and other foreign assets. In reality, the yen rose because of Japan's growing monopolization of vital manufactured products. As the yen rose on foreign exchanges, America had little choice but to reach into its pocket to pay ever higher prices for Japanese goods — particularly for sophisticated parts and production machines. By contrast, in former times America would have had alternative American or European suppliers to turn to.

Even the MITI has tacitly acknowledged that monopoly is now a critical factor in Japan's foreign trade. In an analysis in May 1993, it reported that recent increases in Japanese exports had been due mostly to higher prices that American and European buyers were being forced to pay because they had no other sources of supplies. The MITI added: "Where exchange rate appreciation is passed on in higher prices, the quantity of [Japan's] exports seems to be little affected." Japan's exports, it said, were benefiting from "the increased integration of Japanese exports into her trading partners' economies." Failure to understand the extent of Japan's monopolistic leadership led American commentators to assume that Japan's exports would soon be priced out of foreign markets with disastrous consequences for Japanese employment. Yet as in previous world recessions, in the early 1990s Japanese employers resisted cutting their work forces and instead applied their excess workers to increasing the quantity and quality of the goods they produced. And producing more and better goods is, of course, the essence of economic growth. Thanks to Japan's constantly lengthening quality lead, the yen, moving in wavelike motions, establishes new high-water marks every three to five years.

Perhaps the most startling fact of the early 1990s was that American companies like IBM, Xerox, Apple Computer, Boeing, and Kodak *increased* their purchasing of components and equipment from Japanese corporations while cutting jobs in the United States. In the past American corporations could always excuse such "outsourcing" by saying they were getting routine chores done in cheap-labor countries. But, with Japan's labor costs now as much as 50 percent higher than America's, Japan is no cheap-labor economy. The new trend amounts to a historic admission that America has lost its ability to make sophisticated manufactured goods. In fact, the then Apple Computer chairman John Sculley said as much in an interview with the *Nihon Keizai Shimbun* in 1993, frankly disclosing that any American effort to restrict imports from Japan would virtually shut down Apple.

In perhaps the most significant example of corporate America's dependence on Japan, IBM announced a flurry of agreements in which it will depend on Japanese competitors for critical components and equipment. IBM's willingness to abandon its once fiercely defended manufacturing independence is the biggest success yet for Japan's so-called kyosei movement. This movement was publicized in 1992 by Sony Corporation chairman Akio Morita, who was evidently acting on behalf of Japan's powerful Keidanren industrial federation. Kyosei is officially translated as "symbiosis," but in this context it has the connotation of mutual prosperity. Stripped of rhetoric, the concept is that the West's major corporations should work with Japanese counterparts in cooperative rather than competitive relationships. These relationships, described as partnerships, are said to work to the benefit of both sides — and they do. They serve the short-term interests of American corporations and the long-term interests of the Japanese.

In the early 1990s, Japan proceeded rapidly to establish dozens of important global partnerships with major American corporations. In the long run these arrangements will serve powerfully to boost Japan's growth strategy. In almost every case the Japanese partner does most or all of the advanced manufacturing. The American side generally confines itself to design, software, and other "creative" activities that bestow few long-term competitive advantages. Thus Japan has been moving to establish the sort of global division of labor dictated by its Monopolistic Supergrowth strategy.

These kyosei deals, which we will look at in detail in Chapter Two, serve decisively to undermine Washington's ability to conduct an independent trade policy. If Washington wants to use the ultimate sanction of tariffs against Japan, it will have to fight not only Japan Inc. but large sections of America Inc. as well. Without the big stick of tariffs to wield, the United States has essentially no bargaining power to establish real, as opposed to token, access for advanced American products in Japan.

In high finance also, the balance of power shifted dramatically to the Japanese side. The New York–based McKinsey management consultancy has estimated that Japanese holdings of U.S. bonds doubled between 1989 and 1993. McKinsey's then partner Kenichi Ohmae, who often articulates the Japanese establishment's positions in U.S.-Japan relations, bluntly read the riot act to the Clinton administration about America's weak bargaining position. Writing in the *Wall Street Journal* in May 1993, he said that if America insists on trying to increase its exports to Japan, Japan would retaliate by ordering its financial institutions to sell American bonds, which would "trigger a crash."

Ohmae was explicitly stating a threat that Tokyo has been hinting at for several years, most notably in veiled references by officials of the Japanese Finance Ministry. Each year that goes by, the threat takes on a greater significance for Washington officials. Of course, Japan is unlikely to go so far as to trigger a crash, but it doesn't have to. Even a small amount of Japanese selling can precipitate a distinctly uncomfortable rise in American interest rates. In fact, after President Clinton and Prime Minister Hosokawa failed to reach agreement on trade in February 1994, American fixed-rate mortgage interest rates jumped by 1.7 percentage points in just three months. Japanese officials frankly acknowledged that much of the rise in interest rates had been triggered by Japanese investors selling American bonds.

Tokyo is now evidently less inclined than ever to make anything more than token concessions on trade. As recently as 1990, top officials of the Ministry of Finance offered a compromise settlement of the long-running U.S.-Japan trade argument. Japan would promise to keep its current account surpluses to below 2 percent of gross national product indefinitely, provided the United States would stop trying to restructure Japan's internal economy. America's then top trade negotiator Carla Hills spurned the offer. Within weeks of Hills's response, Japan's trade surpluses started soaring. The result was that by 1992 they had exceeded 3 percent of gross national product and were still rising.

When the Clinton administration took office, its rhetoric suggested it would stand up to Japan on trade. A closer look revealed a different picture. The central objective of the administration's policy turned out to be merely to get Japan to reduce its current account surpluses gradually over four years to 2 percent of gross national product. The administration was trying to get the Japanese to do by 1997 what the

Japanese had voluntarily offered Hills in 1990! This time Tokyo was having none of it.

Commenting on the ongoing trade talks in July 1994, the influential economist Rudi Dornbusch said, "It is now clear the administration will settle for anything, anything at all, just to get a deal. Anything at all means practically nothing." Dornbusch was amply vindicated when the two sides unveiled an agreement in October 1994. Like previous failed agreements, this one was long on talk of change in Japanese regulatory behavior; conspicuously absent was any firm commitment by Tokyo to put a ceiling on Japan's surpluses. Given the fervor with which American officials had at the outset advertised their intention of establishing numerical targets, the agreement was not only a humiliating climb-down for the Clinton administration but a historic acknowledgment that the balance of economic power in the U.S.-Japan relationship had passed to Tokyo.

For Americans who care about their country, Tokyo's recent negotiating record will add powerfully to unease about the U.S.-Japan relationship. This book will do nothing to alleviate their bewilderment at Washington's handling of the American side of the relationship in the last half-century. But what of the Japanese side? What are Tokyo's true motives? Many otherwise generous-minded Americans are understandably beginning to ask some sharp questions.

As far back as the early 1980s, the American journalist Marvin J. Wolf purported to resolve the doubts in his book *The Japanese Conspiracy: Their Plot to Dominate Industry Worldwide and How to Deal with It*. If nothing else, the book's title won points for shock value. But, like most American authors who write about Japan, Wolf had never lived in the country. This was an obvious handicap in addressing such a delicate question as the motives behind Japan's policies. The truth is that the question can be answered only after making a thorough study of both the history of U.S.-Japan relations and of the profound cultural gap that separates the two countries.

As we elucidate the secrets of Japan's success in later chapters, we will assemble the evidence on both sides of the conspiracy question. In the final chapter, we will give our verdict on Japan's motives. But for now we must return to our main theme. First we will assess key Japanese strengths that Western observers persistently overlook.

2

Hidden Strengths

Whenever the Japanese and American economic systems clash, Americans issue the same call: "Japan must change." This call was first heard in the 1850s when President Millard Fillmore sent gunboats to open the Japanese market. It was repeated in the 1930s when American manufacturers accused Japanese industry of using cheap labor to undermine the world trading system. And again in recent years, with Japan's surpluses hitting unheard-of records almost every month, Americans renewed their familiar cry. Their message was conveyed most pointedly by the economic commentator Leonard Silk. He recently warned that if the Japanese do not change their economic ways, an angry United States would retaliate and deal a "severe blow" to the Japanese economy.

Fighting words — but will they be heeded in Tokyo? Probably not. The Japanese attitude was well articulated in 1993 by Kazuo Nukazawa, the gritty managing director of Keidanren, Japan's powerful federation of business leaders. "We Japanese feel we have been pretty successful," he said. "Why should we change? Others who are doing worse than us should change, not us."

The point was made even more strongly by the former top Japanese bureaucrat Yukio Okamoto in 1994. In an address to foreign businessmen, he said that young Japanese officials now openly condemn America's effort to change Japan's economic behavior as an "outrageous" interference in Japan's internal affairs.

Japanese economic leaders in the 1990s are not only more convinced than ever of the wisdom of Japanese economic policies but, overlooked by the West, they enjoy unprecedented strengths that buttress their determination not to blink first in trade confrontations. Here follows an assessment of some of these hidden strengths.

Focus on manufacturing

Japan has often been criticized by American commentators for its "slowness to make the transition to a services-based economy." Japanese leaders know better. They know that by dominating global manufacturing, Japan is becoming the indispensable hub of the world economy. They have therefore been working with new vigor to promote their manufacturing industries in recent years. Between 1980 and 1993, Japan increased its manufacturing work force by 14 percent — at a time when America's manufacturing work force declined by 11 percent.

The result is that, with just one-half of America's population, Japan now boasts fully three-quarters of America's manufacturing work force. Add the fact that Japanese corporations recently have been investing two to three times as much per worker as corporate America and it is not surprising that Japan has now surpassed the United States in total manufacturing output.

Japan's enormous productivity in manufacturing has enabled it not only to become self-sufficient in most manufactures but to become so prolific an exporter that it is establishing global monopolies in a rapidly expanding range of vital products.

This picture of Japan's manufacturing invincibility may come as a surprise to readers of the American press. How can we reconcile it with reports that a resurgent America has turned the tables on a struggling Japan? Such reports are loaded with inconsequential anecdotes and remarkably short on hard numbers. One example is a *Business Week* article in 1993 that reported American corporations were beating back Japanese competitors "from sea to shining sea." As evidence, *Business Week* pointed in the first instance to Apple, IBM, and Compaq, which were said to be unbeatable in laptop computers. Yet in truth, like the rest of the American computer industry, these companies "source," or buy, most of their laptops from Japan. Elsewhere, *Business Week* reported that Hewlett-Packard was "murdering" the Japanese in laser printers. This sort of death, however, holds no sting for the Japanese, because Japan supplies the most sophisticated components in Hewlett-Packard's printers.

As with many "resurgent America" stories, the Hewlett-Packard printer story has grown with the retelling. As recently as September 1994, it was given front page treatment in the *Wall Street Journal* as the showcase example in a series titled "America Ascendant: U.S. Companies' New Competitiveness." But the *Journal* didn't mention H-P's dependence on Japan's laser technology, let alone the fact that H-P's much-ballyhooed inkjet printers are made in Singapore.

Perhaps the most egregious myth of America's manufacturing comeback concerns the semiconductor industry. In 1993, as reported by the *Wall Street Journal* and other leading newspapers, America staged a "remarkable turnaround" by recovering its former position as the world's largest maker of semiconductors. This news, which was based on a survey by the Dataquest statistical organization, came as a surprise to well-informed observers such as the American Electronics Association, whose figures showed that America's worldwide trade in semiconductors had actually slipped into deficit in 1993. In truth, the American semiconductor revival story was little more than a hoax. Unknown to the American press, Dataquest's figures were for *shipments,* not production, of semiconductors. A large proportion of Japan's output of semiconductors was categorized as "American" because, under Dataquest's rules, semiconductors made by the Japanese for sale by American semiconductor companies count as American shipments. The true story of the 1990s was that American semiconductor companies were getting more and more of their sophisticated semiconductors made in Japanese foundries. There are no accurate figures for this outsourcing phenomenon but few doubt that if semiconductors were classified by country of manufacture, far from falling behind in 1993, Japan probably extended its lead.

Of course, some companies have scored genuine successes in recent years. But such successes are isolated and — a point of critical importance to the theme of this book — they are rarely attributable to an unbeatable American edge in manufacturing. Typically they are in industries that for legal or other non-market reasons are sheltered from Japanese competition. A case in point is the Intel microprocessor company. Sadly for American hopes for a general manufacturing comeback, Intel's success is quite unique. While Intel is indeed a sophisticated company, it is admired today for the same reason that Xerox and IBM were once lionized as symbols of American superiority: it is a monopoly. As such it can afford to do things in style. Its success stems largely from its luck in the early 1980s in acquiring exclusive rights to sell microprocessors for IBM-standard personal computers.

A telling sign that Intel's success does not rest primarily on a manufacturing lead is that Taiwanese competitors have been making cut-price clones of its chips. In fact, an increasing proportion of Intel's manufacturing these days takes place offshore: Intel's much-publicized Pentium chip, for instance, is made in Ireland as well as the United States. Some of Intel's products are actually outsourced from Japanese companies such as Matsushita, Sharp, and Nittetsu. The critical point is that while the products carry the Intel brand, the jobs are in Japan, and the crucial manufacturing equipment used to make the products is Japanese.

The Japanese are underwhelmed also by the reported comeback by the American auto industry. As they know only too well, America is sourcing a rapidly increasing number of sophisticated components from East Asia. Chrysler, for instance, buys many of its engines from Mitsubishi. Rarely has the hollowing out of American industry been so embarrassingly clear as when General Motors in 1992 filled an order from Honda Motor for batteries. The order was part of a deal concluded by President George Bush in which Japanese industry agreed to create jobs in America by importing American products. When Honda took delivery of the batteries, it discovered they were made in Korea.

The American press has also been reporting that American corporations are exporting more. But what exactly are they exporting? Increasingly, products assembled from made-in-Japan parts. Even such traditionally strong exporters as Xerox, Caterpillar, and Boeing now depend on Japanese parts. If the *Economist* is to be believed, up to two-thirds of the components in some Boeing planes, for instance, are made abroad, chiefly in Japan.

Many American commentators maintain that the United States still leads in the most "sophisticated" forms of manufacturing. Many of the products Americans have retreated to are sophisticated only in the same sense as a Rolls-Royce is sophisticated: a Rolls-Royce may be highly prized by discerning owners, but the cottage industry techniques employed in making it hardly seem sophisticated to a company like Toyota. This Rolls-Royce syndrome — characterized by short runs, special designs, and old-fashioned labor-intensive production techniques — is apparent in many areas of dominance claimed by the American electronics industry.

By contrast, the Japanese electronics industry specializes in Toyota-style operations, characterized by vast investments in new factories, highly efficient manufacturing processes, and enormous production runs. The Toyota syndrome is perhaps best seen in the Japanese semiconductor industry, which specializes in mass producing the world's most powerful memory chips. The techniques required are way ahead of those used even by Intel and other leading American makers of microprocessors. Specifically, the Japanese use purer materials than the Americans, and their lithography achieves much finer miniaturization of semiconductor circuits. As of 1994, the only two companies in the world that had announced plans to make one-gigabit memories, which will hold an astounding one billion bits of information, were Japanese — NEC and Hitachi. Commenting on their plans, the *Wall Street Journal* was characteristically condescending: "Although U.S. chip makers are the world's top producers of microprocessors and other profitable, sophisticated chips, the Japanese are still ahead in brute manufacturing technology — the kind needed to make chips that have circuits with extremely small lines." In reality, the one-gigabit chip will require "brute" technology several generations more advanced than that used in Intel's Pentium. Although the *Journal* characterizes Japan's advanced memory chips as "commodities," they are in fact the very opposite: a Japanese monopoly.

If American manufacturers had really turned the tables on the Japanese, international trade figures should surely confirm this. These figures are a notable omission in most American comeback stories, and for good reason: in virtually every category where American manufacturers are said to be doing well, the trade figures show the Japanese are palpably doing even better. Take semiconductors. As of 1993, America's bilateral deficit in semiconductors and transistors totaled $4 billion. In computers and peripherals, the bilateral deficit was $9.9 billion. And in automobiles and auto components it was $33.7 billion. Even in telecommunications, where the Americans are indeed strong, the Japanese are stronger still. Powered by a seemingly insatiable American appetite for telephone switches, fax machines, and cellular phones, America's bilateral telecommunications deficit totaled $3.7 billion in 1993.

Why has Japan been so successful in increasing its manufacturing base? The answer lies in its successful war on service-ization.

The war on service-ization

Japan has been working hard to ward off service-ization, the tendency for marginal or counterproductive service activities to preempt ever more of the economy's labor. Japan's success is immediately apparent in the overall numbers: the service economy accounts for only 60 percent of the work force in Japan versus fully 72 percent in the United States.

Some of Japan's most important manpower savings are in information services and finance, activities whose increasing share of the work force in the United States is ironically considered by American policymakers to be the cornerstone of America's future prosperity.

The statistical category of finance, insurance, real estate and business services accounts for only 7.7 percent of Japan's total work force versus 11.0 percent of America's. Manpower savings in this category alone provide Japan with about two million above-average workers for its manufacturing economy.

Within this category, Japan's most spectacular victory has been in legal services. Even after adjusting for the fact that certain types of legal work are performed by separate professions in Japan, Japan's legal services industry preempts only about 50,000 professionals versus 777,000 in the United States. On a proportional basis, the streamlining of Japan's legal system provides more than 330,000 high-grade draftees for the manufacturing labor force.

The Japanese authorities tightly curb the supply of legal services by controlling entry to the profession. In a typical year only one in fifty would-be lawyers succeeds in gaining admission to Japan's legal training institute. Meanwhile the authorities curb demand for legal services by, for instance, discouraging class actions. And the government has deliberately structured the court system so that even the simplest lawsuit takes years or even decades to litigate — a powerful deterrent to most would-be litigants.

But how can a complex society get by without lawyers? Actually, very easily. Japan has various informal but efficient ways of arbitrating grievances. The secret in part is the hierarchical nature of Japanese society. In the case of commercial disputes, for instance, there is generally some higher authority whose bona fides as an arbitrator will be accepted by both sides. Banks, major industrial corporations, and, in the case of the most intractable disputes, government agencies often act as arbitrators in commercial disputes. Because such organizations enjoy exceptional power in Japanese society, their rulings are generally respected.

Prevention is better than cure, of course, and at every level in Japanese society life is arranged to prevent disputes from arising. Japanese companies, for instance, rarely do business with strangers except where introductions have been performed by trusted intermediaries. Each side's loyalty to the intermediary serves as a restraining force, and in the event of dissension, the intermediary can probably break the deadlock.

Advertising is another area of the information services sector where Japan achieves spectacular manpower savings. The big cartels that control Japan's main industries generally curb their members' advertising spending. Japan's big banks use cartel-driven advertising "ceasefires" to minimize their advertising spending. Much to the chagrin of the Japanese media, such ceasefires are often blessed or even imposed by government officials.

The Japanese advertising industry is organized to tap the full benefits of scale economies. The Dentsu advertising agency alone accounts for about 25 percent of all advertising in Japan, yet it employs fewer than six thousand people. On average each Dentsu employee generates about $1.8 million of advertising versus only $425,000 at the WPP advertising giant, Madison Avenue's biggest player. Is this an apples to apples comparison? Perhaps not. A truly accurate study would require a whole book all its own. But the available evidence indicates that advertising preempts much less labor in Japan than in America. By this writer's estimate, advertising manpower savings contribute at least 40,000 draftees to Japan's manufacturing labor force.

Japan also achieves great manpower savings in such information-era businesses as the media, public relations and lobbying, direct mail, and recruitment and executive search. In the media, for example, Japan has only 124 daily newspapers versus 1,642 in the United States. The growth of television has also been contained by tight limits on the number of television channels. Fewer than twenty channels are available to most viewers.

Japan's war on service-ization has also been notably successful in banking, a surprising victory because American policy analysts have long assumed that Japan is uncommonly inefficient in financial services. In reality, as *Forbes* magazine's senior editor Richard L. Stern has documented, Japanese financial institutions are startlingly lean organizations. Measured by assets per employee, Japan's major banks are nearly ten times more efficient than equivalent American banks. Take Japan's biggest bank, Dai-Ichi Kangyo. It recently needed only 19,000 employees to run an institution with assets of $503 billion. By contrast, Citicorp needed 81,000 employees to manage assets of $217 billion. As of 1991, Japan's commercial banking sector's personnel costs per $100 of assets averaged just 47 cents, less than one-third of the American figure of $1.55. Knowledgeable observers point out that American banks have for decades been consistently far more profitable than their Japanese counterparts. But international comparisons of bank profits are largely meaningless because of differences in regulations, accounting practices, tax systems, economic structures, and industrial policies. A key reason for the Japanese banks' low profitability is that they subsidize their keiretsu affiliates with exceptionally low interest rates on loans.

Japan also saves considerable manpower in the securities industry. On Richard Stern's numbers, the Japanese securities industry employs only one-fifth as many workers as the American industry. In the minor financial professions such as accounting, investment management, and tax consulting, Japan's manpower savings are even more spectacular. Japan gets by with less than one-tenth of America's proportion of accountants, for instance.

How can Japan function with so few financial workers? Partly because of Japan's "big is beautiful" logic. The Ministry of Finance regulates the financial system to maximize the amount of money concentrated in the hands of just a few giant banks and fund management houses. Meanwhile the MOF has kept a tight lid on exotic new financial instruments such as futures and other "derivatives." Although securities firms say such instruments make an economy more efficient, the MOF does not agree: it sees such instruments principally as ploys by which the securities industry creates transactions whose costs are borne ultimately by millions of unwitting participants in pension funds and mutual funds.

Japan has also been extremely successful in minimizing government bureaucracy. Because most government officials are given strong powers (they effectively write the laws under which they operate and their policies are largely free from legal challenge), their decision-making processes are streamlined and effective.

A case in point is law enforcement. Japan gets by with significantly fewer police officers than the United States. Here a decisive factor is that the law is stacked in the police's favor: gun control is very strict, the police enjoy robust powers to interrogate suspects, and the courts take a firm line with defendants. (Is this a good way to run a country? As elsewhere in this book, our purpose here is not to judge the wider philosophical questions; it's to show why Japan boasts proportionately far more manufacturing muscle than the United States.)

Meanwhile Japan gets by with a significantly lower ratio of teachers than the United States. Many factors are at work here, but a key one is probably that curriculums are set nationally, thereby minimizing the need for administrative bureaucracies in individual school districts.

Japan's government health care system is highly efficient thanks to a sharp eye on transaction costs. Coverage is universal, which minimizes the need for labor in medical insurance and allows the government to focus single-mindedly on preventive medicine. Doctors are well protected against malpractice suits. Taking the United States as a benchmark, Japan's manpower savings in nurses and doctors alone amount to more than 500,000 people.

Japan has also organized its economy to discourage the proliferation of various sorts of repair services. In the auto industry, tough certification rules ensure that most cars on Japan's roads are quite new. The Japanese auto distribution industry markets used cars in places like the Russian Far East. This pattern maximizes the number of workers the economy supports in making cars and reduces employment in the auto repair industry.

Many foreigners mistakenly believe Japan wastes a great deal of labor in distribution. However, their view is based largely on how Japanese distribution appears to foreign shoppers — and foreigners do much of their shopping at a few department stores in central Tokyo that offer lavish service. Foreigners are also influenced by the fact that, for historical and cultural reasons, Japan's city centers are full of tiny stores typically run by octogenarian proprietors. Although such stores look inefficient, they preempt remarkably little able-bodied labor.

In reality, the authorities have used various regulatory devices to curb the overall size of retailing in Japan. Auto retailing is probably the most cartelized of all areas of Japanese distribution. This industry preempts just 514,000 workers in Japan versus 1,996,000 in the

United States. Thus with one-half America's population, Japan needs little more than one-quarter of America's total automobile sales force. The food retailing industry employs only 669,000 in Japan versus 3,204,000 in the United States. In general merchandise retailing, Japan gets by with only one-sixth of America's employment total, 405,000 workers versus 2,426,000.

Japan's combined employment in both retailing and wholesaling is 11,183,000 — a mere 44 percent of America's 25,328,000. Its manpower savings in distribution alone contribute nearly 1.5 million workers to the manufacturing sector.

Adding up Japan's various antiservice-ization policies, we can hardly be surprised at its exceptionally large manufacturing labor force.

Japan's productivity lead

Although the West has heard much about Japanese productivity over the years, the full extent of Japan's advantage is one of the least understood and most significant facts of Japanese economics.

American policymakers are confused on this subject, maintaining that Japan's productivity story is quite patchy. They say that Japan enjoys high productivity only in a narrow range of export-oriented industries. Productivity in most other Japanese industries is supposedly quite low, so much so that Japan ostensibly lags behind the United States overall. In one extreme view put forward by the *Economist,* American labor is supposed to be, on average, nearly twice as productive as Japanese labor.

Like the rest of the press, the *Economist* is greatly influenced by superficial factors. Its editors make much of the supposed excessively lavish service observable in a few special circumstances in Japan. They have also commented adversely on the relaxed, even unhurried, atmosphere in many Japanese offices. The *Economist* seems to assume that the only way Japanese workers can outproduce their American counterparts is by emulating the frantic work pace of the hapless Charlie Chaplin in *Modern Times.* Yet a frantic work pace has little to do with Japan's superiority any more than it explains why Americans are more productive than Bangladeshis. The Japanese outproduce Americans partly because Japan invests two or three times more in each job than America does and partly because, thanks to the long-term relationships of the keiretsu system, the entire Japanese economy has been structured to keep transaction costs to a minimum.

One thing is clear: comparing productivity in economies as different as the United States and Japan's is fraught with pitfalls. The outputs in many cases are very different (how do you compare sushi with hot dogs?). The corporate structures are different (many Japanese manufacturers control their retail outlets, whereas their American counterparts are denied this option by American antitrust law). Consumer standards are often different; in frills like service and packaging, Japanese consumers are more demanding than Americans.

Adding to the measurement difficulties are the vested interests of those involved in making productivity comparisons. American economists are generally intent on proving America still leads in overall productivity. Otherwise, they would have to question their entire free market belief system.

On the Japanese side, too, there is pressure to show the United States in a good light. Take the Japan Productivity Center. Founded in 1955 with financial support from Washington, its mission has been to help raise Japanese productivity to American levels. If it admitted that Japan surpassed the United States in productivity years ago, it would be out of a job.

The Japanese traditionally believe in flattering their customers, and no customer is more important than the United States. Just as a smart Japanese executive deliberately contrives to lose when playing golf with an important customer, Japanese officials probably consider it good manners to save America's face in the productivity league tables.

The ultimate source of confusion on this issue is undoubtedly Japan's trade lobbyists in Washington. They have a notably contradictory agenda. On the one hand, lobbyists for a few major Japanese export corporations often emphasize these corporations' efficiency because superior productivity is an important defense against allegations of dumping. On the other hand, out of a concern to minimize the damage to America's economic ego, they maintain that Japan's exporters are a narrow segment of the Japanese economy and that other Japanese industries are notably inefficient. Japan's lobbyists, like Europe's, know that flattering America is simply good business. A confident America is a big-hearted America — an America that not only magnanimously overlooks foreigners' trade barriers but continues even in the 1990s to make large transfers of military technology to those same foreigners.

The lobbyists' double-edged story of Japanese labor productivity has been widely embraced by American economists because it dovetails so nicely with Western competition theory. Economists want to believe that Japan's export corporations learn efficiency by competing in the American market while Japan's domestic industries, operating in a cartelized home environment free from American competition, remain inefficient.

But when Americans measure Japan by Western theory rather than by on-the-spot observation, they generally grasp the wrong end of the stick. Theory has led them mistakenly to disparage the efficiency of, for instance, the Japanese cigarette industry. The industry's productivity was described as "very weak" by the Washington-based McKinsey Global Institute in 1992 and as "particularly weak" in a 1994 *Wall Street Journal* op-ed piece.

Neither of these comments was supported by data or source material. As with many myths about Japanese productivity, the point evidently seemed so obvious that it did not need substantiation. Certainly the structure of the Japanese tobacco industry could hardly seem more economically incorrect to believers in American-style capitalism: the industry is dominated by Japan Tobacco, a government-owned monopoly run by retired government bureaucrats. Meanwhile, the American tobacco industry is widely regarded as one of America's most efficient exporters.

As it happens, tobacco is one of the very few industries where a comparison of output volumes is readily available. The numbers are a startling rebuke to American conventional wisdom. Japan Tobacco needed just 19,100 workers to produce 286 billion cigarettes in 1991. By comparison, American tobacco manufacturers employed 61,691 to produce 695 billion. Thus annual output per worker at Japan Tobacco, at 15.0 million cigarettes, was 34 percent higher than the American industry's 11.2 million. Of course, for a fully accurate comparison, one would need to do much fine-tuning, using information that is not disclosed to the public. Even if such information were available, however, it probably would not affect the overall comparison very much, and under no circumstances could it conceivably alter the comparison so much as to make Japanese productivity look "particularly weak."

One of the most egregious myths of Japanese productivity is that Japanese white-collar workers are supposed to be particularly inefficient. Again, this allegation is considered by American observers to be so obviously true that no figures or sources are needed — and certainly none is quoted. But the figures are available and they're a stinging rebuke to American hubris: according to the University of California scholar Richard Rosecrance, Japanese corporations typically run their business with only one-sixth of the ratio of white-collar workers of equivalent American corporations.

Many American observers consider Japanese banks inefficient. In 1993 Bill Lewis, head of the McKinsey Global Institute, suggested that Japan's bank workers were only half as productive as their American counterparts. A similar suggestion has come from American Enterprise Institute scholar Karl Zinsmeister. Neither Lewis nor Zinsmeister seems to have any evidence to support their assertions. Judged by personnel costs per unit of assets, Japan's commercial banks are more than three times as productive as their American counterparts. In fact, there is probably no other major Japanese industry that has such an efficiency lead over the Americans as banking!

Lewis went on to suggest that Japan's service economy employed 15 million more workers than it needed, a truly bizarre assessment given that the service economy preempts only 60 percent of Japan's work force versus 72 percent of America's.

Lewis and Zinsmeister's comments are a classic example of the way American opinion leaders are misled by the American press's chronically superficial coverage of Japanese economics. The American press routinely dismisses Japanese services as inefficient simply because many services are very expensive in Japan. Thinking in Western terms, the press concludes that Japan's high airfares, for instance, betoken great inefficiency in the Japanese airline industry. This view overlooks the very different dynamics of the Japanese economic system. Japan's high airfares are actually part of an elaborate system of cross-subsidies by which service industries help manufacturing industries. In this case the airlines are required by oil industry regulators to pay high prices for fuel as a way of subsidizing the steel industry (whose fuel costs are correspondingly reduced). The steelmakers in turn pass on the subsidy in low prices for steel supplied to the auto industry. Japanese air travelers, in effect, are helping to build the Japanese auto industry.

Air travelers also subsidize Japan's aerospace industry. Thanks to high fares, Japanese airlines can afford to pay top dollar for American planes, and American plane manufacturers agree in return to transfer technology and provide subcontract work to Japanese aerospace companies. While this may seem complicated, it works because so much of Japanese industry is cartelized, and the bureaucrats enjoy large regulatory powers.

Even productivity experts who engage in rigorous analysis to measure Japan's overall productivity are hardly more reliable. Take the New York University economist Edward N. Wolff. As publicized in a major article in 1992 by Sylvia Nasar of the *New York Times,* Wolff purportedly found that America in 1988 led Japan by a truly astonishing 45 percent in overall productivity. Sadly for the United States, this conclusion was based on a highly controversial methodology: Wolff translated all Japanese production numbers at an artificial exchange rate of about ¥220 to the dollar, thus undervaluing the yen by about 40 percent compared to the relevant market exchange rate.

To get a sense of the limitations of Wolff's method, consider how it measured the legal profession's productivity. Each lawyer's productivity was deemed to be equal to his or her earnings, with the proviso that in the case of the Japanese the figures should be devalued by 40 percent. Typically top lawyers in Japan generate only about half the fee income of their American counterparts, so, as measured by Wolff, they emerged only 30 percent (one-half less 40 percent) as "productive" as the Americans. This slighting of Japanese legal efficiency seems even more absurd when you look at the content of legal work in the two countries. It is not too much to say that American lawyers often undermine societal cohesiveness by aiding and abetting various forms of "legal fraud" such as disingenuous class actions and bogus insurance claims. By contrast, lawyers in Japan see themselves as defenders of collective societal interests and they even tacitly act against their own clients' interests where they feel those clients are being opportunistic.

Wolff's 40 percent yen devaluation was dictated by the logic of the so-called purchasing power parity method of productivity measurement. There are, however, several major problems in using purchasing power parity in Japan. First, American observers consistently underestimate the yen's true purchasing power within Japan. Second, Japanese consumer prices are distorted by a special "investment premium" — a surcharge that the cartels load into their prices to pay for future expansion.

The most significant point about purchasing power parity is that until recently, the method was rarely used by the American media in making comparisons. By contrast, it had had a long history as an economic crutch that helped lift the productivity of subpar economies like Britain, Australia, and New Zealand in world economic league tables. That American economists have resorted to purchasing power parity to beautify America's numbers is a disturbing admission of weakness.

Up to the early 1980s, American policymakers were content to accept that output per capita as translated at current market exchange rates gave a reasonably realistic ranking of productivity among major economies. If we apply the same method today we find that Japan is about 40 percent ahead. Although informed observers would make many minor upward and downward refinements to this number, it is nonetheless close to the truth.

The good life

If the Japanese are so productive, why are they so poor? In fact they are *not* poor. The Japanese people as a whole have a lifestyle about as affluent as that of Americans — in other words, very affluent indeed. That Japan produces such affluence while also handsomely outinvesting and outexporting the United States is the ultimate proof that Japan now leads in overall productivity.

That said, many American commentators still maintain that Japan lags in affluence. But invariably they offer no convincing evidence to support this contention. Moreover, the Japanese people's standard of living is reflected in many important indicators. Japan ranks substantially higher than the United States in the United Nations Human Development Index. The Japanese enjoy the world's highest life expectancy, one of the most unequivocal tests of national well-being. The life expectancy rate at birth for women is now 80.9 years in Japan versus around 79 years in the United States and France and less than 78 years in Germany and Britain. Men now enjoy a life expectancy of an amazing 75.2 years in Japan versus less than 72 years in the United States and Britain and less than 71 years in Germany and France. It is interesting to note that no significant country in Asia comes even close to Japan in life expectancy.

Exaggerated impressions abroad of Japan's poor quality of life have been fostered partly by Japan's ritual modesty. Public relations materials mailed to Japan-watchers around the world are peppered with comments like this one from the English-language magazine *Japan Update:* "On paper, per capita income [in Japan] is the highest in the world, but it doesn't show up in the quality of life." These publications rarely give the other side of the picture: they seem never to note, for instance, that Japan passed the United States in the quality of infant health care as long ago as the early 1960s.

There is only one significant area where the Japanese are clearly worse off than Americans: housing. Housing space per head in Japan is about one-half the American figure. But even here, Westerners have an exaggerated idea of the Japanese disadvantage. For one thing, the Japanese are more efficient in using space than Westerners: for the most part they sleep on futons, thin mattresses placed on the floor which are then folded away in the morning to clear space for daytime activities. In any case, Japan's shortage of living space represents no intrinsic poverty; rather it is a manifestation of the government's policy of suppressing consumption. As we will see in Chapter Six, what the Japanese lack in living space is more than made up for in the much larger proportion of gross national income devoted to industrial investment. Additionally, it is worth remembering that the abundance of high-quality housing in the United States is in part attributable to generous subsidies not available in Japan.

Western visitors tend to judge Japan's cost of living by the prices of Western-style goods in Japanese stores, yet many such goods are exotica in Japan and are naturally more expensive than the staples of Japanese-style living. Also, Western observers are more often than not members of the upper middle class, and they unconsciously look to their class counterparts in Japan as a reference point. This leads to a systematic bias, for people at the top end of the social scale in Japan generally lead modest lifestyles. After all, Japan has one of the narrowest gaps between rich and poor outside Communist China. The incomes of the top one-fifth of the Japanese population are only 2.9 times higher than the incomes of the bottom one-fifth. By comparison the multiple is 9.1 times in the United States and more than 10 times in both France and Britain. As the Tokyo-based consultants Thomas R. Zengage and C. Tait Ratcliffe pointed out a few years ago, the Japanese economy's special achievement is that its *average* standard of living is so uniformly high.

In 1992 Japan surpassed the United States to become the world's biggest market for diamond jewelery. The figures, compiled by the De Beers diamond organization, imply that Japan's per capita diamond purchases now run twice the American rate. The Japanese now drink about 12 percent more spirits than Americans. Japan scores higher than the United States in the percentage of households with telephones (99 versus 94 percent), air conditioners (68 versus 64 percent), and washing machines (99 versus 75 percent). Japan also leads in households with color television sets, videocassette recorders, and microwave ovens. Even in sewage disposal — a category in which Japan lagged badly in the early decades of its Economic Miracle — it has almost caught up, with 89 percent of Japanese dwellings now connected to public sewage services. Japan leads the world in the number of hospital beds per 1,000 population. It has around thirteen beds per thousand people, versus eleven in Germany and a mere six in the United States, the United Kingdom, and France.

There is essentially no poverty in Japan. Some down-and-outs live rough in Japan's cities, but they are a negligible phenomenon compared to the vagrancy problem in the cities of Europe and the United States. Child poverty seems to be nonexistent.

Some of the ways the Japanese use their affluence elude the Western eye or seem inappropriate. Fewer mothers of young children work in Japan. Like Americans in the 1950s, the Japanese regard this as a mark of affluence. Many Japanese spend much of their income on sending their children to cram school. Moreover, the heavy use of perks in corporate Japan tends to conceal much consumer welfare from statisticians: Japanese families, for instance, often take vacations free or virtually free at company-owned mountain lodges.

Even if Westerners are blind to Japan's affluence, the middle-aged Japanese officials who chart Japan's course have, within their own lifetimes, witnessed the most spectacular improvement in living standards in world history. They are not likely to be easily persuaded to abandon the principles that built that prosperity.

The impression that Japan lags behind the United States in consumer welfare serves to perpetuate the American policymaking community's habit of condescending to Japan. Moreover it constitutes one of the great barriers to the United States addressing in a timely fashion the issues raised by Japan's evident rewriting of the rules of economics.

In search of monopolies

Japan's economic leaders aim to establish monopolistic leadership in advanced industries. Their success to date has been greater than most Americans realize and constitutes one of Japan's greatest hidden strengths.

Many of Japan's monopolies are so obscure that they are virtually invisible to American executives and government officials. Take the strange story of epoxy cresol novolac resin, an ingredient in most semiconductors. Almost no one in the United States had heard of this substance before 1993, but things changed fast when an explosion disabled a small factory in the remote Japanese town of Niihama. As horrified American semiconductor executives quickly discovered, the factory accounted for nearly 65 percent of the entire world supply.

Prices of some types of semiconductors doubled on the world market in the following two weeks. Within a month, the Clinton administration was pressing the Japanese to take emergency action to restore production. The closer American officials looked at the epoxy story, the more worried they became. They found that the Japanese also monopolized both the substance known as resolving silica, with which the epoxy is mixed before being incorporated in semiconductors, and the process by which resolving silica and epoxy are mixed. Thus three links of the manufacturing "food chain" in one hitherto unsung subdivision of the semiconductor industry had been monopolized by corporate Japan. Moreover, an alternative technology called ceramic packaging is also a Japanese monopoly.

In the wake of the Niihama disaster, top American companies like Du Pont and Monsanto were urged to get into the business, but they didn't want to compete in a Japan-dominated product category.

Why did the Niihama explosion come as such a surprise to the United States? In mapping gaps in America's technology food chain, Americans have hitherto focused narrowly on a few "critical" technologies of compelling importance to American military security while ignoring unglamorous civilian technologies. Yet these civilian technologies account for a much larger share of world economic output.

How many economically significant monopolies does Japan now have? As this question has never been studied systematically by government officials or scholars, we can only guess. But it seems reasonable to assume that monopolistic leadership is a factor in about one-third of Japan's exports.

Certainly research by Salomon Brothers suggests that Japanese policy has aimed for years to increase America's dependence on Japanese monopolies. In Salomon's view, Japan's principal motive has been to render Japanese industry invulnerable to rising protectionism in the United States.

The major difficulty in identifying Japan's monopolies is that crude statistics in this area are often misleading; qualitative factors are involved to an extraordinary degree. To assess the degree of monopoly one must, for example, distinguish between different production technologies. Often where the Japanese have a real monopoly, the Americans still can claim a presence. Typically one American supplier remains in any particular category who uses "handmade" production techniques for special-order military applications, while leaving the vast consumer market entirely to a Japanese cartel.

Another problem in measuring Japanese monopoly is American corporations' increasing secrecy about their dependence on Japanese supplies. As reported by Marie Pialot, many hollowed-out corporations even swear their suppliers to secrecy. The cover-up is understandable: because wages are now lower in the United States than in Japan, American employers who fire American workers in order to source from Japan are implicitly confessing they have lost the technology race. American defense contractors seem particularly secretive, perhaps because they made large profits in the 1980s by relying on cut-price components imported from Japan while turning their backs on struggling American suppliers. In withdrawing from making certain categories of components, U.S. manufacturers may get a quid pro quo such as a guarantee of below-market prices for several years to come. Such agreements may violate American law, so neither party to the bargain is likely to want to draw attention to the agreement.

Another difficult qualitative question is to what extent control of apparently insignificant components gives Japan a monopoly in a whole industry. Does Japan monopolize the videocassette recorder industry? On paper, no. But in practice, probably yes, because non-Japanese makers are dependent on Japan for vital parts.

In some industries dominated by corporate Japan, a few non-Japanese suppliers exist in Europe or East Asia. But often such suppliers are de facto junior partners in the Japanese cartels, and they are located in countries whose governments turn a blind eye to antitrust concerns. In general, once a Japanese cartel has captured at least 50 percent of the global market, it can be presumed to have established monopolistic leadership.

With these qualifications, let's try to identify some of Japan's monopolies.

The electronic fortress

Probably corporate Japan's most important area of monopolistic leadership is electronics. The seeds of monopoly which Japan has planted here promise a truly exceptional harvest. The Japanese technology expert Masanori Moritani has perhaps put it most succinctly: the silicon revolution, he says, promises as big a transformation in the world economy as all other technologies developed since the eighteenth century put together. This is quite a statement but the evidence that it is true is widely apparent to anyone who has looked at how corporate Japan's control of the electronics industry is giving it growing power to shape dozens of other industries, from robotics and factory automation to cars and aerospace.

These are some of the "chokepoints" that Japanese companies control in the electronics industry:

Flat panel displays. Japan dominates the industry, especially in large high-end products such as thin-film transistor liquid crystal displays. According to the information technology scholar Tom Forester, America's dependence on Japanese liquid crystal displays is a major reason why IBM and Apple Computer have been forced into unequal partnerships with Japanese competitors. Total flat panel sales were about $2.5 billion in 1992 and are expected to reach an astonishing $18 billion by 2000. Japan also monopolizes special flat panel components known as drivers and has a lock on production of liquid-crystal cells (the raw material from which the displays are made).

Laser diodes. These are already indispensable in compact disk players and laser printers and now they are critical components for the new multimedia industry. Japan's global market share is more than 99 percent. Sharp Corporation's share alone is 40 percent.

Compact disk players and CD-ROM drives. Compact disk players need no introduction; their more advanced derivatives CD-ROM (compact disk read-only memory) drives are becoming well known because they are a core technology of the multimedia revolution. Sony has about 40 percent of the global CD-ROM market. Other Japanese makers control the rest. According to an American government expert, the lasers at the heart of CD-ROMs are "about twenty years ahead of the laser technology used in most American weapons."

Supercomputers. The remaining American player, Cray Research, depends on Japan for critical components.

Capacitors. Murata makes 50 percent of the world's multilayered ceramic capacitors, which are essential in almost all electronic devices, and 80 percent of the world's ceramic filters.

The information highway. Although American commentators think of the information highway as an American stronghold, Japan will make much of the relevant hardware, including many of the ultrasophisticated asynchronous transmission mode (ATM) switching systems at the heart of interactive television. The Japanese have leveraged their expertise in video compression to lead a new international consortium that will own most of the patents for future video compression systems: of the eight companies participating in this consortium, four are Japanese (Sony, Matsushita Electric, Fujitsu, and Mitsubishi Electric), two are American (AT&T and General Instrument), and two are European (Thomson and Philips).

Notebook computers. Japan dominates this industry thanks to key monopolies not only in components, notably displays and tiny disk drives, but in such manufacturing equipment as production robots.

Semiconductor materials and equipment. Japan's share of the semiconductor materials industry rose from 21 percent in 1980 to 73 percent in 1990 and is still rising. Japan's market share appears to be at least 80 percent in several crucial items including ceramic substrates, silicon wafers, sputter targets, bonding wire, TAB tapes, lead frames, and mask blanks. Japan also monopolizes the supply of copper foil for printed circuit boards. Disco Corporation makes 70 percent of dicing saws for cutting silicon wafers. Two-thirds of the world's quartz masks are made by Hoya, more than 50 percent of photoresists by Tokyo Ohka Kogyo, and 40 percent of photomasks by Dai Nippon Printing.

Hot-wall oxidation/diffusion furnaces. These are vital in making semiconductors. Japan owes its leadership here in part to American antitrust policy, which blocked two strong American makers from joining forces in the 1980s to compete with a growing challenge from Tokyo Electron.

Cellular phones and pagers. A key area of Japanese dominance in cellular phones is gallium arsenide chips, which operate at higher frequencies and consume less power than silicon chips. Oki Electric is increasing its gallium arsenide capacity by 50 percent in 1995 to keep up with booming demand. Corporate Japan is believed to monopolize the market in surface acoustic wave devices used in cellular phones.

Optical character recognition. Optical scanning equipment allows postal services automatically to sort letters. It is also installed in automated ticket barriers in the world's most advanced subway systems and in vending and change-making machines that accept bank notes. Much of the software in these machines is made in the United States and other Western countries, but the crucial hardware is almost entirely Japanese. The major manufacturer is Toshiba, which got its start in a MITI-sponsored research cartel in the 1960s. Japan also leads in supermarket scanner technology.

Ferrite. High-grade ferrite is a vital material in several high-technology applications, notably the data-reading heads of computer hard disk drives. TDK makes 45 percent of the world's total output in one factory in Kofu, Japan, and even supplies the U.S. Defense Department.

Nickel hydride batteries. These tiny high-tech batteries are vital for cellular phones, notebook computers, camcorders, and other portable electronic gadgets. Leading makers: Sanyo Electric, Matsushita Battery, and Toshiba.

Laser printers. By far the most important component in laser printers is the so-called engine. Canon alone has about 80 percent of the engine market, according to American government sources.

Fax machines. Japan monopolizes this category via control of printer engines and optical readers.

Steppers. These precision machines are vital for making semiconductors and liquid crystal displays. Nikon enjoys close to 70 percent of the booming market for steppers; Canon has almost all the rest.

Military electronics. According to John Stern of the American Electronics Association, twenty-one of America's key weapons systems are "totally dependent" on Japanese suppliers for certain critical components. Japan's ceramic packages, which are designed to resist environmental extremes, encase most semiconductors used in American weapons. Coors Electronic Package, an American company which used to dominate the ceramic package industry, has blamed "state-sponsored trade socialism and foreign government agendas to corner the world market" for the collapse of the American industry. According to Eduardo Lachica, the American defense industry must buy Japanese ceramic packages because American ones would be "prohibitively expensive." Kyocera alone makes 70 percent of the world's ceramic packages and its products are vital to the functioning of such American weapons as the Tomahawk, Patriot, and HARM missiles. At the time of the Gulf War, America defense chiefs were reportedly "sweating bullets" over America dependence on foreign components, particularly those made in neutral-leaning Japan.

More fortresses

Outside the electronics field, the following seem to be some of Japan's most important areas of monopolistic leadership:

Robotics. Pioneered by the Americans in the early 1960s, this industry is now entirely dominated by Japan, which makes at least 80 percent of the world's robots. Fully two-thirds of all the world's industrial robots are used in Japan. Robot makers in Sweden, Germany, and Italy depend on Japan for components.

Microengineering. Japan's microengineering expertise is easy to overlook but it has enabled Japan to establish several important monopolies in electromechanical components. Such components often must be machined to tolerances measured in microns, that is, in millionths of a meter. Such precision is a key reason for the superior reliability of, for example, Japanese videocassette recorders (whose magnetic heads and drums contain dozens of tiny moving parts which wear out quickly if they are not precisely aligned). Olympus Optical recently announced a grinder that grinds steel to a tolerance of one-fiftieth of a micron.

Auto parts. America is hardly extinct in auto parts, but Japan leads in miniaturization. As moving parts get ever smaller, problems of heat and wear are correspondingly exacerbated — and the Japanese are acknowledged masters in making materials which beat these problems. Miniaturization skills helped Japan establish an effective global monopoly in motorcycles by the early 1970s. Now these skills are helping Japanese automakers pack ever more gadgetry into their cars while improving fuel economy through weight reduction. An important area of Japanese leadership is small compressors for automobile air-conditioning systems. Japan leads in sensors, displays, gauges, and other electronic components, which now account for between 5 and 10 percent of the cost of a typical car. The Japanese reputedly have a lock on plastic optical fibers for controlling a car's electronics; compared to traditional wires, optical fibers provide important weight and space reductions. The Japanese reportedly lead in critical future technologies such as lean-burn chemical catalysts, high-capacity batteries, piezoelectric vibrating gyroscopes (for navigation systems), and ceramic engine parts (which will improve efficiency by allowing engines to operate without cooling water).

Auto industry manufacturing machinery. Much was made recently of Chrysler's Neon car, which was described by press commentators as Chrysler's "Japanese car killer." Most reports overlooked the fact that the Neon, like most other advanced American cars, is made using Japanese presses and other sophisticated production equipment. Although Schuler of Germany is still a player in large presses for the auto industry, the category is now led by Japan's Komatsu. Japan leads in so-called squeeze-mold techniques for the mass production of strong, precisely engineered aluminum subcomponents. Honda is the world expert in using aluminum in engines.

Molds and dyes. These seemingly mundane products are an important Japanese stronghold in the production equipment sector. Sophisticated metal molds are required to shape car bodies, bottles, the bodies of appliances, and even the soles of running shoes. Japan's output of metal molds now totals around $15 billion a year, three times the output of Japan's much more visible robotics industry. Japan has about 60 percent of the world mold market and supplies the Detroit Big Three with advanced molds.

Micro-motors. Precise, powerful micro-motors are an important edge for Japan in everything from cameras to CD-ROMs and laptop computers. Most micro-motors are made in East Asia using specialized Japanese manufacturing technology. Mabuchi Motor now makes 900 million micro-motors a year — equivalent to one for every household in the world — and its dollar-denominated sales doubled in the three years from 1989 to 1992.

Bearings. Invisible to the consumer, bearings are a crucial area of Japanese leadership. They are most familiar as ball bearings, but they come in many specialized varieties. Bearings are used to relieve friction in virtually every mechanical process, and Japanese bearings are now vital in precision-engineering applications from videocassette recorders to fighter jets. Because bearings must combine extreme hardness with precise engineering, they are made in highly specialized factories, and monopolistic pressures have always been powerful in the industry. In recent years Japanese companies have leapfrogged over the American and Swedish companies that used to dominate the industry, and the United States now imports about 80 percent of its bearings. Just how strong the monopolistic pressures are in this industry can be gauged from the story of New Hampshire Ball Bearings, an American defense supplier that was taken over by Japan's Minebea in 1985. The takeover was controversial because America's ball bearing capacity had already fallen too low to meet surge production needs of a conventional war. But Ronald Reagan personally decided to approve the takeover in an effort to boost then Prime Minister Yasuhiro Nakasone's standing in Japan. Although Minebea had undertaken to expand in the United States, it instead quickly cut back and allegedly started importing East Asian ball bearings that were repackaged as American-made. Commenting on the alleged repackaging, the Defense Science Board said this "seriously threatens the assured access of the U.S. military." Why would Minebea risk offending the United States in such a serious way? Much of the answer lies in the ball bearing industry's huge monopolistic pressures that make it unprofitable to operate duplicate factories.

Cameras. The camera industry is a classic Japanese monopoly and it has conferred classic monopolistic advantages on the Japanese economy. Thanks to leadership in cameras, Japan rapidly ascended the learning curve in lenses and miniature motors and thus surpassed the Americans in copiers, semiconductor-making equipment, laptop computers, television broadcasting equipment, and a host of other seemingly unrelated products that depend on camera technology.

Machine tools. This is a vast category with probably dozens of subsectors in which Japanese companies have effective global monopolies. Between 70 and 80 percent of high-technology machine tools are made in Japan.

Medical and scientific instruments. Corporate Japan monopolizes a growing number of products in this important category due to leadership in optics, high-performance lasers, and electronics. Japanese companies have long dominated in both conventional and electron microscopes. Olympus Optical alone makes 70 percent of the world's endoscopes. Sumitomo Special Metals, maker of the world's most powerful magnets, supplies key components for advanced magnetic resonance imaging (MRI) diagnostic equipment.

High-technology lamps. Japan dominates the world market in lamps used in copiers and semiconductor-making equipment.

Interferon. Invented by a Tokyo University professor, human interferon is a vital substance for treating cancer and AIDS. The Hayashibara group makes half the world's supplies.

Copiers. The world leaders are the Japanese companies Canon, Ricoh, and Tokyo-based Fuji Xerox. Many of the sophisticated parts in American-brand copiers are made in Japan.

Gears. Japan dominates many categories, most visibly bicycle gears. Thanks to leadership in advanced gears, Japan has a lock on highly efficient contra-rotating propellors, which enable modern ships to cut fuel consumption by about 15 percent.

Wristwatches and watch movements. Japan exports nearly 90 percent of its watch output. Its main monopoly is in analog watches, which have traditional faces and electronic movements. Using high-speed robots in virtually workerless factories, Japan's Citizen Watch alone makes one-fifth of all the world's watches.

Musical instruments. According to one estimate, Japan has 90 percent of the world market.

Electric power generation equipment. This oligopolistic $75 billion industry is virtually invisible to the consumer but is of great geopolitical importance. The Americans, the French, the Swiss, and the Germans are all players, but the Japanese now lead in important categories such as steam turbines. Western suppliers often function as the Japanese companies' junior partners in the booming Asian market.

Ships. The shipbuilding industry is an example of a "smokestack" industry the United States mistakenly has scorned as an industry of the past. Japan leads due to its use of computers in on-site production supervision and in the cutting and shaping of materials. Japan now makes virtually all the world's ships' engines, giving Japanese ship-builders leverage over Korean and European rivals. Japan's new high-technology ships' engines promise to revolutionize warfare. Another area of Japanese leadership is new-generation double-hulled oil tank-ers, which are designed to reduce the risk of environmental disasters. This leadership explains why in 1993 the American shipbuilding in-dustry sought subsidies from the Clinton administration to buy vital manufacturing technology from Japan.

Pollution control equipment. Japan has long considered pollution control one of the key growth industries of the future and has in particular honed its skills in desulfurization and denitration. Japan monopolizes key subsectors such as the specialized equipment needed to control emissions from power stations.

Carbon fiber. Stronger than steel and lighter than aluminum, car-bon fiber has long been a vital material in aviation. Engineers reckon that carbon fiber components typically reduce a plane's total weight by 8 to 9 percent, a key advantage in fuel economy and, in the case of warplanes, in range and maneuverability. Japan is believed to enjoy a monopoly in the special source material from which most carbon fiber is made. Moreover, Japan specializes in new low-cost versions of carbon fiber which are expected to make substantial inroads into the auto industry.

Avionics. Japan leads the world in aviation-related electronic com-ponents.

Titanium. Sumitomo Sitix is the world's leading producer of this increasingly important metal. Titanium's lightness and corrosion re-sistance make it a vital metal in aircraft, chemical plants, nuclear power stations, desalination plants, space and underwater explora-tion, automobile manufacturing, and offshore oil production.

Construction equipment. Most construction equipment sold in the United States is manufactured abroad, generally in Japan. Such American suppliers as Caterpillar and Dresser rely on Japan for dif-ficult-to-make components. The Japanese lead in sophisticated speci-alities such as tunnel-boring.

Lopsided dependencies

Most Americans seem to think America's growing dependence on
Japanese manufacturing is of little significance. Even the fact that
America's most advanced weapons depend on Japanese components
elicits no more than a shrug from the likes of the Brookings Institution and the *Wall Street Journal*. This is globalism, they seem to say;
sit back and enjoy it! The complacency seems to stem from a view
that "mutual dependencies" are unavoidable in the modern global
economy. Just as America is becoming dependent on Japan for some
products, so Japan is supposedly becoming dependent on America for
others.

At first sight Japan does seem to be importing more manufactured
goods from the United States. But on closer examination this trend
betokens no dependence on American manufacturing but merely
growth in "reverse imports." A typical example is American-built
Honda cars that are taking an increasing share of the Japanese market. They are made largely from Japanese parts, and America's main
contribution is to provide inexpensive labor for Honda's assembly
lines.

The truth is that the combination of a huge manufacturing work
force and high productivity enable the Japanese economic system to
aim for almost complete self-sufficiency in advanced manufacturing.
In the last two decades Japan has reduced or eliminated its dependence on America in computers and computer components, telecommunications, machine tools, electronic manufacturing equipment,
and robotics. Perhaps most significantly of all, the Japanese economic
system has been working in a coordinated way to reduce Japan's
dependence on America in aerospace, the last significant manufacturing industry that America leads. Rather than buy American
warplanes, for instance, Japan decided in the late 1980s to build its
own.

Aerospace apart, American trade officials who have studied this
question know of no significant industrial activity where Japan lacks
a full range of manufacturing capabilities.

One reason American policymakers have been unconcerned about
the loss of American manufacturing power is that they believe the
United States can easily get back into lost industries "in a matter of

weeks" in an emergency. This theory has gone largely unchallenged because there are few hard numbers in the public domain that would allow academic economists to evaluate it.

On the rare occasions when the theory has been tested by events, however, it has proved startlingly wanting. One such occasion was the Toshiba military secrets scandal of the 1980s. A Toshiba subsidiary was found to have sold crucial machine tools to the Soviet defense industry. The United States wanted to retaliate by boycotting Toshiba products, but it quickly discovered it could not do so because many major American manufacturers were critically dependent on Toshiba for components. There followed one of the most humiliating episodes in American business history as such high-technology corporations as AT&T, Hewlett-Packard, and Apple Computer lobbied Capitol Hill in Toshiba's behalf. Although the companies were understandably embarrassed to associate their names with such a controversial cause (the estimated damage Toshiba's action had inflicted on American defenses had been put as high as $30 billion), they felt they had no choice. In the end, Toshiba escaped with a slap on the wrist.

A perhaps even more significant admission of American dependency came in the early 1990s, after the small company Japan Aviation Electronics Industry was indicted by the United States Justice Department for selling defense technology to Iran. This time, the company turned out to be so important to America's defense strategy that no less an organization than the United States Defense Department stepped in to plead successfully to get it off the hook.

The message of the Toshiba and Japan Aviation incidents is clear: Japan's manufacturing prowess is rapidly becoming a vital tool of global power.

Japan's new lobbyists

We noted in Chapter One that Japan has invented the kyosei movement to promote partnerships between Japanese and American corporations. Typically all that the Americans bring to the party is their marketing clout in the United States. The true significance of these arrangements is that they institutionalize corporate America's dependence on corporate Japan's manufacturing skills. But the public relations version as presented in the American press is generally that strong and generous American corporations are helping troubled or technologically backward Japanese counterparts.

One such deal between General Motors and Isuzu Motors was presented in the American press as General Motors "teaching" Isuzu how to cut costs. Only later did it emerge that General Motors had agreed to import diesel engines, truck cabs, and complete truck chassis assemblies from Isuzu. Similarly, in the case of a kyosei deal between Ford Motor and Mazda Motor, the press reported that Ford was teaching Mazda to cut costs. Later Ford disclosed it would buy several lines of Mazda-built small cars for sale under the Ford brand name.

Here are a few examples of kyosei in action:

Intel's "flash" memories.   These will function like extremely miniaturized floppy disks and they are expected to enjoy a huge market. Early press reports suggested that these devices would help Intel lead a major American manufacturing comeback in advanced electronics, but in reality Intel is getting the manufacturing done in Japan by NMB Semiconductor and Sharp. Advanced Micro Devices and National Semiconductor are among several other American corporations that have signed kyosei deals to get their flash memories made in Japan.

Motorola's D-RAMs.   Motorola's most sophisticated D-RAMs — 16 megabit chips — are to be made in Sendai, Japan, in a $720 million partnership with Toshiba.

Applied Materials' liquid crystal displays.   These are being made in Japan in a joint venture with the Japanese heavy-equipment maker Komatsu.

Amdahl's next generation mainframe computers. Design and manufacturing by Fujitsu.

Hewlett-Packard's new intelligent network systems. Aimed at the world's telecommunications utilities, these systems will be based on switching systems supplied mainly by Fujitsu under a long-term agreement signed in 1994.

Digital Equipment's notebook computers. Manufacturing by Japan's Citizen Watch.

Harley-Davidson motorcycles. Following negotiations with the Japanese components industry, Harley-Davidson is now reputedly sourcing as much as 20 percent of the components in some supposedly all-American "hogs" from Japan.

Hewlett-Packard's RISC computer chips. Many of these are being produced in a joint venture with Hitachi.

Silicon Graphics' technical computing microprocessors. The world's fastest microprocessors for scientific calculations, they are manufactured in Japan by Toshiba. In a separate deal, Silicon Graphics, America's leading supplier of three-dimensional imaging computers, is sourcing new RISC computer microprocessors from NEC.

Microsoft's computerized television and multimedia decoder boxes. These devices will enable users to play interactive games and go shopping by computer. Much of the manufacturing will be done in Japan by NEC in association with Hewlett-Packard.

Time Warner's new interactive cable technologies. Manufacturing by Toshiba.

These deals all pale in importance when compared with IBM's participation in the kyosei movement. IBM now relies on Hitachi for the so-called engine — the most complex component — of many advanced IBM printers. Many of the smallest and most sophisticated IBM personal computers are made by Japan's Ricoh Corporation. IBM's Notejet printer is made by Canon. Matsushita Electric makes many high-end desktop computers sold under the IBM label. The most sophisticated of IBM's color screens are made in Japan by Toshiba. And in 1994 IBM announced it would buy central processing units and other key parts in forthcoming multimedia computers from Fujitsu.

IBM has entered a $2 billion joint venture with Toshiba and Siemens to develop 256-megabit dynamic random access memories. These chips are three generations more advanced than the 4-megabit chips that are routinely incorporated in today's generation of electronic devices — each has the capacity to store a phenomenal 10,000 pages of typewritten text versus fewer than 160 pages for today's chips.

It is hard not to see these deals as indicating that America's most respected companies have abandoned hope of reclaiming their lead in manufacturing productivity. Certainly up to just a few years ago such deals would have been considered an outright admission of defeat by corporate America. As recently as 1988, IBM's Industry Operations Vice President Sanford Kane said the company was determined to avoid becoming dependent on Japanese partners because "we would be forced to share information and it would be doubtful whether we could get access to state-of-the-art equipment as quickly as our Japanese counterparts."

Seven years later IBM is singing a different song. Like many other American participants in kyosei, it now lobbies against efforts by Washington to get tough with Tokyo on trade.

Merchants of confusion

As we approach the denouement in the contest between the American and Japanese economic systems, one further Japanese strength must be mentioned, and it is perhaps the most surprising of all — the American press. Although the American press is often critical of Japan and therefore is not generally thought of as an advantage for the Japanese side, it is nonetheless Japan's trump card.

Japanese leaders have long resented the American press's condescension toward Japanese administrative methods, but they have used it to Japan's advantage by appearing to agree with the criticisms and erroneous perceptions of American correspondents. They thus create multiple, contradictory versions of the facts of Japanese economic life, and it has become virtually impossible for American policymakers even to begin to find common ground among themselves in discussing the Japanese economic system, let alone agree on an intelligent response to it.

When not actively confusing the American public, the American press has given powerful voice to a crucial theme of Japanese public relations: that the Japanese economic system is trying to reform itself along Western lines.

The American press's influence has been all the more significant because many of America's other windows on Japan are peculiarly inadequate. For instance, most American scholars and authors who study Japanese economics are dependent on Japanese funding. Their research is often based on short trips to Japan organized by various public relations organizations in Tokyo that steer attention away from taboo topics such as cartels. Also, American scholars tend to be too narrowly focused to understand that Japanese society works by an entirely different logic that can be understood only as a whole.

American understanding has not been improved by the American embassy in Tokyo, which has a record of being notably misinformed on Japanese economics. The embassy seems bereft of officials who speak Japanese (at times of trade tension, it cannot even field a Japanese-speaking spokesman to put America's message before the Japanese public).

Meanwhile, American corporations know little of what is happening on the ground in Japan. In most cases they have handed over management of their Japansese operations to largely unsupervised Japanese executives.

Moreover, the few American executives posted to Japan these days rarely stay long enough to get a grip on reality. Although typically they find ordinary life in Japan an enchanting experience, they generally become so disoriented by the business culture that they leave in despair within two or three years. Few of them return. By contrast, American executives who stay in Japan for a long time generally share with the Japanese people a special lack of inquisitiveness about the big picture. For them Japan never ceases to be an enchanting experience, and they come to accept as a right the many privileges the Japanese shower on honored guests.

Ideally, the American press should approach Tokyo as professionally as the Japanese press approaches Washington or Paris. After all, Japan is far more difficult for newcomers to fathom than the United States or France. Among other things, American newspapers should, therefore, invest in years of training for their future foreign correspondents. Most American correspondents in Tokyo have had virtually no such training, and they generally leave within about three years, well short of the five years or so most foreigners need to begin to understand the culture.

It is hard to exaggerate how unreliable the American press is on Japan. Look at how the press has presented the American auto industry's problems in the Japanese market: Detroit allegedly has failed because it refuses to make cars with the steering wheel in the correct position for Japan's left-hand-drive roads. The truth is that, via subsidiaries in Europe, all the Detroit automakers produce cars configured for Japanese roads — yet historically these cars, many of them made to high German standards, have faced even greater difficulty in Japan than Detroit's American-built offerings. In reality, configuration is irrelevant: in the case of makes such as Mercedes-Benz, BMW, and Jaguar, which are available in a choice of steering wheel positions, Japanese buyers have a long history of preferring the steering wheel on the wrong side because, in their eyes, this is an exotic status symbol.

The steering wheel canard is perhaps the most obvious example of how gullible the American press has been in swallowing the Japan lobby's public relations. Suffice it to say that while American journalists have for decades repeated the left-hand-drive story, they have downplayed Japan's deliberate barriers to auto imports. As far back as the early 1980s some commentators even took to describing the Japanese car market as "one of the most open in the world." That this was a little premature was authoritatively demonstrated in 1994 when the consulting firm Booz Allen & Hamilton concluded that remaining trade barriers added as much as 40 percent to the price of imported cars sold in Japan.

The American press's habit of condescending to Japan leads it constantly to make almost unbelievably careless errors. For example, from 1990 to 1994, the press constantly attributed Japan's soaring trade surpluses to Japan's supposed "slump." Tough times had supposedly slashed Japan's demand for imports. Unfortunately, no one in the American press seems to have checked the underlying import trends. In truth, Japan's imports rose. The widening surplus was driven entirely by export revenues, which rose even faster. In the four years, the rise in imports was 15 percent versus a rise of 32 percent in exports. Had Americans known that exports were the driver, they would have seen that the economic slump was a media hoax and that, far from feeling sorry for "poor dysfunctional Japan," they should have been envying Japan's stunning strengths. Virtually the entire Western press made this error not once but many times, most notably the *Wall Street Journal,* which as late as 1994 was still describing Japan as "mired in an economic slump."

The American press's record on covering Japanese banking has been even worse. American correspondents predicted for three years running — in 1991, 1992, and 1993 — that Japanese banks would disastrously fail to meet tight new capital rules introduced under the auspices of the Bank of International Settlements (BIS). All the Japanese banks proved these predictions incorrect each year — but the *Wall Street Journal* led the press in making the same unfounded predictions in subsequent years. The remarkable thing about the BIS story is that, as *Euromoney* magazine pointed out in 1988, acknowledged experts on Japanese finance knew all along that, thanks to special strengths in the Japanese financial system, the Japanese banks would easily meet the BIS requirements.

The fiasco of the *Journal*'s BIS reporting was a classic demonstration of business leader Tadashi Sekimoto's point that American press correspondents in Tokyo seem constantly to place their trust in the wrong sources. In this case, correspondents relied on American securities analysts to "substantiate" their reports. Such analysts are readily accessible but, for the most part, unreliable: typically they don't read Japanese, and in trying to see into the Japanese financial structure, they draw heavily on newspapers such as the *Wall Street Journal*. In a word, they reflect back to the *Journal* the misguided version of Japanese reality that *Journal* writers want to believe.

One of the American press's problems is that its major source of background information on Japan is official English-language translations of selected documents issued by Japanese government agencies, industry cartels, and individual corporations. Such translations are often extremely inaccurate. Errors seem to arise particularly in final editing into idiomatic English, a process generally carried out by recently arrived Australian, British, and American expatriates in Tokyo. Lacking a solid understanding of Japanese politics and economics, such editors often unconsciously introduce their own misconceptions into the finished product.

Another important source of errors is articles contributed by Westerners to Japan's public relations magazines. Such contributors are often distinguished people in the West who have little or no direct understanding of Japan. And instead of correcting any errors, the magazines print a small disclaimer in each issue absolving themselves of responsibility for contributors' accuracy.

The slant of these magazines' coverage was exemplified by a major article on U.S.-Japan trade tensions in Nomura Securities' English-language magazine. It was written by Phillip Oppenheim, a British conservative politician. Under a heading *Double Standard: Who's Really the Unfair Trader?*, Oppenheim painted the United States as highly protectionist and said that Tokyo was "far too deferential" to Western critics of Japanese trade practices. In an ostensible show of fairness, Nomura balanced this article with a commentary from the former California governor Jerry Brown. But Brown addressed himself mainly to tangential matters such as American labor leaders' and environmentalists' concerns about trade with Mexico. To be fair to Brown, he probably had no knowledge of Oppenheim's arguments, but the fact remains that Oppenheim's assertions went unchallenged.

A major problem for American correspondents is that the Japanese generally do not correct foreigners' misunderstandings. For the Japanese, Westerners in Tokyo are "guests of Japan," and one does not correct guests. This misplaced courtesy probably helps explain the *Economist* magazine's embarrassing experience when it launched a direct mail campaign to sell subscriptions in Japan. The mailing piece was written in both Japanese and English and featured an endorsement from a well-known Tokyo banker. In the English-language version, the *Economist* consistently misspelled the banker's name and, in the accompanying Japanese-language version, it mixed him up with another prominent Japanese banker. (The *Economist* called him Yusuke Kashigawe in the English version and Toyoo Gyohten in the Japanese version. The correct name was Yusuke Kashiwagi.) The mailing piece was first sent out in 1992 but, thanks to the evident discretion of the *Economist*'s Japanese contacts and associates, the magazine was still using the uncorrected missive a year later. A similar reluctance by the Japanese to correct errors in editorial coverage may help explain why the *Economist,* like most other Western news organizations, is lax about fact-checking in Japan. The result is a blind-leading-the-blind effect in which foreign correspondents constantly amplify myths created by other foreign correspondents without checking with primary sources.

The press is also hampered by Japanese leaders' tendency to regard journalists as inferiors in the Confucian pecking order who have no right to ask difficult questions. In answer to an inappropriate question, a Japanese official is likely to launch into a sort of soliloquy full of airy irrelevance and deliberate self-contradiction. This is best considered nonsense talk, and it is the polite Japanese equivalent of a curt Western "No comment." A famous remark by Tsutomu Hata, who became prime minister in 1994, provides a good example: asked to justify Japan's restrictions on beef imports, he told journalists that the Japanese had specially long intestines, which make it difficult to digest beef. On that occasion, common sense prevailed and the foreign correspondents laughed. But on topics where correspondents are operating beyond the limits of their own common sense (for example, in writing about the counterintuitive Japanese financial system), they are often blind to the jokes and duly fill their articles with nonsense quotes. In fact such quotes often acquire a life of their own as they are picked up by American scholars and used in the footnotes of erudite papers on Japanese economics.

Japanese sources are particularly likely to resort to nonsense talk where Japan's sovereignty or national security is involved — and both concepts are defined broadly in Japan. In fact, as the authors Joel Kotkin and Yoriko Kishimoto have noted, Japanese leaders quite openly advise their subordinates and social inferiors that the less the West knows about Japan the better. And, unknown to the Western press, ordinary Japanese people not only do not understand how their economy works but do not try to find out. This goes even for most of the official spokesmen and analysts the Western press uses as sources in Tokyo.

American correspondents often place too much trust in the accuracy of Japan's English-language daily newspapers, which are published by the Japanese press cartel. Japanese editors are bound by an ethical system that emphasizes loyalty to the nation and often requires information to be suppressed or subjected to spin control in the national interest.

It should be noted, however, that this spin control is largely limited to economic matters. On such sensitive issues as Japanese war guilt and political corruption, the Tokyo English-language press is often surprisingly frank. Frankness on such issues (which incidentally is echoed by some of Japan's Washington trade lobbyists) can be so disarming that Westerners are blinded to the extensive spin control applied in economic matters.

To make matters worse, many American business publications approach the Japan story with an avowedly political agenda that dovetails with the Japanese economic system's public relations objectives. Probably the worse offender is the *Wall Street Journal*, which seems to regard promoting free trade as a higher ideal than telling the truth. The *Journal*'s editorial pages in particular are notorious for bending the facts about Japan to head off protectionist tendencies in the United States. For many years virtually all the *Journal*'s influential editorial page articles on trade have been written by lobbyists or crypto-lobbyists (such as American lawyers, consultants, and scholars who ostensibly are independent observers but in fact are funded by Japanese corporations and agencies). As late as 1993, one such contributor was spotted still promoting the steering wheel myth.

The *Journal*'s editors hold as a matter of ideology that America's trade deficits — and America's consequent dependence on foreign investors — "do not matter." Impatient with supposedly misguided Americans who are upset by the deficits, they have gone on record as saying that "the best solution for the [American] trade deficit would be to stop reporting it." The *Journal*'s principal commentator on Japan, Brussels-based George Melloan, seems to consider America's trade deficits a good thing. In a bizarre comment in 1994, he implied that the trade deficits bolster American financial markets. "If the U.S. were running a trade surplus," he said, "the rest of the world would no longer be piling up all the dollars that now help prop up the U.S. bond and stock markets." Not even the Japan lobby has come up with a more creative argument for American policymakers to fiddle while Rome burns.

Another publication whose politics have had a particularly pernicious effect on truth is the *Economist*. If anything, the *Economist* has been more influential in propagating error in the United States than the *Journal*. Although it speaks with a British accent, its marketing strategy is geared principally to the United States, which is its main circulation area. And many powerful Americans regard it as the gold standard in economic journalism.

The American press's most important contribution to Japan's public relations policy is to induce Americans to underestimate the strength of Japan's challenge to American economic leadership. In this the American press is often responding to a powerful "bad news" spin in Japanese public relations. As C. Tait Ratcliffe, the president of a Tokyo consulting firm, has pointed out, Japanese business leaders deliberately exaggerate their problems as a pretext for making vital but difficult corporate changes to eliminate waste. Hyped corporate pessimism is used, for instance, as a face-saving formula for triggering early retirements of over-the-hill executives and chopping back corporate entertainment budgets.

The bad-news strategy is also clearly intended for foreign consumption. As far back as 1971, one prominent American businessman in Tokyo noted the habit of the Japanese to poormouth themselves in the presence of foreigners. He characterized this as Japan's "poor little me" complex. Japanese leaders have long sensed that Washington is more tolerant of their trade barriers if Japan is perceived as a poor country. Increasingly, however, they have also seemed to use the poor-little-me strategy to allay Western unease at Japan's growing power. Western anxiety became a critical problem after the yen soared in the mid-1980s. In 1987, the philosopher banker George Soros portrayed Japanese financial strength as "very disturbing" for the future of Western civilization. And in 1990, British Prime Minister

Margaret Thatcher described the possibility that Japan might outperform America in the 1990s as a "disaster." Japan's public relations strategists read the newspapers and can probably draw their own conclusions.

One thing is certain: though Japanese officials are rarely concerned to correct Westerners' mistaken impressions of Japan, they make an exception for writers who present bullish views of Japan's prospects. In 1986 Ratcliffe, who is regarded by many as America's most astute expert on the Japanese economy, was firmly reprimanded after he forecast that Japan would quickly overcome the problems triggered by the yen's massive mid-1980s rise. He was summoned to a chilly meeting in which the Economic Planning Minister, surrounded by top officials, emphasized the supposed seriousness of Japan's problems. Then in 1992, after Ratcliffe had written an article authoritatively rebutting the general view that the Tokyo stock market crash would trigger a banking collapse, the *Mainichi Daily News,* one of Tokyo's semiofficial English-language newspapers, dropped his weekly column. On both occasions Ratcliffe's analysis was vindicated by subsequent events, but this was probably beside the point as far as the Tokyo establishment was concerned.

Ratcliffe had been writing the column for six years when he was terminated. In his final column, he offered this somber insight into how economic information is disseminated in Tokyo:

> Perhaps the one thing that I have sensed over the past six years, much to my dismay, is that somewhere, somehow, informal pressures in Japan for expressing only narrow variations on the general consensus view and keeping communication within prescribed bounds have grown rather than diminished. This is one source of the lack of transparency sensed by the rest of the world about Japan. . . . There are times when many commentators seem to be talking with the same voice. But anyone with access to the flood of data and statistics in Japan can from time to time point to discrepancies between the consensus view and reality.

Apart from a few case-hardened observers like Ratcliffe, foreigners generally need little persuasion to take a pessimistic view of Japan's prospects. The pattern is universal and amazingly long-lived. Anyone who points out the strengths of Japanese economics can expect to be ridiculed or ignored by the American press. In 1970, Herman Kahn's prescient book *The Emerging Japanese Superstate* was dismissed by the *New York Times* as "a silly book." In 1988, Clyde Prestowitz's *Trading Places,* a pathbreaking account of how Japan had passed the United States in key industries, was never reviewed by the *Wall Street Journal.*

Perhaps at no time has the press's pessimism about Japan been more absurdly evident than in coverage of the 1973–74 oil crisis. Distinguished commentators in both the United States and Britain cast Japan as the worst victim of the crisis — and often did so in end-of-the-world terms. The *Economist* reported that with Japanese employers supposedly cutting output by up to 55 percent, "conditions approaching anarchy" might ensue, setting the scene for the military or the extreme left to stage a coup d'état.

In reality, the crisis was a golden opportunity for Japan. Because Japanese corporations were already considerably more energy efficient than their American competitors, they suddenly found themselves the world's low-cost producers in a range of important industries.

The most notable winner was the Japanese auto industry, which benefited both from the Japanese steel industry's energy efficiency and from the low gasoline consumption of Japanese cars. Thus at the very time the *Economist* was talking about the collapse of Japanese manufacturing, the Japanese auto industry was gearing up for the export boom of a lifetime. Almost immediately, Japan passed West Germany to become the world's greatest auto exporter. While West Germany's auto exports fell from 2.2 million units to 1.8 million between 1972 and 1974, Japan's exports shot from 2.0 million to 2.6 million. Japan went on just six years later to surpass the United States as the world's biggest auto producer.

If Japan was so well placed in the mid-1970s, why did the *Economist* think otherwise? We can only conclude that it unwittingly was a conduit of Japan's bad-news public relations. At the time Japan was haggling with the United States and other nations for as big a share as possible of the available oil. Putting on a happy face was not the way to get priority.

Japan's bad-news public relations strategy is so remote from Western experience that we find it hard to credit. What sort of country would resort to such an extreme strategy? A nation with a burning desire to be number one. It is time to consider Japan's greatest hidden strength — its will to win.

3

The Will to Win

In many respects, Japan's greatest hidden strength is its history. And ignorance of Japanese history is one of the main reasons Westerners constantly underestimate the Japanese leadership's will to win.

Dozens of factors go into building a nation's psychology, and any attempt to weigh them is necessarily impressionistic. Nonetheless Japan scholars are largely in agreement on the main historical factors driving Japan. This chapter looks at some of these factors.

An ancient nation — with a mission

Today's Japanese are heirs to one of the world's oldest and most sophisticated civilizations. They are descendants of prehistoric immigrants from Mongolia, Korea, and Polynesia who by the time of Christ had become a recognizable Japanese race. Since then, Japan has been characterized by an unusually high degree of ethnic, linguistic, and cultural unity.

For most of the last two thousand years, the Japanese could legitimately look on Westerners as relative barbarians. They were very early in the use of writing, for instance. They imported the Chinese writing system more than 1,500 years ago and have since consistently enjoyed literacy rates that have put the West to shame. For Japan's ancient leaders literacy was at first primarily a political tool, a means of coordinating the activities of what was by the standards of that time an extensive state. Writing allowed them to adopt from China an elaborate system for registering births, deaths, and marriages in the

seventh century. This system — known as the *koseki* — was a vital
administrative tool used in setting policy on tax, education, and agriculture, and it represented an early example of the care with which
bureaucrats administered Japanese society.

Japan can claim to be the second oldest nation-state after China —
and in many ways, Japan has outdone China in preserving its ancient
heritage. Japan's emperor system, for instance, has outlived China's,
and the Japanse imperial family is by far the world's oldest surviving
monarchy.

Japan is one of the very few countries that has never succumbed to
colonization. From a Japanese point of view, not even Britain can
claim such a record — because Britain was colonized twice, first by
the Romans and a millenium later by the French-speaking Normans.
As we will see, even when the Americans occupied Japan after World
War II, the Japanese never truly lost control of their destiny.

The one period during which Japan slipped seriously behind the
West was between the seventeenth and mid-nineteenth centuries,
when Japanese rulers cut the country off from the outside world at a
time when the West was racing ahead in technical knowledge. This
period and the manner in which it was abruptly ended would powerfully shape Japan's relations with the West down to our own time.

Thus the present-day Japanese see their history in a very different
light from Westerners. While Westerners tend to dwell on inglorious
aspects of Japan's role in World War II, the Japanese see that struggle
in a much larger, and more flattering, context. Japan, in this view, has
been the one country that has consistently led other non-Caucasian
peoples in an epochal effort to moderate — and even to roll back —
the West's claims to global leadership.

First impressions

The West first became aware of Japan's existence from the thirteenth-
century Venetian explorer Marco Polo. Polo never visited the country,
but he'd heard of it during his travels in China. On Polo's testimony,
Japan was a nation of fabulous wealth. He called it Zippangu, which
came from the Chinese and means the source of the sun. Zippangu in
turn was Anglicized as Japan. (The Japanese themselves call the country Nihon or Nippon, which are alternative Japanese pronunciations
of the ideograms the Chinese use to denote Japan.)

The first direct contact between the West and Japan seems to have taken place in 1543. Portuguese traders heading for China were blown off course and ended up on the island of Tanegashima, near Kyushu, the southernmost of Japan's four main islands. A few years later the Spanish made an appearance. One of the most notable early visitors was the Jesuit missionary Francis Xavier, who visited Japan between 1549 and 1552 and reported to his superiors, "These are the best people so far discovered and it seems to me that among unbelievers no people can be found to excel them."

At that time Japan, like China, was in many respects more advanced than Europe; it was already a leader in steelmaking, a technology that must have seemed as impressive then as superconductivity is today. And because of this Japan made the world's best swords. It also led in the production of silver, pottery, copper, and sulfur.

Japan was ruled by the shoguns, its line of military dictators who were nominally subject to oversight by the emperors but were in fact answerable only to themselves. The shoguns quickly became suspicious of the Church of Rome and the threat they believed it posed to Japanese culture. They proscribed Christianity and ordered the expulsion of the missionaries. Then, beginning in the 1610s, they conducted a series of increasingly determined efforts to stamp out Christianity, which ended in the wholesale slaughter of remaining Christians. To ensure Christianity never returned, they set in place comprehensive controls to ban the Japanese people from further contact with the outside world. In 1609, for instance, they ordered the destruction of oceangoing vessels (vessels with a capacity larger than fifty tons).

For the next two centuries Japan was a hermit kingdom whose only contact with the West was via a single trading post on a small island near the city of Nagasaki. There, Dutch merchants were given a monopoly on Japan's trade with the West. This arrangement was the forerunner of Japan's cartelized mercantilism, which in liberalized form survives to this day. The Dutch were allowed to send only one ship each year, and Japan's imports seem to have been confined mainly to medicines and books. Meanwhile a small group of Japanese scholars, who had made a special study of the Dutch language, read Dutch books and thereby monitored the outside world.

A memorable slight

The shoguns seemed intent on maintaining Japan's isolation indefinitely when the United States in the mid-nineteenth century inter-
vened decisively. Washington ostensibly wanted to open Japan to the
benefits of multilateral trade — but unfortunately its bullying approach could hardly have been more at odds with the spirit of freedom at the heart of Western economics.

The American initiative came from President Millard Fillmore,
who in 1852 dispatched a small U.S. naval expedition to Tokyo under
the leadership of Commodore Matthew Perry. The story of Perry's
mission has been imprinted as vividly on Japan's collective psyche as
the Boston Tea Party has been on America's. When Perry's black-
painted ironclads finally reached Tokyo Bay on July 8, 1853, they
caused an immediate sensation. They were bigger than anything the
Japanese had seen before. On first sight of the strange black hulls,
frightened fishermen, in the words of one contemporary account, fled
"like wild birds at a sudden intruder." By nightfall, news of the
strange visitors had sent the shogun's capital of Tokyo (then known
as Edo and already probably the world's largest city) into pandemonium.

The following morning the Americans were amazed to find themselves surrounded by high-prowed junks full of artists busily sketch-
ing everything in sight. As Perry later learned, woodblock copies of
these sketches of the "hairy barbarians" would be marketed within a
week in Tokyo.

Later the same day, large barges appeared carrying local officials
dressed in stiff ceremonial robes. Also on board were some of Japan's
experts in Dutch studies. Thus, haltingly, with the help of a Dutch-
man among Perry's crew, the Americans plunged into Washington's
very first round of trade negotiations with Tokyo.

The Japanese were bargaining from a position of abject weakness,
but they showed themselves from the start to be tough and resourceful negotiators. Their strategy then, as later, was to play for time.
First, they tried unsuccessfully to get the Americans to cease direct
contact and negotiate instead via designated Dutch and Chinese intermediaries. Then they told the Americans to go to Nagasaki, six
hundred miles away. Perry held firm, and eventually the Japanese

resigned themselves to having to negotiate in earnest. In anticipation of this contingency, they had carefully conserved some negotiating leverage by insisting that the Americans stay cooped up in their ships until a treaty was concluded. Then in a witty — but unsuccessful — attempt to undermine Perry's bargaining position, they sent word to his men that plenty of female companionship would be available onshore once a treaty was concluded.

But Perry, a stern New Englander, refused to be hurried, and eventually he succeeded in breaking the shogun's intransigence. The shogun finally agreed to open two ports to American ships and to allow American consuls to live in Japan. After word spread in Europe of Perry's negotiations, several European powers pressured Japan for similar trade favors, and the intimidated shogun quickly signed treaties with, among other countries, Britain, France, and Russia.

The Perry mission left the Japanese with an abiding sense of grievance. Westerners rarely see this because they regard trade as mutually beneficial, and Japan's isolation has always seemed deeply unnatural to the Western mind. But Perry's action was not as idealistic as it has often been portrayed in modern Western accounts. A telling indication of his aggressive mindset is a note he made in his diary at the time, expressing the hope "that our present attempt to bring a singular and isolated people into the family of civilized nations may succeed without resort to bloodshed."

True, Perry had been specifically instructed not to shoot first by Fillmore. Moreover, the Americans had a good pretext for negotiating with the shogun because in the past American sailors shipwrecked on the Japanese coast had suffered great hardship trying to get out of Japan. Yet Perry was hardly blameless in that he used the *threat* of force to play on Japanese fears. The Japanese had good reason for concern. After all, a few years earlier in 1839, the British had invaded China in support of British merchant houses like Jardine which peddled opium to the Chinese people.

Perry and his successors bargained successfully for Japan to throw itself open not only to Western diplomats but to Western travelers and, most troubling of all from a Japanese point of view, Western merchants. As the Japanese knew well from their careful monitoring of Western contact with other parts of Asia, once Western merchants got established in a country, colonization would generally follow. Enjoying a near monopoly on trade, the Western merchants would prosper and they would use their money to buy the cooperation of the local administrative and business classes.

That this process ultimately was not played out in Japan is a reflection of the specially effective leadership which was soon to emerge in Japan. Almost from the start, the samurais, Japan's hereditary caste of warrior/administrators, rejected the treaties as inimical to Japan's interests. Among other things, the treaties compelled Japan to agree not to impose tariffs higher than 5 percent on imports from the West. For many years thereafter, Japan's customs duties were administered by the Western powers. Yet Japan received no corresponding guarantees of privileged access to the West's then heavily protected markets (America, for instance, maintained tariffs of more than 30 percent during most of the nineteenth century). As the author Richard Halloran has recorded, the Japanese did not establish full control over their own customs administration until 1911.

Perhaps even more galling for a touchy and impoverished nation was the insulting symbolism of the treaties' so-called extraterritoriality clauses. Under the extraterritoriality system, foreign residents of Japan were exempted from Japanese law. When they were accused of offenses they would be tried by fellow Westerners in special extraterritorial courts established on Japanese soil. For these and other reasons, the treaties became known to the Japanese as the Unequal Treaties.

The leading British historian Sir George Sansom has given perhaps the fairest summing up of the Americans' ethical position in pressuring Japan:

> Like most Western people at that date, they were thoroughly confident, not to say complacent, as to the rightness of their views and the perfection of their culture. Whether the Japanese liked it or not, the West proposed to confer upon them the benefits of Western civilization. It was good for them. Perry therefore would have felt no misgivings on moral grounds if he had been obliged to use force.

In the event, although Perry held his fire, subsequent visitors were less restrained. In 1863, for instance, the French and British navies jointly bombarded the town of Kagoshima. In 1868 the British assembled a large fleet off the port of Kobe in an effort to hurry along some trade negotiations.

The high-handed behavior of some of Japan's first Western residents added salt to Japan's psychological wounds. Some British residents of Yokohama, for instance, reportedly adopted a peculiarly distasteful way of impressing the "natives": they made a habit of buying bags of one-sen coins (a sen is one-hundredth of a yen) before going on picnics in the countryside. Then, to the mirth of other picnickers, they threw the tiny coins into the air and watched as the penurious villagers scrambled for them.

Characteristically, the Japanese usually hid their resentment, but underneath they often boiled with anger at the West. Something of their true psychology can be gleaned from *Shorai no Nihon* (*The Future Japan*), a best-selling polemic published by a young essayist, Soho Tokutomi, in 1886. This is Tokutomi's ironic comment on Britain's conquest of Burma the previous year:

> When a peasant dies in a country village there is always someone to shed a tear; why then does everyone in the world turn a blind eye to the death of such a great country as though one knew nothing about it? I suspect that just as plants exist for the sake of animals, and animals exist for the sake of human beings, so perhaps Asia exists for the sake of Europeans.

Even in the mid-nineteenth century, few countries were more advanced than Japan. Japan had 16,000 schools at the time of Perry's arrival. When it started its modernization drive in the 1860s, about one-third of its adult population could already read and write — compared to fewer than 25 percent in Britain, the preeminent Western economy.

Japan was an orderly country with a strong police force and an elaborate administrative system. The era of seclusion had been a time of social and political innovation. The shoguns had evolved highly creative methods for controlling the population, albeit methods that hardly conformed to Western ideals. The shogun's first concern had always been to keep potential rivals under his thumb. One element of such control was the system of *sankin kotai*, "alternate attendance," in which the feudal lords were required to maintain a home in the shogun's capital of Tokyo and spend each alternate year there. More important, they were required to leave their wives and children there at all times. In effect, the shogun tacitly held his rivals' families hostage.

The families could not easily flee because the shogun's officials maintained hundreds of checkpoints on Japan's roads, and travelers were required to carry identification papers. Consequently, although the feudal lords spent half their lives in their home regions far from the shogun's capital, they knew they would pay a terrible price if they fomented trouble while out of his sight.

Meanwhile, the authorities used the *goningumi* system to control the general population. Goningumi literally means "groups of five people." Under this system, the nation was divided into groups of five families. Whenever one family flouted authority, all five families would be punished. In effect, individual families were pressured to police one other.

Using a massive army of secret police, the shoguns enforced detailed regulations prescribing everything from what people could wear to what they could say. Travelers were told how far they could travel, and farmers obediently followed instructions on which crops to grow. In essence, Japan was the first police state — and the first planned economy.

However unpleasant some aspects of the shogun's rule may seem to modern Westerners, the Japanese were understandably outraged at being treated as a "semibarbarous" nation (the epithet had been used in Washington correspondence relating to the Perry visit). Moreover, Japan's preexisting administrative mechanisms and its culture of obedience helped it later to halt and then to roll back Western penetration of its economy. Although the outward presentation of Japanese administration has changed greatly since the shoguns' time, many of the carrot-and-stick control mechanisms invented in the era of isolation are still visibly at work in Japanese society today, albeit in somewhat more subtle forms.

As Karel van Wolferen has noted, Japan continues to this day to consider itself "in the world but not of it." Japan would probably today be a less aloof nation had it been allowed to rejoin the world of its own free will. Of course, time has somewhat soothed the Japanese people's sense of grievance, but the events of the 1850s have afforded successive generations of Japanese leaders a perfect pretext to ignore, misinterpret, and generally circumvent the West's self-proclaimed universal rules of economic, political, and social behavior.

The technology race begins

Faced with the West's trade demands, the shogun's officials began a historic reappraisal of Japan's position in the world. They reasoned that Japan had fallen prey to Western coercion not because its civilization was inferior, as Westerners assumed, but merely because it was poor. And it was poor mainly because it was technologically backward. Japan had cut itself off from a tremendous, and largely unexpected, potlatch of technological progress in the outside world during its 250 years of isolation.

Almost from the moment the shogun's officials sensed Perry would not be deflected, therefore, they launched major efforts to "Westernize" the country. This Westernization was not, however, driven by unconditional admiration of the West. In reality, what Japan admired was not Western culture but Western technology, and in particular Western armaments. Because Japan did not have the armaments to defeat the West, it would instead have to use its wits — and its charm. The Japanese authorities launched an elaborate program of welcoming Westerners to Japan's shores with the dual objectives of acquiring Western technology and of generating goodwill among Western elites.

Japan's mindset was encapsulated in a slogan that the Japanese mass media urged incessantly on the people in the later decades of the nineteenth century: "*Fukoku, kyohei*" — "Let's build a rich country and a strong army."

In sharp contrast to modern Japan's habit of modestly abjuring any aspirations to world economic leadership, early prophets of Japanese economic power innocently left nothing to the imagination. In 1886, for instance, a former Finance Ministry official, Shigeyasu Suehiro, published a best-selling novel that suggested that Japan in the year 2040 would be the hub of world commerce. No longer an outpost at the end of the world, Japan would be so rich that ships flying the proud flags of the European powers would flock to its harbors. (If Suehiro returned today he would be pleased to discover not only that the port of Tokyo-Yokohama is by far the world's largest but Japan, via flag-of-convenience registrations, now owns most of the world's shipping.)

Japan's leaders analyzed Western technology, focusing on the intellectual and societal forces that produced it. Although Japan was hardly more economically significant than, say, Vietnam is today, it dispatched top-level officials on dozens of missions to study Western civilization from top to bottom. Nothing, no matter how apparently trivial, escaped their notice. They carefully reconciled each mission's findings with previous missions and thus established a fully coherent understanding of how the pieces fit together.

Right from the start, Japan began coaxing the West's mighty enterprises to transfer technology. Typically, Japanese officials insisted that in return for buying a steam engine or a ship from the West, the manufacturer should employ some workers seconded from Japan for a period of instruction in how to build steam engines or ships. Such workers were generally professional engineers, and they made sure that by the time their tour of duty was completed they had mastered the technologies they saw.

Japanese engineers were sent to England to work in the booming Lancashire cotton industry. Soon the Japanese government established a model cotton mill near Osaka which was used as a technology transfer tool in showing private entrepreneurs how to get started in the industry. Within decades Japan surpassed Britain to become the world's largest cotton goods exporter.

The speed with which the Japanese reorganized their society was astounding. Their priorities followed a typically pragmatic Japanese line of thinking. The very first task was to establish a navy to counter Western bullying. Within weeks of first sighting Perry's ironclads in 1853, the shogun repealed the isolation-era ban on the building of oceangoing ships. In 1857, Dutch engineers were invited to Japan to direct the building of a state-of-the-art ship repair yard. Then in 1865 the Japanese built their first modern shipyard. This was the birth of Japan's modern shipbuilding industry, which today makes nearly 50 percent of all the world's ships.

Defense concerns also spurred the government to pursue a crash program of railroad building. With the help of British capital and expertise, Japan opened its first railroad in 1872.

From the beginning, the government understood that exports were the key to building a strong Japan. This meant going head-to-head with Western manufacturers in making goods to Western specifications. Thus began Japan's habit of copying Western products lock, stock, and barrel. The *American Annual Cyclopedia* noted the pattern as early as 1861, reporting that the Japanese "imitate perfectly our manufacturers." Japan's tendency to copy has created the myth that the Japanese lack creativity — but they thought that copying was a matter of common sense. Relieved of the burden of having to come up with original designs, Japanese manufacturers concentrated all their creative talents on the far more economically effective task of beating Western rivals in productivity.

The Japanese also took to copying entire Western institutions. They created the Japanese navy as a virtual replica of Britain's Royal Navy. The Japanese army was first modeled on the French army — but then in the 1880s instructors from the German army were imported to teach German military principles.

Japanese officials identified the Bank of Belgium as the world's best-structured central bank; this became the model for the Bank of Japan. Japan's first Western-style doctors modeled their profession on German lines.

If Japan was to build an invincible labor force, it needed the best education system. Therefore, in 1872, it introduced compulsory universal education and modeled its school system loosely on that of France's.

The investment paid off. The high level of literacy in Japan helped to speed the adoption of Western technical knowhow at every level in Japanese manufacturing. The government established teams of planners and technicians to translate manuals and instruction books for operating imported European and American production machinery. Japan quickly seized a world lead in silk production after the government distributed thousands of pamphlets on French silk-industry techniques.

Japan's newly established banks and manufacturing corporations offered ten times Western salary levels to Western engineers to transfer Western knowhow to Japan. By 1876, some four hundred foreign experts were working in the government service, many of them in the Department of Public Works. Americans, for instance, taught the Japanese their first lessons in modern farming and seismology.

Japan made an early start in sophisticated science by establishing the Telegraph Insulator Laboratory in 1876. The Imperial College of Engineering was founded in 1877 with the help of British experts and it became the first college in the world to offer degree courses in electrical engineering. Charles Dickinson West, an Irish mechanical engineer, helped found Tokyo University's engineering department and showed the Japanese how to make ships' engines, a technology in which Japan today enjoys a global monopoly.

No detail of the modernization process was overlooked. Early on, the Japanese decided they needed to look Western if they were to get more respect from Western diplomats and businessmen. Senior officials led the country in adopting Western hair styles. Within a few years, virtually every male had followed suit. Japanese men also quickly discarded their kimonos. Government officials switched to Western clothes in 1870. Then Western clothes were introduced at Emperor Meiji's court, and soon the entire elite wore Western clothes, albeit ill-fitting ones at first.

Next it was time for Japan's cities to undergo a makeover. Tokyo's flimsy wood and paper architecture did not seem to befit the capital of an aspiring Great Power. Builders were sent abroad to study Western architecture. The Mitsubishi organization built an entire bricks and mortar business district on swampy coastal land formerly attached to the Imperial Palace in Tokyo. The development mimicked the financial district of London and was promptly dubbed Londontown. Rebuilt after World War II and renamed Mitsubishi Village, it is now, even at post-crash valuations, the most valuable real estate in the world.

For public buildings, the Japanese copied Victorian British designs, which were in turn copies of Roman temples. The Japanese built Tokyo's main railroad station as a replica of Amsterdam's, and the Tokyo station in turn served as the model for Seoul's.

The Japanese found their traditional Chinese calendar caused confusion in foreign trade, so on January 1, 1873, they moved to the Western calendar (and to the Western concept of a seven-day week). They even reformed family law, eliminating polygamy and adopting the Western concept of the nuclear family.

The earliest Western influence on Japanese economic policymakers was *Outline of Social Economy* by William Ellis. This appeared in Japanese translation in 1867, and it summarized the ideas of Adam Smith, David Ricardo, and other members of the British school of economics. Soon, however, the Japanese became aware of an opposing German school pioneered in the 1840s and 1850s by Friedrich List and Wilhelm Roscher, who preached that intelligently arranged tariffs can speed a country's growth. The tension between the two philosophies was resolved in the 1880s when supporters of the German school seized leadership in the bureaucracy.

Trade apart, however, the Japanese remained largely convinced by the case for Western capitalism. By the early 1900s they had created a freebooting capitalist system that was virtually a replica of Britain's, complete with titled plutocrats, Rolls-Royces, a hire-and-fire labor market, and even bitter labor disputes.

All in all this was the time when Japan most closely resembled the West.

Votes without democracy

Japan's modernization drive would not have proceeded so fast but for a political upheaval in the late 1860s that overthrew the shogun's administration. The revolution was instigated by Japan's samurais, who were outraged at the administration's weakness in agreeing to the Unequal Treaties. The rebels defeated the shogun's troops and swept him aside to establish a new administration headed unequivocably by the emperor. The episode has become known as the Meiji Ishin — the Meiji revolution. This new government, a junta led by young samurais, set out to rescind the Unequal Treaties and to buttress Japan's defenses against the West.

A great deal of political reform quickly followed that was more cosmetic than real. Because Westerners rationalized their imperialism on the grounds that they were bringing Western freedoms to oppressed and ignorant foreign peoples, Japanese leaders decided to preempt foreign interference by establishing government institutions that in appearance, if not in function, mirrored those of the West.

First a bureaucracy was established along Western lines with major ministries emerging in more or less their modern form in the early 1870s. The junta's supreme leaders established a cabinet modeled after Britain's in most respects except that it was composed of unelected oligarchs. Emperor Meiji moved from his secluded residence in Kyoto to take over the former shogun's splendid palace in central Tokyo. Mimicking European monarchs, he embarked on a career of state ceremonies and public proclamations.

Next on the Westernization agenda was democracy. In East Asian eyes, the Western concept of rule by the people seems strange because it empowers the benighted (a healthy majority in any society) to overrule the intelligent and the informed. Nonetheless Japanese leaders felt they had to pay lip service to Western democratic rhetoric.

Thus they modeled Japan's parliamentary arrangements on those of the Kaiser's Germany.

After a new national constitution was promulgated in 1889, the first diet elections were held in 1890 — but only after essentially un-repealable constitutional rules were installed giving unelected officials effective control over the national budget. By this expedient, the civil servants retained great patronage powers, which they used liberally to reward politicians and businessmen for cooperating with the government's "transcendental" — nonpartisan — policies.

As part of the effort to fight the Unequal Treaties, Japan's ancient but, to Western eyes, quirky legal system also was given a new look. The new system was modeled superficially on French Napoleonic law and rendered the West's extraterritorial courts in Japan redundant. To this day, however, the philosophy underlying Japanese law has hardly changed. In the words of James Feinerman, a professor of law at Georgetown University and an authority on Japanese law, Japan is a society "ruled by men, not by laws." Judges often seem to ignore the statutes in favor of their own intuitive ideas of natural justice.

At the end of the day, Japan squared the circle: under the guise of establishing Western-style institutions, it in reality established the prototypical strong state that has since become the model for other East Asian growth economies.

The birth of Japan Inc.

Soon after the shogun was overthrown, the government began laying the foundations of modern Japanese business. The first step was to persuade the samurais to enter trade, an activity they had previously considered beneath them.

One of the first samurais to take the plunge was Yataro Iwasaki, a young bookkeeper for a small trading company owned by a local feudal government. As the revolutionary leaders in Tokyo began abolishing the feudal system in the early 1870s, Iwasaki stepped forward to buy the company at a firesale price. The company's only ostensible assets were six small steamships, but he was aware that it had hidden assets that had never been disclosed to the shogun's regulators. This purchase launched the Mitsubishi group, which today accounts for nearly 10 percent of Japan's GNP and is probably the world's largest single commercial organization.

Iwasaki had good contacts in the new government and used them to garner valuable government military contracts. In particular, he made his ships available for an attack the government launched on Taiwan in 1874. Taiwan had been a loosely attached protectorate of the moribund Chinese empire and it fell easily to the Japanese. This was Tokyo's fateful first stab at imitating Western imperialism.

Iwasaki's next big opportunity came in international shipping. At this time two foreign companies, American-owned Pacific Mail Steamship Company and British-owned P&O Line, monopolized Japan's main shipping routes. The new government decided Japan had to establish control over its shipping routes. The government therefore staked Iwasaki to take on the Americans and the British. He launched a rate war that quickly forced them to withdraw. The Japanese had guessed right: if they used the military-style tactic of concentrating their economic firepower, even the most powerful Western opponents would quickly scatter. It was the first victory for Japan-style industrial policy, and probably no victory since has proved so consequential. Establishing Japanese control of shipping was the vital first step for Tokyo in building an inventive system of nontariff barriers to get around the trade provisions of the Unequal Treaties. The victory marked the birth of Japan's system of neomercantilism.

Almost from the start, Iwasaki began to pump his monopolistic shipping profits into related fields, notably banking, insurance, warehousing, trading, shipbuilding, and mining. In the process he built a vast conglomerate which became a prototype of the Japanese business form, the zaibatsu. Four great zaibatsus — Mitsubishi, Sumitomo, Mitsui, and Yasuda — went on to dominate Japanese industry in the first half of the twentieth century. After World War II the zaibatsus were broken up by the Americans, but this proved fortuitous for Japan because it gave the civil servants a chance to reinvent the zaibatsus in a new, more suitable form that paved the way for the introduction of the full Big Logic system.

Expansion and confrontation

For Americans, the war with Japan began on December 7, 1941, the day Japan bombed Pearl Harbor. From a Japanese point of view the war's beginnings went back decades before 1941, and the causes ran deep. A major factor was Japan's decision in the 1870s to build an overseas empire to match those of the Great Powers. In one of the great ironies of history, Japan's first efforts at expansionism were encouraged and facilitated by Westerners, most notably the American consul Charles LeGendre. But when Japan showed aptitude for the great game of imperialism, its expansionism quickly upset the West.

U.S-Japan relations started to unravel after the Japanese defeated the Russians in 1905. It was the first time in centuries that a non-Western people had vanquished one of the West's great nations, and many Westerners saw it as the beginning of the end of Western colonialism. But for the moment, America pressed ahead with expansion in the Pacific, having annexed first Hawaii and later, much more threatening for Japan, the Philippines. America's war to take control of the Philippines cost the lives of perhaps as many as one million Filipinos.

As early as 1908, scholars and authors in the United States began predicting a struggle between the United States and Japan. By 1911, the American press was whipping up such anti-Japanese feeling that talk of war was becoming commonplace. The press was upset by large-scale Japanese immigration and by Tokyo's clinching of an advantageous trade agreement with China.

Race tensions emerged explicitly in 1919 when the Japanese proposed a proclamation of the equality of the races at a post–World War I summit in Versailles. Viewing the Japanese proposal as a veiled attack on Western colonialism in East Asia, the Western powers quashed it.

Japan's own colonialism in China and Manchuria was soon to become the subject of increasing controversy in the West. Westerners these days tend to condemn Japan out of hand for its colonization efforts on the Asian mainland, but that viewpoint conveniently overlooks the fact the Japanese were merely copying the West. The Western powers had already carved up China: even Shanghai, China's largest city, was run under the joint administration of Britain, France, and the United States.

The West was in fact a party to Japan's involvement on the Asian mainland because, in a general redrawing of maps after World War I, Britain and the United States had ceded Germany's former territorial privileges in coastal China to Tokyo. In the early 1930s, Western business interests had actually connived with Japan against China in the hope that the Japanese would "keep the Chinese in their place." The United States and other Western governments actually helped Japan by selling vast supplies of war materials to it while denying war supplies to the beleaguered Chinese.

Rumors of vast atrocities by the Japanese army, however, alienated the public in the West. As tensions increased in the 1930s, Tokyo transmitted a now-or-never ethos down the line in trying to consolidate its military advances. Normal rules of civilized behavior were suspended as the generals strove to achieve objectives in the field by any and every means. According to the author Arnold C. Brackman, Imperial Japan wiped out about six million people in China alone.

Trade competition added to U.S.-Japan strains. After Japan devalued the yen in the early 1930s, Japanese manufacturers flooded the world with cheap exports. By the late 1930s, Japan accounted for 40 percent of all the world's cotton cloth exports, for instance. In a move that brilliantly anticipated the revolutionary economic thinking of John Maynard Keynes, Japan in 1932 began running large budget deficits to stimulate the domestic economy. Thus in the five years to 1935, Japan's manufacturing and mining output jumped by 49.6 percent, versus a decline of 6.3 percent in the United States. Japan's boom, however, came at the fateful cost of infuriating American business interests.

Meanwhile, the West was building a strong moral case against Tokyo over such "incidents" as the massacre of perhaps as many as 250,000 Chinese soldiers and civilians in the Rape of Nanking in 1937. The Americans led the West in embargoing Japan's supplies of oil, a controversial decision at the time. America's ambassador in Tokyo was among the dissidents who thought Washington was courting "sure disaster." As the West tightened the embargo and Japan's oil stock dwindled, Tokyo felt it had no choice. Its reaction was war. It attacked Pearl Harbor and quickly overran much of East Asia, most notably the oil-rich Dutch colony of Sumatra.

From the start, the Japanese fought with astounding ferocity. In a careful program of indoctrination, they had been trained to fight willingly to the death. To be taken alive, they were told, was not only a disgrace but a capital offense in Japanese law. In keeping with this ideology, Tokyo had not ratified the 1929 Geneva Convention on prisoners of war.

In the event, the fearlessness the Japanese displayed in the face of certain death was probably unprecedented in military history. After the battle of Tarawa in the Gilbert Islands in 1943, for instance, only 8 Japanese of a total garrison of 5,000 were taken alive. Japanese morale began to sag only in June of 1945 in the battle of Saipan, Japan's last remaining major offshore fortress in the Pacific. Even then only about 1,000 Japanese surrendered of a garrison of 27,000.

By contrast, Allied troops surrendered in large numbers from the beginning. In the first two months of the war, 130,000 British troops surrendered in Malaya alone. In captivity, Allied soldiers discovered the other side of Japan's no-surrender ideology. Prisoners of war who became a nuisance to their Japanese captors — perhaps because food was running out or merely because they could not march fast enough — were shot without a second thought.

In the years immediately before Pearl Harbor, Westerners had taken Japan for a paper tiger. As recounted by the historian Malcolm Kennedy, Western economists played a characteristic role in the late 1930s by portraying Japan as heading for financial collapse "within six months." Needless to say, they were wrong.

Though Japan enjoyed less than one-tenth of America's industrial might, it partially made up for this disability by accumulating a vast stockpile of weapons and ammunition. Thus by 1941 Japan had built up the largest and best-equipped naval air force in the world. Many of its naval vessels were faster than the American equivalents. Japan's torpedoes, star shells, and parachute flares performed better. The famous Mitsubishi Zero planes, which ironically had been built with the help of American aircraft technology transferred before the war, proved to be unsurpassed in their maneuverability and long cruising range.

The Americans' surprise was as nothing compared to that of the British. Members of the British officers' club in Singapore had spent the final months before Pearl Harbor chortling at the thought of attack from the apparently impotent Japanese. In the first month after Pearl Harbor, however, the Japanese raced through the British colony of Malaya and then in a matter of hours took Singapore, Britain's most heavily protected fortress in the East. They had thought of everything, down to caches of bicycles along their troops' projected route through Malaya. After the British surrendered, they were dismayed to discover they had outnumbered the Japanese three to one. The Japanese had pulled off one of the most daring bluffs in all military history.

In prewar days the Japanese had saturated Singapore with spies, and they probably understood the city's weak points better than the British. They had even infiltrated the British officers' club. The "Chinese" headwaiter there had always shown markedly pro-British sympathies, but he turned out to be a West Point–trained colonel of the Japanese secret service.

If the West underestimated Japan's ability to start a war, Japan underestimated the West's ability to finish it. Japan knew from the outset that in a prolonged war it would be overwhelmed by the "factories of Detroit and the oil wells of Texas," as one Japanese military leader had put it before Pearl Harbor. Japan, however, staked everything on Hitler's view that the Americans had been emasculated by soft living and would sue for an early peace. Thus Tokyo's strategy was to overrun so much territory that it could negotiate for peace on equal terms with Washington. At first, Japan's campaign went better than expected. By the summer of 1942, Japan controlled an astonishing one-seventh of the surface of the globe. But once the Americans had the bit between their teeth, they proved unstoppable.

By the middle of 1944 Japan's generals knew they were beaten, and by early 1945 they were desperate for a negotiated peace. The Allies, however, pressed on for what amounted in Japanese eyes to unconditional surrender. They repeatedly fire-bombed Tokyo in the spring of 1945: in just one night alone, up to 90,000 civilians are believed to have died. Then in August 1945 they dropped atomic bombs on Hiroshima and Nagasaki, wiping out more than 200,000 lives.

Was the bomb militarily necessary? Many argue that the atomic bomb in the end saved more lives than it sacrificed. Before Hiroshima, Japan's leaders understandably would not hear of surrender because they knew they would in effect not only be signing their own death warrants but putting the emperor system in jeopardy. Without the bomb, the war might have gone on for several months longer. But some historians think the time advantage the Americans won was not large. The Princeton Japan scholar Marius B. Jansen has argued that the Japanese were already defeated before Hiroshima. Japan had been cut off by American submarines from vital sources of food in its colonies and was on the brink of starvation.

Whatever the morality of using the bomb, the public relations consequences have proved counterproductive for the United States. For one thing, the bomb made it harder for the Americans to win genuine support in Japan for a move to establish a truly Western political system after the surrender.

More important, perhaps, has been the long-term effect the bomb has had on American psychology. Guilt about Hiroshima and Nagasaki seems to have inhibited succeeding American administrations in their efforts to stand up to Japan on trade. The final verdict of history may be that the United States overplayed its hand in August 1945.

The legacy of war

Almost from the moment that Emperor Hirohito announced Japan's surrender on August 15, 1945, the Americans decided to let bygones be bygones. But seen from a Japanese point of view, the war's aftermath continues to this day: Japan's response to the shame of defeat has been sublimated in economic competition. In fact, some observers see a hint of revenge in Japan's constant economic overachieving. This has been expressed most clearly by the Tokyo-based historian Ivan Hall, who in 1992 talked of a "deliberate, humorless, and relentless economic war" conceived as retaliation for the 1945 defeat.

Hall's view is broadly shared by the Australian-born author Russell Braddon, who was taken as a prisoner of war by the Japanese in World War II. Braddon cites his wartime conversations with his Japanese captors as evidence that Japan's leaders regarded the Pacific War as just one manifestation of a continuing, multifaceted struggle against the West. It is a matter of record that in the last two years of the war, the Japanese military in combination with the media and the business community began preparing the people to regard the coming defeat as merely a new phase of the struggle against the West. This campaign reached a crescendo in late August 1945, an interregnum period after Japan had surrendered but before the American occupation began. Official posters displayed everywhere said: "Never has great Nippon known defeat. The present difficulty is but a stepping stone to the future. Rally around the Imperial throne and fight on, for this is a one-hundred-year war." The posters were taken down just before the Americans landed.

The Japanese themselves occasionally admit that wartime defeat has spurred them to economic overachievement in the postwar era.

The Japanese computer industry, for instance, seems to have benefited from this dynamic. According to the top Japanese banker Hiroshi Takeuchi, Japanese computer buyers gave strong support to Japan's fledgling computer industry three decades ago partly because they felt that Japan was still a pariah nation and needed to be self-sufficient in computers.

Japan's sense of insecurity is not entirely unwarranted. Washington makes clear that it trusts Japan less than other allies. This subtext to Washington's Japan policy is rarely explicitly evident but can be seen in the fact that the Washington establishment seems to see nothing amiss when the *Washington Post* implies, as it has done in recent years, that the United States should keep large military bases in Japan to stop Japan going militarist again.

In typical Japanese fashion, Japan's leaders have turned adversity to advantage. Tokyo has understood that Americans are highly reluctant to use normal trade sanctions against Japan because of a fear that an angry Japan might overreact and "revert to type." Thus top officials in Washington are easily persuaded by the Japan lobby to handle Tokyo with special "understanding." As recently as June 1993, the Clinton administration's "get-tough" trade negotiators were publicly talking about the need not to go "too far" in pressuring Japan. By contrast, Washington's trade negotiators deal far more harshly with much poorer, less stable countries such as Brazil and India.

The occupation: a myth is born

On the morning of August 30, 1945, MacArthur's plane took off from the Philippines, and by early afternoon it had entered Japanese airspace. Dropping down from a clear sky, MacArthur caught a picture-perfect view of Mount Fuji before landing a few minutes later at an airbase on the outskirts of Tokyo. Puffing his trademark corncob pipe as he emerged, he slowly took in the scene and murmured: "As they say in the movies, this is the payoff." The occupation had begun the way it was destined to continue — in a blaze of MacArthurian triumphalism.

Tokyo's plan for dealing with MacArthur quickly became apparent. Everyone has a weakness and MacArthur's was vanity. Tokyo perceptively determined to treat MacArthur as an ersatz emperor, lavishing on him all the pomp and splendor he evidently craved. The substance of power, however, would remain firmly in other hands (it should be remembered that emperors have always been accorded a purely ceremonial role in Japan). MacArthur's first taste of imperial splendor came as his entourage left the airbase for his luxury quarters in a Yokohama hotel. Japanese soldiers lined the route, each one facing away from the entourage. Some in the American party may have taken this as an insult, but MacArthur knew that for the Japanese it was a reverential posture. It had been previously reserved only for Emperor Hirohito, the Son of Heaven, on whom the Japanese were not allowed to gaze directly.

The Japanese press too treated MacArthur as an honorary emperor and turned his every move into a media circus. Photographs of him setting out for his office in the morning quickly became a media cliché — so much so that soon crowds of ordinary Japanese were mounting a vigil outside his residence each morning waiting to catch a glimpse of the American Caesar. In truth there were few rival diversions for the Japanese in those desperately poor days. But drunk on all the attention, MacArthur quickly concluded that he had wrought a cultural sea change in Japan. Thus was born the myth of Japan's "Americanization," a myth on which American policy has been predicated ever since.

On the first anniversary of his landing in Japan, MacArthur was to give the *Nippon Times* this retrospective on the defeated nation's first year of reform: "A spiritual revolution ensued almost overnight, tore asunder a theory and practice of life built upon two thousand years of history and tradition and legend. . . . This revolution of the spirit among the Japanese people represents no thin veneer to serve the purposes of the present. It represents an unparalleled convulsion in the social history of the world."

On the Japanese side, too, the occupation was presented almost from the start as an idyllic, almost magical reconciliation between bitter foes. True enough, there is much to celebrate about the occupation. The Americans came out of it as remarkably magnanimous people. Within months of the surrender, ordinary citizens in the States were showering Japan with food parcels; moreover, most American occupation officials behaved in an exemplary way.

The speed with which the Japanese took to some aspects of American culture was amazing. Overnight, everyone seemed to be using — or more often misusing — the English language. Officialdom gave the lead. The government-owned tobacco company, for instance, marked the new era with the launch of two English brand names, Peace and Happy.

The Japanese people's willingness to follow the officials' lead was even marked by new fashions in babies' names. Whereas parents had only a few months previously been giving their babies martial names like Takeshi ("warrior") or Katsuko ("victory girl"), now conciliatory names such as Yasuo ("peace man") and Kazuko ("harmony girl") became the vogue.

Even Prime Minister Shigeru Yoshida, an English-speaking former diplomat, cultivated a Western style. Modeling himself on Winston Churchill, he wore Savile Row suits, smoked fat cigars, and rode around the war-pulverized Japanese capital in a Rolls-Royce.

By 1947, MacArthur was so confident of the Japanese people's acceptance of American values that he gathered his men for a spectacular Fourth of July parade right past Emperor Hirohito's palace. The following week, the celebrations were featured as the top item in the movie newsreels shown in Japanese cinemas, complete with a short explanation of the American Revolution.

But the idea that two countries as different as the United States and Japan could achieve an easy partnership seemed from the start to be doomed to disappointment. On virtually every issue of culture and philosophy, Americans and Japanese were positioned then as now at opposite extremes of the world spectrum (with Europe, Russia, and China generally positioned somewhere in between and usually in time zone order). Whereas Americans, for instance, believe in having everything out in the open, the Japanese prefer to read between the lines. Whereas contradictions in public presentations of reality generally provoke serious discomfort in the United States, they are accepted as an essential lubricant of human relations in Japan. Whereas Americans view the world as a battle between clearly identifiable right and wrong, the Japanese see ethical issues as a study in various shades of gray. Whereas Americans believe in stop-at-nothing crusades and Pauline conversions, the Japanese believe in bending like a reed and striking while the iron is hot.

In short, the stage was set for a double take. The Americans, in their eagerness to believe in miracles, projected onto the Japanese a much more thorough commitment to Westernization than was actually there.

The Americans seemed to have been totally disarmed by the

friendly reception they received in Japan. Unconsciously assuming that Western patterns of behavior are universal, the Americans had expected to be treated with hostility or at least sullenness by the defeated Japanese. But Japanese leaders, in a classic demonstration of Japanese culture, had decided to spring a pleasant surprise. A week before the occupation began, they launched a major press campaign tutoring the Japanese on how to make the forthcoming encounter as friendly as possible for all concerned — and virtually every Japanese citizen complied.

As recounted by the occupation historian Harry Emerson Wildes, no one was more charmed than MacArthur. MacArthur had come to Japan with vengeance in his heart, determined that for the next twenty-five years "the Japanese will have a hard enough time eating." Almost immediately, however, he began backing away from this stance. And within just two weeks, he announced his conviction that the Japanese, on the strength of a few days' contact with the GIs, had become firm admirers of "the free man's way of life in actual action."

On the face of it, the idea that Japan was Westernizing itself was always unlikely. After all, Japan had already had ample opportunity to embrace Western norms but had, as we have seen, deliberately rejected the Western model. Instead it had studiedly chosen to graft specific admired elements of Western civilization onto a sturdy root stock of Japanese Confucianism. From the moment the atom bomb destroyed Hiroshima, however, the Japanese found it expedient to make an outward display of cooperation with America's agenda. Japan decided to play the model prisoner, gracefully putting up with every indignity the quicker to regain its freedom.

Of course, we must not exaggerate Japan's insincerity in cooperating with the occupation's agenda. In truth, many of Japan's postwar changes in areas such as education, labor law, and agriculture were quite sincere. In fact, they would undoubtedly have been instigated anyway even if the Americans had never occupied the country. After all, the transition from war to peace would inevitably have entailed a complete psychological and economic makeover. Occupation or no occupation, Japan no longer had any need for most of the draconian wartime controls and, left to its own devices, it might well have quickly resumed its sunny disposition of the early 1920s.

That said, it is clear that most of the time there was no true meeting of minds between the Americans and the Japanese. A telling sign of the occupation's mindset was the Americans' tendency to regard their Japanese counterparts as comically irrational or even stupid. One American brigadier, for instance, even told the *Philadelphia Bulletin*, "Dumbness has been bred into these people." The Japanese often *seem* irrational to Westerners. But when the Japanese say something that does not make sense, the Western listener may well be missing some important piece of the Japanese cultural jigsaw — or the Japanese may simply be giving their idea of a polite "no comment."

In effect the Americans were wrestling with the shogun's ghost. In a country where for centuries one could lose one's head for saying the wrong thing, the art of speaking ambiguously was second nature. It has remained so to this day.

Moreover, the Japanese people often display an ability to mount elaborate cast-of-thousands rituals in which everyone is merely acting a part. This "situational" aspect of Japanese behavior was noted at the time of the occupation by the leading American anthropologist Clyde Kluckhohn, who pointed out that the Japanese people's concept of appropriate rules of behavior is highly influenced by context. When in the 1930s the Japanese people were assigned bit parts in a police state melodrama, they performed to thespian perfection. When MacArthur prescribed a switch to democratic mode, everyone talked individualism and acted out noisy scenes of political pluralism.

This theatricality is apparent in Japan even today. Japanese gangsters, for instance, model themselves on their Chicago counterparts of the 1920s: wearing loud double-breasted suits and puffing chunky cigars, they drive large American-made limousines (for decades the gangster market has been virtually the only bright spot for Detroit in Japan). Japanese weekend artists solemnly don French-style berets and strike Gallic poses as they paint scenes like the Bank of Japan building. Japanese golfers wear plus fours and share with Japanese politicians the habit of shaking hands often (shaking hands is, of course, a theatrical gesture in a country where people normally bow).

This Japanese role-playing sometimes seems farcical, and people have been making fun of it since W. S. Gilbert wrote *The Mikado* in 1885. But in all the mirth, Westerners tend to miss the point: the role-playing reflects an earnest concern on the part of each Japanese to behave as society expects him or her to behave. Drilled into every child at school, this concern makes the Japanese a particularly malleable people in the hands of their leaders. In the blunt words of Keyes Beech, at one time a Pulitzer Prize–winning correspondent who covered Tokyo in the 1960s, the Japanese will "go anywhere they are aimed."

The Japanese people's theatricality is rooted in a highly institutionalized dichotomy between what the truth is and how that truth is described for public consumption. The public version, called the *tatemae,* is often fanciful and is invariably misleading. True reality is called the *honne* and is generally disclosed only to superiors and other "insiders" with a well-recognized right to know. Insidership is a relative term: sometimes the insiders are members of a company, sometimes of an industry cartel, sometimes (as in dealings with foreigners) the entire Japanese establishment. Much of what passes for political reporting in the Japanese press is really tatemae, and the only thing certain is that the real meaning is different from what the papers print.

To keep up with what is going on in Japan, it pays to be a mindreader. Sophisticated Japanese cultivate a style that is intended to exclude the uninitiated. Ambiguity is piled on irony. Speakers use nonverbal signals — called *haragei* ("belly talk") — to convey their real meaning. Significant pauses, for instance, may say far more than words.

Western residents invariably take many years to begin to see through the ritual. The occupation forces, like thousands of subsequent American arrivals in Japan, never completed their education. In 1951 Robert B. Textor, one of the occupation's few Japanese-speaking officials, published *Failure in Japan,* a debunking account of the occupation. Textor describes a Japan that vividly evokes the problems conscientious diplomats and foreign correspondents still encounter to this day:

Huge obstacles to finding and appraising the facts are to be found in Japanese culture. . . . The Japanese have been "standing inspections" for a thousand years longer than we. They have had centuries of experience in pleasing their superiors. Their deep sense of hierarchy, their frequent preference for propriety over rectitude and sometimes over logic lead them to give answers to the casual American visitor which are not always in line with objective fact. There are vast areas of behavior about which the ordinary Japanese may be unwilling to talk freely. Some types of question in the realm of government or sociology that a Westerner in official capacity would gladly answer in detail, his Japanese counterpart will tackle reluctantly or not at all. . . . The Japanese language alone is a formidable barrier to getting accurate information. Their information gathering and collating techniques differ weirdly from our own. To be reliable, information usually has to be checked several times, often in varied contexts. Assembling accurate information takes time and some specialized skills.

In short, the Americans got the runaround. In the eyes of Japanese leaders, deceiving the occupation was a matter of self-defense — a strategy that any other proud, well-organized nation would have attempted in the face of an occupying army. By making a show of complying with some welcome new ideas (such as the abolition of inefficient serf-like conditions in agriculture), the Japanese hoped to ward off more fundamental reforms that would "contaminate" their cultural and governmental institutions. Their fears were hardly groundless: injudicious outside attempts to impose Western ideas on Asian culture do seem to have created many problems in places like the Philippines and Iran.

A two-thousand-year nadir

The occupation's most visible achievement was to arraign more than five thousand Japanese officers, soldiers, and civilians for war crimes. At least nine hundred were executed and nearly five hundred were given life imprisonment.

The war crimes proceedings reached their denouement in the early morning of December 23, 1948, when the Americans hanged Japan's wartime leader, Hideki Tojo, at Sugamo Prison in Tokyo. Also hanged that morning were six other top wartime leaders. Before mounting the scaffold, Tojo and three other condemned men shouted three times in unison, *"Tenno heika banzai"* — may the Emperor live ten thousand years.

For Americans, justice had been served. From a Japanese point of view, the message was different: the will to win had prevailed even at this nadir in Japan's two-thousand-year history. Tojo had consciously offered himself as a sacrifice to shield Emperor Hirohito. The other accused war leaders also tried to present a front of decorum and fortitude. As the commentator-philosopher Taichi Sakaiya has pointed out, not one of the thousands of Japanese accused of war crimes had attempted to flee the country before the Americans caught up with them. This contrasted markedly with the behavior of the Nazis. In facing their fate with resignation, Japan's leaders were in effect sending the same message the young kamikaze pilots had sent: the Japanese are different.

American hubris — and Japanese hope

The lasting consequence of the occupation's effort to root out the militarists was a power vacuum within Japan as thousands of identifiable sympathizers with the military were purged from government ministries and large corporations. Japan's military forces were, of course, immediately disbanded. Even more significant in terms of Japan's subsequent economic history, the powerful families who owned the zaibatsus were effectively expropriated. This removed the one major power group that might have stood in the way of the civil servants' revolutionary new economic program for recovery. The Americans had unwittingly functioned as the catalyst in ending capitalism's reign in Japan: as the former top MITI official Koji Matsumoto has pointed out, the permanent elimination of capitalist control over the economy was essential for Big Logic Economics to work.

The Japanese civil servants soon discovered a geological fault line in the occupation's philosophy: New Dealers, who wanted to reform Japanese economic and social practices, were opposed by right-wingers who wanted to build up Japan as a bulwark against the Soviet Union. Operating under the patronage of the occupation's right-wingers, the Japanese leaders found they could ignore the New Dealers with impunity.

This fault line helps explain some stunning reversals of the occupation's original aims. A case in point is shipbuilding. An American commission had recommended in the fall of 1945 that Japan's shipbuilding industry be contained to ensure that Japan could never again become a naval rival of the United States. Within two years, however, the occupation had been persuaded to approve Japan's first gambits in what would be a stunning comeback in shipbuilding. Less than a decade later, Japan had passed Britain to become the world's biggest shipbuilder.

The occupation's reform efforts were also hindered by a mixture of hubris and naiveté, a potent brew that has always bedeviled American relations with Japan. The naiveté began at the top: in an unconscious admission of utter *Innocents Abroad* credulity, MacArthur publicly characterized the Japanese as children. Giving evidence to a congressional committee in 1951, he offered this assessment of Japanese culture: "Measured by the standards of modern civilization, they would be like a boy of twelve, as compared with our development of forty-five years." The full significance of this comment is only apparent when you realize that virtually the only Japanese citizens MacArthur ever got to know were Japan's highest civil servants — in other words, the most resourceful and adroit graduates of the world's most competitive educational system. Their estimate of MacArthur's mental age is not recorded!

Top American officials not only could not speak or read the Japanese language, they felt that even to attempt to understand Japanese culture would hinder their purpose in remaking Japan on Western principles. MacArthur exacerbated the occupation's blind spots by sending many of America's Japan experts to Korea. In a notably counterproductive fit of Western individualism, he cast them aside because he was uncertain of their loyalty to him personally.

This cleared the way for Japanese leaders to shape American opinion to suit their own agenda. It was at this time that they began their practice of exaggerating Japan's economic problems. According to a report in the *New York Herald Tribune* in October 1947, Japanese industrialists were engaged in a carefully concealed but concerted effort to slow down reconstruction so as to win sympathy abroad for "poor Japan." The goal was to minimize Japan's reparations bills and to maximize its receipts of aid from the West. In the event, Japan was to succeed extraordinarily well in both objectives.

The occupation made almost no contact with the real Japan. This was amply illustrated by the plight of one Japanese diplomat who, under the nose of occupation officials, was victimized by his superiors at the Ministry of Foreign Affairs. He was Chiune Sugihara, who in his capacity as vice consul at Japan's mission to Lithuania in 1940 had deviated from official policy by issuing visas to six thousand Jews fleeing from the Nazis. When he finally returned to Japan in 1947 after a period of detention in the Soviet Union, Sugihara was forced to take early retirement for his breach of discipline. To support his family in the miserable years that followed, he was forced to take a job as a door-to-door salesman of light bulbs. He was finally forgiven by the Japanese establishment only posthumously in 1991 when the Ministry apologized to his widow. The occupation clearly knew nothing of Sugihara's plight — and, fearing further victimization if he rocked the boat, Sugihara had kept his silence.

Much of the early history of the occupation was colored by the fact that MacArthur was grooming himself for a possible run for president of the United States in 1948. Thus reform of Japan often took second place to MacArthur's personal public relations agenda. Japanese officials were told that whenever they disagreed with MacArthur there must be "no sign to the world of dissension."

MacArthur limited his interviews to journalists who could be counted on to produce adulatory reports. And American scholars and authors were induced to write euphoric books on the occupation with titles like *The Conqueror Comes to Tea, Fallen Sun,* and *Star-spangled Mikado.*

The author Robert B. Textor, an occupation official, documented the extraordinary lengths to which MacArthur controlled how the occupation was presented in the Western press. The *London Times*'s Tokyo correspondent was told he would be classified as "a security risk" if he did not cooperate with the myth-making agenda. Similar pressure was applied to correspondents for CBS and McGraw-Hill. Other news organizations blacklisted or victimized by MacArthur included the *Christian Science Monitor,* the *San Francisco Chronicle,* and *The Nation.*

Occupation public relations officials quickly developed an extraordinary system for "anesthetizing" (to use Textor's word) the countless American dignitaries who visited Japan on fact-finding missions. The formula included minute-by-minute chaperoning by army officials, extraordinary accommodations in the ancient capital of Kyoto, and a virtual commandeering of Japan's then limited fleet of VIP limousines. Schedules were packed with flower arrangements, dancing girls, and extended drinking sessions. The visiting dignitaries became known to occupation officials as "feather merchants" (for reasons that Textor did not explain). Textor commented, "Perhaps never in history has the army's passion for 'eyewash,' orderliness, and showmanship been afforded freer vent than in occupied Japan."

The final verdict on the occupation is that it was an important wrong turn for the United States. By encouraging Washington to believe that the whole world was rapidly converging toward American values, American policy toward Asia in general and Japan in particular has been based on an illusion for four decades. MacArthur is principally to blame. In March 1949 he told the *Osaka Mainichi* newspaper: "Now the Pacific has become an Anglo-Saxon lake." Talk of this sort initiated a terrible vicious circle in U.S.-Japan relations that is still evident even in the 1990s. Encouraged by MacArthur, the American press proclaimed not only America's special destiny of global leadership but Japan's enthusiastic acceptance of that destiny. American diplomats then picked up the theme and played it back to the American press. The painful truth is that all along the Americans were talking only to themselves.

If the occupation encouraged the United States to rest on its laurels, the effect on Japan could hardly have been more different. The cocktail of emotions the Japanese experienced during that time has never been fully understood in the United States, but in a word it sharpened their will to win. The anthropology scholar Harumi Befu has suggested that American behavior during the occupation was colored by attitudes of superiority. Although this may overstate the Americans' insensitivity — after all Japanese leaders seem to have gone out of their way to encourage such attitudes — it is clear that the war and its humiliating aftermath left the Japanese with a large chip on their shoulder.

In view of the extensive retrospective efforts by American cold war ideologues to bowdlerize the history of the occupation, it is well to remember that not all the occupiers behaved in an exemplary way. In fact, the experience proved a subtly corrupting experience for America. The occupation often placed quite ordinary and inexperienced American soldiers in a position to wield unaccountable power over Japanese citizens. It was a formulation that recalls the British historian Lord Acton's epigram about the hazards of absolute power.

A Japanese-speaking American who lived in a provincial city in Japan in the late 1940s reported a tendency for the "small fry," as he described lower-ranking occupation officials, to treat the Japanese arrogantly. In a letter to Textor in 1949, this informant wrote: "There will be jeeps and private occupation cars crawling along the roads followed by a long line of Japanese taxis, trucks, and cars, and if one of them tries to pass, the Americans will halt him and give him Hell." This informant also highlighted the habit of some GIs of stopping women passersby "just for a lark" and hauling them into a military clinic for a venereal disease check. He commented, "I know there is a definite reaction setting in on the part of the Japanese. Not the kind of reaction that breeds violence, but a quiet (and rather deep) scorn."

Of course, such arrogance was displayed by only a tiny minority of American servicemen, and it was nothing compared to what Japan's Imperial Army had been meting out in China a few years earlier. But the Japanese, like everyone else, have selective memories.

The truth is that the relationship between occupier and occupied, like that between landlord and tenant, is fated to be an awkward one. Although ordinary Japanese citizens to this day fondly remember the GIs' kindness and chivalry, the Tokyo elite's memories were not unalloyed bliss. The elite's discomfiture was usually well hidden at the time, but it has cast a shadow over U.S.-Japan relations in the post-occupation era.

The lobbyists come calling

In terms of realpolitik, perhaps the most damaging consequence of the occupation for America has been that it bred an abiding cynicism among Japanese leaders about the ethical standards of American government officials.

Early in the occupation, a highly organized lobbying system developed in Tokyo to help Japanese interests influence occupation policy; and far from distancing themselves from this system, some occupation officials seemed to embrace it. They acquiesced, for instance, to an arrangement whereby ordinary members of the Japanese public were not permitted to talk to the Americans directly but were required instead to go through specially designated Japanese intermediaries. This arrangement obviously gave the intermediaries great power. Moreover this system sometimes seems to have involved payments by members of the Japanese public, an arrangement which almost guaranteed that occupation officials heard only from the wrong sort of people.

Conflicts of interest abounded. Tellingly, some occupation officials openly talked about their hopes of staying behind to form an American zaibatsu after the occupation ended, a bizarre ambition for an organization dedicated to ridding Japan of its powerful zaibatsus.

Some American officials seem to have profited personally from the misfortunes they inflicted on the Japanese elite. A notable example was the head of the occupation's Economic Section. At one point in negotiations with Mitsui representatives, he gestured out his window to some shabby passersby and vehemently announced: "The Mitsui family shall not live better than those people." It sounded like the fashionable egalitarianism of the day, but in fact the American, who in private life ran textile businesses in the United States, had somehow come to own a large block of shares in a Mitsui textile company. The author, John G. Roberts, commented on this shareholding:

> Such acquisitions were not rare. Some occupation officials used their authority to extort securities, real estate, and works of art from Japanese owners reduced to desperation by the freeze on securities and bank accounts or went into "partnership" with businessmen seeking privileges. Quite a few of those carpetbaggers, especially Japanese-speaking American lawyers, became landed gentry by such means and still [in 1973] live in Japan as millionaires.

It is noteworthy that in the post-occupation era some of these Americans pursued second careers in Japan advising American corporations on how to penetrate the Japanese market. Was this advice always reliable and frank? The question is unavoidable, given how heavily compromised the advisers were — and how absurdly accident-prone American corporations proved to be in post-occupation Japan. One prominent Washington official was publicly accused in Japan of open graft. He was W. R. Hutchinson, a lawyer who, while a member of a five-man Washington commission on the zaibatsus, allegedly offered himself as a lobbyist to the Mitsui group. His fees were so high that the Mitsui men felt obliged to share the burden with several other zaibatsus.

Perhaps the most startling example of how conflicts of interest marred American reform efforts was the so-called Draper-Johnson Mission, a highly influential inquiry team sent out by Washington in 1948 to help shape future American policy toward Japan. The mission seems to have owed its genesis to efforts by the investment banking house Dillon, Read and other American business interests to promote commercial ties with Japan. Washington had been panicked into forming the mission after a leaked report by a former Dillon, Read executive had portrayed the occupation's efforts to reform Japanese business as "tragic." On the strength of this report, *Newsweek* and other media organizations argued that Japan would fall into the communist camp if the occupation persisted with efforts to break up the zaibatsus. The mission's leader turned out to be United States Army Undersecretary William H. Draper, a former and future executive of Dillon, Read who had a serious conflict of interest. Dillon, Read was trying to recover a major loan it had made before the war to a Japanese electric power utility. As recounted by John G. Roberts, Draper seems to have used the occasion of his visit to Japan to establish participation for Dillon, Read in the launch of the Alaska Pulp Company, one of the first major Japanese investments in the United States in the postwar era.

Whatever Draper's motives, the end result is that his mission produced recommendations so favorable to Japan that they might have been penned by the Tokyo bureaucracy. For one thing, the mission recommended that Japan's reparations to victims of Japanese military aggression be cut by three-quarters. Japan's burden of reparations seems to have been whittled down to only about $1 billion. Certainly it represents only a minute fraction of the $72 billion that has already been paid or has been promised under Germany's continuing reparations program.

The mission definitively opposed the occupation's plans to break up the big Japanese banks. The fact that the banks lived to fight another day proved invaluable for the Japanese economic bureaucrats later on when the occupation ordered the sale of the broken-up remains of the old zaibatsus. According to the Americans' script, shares in the new companies formed from the breakup should have been dispersed widely among the Japanese public. In the event, the shares were bought heavily by the still vastly powerful banks, helping Japanese economic leaders resurrect the zaibatsu system in keiretsu form almost as soon as the Americans left.

Another crucial favor the mission rendered to Tokyo was to advocate a so-called reverse-course strategy in which the United States should switch from regarding Japan as a former enemy to building up the Japanese economy as a bulwark against communism. In this too the mission's message was to prove stunningly influential: in short order, the vast American market was thrown open on preferential terms to Japanese exporters and large amounts of American taxpayers' money were being pumped into teaching the Japanese the secrets of American industrial success.

The biggest surprise of all is that the mission came up with such dramatic policy recommendations after a stay of just three weeks in Japan. It was a style of "businesslike" Washington decision-making that the Japanese were soon to become very accustomed to — and very comfortable with.

The miracle

The strength of Japan's will has rarely been more apparent than in the boldness with which Japanese leaders planned the spectacular post-war recovery.

Defeated by the awe-inspiring productivity of America's capitalist system, Japanese leaders nonetheless boldly decided they could leap-frog to a new economic system that would outdo capitalism. Setting their faces against all capitalist theory, they perfected the cartels, the lifetime employment system, and the other now-familiar institutions of Big Logic Economics. Tokyo had experimented with most of these tools before — and now it moved decisively to cross an economic Rubicon by effectively abolishing capitalism.

Ironically, the United States powerfully encouraged this challenge to capitalism. It had largely excluded Japanese exports before the war, but it now welcomed them with open arms. This produced a qualitative change in the world economy which Americans have never fully understood. A huge home market had been one of the key hidden advantages American corporations enjoyed in racing ahead of foreign competitors in the first half of the twentieth century — no other country had such a large population of educated and productive people as the United States. Thus corporate America could amortize its research and development and other up-front costs over a uniquely large home market. Now at a stroke, the advantage of market size moved to the Japanese — whose effective home market was Japan *plus* the United States. Given that the Japanese market remained almost impenetrable for American goods, corporate America found itself in the post-war world playing with a handicap, particularly in research-intensive products such as electronic goods.

America was so eager to see Japan succeed that at times it gave the Japanese even better access to the American market than American manufacturers enjoyed. The Pentagon, for example, gave the Japanese a de facto dispensation from its normal rules restricting defense suppliers from using American military technologies in consumer products.

American policymakers didn't think very much about their policies at the time. In their eyes they were being charitable to an underdeveloped country. Certainly what American observers saw in Japan in the fall of 1945 was a country which, on the surface at least, was poorer than many Third World countries. It had lost more than 80 percent of its shipping tonnage and had virtually no hard currency. As a result Japanese manufacturers could not import even essential materials, and whole factories closed down for the want of normally insignificant parts.

Homeless orphans roamed the streets. About six million returnees from the war and from the colonies flooded into the main cities and put almost unbearable pressure on the country's supplies of housing and food. With the sewage system out of commission because of bombing, oxcarts reappeared to provide an ancient solution for Tokyo's sanitation problems. One of the American army's first activities was to spray lines of louse-ridden people with DDT — an unheard-of plight for the Japanese, who in normal times were fastidious about personal hygiene.

For several years the only food available in reasonable quantity was sweet potatoes, a vegetable that many older Japanese cannot look at now without a tinge of nausea. The effects of food shortages are still visible today: an official survey recently found that Japanese men born between 1932 and 1942 are on average only five feet three and a half inches tall, a full three inches shorter than their sons born twenty-five years later, in more nutritionally favorable times. Significantly, the top civil servants who make the decisions today on Japan's food policy come from the generation that as children experienced indelible memories of food shortages.

Gasoline was so scarce that the only taxis available were Rube Goldberg contraptions that somehow ran on charcoal. At sixty yen, the minimum fare was four times the standard lunch of those days, a cup of noodles.

In characteristic style, the Tokyo bureaucrats began working on recovery literally the day that Japan surrendered. In the two weeks between the end of the war and the beginning of the occupation, the bureaucrats made massive transfers of wealth to the zaibatsu companies via sales of army surplus materials and payments of war indemnities. As recorded later in a controversial book by the occupation official T. A. Bisson, such transfers were in most cases conducted on terms so favorable to the zaibatsu that in many cases they amounted to a free gift. Who benefited from this generosity? Not the zaibatsu owners, who were destined to be expropriated within weeks. The true beneficiaries were the hired managers of the zaibatsu, whose personal prestige in Japanese society was a function of the power of the companies they worked for. Given the favor-for-favor etiquette that is such a factor in Japanese administrative culture, these managers were put under an obligation to support the officials' efforts to reorganize the structure of the economic system. Ever afterwards, Japanese officials and corporate executives remained solid partners in promoting economic progress.

The civil servants' position was enhanced at the outset by the fact that the American occupation had to work through them in implementing change. That gave the officials an effective veto on the occupation. The civil servants first concentrated on rebuilding heavy industry and infrastructure.

Money was poured into new steelmaking facilities, civil engineering works, mine development, and electrical power generation plants. Thus by 1951 Japan had boosted its industrial output back to the levels of 1935, the last year before the economy had been put fully on a war footing. By 1951, American purchases of parts and services for the Korean War had helped trigger a miniboom in Japan. But it was not until 1955 that the economy really took off. In the next two decades economic growth averaged a stunning nine percent a year. In 1961 alone, GNP grew by 14.6 percent, surely the fastest growth any major nation has achieved in history.

The Japanese civil servants' ability to mobilize resources on a colossal scale became apparent in the coordinated development of a cluster of steel-related industries ranging from mining to automobiles. The first move was to rebuild steel foundries; their steel was then used to build shipyards and make ships. The ships enabled Japan to import more iron ore and produce more steel and ships. Corporate Japan went on to build port facilities both in Japan and in mining countries such as Australia. Eventually Japan began financing new mines in Australia and elsewhere. And, of course, the mines created a new market for excavation equipment, made from Japanese steel. By creating both products and markets, Japan carefully climbed up the economic league tables.

Another important market for Japanese steel was Japan's fishing fleet, which quickly grew to become the world's largest. By the mid-1970s, Japanese trawlers were taking one-seventh of the world's fishing catch — not bad for a country that accounted for only one in fifty of the world's population. And, by maintaining high trade barriers against beef, the civil servants ensured a ready market for the trawlers' catch.

By the early 1960s, Japan was outinvesting the United States in the steel industry. How would the resulting production be sold? The answer would soon become abundantly apparent: the Japanese were going to make cars. It didn't matter that the Japanese auto industry was at that time tiny and primitive, working mainly with hand-me-down British and French designs. Japanese banks poured vast amounts of money into the fledgling car companies to push them up the technology gradient. Meanwhile the civil servants went about inventing a home market for cars, no mean feat given that, in the view of an American research mission in 1956, Japan's roads were the worst in the industrialized world. The authorities suddenly unveiled a vast road-building program keyed to the 1964 Tokyo Olympic Games. In the space of a few years, expressways were threaded through Tokyo's congested downtown areas and out to other cities. The road-building created vast new demand for steel, resulting in more iron ore imports, more foreign port facilities constructed with Japanese steel, more Japanese exports of heavy equipment to foreign mines, and more demand for ships.

The first major overseas market for Japanese cars was Australia. As Japan had been a big customer for Australian minerals, it pressed Australia to buy its cars — and Australia, with no real auto industry of its own, duly obliged.

Tokyo pushed its steel policy even further when oil refiners in Japan started benefiting from the new Japanese motoring boom. The refiners, mainly offshoots of American and European corporations, were told that in return for their continued right to prosper in Japan, they should equip their worldwide fleets with Japanese ships. In the space of a few years, most of the world's oil industry moved over to Japan-made supertankers.

Similar stories of state-sponsored success can be told about dozens of other Japanese industries. In quick succession in the 1960s, Japan achieved global leadership not only in shipbuilding and steel but in cameras, radios, stereos, and black and white television sets. In the 1970s came copiers, VCRs, color television sets, various computer peripherals such as dot-matrix printers, and, of course, cars. In the 1980s, the big new products were compact disk players, semiconductors, nuclear power plants, video cameras, fax machines, machine tools, laptop computers, and supercomputers.

In the 1960s, Japan had passed both Britain and West Germany to become the third-largest economy, behind the United States and the Soviet Union. In the early 1980s, it surged past the Soviet Union.

The lessons of history

It is worth standing back and reviewing how profoundly history has shaped modern Japan.

Japan "Westernized" itself not out of choice but because it had to. And most of what has been called "Westernization" would be better termed modernization: Japan's Westernization was limited largely to economic and technological matters. There is little here to support the so-called convergence theory propounded by most of the American and British press, the idea that because Japan modernized itself in the last 140 years it is destined to become more and more Western in its approach to life. The convergence theory makes the false assumption that because the Japanese needed to import Western technology they necessarily feel a similar need to import Western individualism. If the Japanese ever felt any misgivings on this score, they have resolved them to their own satisfaction in the last fifty years as Japan has gone from strength to strength driven by highly non-Western political and social institutions.

In truth, the world as Japan sees it today is divided by two great — and ultimately incompatible — cultures. The standard bearers of these cultures are America and Japan, respectively. Historically, Eastern culture has been the more successful and significant. Under Japan's leadership, Eastern culture is now reemerging after four hundred years of eclipse as the world's leading culture. Coming fresh to the problems of economic development, Japanese leaders have never felt bound to follow the West's path. They have been prepared to follow that path only if it seemed right for Japan. Above all, the Japanese have felt no need to be bound by Western rules just because the West unilaterally declared these rules to be universally applicable. Just as the West wrote the rules to suit Western conditions, Japan feels an equal right to set the rules to suit itself.

4

The Invisible Leviathan

It is axiomatic that for Japan's Big Logic system to work, it must be supervised by intelligent and disciplined public officials. But how exactly does government work in Japan? This is one of the most hotly debated questions in Japanology.

At the heart of the mystery is the impression that Japan's electoral politics are constantly engulfed in scandal and disorder. For a century "money politics" scandals have been a recurring theme in Western press coverage of Japanese administration. Every few years Japan seems to launch new political reforms that will supposedly end the money politics system. But within a few years, the symptoms of money politics seem to return more vigorous than ever.

In 1994, politicians in Japan were in the midst of yet another program of reform. This followed an election in July 1993 that ended the Liberal Democratic Party's long reign as Japan's permanent party of government. Inevitably, expectations were aroused in the West that Japan was finally going to adopt a more Western approach to economics and politics.

"The Great Tokyo Earthquake" was how the *Wall Street Journal*'s editors described the election result. In the *Journal*'s view, Japan's perennially neglected consumers had finally asserted themselves and would insist that their interests should henceforth take precedence over those of the bureaucracy and big business.

Yet if this was an earthquake, it was one whose tremors seemed more noticeable the farther you were from the epicenter. For those in Tokyo, the ground did *not* move. The election result looked very much like business as usual: a weak diet overshadowed by a strong bureaucracy. If anything the new cabinet was even weaker than its predecessors because it depended on the support of a fragile coalition of seven parties.

Certainly there would be important changes in Japan. Change is a constant in a country that has been consistently outpacing all others in its economic and social development for more than a century. But the new diet was in no position to make changes without the say-so of other more influential Japanese power centers in Japan's distinctly non-Western power hierarchy. As the leading Japan scholar Chalmers Johnson has pointed out, Westerners who in 1993 expected a big move toward Westernization in Japan were unconsciously making a crucial assumption that change in Japan is inevitably toward Western political and economic norms. This assumption is simply false.

In this chapter we will look at how Japan's bureaucrats dominate the Japanese power system. In the next chapter, we will look at how the politicians and other interest groups in Japan fit into the system. Only then can we accurately assess the significance of the 1993 election result.

The path to power

Power in Japan may work in mysterious ways, but we are not completely bereft of clues to solving the enigma. One of the most important clues is the career aspirations of Japan's most ambitious young people. Here things are remarkably clear. All of Japan's brightest young people fight to get into Tokyo University, and the very best of them invariably opt to study law. Where do Tokyo law students go when they graduate? The trail leads directly to a grim six-floor fortress-like building in the Kasumigaseki administrative district of central Tokyo. Kasumigaseki literally means "foggy gate," and it stands just across the moat from the emperor's palace. Most foreigners don't recognize this building because it is one of the few in central Tokyo that does not carry any English-language identification. Its name is displayed only in three barely legible Chinese ideograms. This is the Okurasho — literally, the Ministry of the Big Storehouse. In English, we call it the Ministry of Finance, or, among initiates, the MOF.

The Ministry of Finance hires only about twenty people each year for its elite track. These recruits are quite distinct from the thousands of ordinary graduates the MOF hires each year, and they are the ultimate winners in the world's most grueling educational rat race. They will be acknowledged as such by their Tokyo University peers for the rest of their lives.

The Ministry of Finance is the pinnacle of day-to-day public administration in one of the world's most hierarchical societies. It is so far above the clouds that many ordinary Japanese have little idea of its significance. Even fewer foreigners understand. Yet everyone at the top level in Japan's administrative and commercial life understands. So do Japan's most ambitious *kyoiku mamas* — education-obsessed mothers. In their eyes, the Ministry of Finance is the crock of gold at the end of the educational rainbow. A son who wins entry to the MOF's elite track at the age of twenty-two or twenty-three confers as much distinction on his family by that act alone as he would if he had won a Nobel Prize.

To Westerners unfamiliar with Eastern attitudes to power this may seem like hyperbole, but it isn't. MOF men truly are Nobel caliber — brilliant, creative, tenacious, public-spirited. Many of them would probably win Nobel Prizes if they chose the sort of careers that catch the eye of the Royal Swedish Academy of Sciences. Not only are they recognized in elite circles in Japan as the country's finest, but they enjoy a dimension of prestige few Nobel laureates can claim: immense power. Power is the defining feature of status in Japan; by comparison, fame and fortune, which many of the West's finest pursue, are regarded askance in Japan. Fame signifies an attention-seeking, frivolous personality; and great wealth is regarded less as a measure of a person's contribution *to* society than of his ability to cut corners in taking *from* society.

Once on the elite track in the MOF, the big prize is to become the *jimu jikan* — the administrative vice minister. The title is a classic example of Japanese false modesty, for the MOF administrative vice minister is without doubt Japan's most powerful officeholder. Officially the administrative vice minister reports to the Minister of Finance, who is a political appointee; in reality, the administrative vice minister effortlessly outranks the Minister, who is usually little more than a figurehead.

Virtually unknown abroad, the MOF stands head and shoulders above all other agencies and institutions in Japan. Beneath it lies an intricate power pyramid. The layer of power immediately under the MOF is made up of the big banks, a group of key bureaucratic agencies of which the Ministry of International Trade and Industry is the best known in the West, and the Cabinet. The next layer includes big industrial corporations, lesser bureaucratic agencies, the securities industry, the press, and the main political parties.

This power structure does not, of course, bear much resemblance to Japan's presentation of itself as a Western-style democracy. Elected representatives in Japan acquiesce in a role as part ombudsmen and part lobbyists. Their main job is to intercede with the bureaucrats on behalf of local pressure groups and special interests. They also function as the government's human face in presenting official policies to the governed. They are really, then, the government's public relations men. Their first duty is to deflect domestic and foreign political pressures away from the civil service decision-makers whose policies they explain. These decision-makers are thereby left free to get on with running Japan — and increasingly the world — shielded by the politicians from having to bother directly with the public relations side of power, which is a major distraction for key decision-makers in the West's pluralistic power systems.

Japan is, of course, not the only country with a strong bureaucracy. It shares this characteristic with most of Europe's advanced societies, notably France, Germany, Switzerland, and Austria. A strong bureaucracy is also a feature of East Asia's most successful societies including Taiwan, South Korea, and Singapore.

The Japanese civil service's power, however, is in a league of its own. For a start, Japanese civil servants enjoy the priceless advantage of the moral high ground. As a Confucian society, Japan is avowedly paternalistic, and there is little sympathy for the essentially alien view that supreme power is rightfully the prerogative of elected representatives. Thus the bureaucrats do not have to apologize for overruling populist tendencies. In fact, they are free to act quite harshly if necessary in suppressing such tendencies. Their actions will be judged only in terms of how well they serve the overall national interest. Their objective is to achieve the greatest happiness of the greatest number of people. Moreover, they take an extremely long-term view in that they seek to represent the interests not only of today's Japanese but of future generations.

Some might imagine that elected representatives would bridle at this system of arbitrary civil service power. But, like most other members of the Japanese elite, they are not at heart great admirers of Western democracy. They believe in the Japanese principle of *wa* — harmony. In contrast with Western culture's concern to encourage a diversity of opinion, the search for wa pressures people to play down their differences and to seek to create a common front even where there is considerable disagreement under the surface. Ultimately the pressure to conform must come from a strong central authority — hence the need for a civil service that enjoys considerable power to overrule an excitable and often benighted electorate.

This system of bureaucratic supremacy does not prevent Japan's elected representatives from speaking as if Japanese power were driven by American-style populist pressures. And occasionally they make a show of token resistance to the civil servants, even to the extent of engaging in Western-style pluralistic uproar.

Why would politicians consent to take part in Japan's elaborate democratic rituals if they know that they enjoy little influence over national policymaking? Actually, this comes very naturally in a country where people are noted for theatricality in their public behavior. In any case, role-playing of this sort comes with the territory in many of the world's political systems. Even in the American political process, the gap between illusion and reality can be wide. American politicians often tailor their voting in Congress to please lobbyists and vested interests — yet they are quite as adept as Japanese politicians at pretending their voting springs from a pure concern to represent the people's will.

Japan is hardly alone as a society where an elite group enjoys enormous power to overrule the electorate's wishes. Even Britain is often undemocratic in this sense. If the British democratic system truly represented the people's will, Britain would long ago have restored capital punishment and would have withdrawn from the European Union. In fact, British political leaders of the left and the right have generally cooperated with each other in a successful effort to resist the popular will on both issues. In America, lobbyists and other vested interests are often successful in persuading politicians to overrule popular sentiment. A recent case in point was Congress's approval for the North American Free Trade Agreement, which seemed to be opposed by a majority of ordinary Americans. That said, Japan's version of elite rule is not an occasional aberration but the linchpin of the country's administration.

Interpreting Japanese power: the Tower of Babel

Over the years many attempts have been made to explain the mysteries of Japanese power. Most such theories have overlooked the MOF and led Westerners down a series of blind alleys.

One of the most enduring theories is that Japan is run by big business. This myth seems to have originated among foreign executives resident in Japan. It is easy to see how a superficial view of Japanese policymaking might sustain the illusion. A foreign company, for instance, may try unsuccessfully for years to get established in Japan; as a last resort it decides to do a joint venture with a Japanese company. Suddenly this partnership opens all doors: officials are magically persuaded to cut through red tape, politicians give their blessing, and even the Japanese media sing the foreign company's praises. Thus Japanese corporations seem almost all powerful. But this is far from the case. The Japanese partner merely understands the civil servants' industrial policy and so can reposition the foreign company's project to win official support. This support is reserved mainly for projects that transfer important new technology to Japanese soil. A Japanese partner can quickly identify those pieces of a foreign company's technological endowment of particular interest and arrange for them to be transferred to a Japanese joint venture. In a word, therefore, big business enjoys no magic touch and is clearly a secondary player in the Tokyo power game.

Nonetheless, as in many other aspects of Japanese policymaking, it suits the civil servants for the West to think that big business is in charge. This shields them from accountability for their controversial policy agenda, most notably mercantilist trade policies.

The most extreme form of the big business myth was the widespread view a few years ago in American and European circles that Nomura Securities, Japan's biggest securities firm, was the country's most powerful organization. Nomura was held to be virtually running the Ministry of Finance, which for a while became known to foreigners as the Kasumigaseki branch of Nomura Securities. To those who understand the Japanese educational hierarchy, the idea that Nomura was all-powerful was always an unlikely theory. Big as it is, Nomura finds it difficult to recruit more than a few Tokyo University graduates each year. And without Tokyo graduates, it is by definition out of the loop of supreme power in Japan.

Characteristically, MOF officials did nothing to discourage the Nomura-runs-Japan story; in fact, they often encouraged the myth. One unnamed senior MOF official described Nomura's supposed hold on the MOF in an interview with the author Al Alletzhauser in these extravagant terms: "Nomura is the Ministry of Finance. We consult them on our every move and even let them draft legislation."

Alletzhauser took this to mean the patients were running the asylum. However, the MOF man left much unsaid. Although it is true that Nomura drafts the MOF's securities regulations, it does so only in collaboration with the other Big Four Japanese securities firms. More important, the Big Four are expected to draw up legislation that takes MOF policy concerns fully into account. Such procedures for drafting legislation are the norm in many industries and do not betoken any weakness in the civil service. Rather the reverse —particularly in the case of the MOF. The securities firms are kept on such a short leash by the MOF that they would not dare take advantage of their regulation-writing function to advance their private agendas. The analogy is not with patients in an asylum but with pupils at a traditional boarding school. Some of the pupils are appointed prefects and must keep order when the teachers are absent. If any pillow fighting breaks out, the teachers have someone to hold responsible.

Nomura's secondary position in the Japanese power system became amply apparent in the Nomura scandal of 1991, just a year after Alletzhauser's book was published. The MOF orchestrated a campaign denouncing Nomura's chairman and president in the press and then forced them to resign. Yet the charges against Nomura were essentially trumped up and the campaign represented one of the most remarkable displays of arbitrary civil service power in Japan in recent years.

One of the most enduring media myths about Japanese power is that the country is run by the Ministry of International Trade and Industry. This myth dates to the 1950s and 1960s, when foreign companies found the ministry barring their way when they tried to establish operations in Japan. Among the problems with the MITI theory is that the Ministry and its clientele have always been beholden to the MOF in the crucial matter of the disposition of Japan's savings flows.

In recent times another myth has superseded the mighty MITI story — the void-at-the-top theory. This states that the various power centers in Japan are constantly warring inconclusively with each other and that no one power center ever establishes permanent superiority over the others. Thus Japan is utterly leaderless, and everyone at the top supposedly spends much of his time countermanding everyone else's orders. This theory too seems to have originated with foreigners in Japan. Foreigners who are exposed to Japan's often byzantine import procedures, for instance, often come away convinced that Japan is at heart anarchic. An importer may need to get permission from several government agencies before an import consignment can be cleared through customs. Conflicting regulations can easily derail an import transaction. Adding to the impression of anarchy is the fact that sometimes even industrial cartels may have veto power over certain categories of imports. To top it all, a standard means of cutting through the gridlock at the customs is to make an appropriate campaign contribution to a politician who has influence with a relevant government agency.

From a Western point of view, all this is chaotic to the point of irrationality. But when you understand Japanese economics, you immediately see that there is method in the madness: administrative gridlock generally affects only products that Japanese policymakers evidently do not wish Japan to import. By discouraging imports of most consumer goods, Japan boosts its all-important savings rate. The truth of the import story is apparent when you look at how Japan deals with imports of raw materials such as iron ore that are essential for Japanese industry. In contrast to consumer imports, such imports seem rarely if ever to be held up by governmental gridlock.

Some void-at-the-top theorists maintain that the MOF is incapable of mounting coordinated policy because it is itself hopelessly divided by internal rivalry. In reality, few government agencies enjoy stronger cohesion than the MOF. Certainly the various bureaus within the MOF compete with each other for turf, but always there are officials at higher levels to resolve disputes amicably. Like well-managed Japanese corporations, the MOF uses the special atmosphere created by lifetime employment to ensure internal cooperation: in aspiring to the ultimate top job as jimu jikan, up-and-coming MOF men are naturally heedful of instructions from their superiors to cooperate with one another. People get promoted in Japanese organizations by knowing when to compromise and how to get along with their lifetime colleagues.

A variant on the void-at-the-top story is the idea that various vested interests such as the farmers enjoy tremendous veto power over national policies and use it to pursue self-serving agendas at odds with the common good. In truth, every time a particular lobbying group seems to be in control of policy, this is merely because the group's agenda is congruent with the bureaucrats' own policies. In such cases, the bureaucrats often find it convenient to attribute their policies to the lobbying group as a way of deflecting the complaints of parties aggrieved by such policies.

It is interesting to take a closer look at the farm lobby, which supposedly has the power unilaterally to force the Japanese people to pay six times the world price for rice. But how strong is the farmers' lobby really? Japan's farm population has been deliberately reduced by three-quarters in the last four decades as a direct result of a variety of policies detrimental to farm interests. In particular, the government has virtually shut down Japan's once-huge silk industry. The government saw no point in keeping the industry on a life-support machine after it became noncompetitive in the 1950s, and today Japan imports most of its silk from Thailand and other countries with cheap labor. That Japan's rice industry has not been shut down is less a reflection of the farmers' clout than of the bureaucracy's concern to maintain food security. If Americans lived in a country that nearly starved in 1945, their government might also be concerned to promote food security.

There is a key point here that Americans find difficult to grasp: the direction of causality between policymaking and lobbying is reversed in Japan. Whereas in America vested interests tend to create policy, in Japan, policy tends to create vested interests. In the case of rice, for instance, a preexisting policy of promoting rice production fosters the continued existence of a vociferous lobby in favor of this policy. If the rice promotion policy were to be abandoned, the rice lobby would dwindle as fast as the silk lobby did in the 1950s.

The view that vested interests can divert the course of the economy has been knowledgeably rebutted by the Japanese political scientist Kanji Haitani, who has pointed out that such groups enjoy no fundamental power but are merely humored by the bureaucrats with "minimally necessary compromises."

Many believers in the void-at-the-top theory have pursued a false scent in search of explanations for Japan's pattern of economic overachievement. "Cultural differences" has become a catch phrase to explain Japan's many economic peculiarities. This in turn has quenched curiosity in the West about whether the Japanese have consciously gone about designing better ways of generating economic growth. As Karel van Wolferen has pointed out, Japan's culture is to a far greater degree than that of other countries a conscious creation of the authorities, who have always controlled the extent to which both foreign and home grown ideas could be disseminated within the country.

For the present, the question is who shaped Japan's economic culture. A look at the MOF's history will leave little room for doubt.

The making of a Leviathan

The MOF's roots run deep in Japan's history of bureaucratic rule. Its Japanese name, the Okurasho — the Ministry of the Big Storehouse — is a reference to the fact that taxes were traditionally paid in rice. The name first made its appearance in the seventh century and was revived in 1869 in the wake of the Meiji revolution. The Meiji oligarchs inherited much of the shoguns' government machinery, and we can presume that the shoguns' tax collection department was an element in this inheritance.

As far as one can tell, therefore, the modern MOF is the present-day successor of a tax collection agency with a history going back many centuries.

From the 1870s onward, the MOF was widely recognized as a pivotal agency of Japanese power. The MOF's characteristically non-Western approach to industrial development was apparent from the start of Japan's economic drive in the nineteenth century. Whereas most other economically backward countries imported capital heavily, the MOF considered this a critical error. Two small loans were raised abroad in 1870 and 1873, but for the next twenty-five years the MOF maintained a virtual ban on foreign capital entering Japan. The MOF also led the Japanese establishment in eschewing as much as possible direct investment in Japan by foreign capitalists.

Thus the MOF rejected one of the most cherished principles of Western economics — that unrestricted transfers of capital across borders serve to boost "efficiency" in recipient countries. MOF officials saw things differently, forming their opinion from practice, not the-

ory. They were influenced in particular by the slow death of the old
Chinese and Ottoman empires in the latter decades of the nineteenth
century. Both empires had thrown themselves open to foreign capital,
which in the Japanese view had led to corruption and demoralization.
The foreign investors formed alliances with the local elites, who became in effect lobbyists for foreign capital. Foreign money quickly
suffused government and largely disabled independent policymaking.
Soon the local elites came to identify with the foreigners and adopted
foreign manners. As viewed by the Japanese, foreign money decapi-
tated these once-proud empires.

The MOF's antagonism to foreign investors was apparent from the
start. In 1874 it defied the London financial establishment in an
international incident involving a capital-raising attempt by a British-
owned timber business in northern Japan. The MOF blocked the
capital issue. Deprived of the necessary expansion capital, the firm
stagnated and finally shut its doors in 1883.

Virtually all the key protagonists who led Japan in its first steps
toward industrialization worked at the MOF in the 1870s and then
fanned out into key positions throughout the Japanese establishment.
The modern MOF's first recruits included no less than four of the
half-dozen or so supreme oligarchs who were to dominate Japanese
government for the next half-century — Toshimichi Okubo, Hirobumi Ito, Shigenobu Okuma, and Masayoshi Matsukata.

Okubo was the first of the four to achieve supreme responsibility:
he served as the nation's foremost political leader in the 1870s. He
was in effect the prime minister, although that title had not yet been
created. He has been dubbed the Bismarck of Japan for his leading
role in introducing modern industries and for laying the foundations
of Japan's foreign policy. He is credited with coining the popular
political catch phrase of those days, Fukoku, kyohei — rich country,
strong army.

In 1885 Hirobumi Ito became Japan's first official prime minister.
Ito was a bureaucrat, not a politician — this was before Japan had
elections — and he truly headed the government (in contrast with
today's politician–prime ministers who typically are no more than
figureheads). Ito was perhaps the greatest holder of this office to date
and he was recalled to serve as prime minister in later years three
times. He crafted Japan's first constitution and invented many of the
counterintuitive political arrangements by which Japan continues to
be governed today.

Shigenobu Okuma achieved a special place in Japanese history because he is regarded as the father of modern Japanese mercantilism. He served as prime minister briefly in 1898 and again between 1914 and 1916.

Masayoshi Matsukata founded the Bank of Japan in 1882 and laid the groundwork for the modern Japanese system of government finance. He served as prime minister twice in the 1890s.

Many other early MOF men also made distinguished contributions to Japan's economic progress. Perhaps the most significant was Eiichi Shibusawa. As a young man at the MOF, Shibusawa fostered the development of commercial banking and thus laid much of the groundwork for Japan's rapid industrialization in the late nineteenth century. He resigned from the MOF in 1873 to go into business in partnership with the Mitsui merchant house. One of his first moves was to establish Dai-ichi Kokuritsu Ginko (First National Bank). This was the forerunner of Dai-Ichi Kangyo Bank, which in the 1980s passed Citicorp to become the world's largest commercial bank. As recounted by Kyugoro Obata, Shibusawa successfully opposed Mitsubishi founder Yataro Iwasaki's efforts to introduce Western individualistic management methods into Japan; instead, he pioneered modern Japan's characteristic system of collective management responsibility. Finally, as we will see in Chapter Seven, in the autumn of his career he played a key role in the invention of Japan's lifetime employment system.

The MOF seems to have ruled in a comfortable partnership with Japan's other key agency of those times, the Home Ministry, which supervised the police and the country's local authorities. In fact, the Home and Finance Ministries had started as one unit before being split in 1870. The only effective power which stood above these agencies was the Privy Council, a self-perpetuating committee of oligarchs who advised the emperor on matters of state. Most of the Privy Council's members were top civil servants or military leaders.

The MOF enjoyed great sway over other ministries because it had the constitutional right to determine the national budget largely free from backseat driving by elected representatives. In the first decades of the twentieth century, however, the military began to increase its power. After some initial resistance, Finance Ministry officials seem to have acquiesced in huge defense budgets from 1936 onward. The MOF put up the money for semiofficial corporations formed in the 1930s to develop the natural resources of Manchuria and northern

China. The Industrial Bank of Japan, then partially owned by the MOF and an acknowledged instrument of MOF policy, financed the Imperial Army's huge military and economic activities in Manchuria.

Before World War II, the MOF acquired sweeping regulatory powers over Japan's savings system and used them to force-feed capital to Japan's war industries. These powers remained on the books after the war and enabled the MOF to take control of the postwar economy. The MOF's control of savings started tightening after 1933 when companies were circumscribed from issuing bonds. They were, therefore, forced to rely on the banks for expansion funds. Then the Emergency Funds Regulation Law in 1937 allowed the MOF to close the loop by giving itself massive statutory powers to monitor and veto the banks' lending activities on a loan-by-loan basis. At the same time, the MOF acquired draconian powers to control corporations' dividends and to veto institutional investors' purchases of corporate bonds.

The immediate effect of these measures was not only to break down the previously sacrosanct secrecy of the banks but to put Japan firmly on a noncapitalist trajectory. Meanwhile, the Ministry of Commerce obtained power to appoint the top executives of major private companies. Many of these powers were formally dismantled after the war but, in a pattern similar to Japan's onion-peeling approach to trade liberalization, they have been superseded by a powerful system of nonstatutory and largely invisible "guidance" of the nation's savings flows.

From the moment the war ended, the Finance Ministry moved decisively to implement a carefully conceived contingency plan to cope with defeat. On August 15, 1945, the day Hirohito announced Japan's surrender, top MOF officials met to organize a gigantic printing of bank notes. The program began within hours in printing factories throughout Japan, and it is believed to have continued for several weeks. The MOF was so desperate to lay in a stockpile of money before the American occupation authorities arrived that it even resorted to the unprecedented expedient of requisitioning privately owned printing companies — Dai Nippon, Toppan, and Tokyo Shoken Insatsu — to assist in the program.

The MOF's concern was to make sure that it retained ultimate control of the financial system after the Americans arrived. But within days MOF officials learned of a mortal threat to this strategy: the

American army had its own plans to issue American military currency as legal tender in Japan, just as it had earlier done in the Philippines, Korea, and Okinawa. The Americans had even printed yen-denominated notes in advance in the Philippines in anticipation of Japan's surrender.

The MOF reacted with determination in the face of this unheard-of threat to its financial hegemony. It mounted its counteroffensive in a meeting between MacArthur and Foreign Minister Mamoru Shigemitsu in Yokohama on September 3, just a day after Japan had formally signed a surrender agreement in a ceremony on board the battleship *Missouri* in Tokyo Bay. It was MacArthur's first significant meeting with any Japanese official and, according to occupation historian Richard B. Finn, the currency dispute topped Shigemitsu's agenda. MacArthur agreed without a fuss to allow the MOF to retain its currency powers. He was clearly unaware of the MOF's printing activities and no doubt regarded the whole question as a trivial detail. He could not have been more wrong. The MOF knew that its control of the currency (and of the closely related matter of the creation of credit) was a key lever of power. It was soon to make good use of this power to establish itself as the supreme organ of Japanese government.

The MacArthur-Shigemitsu meeting was notable for the fact that it was Tokyo's first success in the post-1945 era in lobbying the Americans. A pattern was set. As in subsequent lobbying activities, the Japanese had studied the issues and knew exactly what they wanted. The Americans were unprepared and therefore threw away vital negotiating leverage in a show of innocent affability.

In the immediate aftermath of war, the MOF still had many important power rivals in the Japanese establishment. But this was soon to change. The MOF's rise to sole leadership began in the fall of 1945 when the occupation pushed ahead with breaking up the zaibatsus. The old zaibatsu families had been extremely powerful in prewar Japan, and their wealth made them formidable rivals for the civil servants. The Mitsui family, for instance, was said to have been even wealthier than the Rockefellers. That does not seem overstated given that they owned eighty major corporations with a total work force of 1.8 million people. Certainly they were plutocrats of the old-fashioned sort who controlled countless politicians. In prewar days they had traveled in style around the world and had established a network of friendships with important people in the United States and Britain.

When MacArthur moved to break up the Mitsui group and the other major zaibatsus, the Japanese establishment protested loudly. But privately, the MOF and other elements of the bureaucratic establishment seem to have been far from upset. The MOF in fact played a key role in breaking up the zaibatsu families' power. The method of the breakup was for the government to acquire the zaibatsu families' entire stock holdings in exchange for special issues of government bonds. Then, in 1946, the MOF delivered the coup de grâce in the form of a savagely high wealth tax. The head of the Mitsui family, Hachiroemon Mitsui, ended up paying taxes totaling a calamitous 91 percent on his assets.

The wealth tax was only the beginning of the bad news for the zaibatsu families. Releasing new bank notes into circulation literally by the ton, the MOF detonated hyperinflation. By 1949 the yen had lost 95 percent of its August 1945 value. There was no way the zaibatsu families could escape impoverishment because, under the MOF's rules for the zaibatsu breakup, they were not allowed to sell their bonds. Official accounts of the occupation have treated the inflation as if it were an act of God, but many astute observers at the time saw it as a deliberate strategy by the Japanese government. This view was expressed publicly by T. A. Bisson, the deputy head of the occupation's Government Section, in 1949. Certainly the inflation was avoidable because Japan, like Britain, ended the war with a fully functioning government.

The inflation was touched off by large lump-sum payments made to enlisted men in the aftermath of the surrender. Then, in 1947, when the inflation seemed to be subsiding, the MOF reignited it by expanding bank credit. In particular, it funded the setting up of the Reconstruction Finance Bank by printing money. As recounted by the former Bank of Japan economist Kazuo Tatewaki, the new bank "contributed significantly to the postwar accelerating inflation."

Financing the new bank with printed money was a classic power play. At a stroke the MOF not only marginalized the zaibatsu families (via inflation) but enormously increased its patronage in the economy via its ability to direct vast amounts of credit to Japan's then struggling corporations. The inflation also had the advantage of reducing the real burden of the government's war debts to trivial proportions.

The towering irony of MacArthur's destruction of the zaibatsu families' influence was that this was exactly what Japan's militant anti-Western bureaucrats had advocated in the 1930s. These bureaucrats, who came to be known as the New Bureaucrats, came to question the wealth-creating efficacy of capitalism while jump-starting industrial growth in the Japanese colony of Manchuria. In September 1940, they launched their post-capitalist ideas in the home islands of the empire when they published the Economic New Structure manifesto. This advocated that the owners of industry — the zaibatsu families — should be stripped of all power to control industry. The New Bureaucrat movement seems to have started at the Ministry of Commerce and Industry (the 1930s forerunner of the MITI), but by 1940 ultranationalist MOF officials such as Hisatsune Sakomizu, Kazuo Aoki, and Naoki Hoshino were prominent among its leaders and thinkers.

At first the zaibatsus successfully resisted expropriation, and they even staged a "sitdown strike" against government controls in 1943–44. This was finally resolved when the government backed off. It's interesting to note, however, that in the aftermath of the war, the zaibatsu families made little or no further attempt to resist expropriation. The reason may have been that they tacitly admitted that their earlier resistance to the bureaucrats' reorganization efforts had exacerbated bottlenecks in war industries and thus had hastened Japan's defeat.

After the zaibatsu families were discredited and impoverished, the MOF's only remaining power rival was the Home Ministry. But the Home Ministry's days were numbered. It had achieved considerable notoriety abroad because it regulated the Kempeitai, Japan's feared secret police. It was also regarded correctly by the Americans as the organizing force that controlled the diet in the 1930s. Early on in the occupation, MacArthur fired many top Home Ministry officials, and he later shut down the entire ministry.

MacArthur then acted to curtail the power of Japan's cartel of commercial banks by barring them from securities underwriting, an important source of banking power in prewar days. Modeled on America's Glass-Steagall Act of 1933, MacArthur's Securities and Exchange Act of 1948 could not have suited the MOF better. At a stroke, MacArthur powerfully buttressed the MOF's policy of maintaining artificial barriers between the various institutions of Japanese finance. With the creation of many different financial cartels to look after different, narrowly defined financial functions, the MOF's powers of regulatory control were correspondingly enhanced. In this, the MOF was implementing one of the most important principles of Japanese power: Divide and rule.

Even MacArthur's elaborate efforts to purge ultranationalist officials from the civil service worked to the MOF's advantage. Whereas other ministries lost so many key officials that they were gravely weakened, the MOF managed to emerge from the purge virtually intact. It lost just nine officials, by far the least of any ministry. By comparison, the Transportation Ministry lost 587 officials, though its work force was smaller than the MOF's.

The occupation made a feeble effort to shake up the MOF and other government agencies by trying to infuse some new blood into them. It prescribed written examinations for all top civil service positions. Thus incumbents were required to sit down to compete with outsiders for their own jobs. As recorded by the scholar B. C. Koh, however, the effort was secretly frustrated by the incumbents, who pressured outside candidates to stand down. In a classic demonstration of the Japanese public's obeisance to the civil service, virtually all qualified outsiders obeyed the request, and of 175 top jobs filled on the strength of the examination results, only one went to an outsider. The MOF's survival in pristine form thereby became a certainty.

MacArthur imagined that the Ministry of Finance would be subject to the firm supervision of elected representatives. But, in a major miscalculation, he delegated the task of crafting Japan's post–World War II electoral system to Japanese civil servants. They duly proceeded in 1947 to copy the rules virtually verbatim from the prewar system. This constituted a recipe for weak popular representation, and it opened the way for the civil servants to strip the diet of virtually all power in economic matters.

With all other power centers eliminated or weakened, the MOF emerged from the occupation as the one prewar institution positioned to fill the power vacuum after the Americans left. MacArthur had unwittingly created a Leviathan.

Authority as an economic force

Before we detail the MOF's workings, we must take time out to address an important mind block that inhibits many Westerners from seeing the reality of Japanese economic administration. Laissez-faire theoreticians hold that all government intervention in the economy is destined to fail. This proposition is associated particularly with the late Friedrich von Hayek, the Nobel Prize–winning Austrian economist who has been one of the greatest influences on American economics in the twentieth century. Hayek's thesis was that a market economy is constantly processing an almost infinite amount of economic information. Thus for bureaucrats to outthink the market, they would supposedly have to engage in the hopeless task of trying to process a similarly large amount of information.

As far as Japan is concerned, Hayek's theory sets up a straw man. Neither the MOF nor the wider Japanese bureaucracy have been so naive as to try to outthink the market on the scale Hayek postulated. Far from it. Their policies are simple and virtually self-enforcing. Thus the Japanese economic system runs on autopilot most of the time. The cartels and the keiretsus, for instance, automatically reinforce the logic of mercantilism. The obligations of the lifetime employment system automatically force companies to think in long-term ways and to invest for the future.

The education system provides a good example of the Japanese bureaucracy's eye for streamlined administration: by law Japan's schools all teach exactly the same curriculum. This makes it easy to identify schools whose performance is lagging and it also generates economies of scale in everything from textbooks to teacher training. Because the educational curriculum changes slowly, and then only in response to national economic goals rather than teachers' whims, it is a well-oiled machine whose workings have been perfected by *kaizen* — continuous improvement.

An essential ingredient in Japanese administration is arbitrary authority. In Japan, as in other Confucian societies, people live in fear of retaliation if they stand up to the bureaucrats. The Japanese bureaucrats have honed their power so carefully that it is almost invisible to most Westerners, even those who have lived many years in Japan. Deference to authority is more readily apparent in other East Asian societies. Perhaps the clearest example in recent years has been the changing behavior of the Chinese elite in Hong Kong. In the early 1990s, to the amazement of Western residents, virtually all of Hong Kong's Chinese elite backed away from previous support for pluralist democracy and started emulating the obedience to authority that is a hallmark of Japanese society. The Hong Kong Chinese were driven by concern not to get on the wrong side of top bureaucrats in Beijing, who are scheduled to establish sovereignty over Hong Kong in 1997. The extent of this concern became dramatically obvious in 1993 when two prominent anti-Beijing members of the Hong Kong Chinese community wanted to bring a libel suit against a key Hong Kong–based agent of the Beijing government. No less than eighteen of Hong Kong's top law firms refused to take the case.

In Japan such an incident would be unthinkable — but not because Japanese law firms are more willing than their Hong Kong counterparts to confront the bureaucracy on a taboo issue. Rather, no Japanese dissident would be so crass as to canvass eighteen law firms. One rejection would be enough.

The fact is that though the Japanese bureaucracy is sufficiently sensitive to Western opinion to entertain occasional token legal challenges to its authority, there are definite limits beyond which ordinary Japanese know it is dangerous to go.

The MOF's empire

Measured merely by its immediate formal powers as enshrined in Japanese law, the MOF is a titan among government agencies. In regulating the financial system alone, it gathers together under one roof powers which in the United States are dispersed among the Federal Reserve, the Department of the Treasury, the Federal Deposit Insurance Corporation, the Office of the Comptroller, and the Securities and Exchange Commission. The MOF controls the Japanese tax system through the National Tax Agency, which is a MOF division.

The MOF's most important statutory power is its control of the national budget. Its budgetary powers were enshrined in Japan's first constitution a century ago and have been only slightly reined in since. In the 1930s the military authorities unsuccessfully attempted to curb the MOF's budget-writing power. When MacArthur attempted a similar effort to curb the MOF's budget powers after World War II, he too was destined to be disappointed. He specified in the postwar constitution that responsibility for the budget would in future rest with the diet, not the MOF. But in 1947, just as the Constitution took effect, the diet passed a new finance law that restored most of the MOF's prewar prerogatives. The MOF's power, like that of other civil service branches, was protected by a special "nontariff barrier" in the form of the civil service's monopoly on the skills needed to draft Japanese law. To this day virtually no one outside the Japanese civil service can draft legislation. In the words of the Japanese political scientist Kanji Haitani, control of the budget is "deeply entrenched in the bureaucracy of the Ministry of Finance."

MacArthur halfheartedly tried to create a counterweight to the MOF by specifying that an independent agency, the Economic Stabilization Board, be charged with planning the economy. In a classic demonstration of bureaucratic finesse, however, the MOF promptly embraced the rival organization and parachuted in many of its elite officials to run it.

To this day MOF officials draw up the main lines of the budget in intense negotiations with civil servants in other ministries. The MOF takes some soundings in the diet beforehand, but elected representatives are largely excluded from the civil service negotiations that produce the *Okurasho gen-an,* the Finance Ministry draft budget. The elected representatives' hands-on involvement begins only after the budget's basic shape is already a fait accompli. Even then their powers to make amendments to the draft are limited to small pork barrel items on the spending side: the MOF jealously guards its taxing privileges, which are its most impressive lever of power.

The MOF's true role as Japan's preeminent power center is not generally talked about in public. The attitude seems to be that those who need to know already know, and everyone else is better off not knowing. Nonetheless authoritative sources have several times over the years acknowledged the MOF's anchorman role in Japanese society. One of the clearest descriptions in print of the MOF's power has come from the prominent journalist Takao Kawakita, who has reported that the MOF dubs itself "the Ministry of the Ministries."

In a book published in 1989, he said, "The basis of the MOF's influence is its ability to allocate a huge proportion of the national budget, which amounted to ¥56 trillion [around $500 billion] in 1988. This gives it the power of life or death over other ministries as well as over the industries under its jurisdiction. And at the same time because of its expertise, it makes puppets of greedy politicians."

For many years after World War II, Tokyo's English-language public relations industry avoided references to the MOF's pivotal role. But the taboo has recently been breaking down. One of the earliest signs of perestroika emerged in the semiofficial *Encyclopedia of Ja-*

pan, published in 1983, which described the MOF as Japan's "most important and prestigious organization." MOF officials, it added, are considered an "elite within the elite."

A striking outward sign of the MOF's preeminence is the protocol for budget negotiations with other ministries. The rule, as reported by Takao Kawakita, is that other ministries must send an official two ranks higher than the MOF official they are meeting. This means a senior MITI official, for instance, must suffer the indignity of being treated as an equal by a MOF official who may be fifteen years his junior, a remarkable anomaly by Japanese standards.

As the American political scientist John Creighton Campbell has pointed out, the MOF's power over other government agencies is enhanced by the fact that virtually every new government policy in Japan is screened in the first instance for its budgetary implications, even if these are negligible. Other agencies must even get the MOF's permission merely to reassign money from one purpose to another.

As Campbell has recounted, the MOF also stiffens the backs of the entire civil service to resist pressures from partisan groups and special interests. He has reported that MOF officials are disdainful not only of politicians but of civil servants who are sympathetic to politicians or to sectional interests. On one occasion, for instance, a Ministry of Transport official overly sympathetic to the taxi industry was silenced by a MOF budget official with this withering putdown: "You are no better than your boss, the cabdriver."

The MOF also enjoys considerable direct executive control over the Bank of Japan, which is Japan's equivalent of the United States Federal Reserve Board. Ostensibly the Bank of Japan is an independent entity with a mind of its own. But in reality the bank's independence is merely a convenient fiction that allows the MOF to distance itself from unpopular but necessary monetary measures and to parry foreign pressure for changes in Japanese financial policies. Under the Bank of Japan Law, the MOF enjoys wide powers to supervise the bank, to dismiss the bank's officers, and to change the bank's articles of association. More than half of the Bank of Japan's twenty-six governors since its foundation have been ex-MOF men. By contrast only eight have come from the bank's internal ranks.

One of the most significant aspects of the MOF's power is its control over Japan's defense system. The story of how the MOF imposed its hegemony over Japan's Defense Agency offers an interesting insight into Japanese-style power in action. The Defense Agency was founded by MacArthur in the early 1950s as a police reserve, and its top jobs were originally monopolized by nominees from the National Police Agency. But the MOF used its budget power as a bargaining chip in persuading the new agency to accept young MOF men on secondment. As recounted by *Zaikai Tembo,* these secondees gradually wound their way up through the agency. The result is that for many years the top officials of the agency have been MOF men.

Another important pillar of MOF power is Japan's Board of Audit. Virtually unknown outside the Kasumigaseki district, it is widely feared by civil servants. The Board of Audit functions as the MOF's eyes and ears in monitoring how the nation's money is spent. No waste, however trivial, seems too insignificant for the board's attention — and, by extension, the MOF's. John Creighton Campbell recounted an occasion when the MOF caught the Defense Agency red-handed in a memorable misappropriation of funds. The agency had ordered two flagpoles for an army barracks and then somehow had forgotten to use them. The MOF was implacable. One of its officials indignantly commented: "This indicates our evaluation of Defense Agency requests has been too lenient; so this year we will evaluate them much more carefully." The upshot was that the MOF refused to grant the Defense Agency any budget increase in the subsequent year, ostensibly because of this one tiny misallocation of resources. The MOF's indignation may have been staged merely as a pretext to clip the Defense Agency's wings, but the episode illustrates the proprietary hand the MOF uses to guard the public purse.

Another source of MOF power is *amakudari* — the civil servants' practice of taking important second careers in their fifties after they retire. The term literally means "descent from heaven," which speaks volumes about the civil servants' feelings when the time comes to leave their ministry to become chairman of an influential public agency, a giant bank, or a major corporation. No job outside, no matter how lucrative or prestigious, confers as much power and satisfaction as staying on at the Ministry.

Nonetheless, retired officials take their second careers very seriously, and amakudari provides the ministries with an old-boy network that maintains a vital two-way information flow between the rulers and the ruled. The hidden dynamic of this system is that in

Japan, unlike many Western countries, retired officials in Japan are expected to remain loyal to their old ministries for life.

Amakudari is patterned closely after the retirement system developed by the military authorities in the 1930s to establish control over important industries. In those days hundreds of retired army and naval officers were given key positions in zaibatsu head offices as well as in steelmaking, shipbuilding, and a host of other key areas of the private sector.

The American and British press have often imagined that the amakudari system is a form of corruption because, allegedly, private companies can influence civil servants by dangling offers of highly paid post-retirement jobs. But this interpretation overlooks a hidden but vital aspect of the system: even after retirement, Japanese civil servants remain answerable to their former ministries and must not accept post-retirement jobs without the approval of their former colleagues. Even former MOF administrative vice ministers are not exempt from this supervision: in their case, their post-retirement jobs must be approved by the current administrative vice minister.

Characteristically, ex-MOF men prefer if possible to take retirement jobs in public agencies, even though they could earn much more in the private sector. The attraction of public sector jobs is that they carry more power. As of 1994, only one of the last eight MOF administrative vice ministers was working in the private sector. This was Yasuo Matsushita, who was chairman of Sakura Bank. The Sakura job was only a way station for him; he was expected to be appointed governor of the Bank of Japan within a few months. The other seven former MOF administrative vice ministers were heading agencies such as the Fair Trade Commission, the National Finance Corporation, the Overseas Economic Cooperation Fund (it administers the world's largest foreign aid budget), the Japan Development Bank, and the Export-Import Bank of Japan.

Another favorite perch for former top MOF men is running the Tokyo Stock Exchange. The exchange's last five presidents have been MOF administrative vice ministers, which helps explain why the exchange has long functioned virtually as a division of the MOF.

The MOF's control of the budget and the civil service gives it great leverage over politicians. This is not always apparent on the surface in Tokyo because the MOF is adept at drafting budgets that contain unnecessarily unpopular provisions for use as bargaining ploys. It later makes a show of bowing to pressure from politicians in removing the offending provisions, thus preserving the impression that the popular will prevails. The politicians' powers are largely limited to influencing spending on such local construction projects as bridges and railroad stations.

The MOF's high-handedness in disregarding the politicians' wishes was notably apparent in the summer of 1989. The LDP's popularity was at a low ebb and, facing an imminent election, LDP leaders wanted to exempt food from the MOF's unpopular consumption tax to placate increasingly hostile public opinion. The MOF turned down the idea, and LDP leaders had to renege on their pledge, saying that the exemptions list could not be extended because it had been compiled "after extensive debate within the party."

Another occasion when the MOF memorably flexed its muscles in public came in the early 1990s when the Bush administration pressured Japan to help pay for the Gulf War. Concerned about the American public's increasingly sullen attitude to Japan's quasi-neutral stance, the MOF decided in the end to contribute $13 billion and paid for this via a 2.5 percent surtax on corporations. Neither the LDP nor corporate Japan seems to have opposed the MOF's decision.

The MOF's budget system effectively casts politicians in the role of lobbyists interceding with the civil service on behalf of local and national vested interests. In many such cases, the politicians are acting on behalf of construction companies soliciting public works contracts. In theory, the government is required to put contracts out to open bidding, but in practice it generally canvasses bids only from a charmed circle of "authorized" local and national firms. According to the Japanese writer Shunji Taoka, 99 percent of contracts are allocated on this "invitation only" basis. The "invitations" are issued by the Ministry of Construction, but the MOF retains ultimate control thanks to its domination of Japan's budget-making.

Another key area of MOF sway over the politicians is overseas aid, which is controlled by MOF-dominated agencies. Disbursements of aid are often made on the understanding that the recipient country will make contributions to the reelection campaign funds of specified Japanese politicians. In the case of some recent Japanese subventions to Indonesia, for instance, up to one-third of the money is said to have returned to Japan in the form of political contributions.

The MOF's foreign aid mandarins have the power even to overrule

Japanese prime ministers. As Richard Halloran has recorded, they memorably snubbed Eisaku Sato, one of Japan's most powerful post-war prime ministers. Sato was preparing for an important tour of Southeast Asia, and he decided to make some concrete gesture of atonement for Japan's previous military record in the region. He therefore announced publicly he would distribute economic aid total-ing $100 million in the countries he planned to visit. But the MOF said Japan could not afford such aid, and Sato had to make the tour empty-handed.

According to the scholar Robert M. Orr, Jr., Japanese aid now accounts for 15 to 20 percent of the entire government budget of almost every East Asian country. Clearly, therefore, when the MOF speaks, East Asia listens. At home too, the MOF's foreign aid pro-gram, now the world's largest, is an attention-getter. In particular, Japanese construction and engineering companies are constantly lob-bying the MOF to secure the vast construction contracts which are at the heart of most Japanese aid projects. The standard way for Japa-nese corporations to secure the business is to contribute to the reelec-tion campaign of politicians in favor with the MOF.

A key to the MOF's practical efficiency in getting things done is that MOF men are the acknowledged leaders of the Tokyo University old-boy network, which dominates top positions in big business. Graduates from certain other prestigious universities such as Kyoto, Keio, Waseda, and Hitotsubashi are also recruited in large numbers for fast-track jobs in Japanese business. But Tokyo men tend to do disproportionately well in the final cut.

Tokyo University accounts for up to 60 percent of top executives at the major banks and major trading houses, which are the keystones of the keiretsus. At the giant manufacturing companies, the Tokyo University ratio is somewhat lower but still very important: probably 30 to 40 percent of top positions in some such companies are held by Tokyo men.

And, of course, Tokyo men utterly dominate the top positions in the civil service. Of the fifteen or so top positions at the MOF, prob-ably thirteen or fourteen are held by Tokyo men. At the MITI and the Ministry of Foreign Affairs, the ratio is slightly lower, perhaps ten out of fifteen; and at Industrial Bank of Japan, Japan's most powerful bank and the government's main private sector lieutenant in admin-istering industrial policy, typically two-thirds of the directors are Tokyo men.

The everyone-knows-everyone-else factor is further enhanced by the fact that promotion in major Japanese private and public institutions is based strictly on seniority. Generally, the top people in the various organizations are in their mid- to late fifties. Thus, at the time when a man has reached the top of the MOF, his old classmates from Tokyo University will be moving into top positions throughout the civil service, banking, and industry. The effect is all the more powerful because most of the people who rise to the very top come from one department at Tokyo University, the law department.

Tokyo University's dominance is not an accident. The university took its modern form in 1877 when top schools from the shogun's era were amalgamated to form a single institution deliberately designed to create a tightly knit overachieving elite that would dominate the country's leadership. The success Tokyo men enjoy in getting into elite-track jobs in the civil service has long been a matter of some controversy. Tokyo University graduates have always benefited from favoritism via a strong old-boy network; in fact, for many years Tokyo University graduates were exempted from taking the entrance examination to join the higher civil service. Although this preferential treatment was withdrawn before World War II, the feeling has lingered in Japan that the civil service examinations are deliberately tilted to favor Tokyo law students. Until recently, Tokyo University law professors were disproportionately represented among the examiners. This of course not only gave Tokyo graduates an advantage in anticipating examination topics but in playing to the examiners' biases. Such overt skewing of the examination system is less of a factor these days — but only because of a conscious policy of affirmative action aimed at giving at least token representation to other universities.

Given Japanese respect for the logic of group strength, however, there is still a feeling that the civil service works best if its upper ranks are dominated by people who have known one another since student days. The system has been designed to create the atmosphere of a village — for the good reason that villagers keep an eye on their neighbors and punish those whose behavior strays too far from the community's norms.

The MOF's ties to the financial institutions are particularly close and work to the benefit of both sides. The financial institutions throw their immense resources behind the MOF; in return they benefit disproportionately from the MOF's favor. Thanks to cartel-based fee scales approved by the MOF, the big banks' employees enjoy some of the highest salaries in the private sector. The head of the Canon company estimated a few years ago that salaries at the big banks ran fully 70 percent higher than for equivalent people in Japanese industry. That is a startling gap in Japan, where salary grades are highly systematized and the range between the lowest and the highest is deliberately compressed as part of industrial policy. These days, a typical graduate employed by one of Japan's big banks can expect a compensation package worth about $90,000 by his mid-thirties.

The MOF's seven hundred or so career officials rely on the rest of the Japanese civil service as their agents in steering the economy. Because the system is structured hierarchically, there are few overlapping functions between agencies, and turf battles can usually be resolved satisfactorily before they create major disruption. Thus administration can be streamlined to a degree hard to emulate in the West. The OECD calculates that in relation to the nation's population, Japan's ratio of civil servants is only about one-half America's and little more than one-third that of France. In fact, the MOF has set clear limits on the size of the total civil service and adheres to them. In the 1980s alone the MOF succeeded in cutting the Japanese civil service's total staff numbers by 3.7 percent; Japan's entire complement of elite-track civil servants recently totaled just eighteen thousand.

A basic motif of the Japanese civil service's minimalist approach is to force *jishuku,* or self-control, on its clientele. The civil servants require industries, cartels, and social organizations to police themselves in return for various privileges. Everyone knows the major rules of Japanese-style success. Cartels, for instance, don't need to be told to avoid importing components that can be sourced at home, and cartel members can be trusted to monitor one another's observance of the rules.

The politicians are not necessarily always delighted to rubber stamp the MOF's policies, but when a politician resists the MOF he does so only on issues that matter greatly to him personally, either in terms of his local electoral support or his ability to deliver the goods for his financial backers. Such issues tend to be local or at least narrowly focused ones. On the biggest issues — the overall framework of economic policy, for instance — the MOF enjoys almost complete freedom to operate in the national interest without worrying about the usual short-term political pressures that often blow Western governments' attempts at industrial policy off course.

The levers of power

On the few occasions when the carrot doesn't work, the MOF finds that the stick usually does. The MOF has often proved a resourceful taskmaster in overseeing economic policy.

Its biggest stick is selective enforcement of the law. Civil servants write strict regulations but give Japanese citizens considerable discretion to bend the rules. This policy sounds generous, but it is actually a formidable, sometimes even frightening, tool of power because officials reserve the right to tighten enforcement on anyone who displeases them at any time they want.

Selective enforcement is particularly effective in tax matters. Officials generally turn a blind eye to certain "acceptable" kinds of tax evasion but simultaneously enforce the tax code strictly against those who do not respect the MOF's general guidelines on national economic development.

The concept of selective enforcement as a tool of power was invented by the tax officials of the shogunal bureaucracy. Farmers were nominally required to pay 60 percent of their rice harvest in tax, but in practice tax collectors generally allowed farmers to understate harvest yields. Thus the effective rate of tax was often reduced to as little as one-third of the official rate. As the former Japanese bureaucrat Taichi Sakaiya has recorded, the tax officials generously based their assessment on a "test harvest" conducted on a patch of poor land. Moreover, in threshing the stalks of the test harvest, the farmers were permitted to do an incomplete job, leaving plenty of grain hidden in the stalks. And they often were permitted to till "hidden" fields that the tax collectors did not officially know about. While the test harvest was being conducted, the farmers entertained the officials by plying them with cups of tea. Officials usually allowed themselves to be deceived in this way, but they reserved the right to open their eyes in the case of any particular farmer who was dilatory about cooperating with shogunal policy in other respects.

In modern times, the MOF uses selective enforcement not only in tax matters but in banking and securities regulation. Moreover the technique is now promiscuously applied by other agencies of the Japanese civil service. A classic example of the indirect way in which selective enforcement works occurred some years ago when the government wanted to stop retail pharmacies from opening new branches. Officially the government had no direct powers to forbid such expansion, but it did so anyhow and instructed pharmaceutical manufacturers to boycott any pharmacy that ignored the prohibition. The manufacturers had to cooperate because, as they knew only too well, the government could retaliate against them by obstructing their applications for the approval of new drugs.

There has been much confusion over the nature of the links between the MOF and the National Tax Agency, which collects Japan's taxes. The agency has even been commended by the *Economist* for its apparent independence from the MOF. This is a classic example of how foreign correspondents tend to grasp the wrong end of the stick when they lack basic language skills. Anyone who checks the Japanese-language handbook of the Tokyo bureaucracy discovers that the top three officials at the National Tax Agency are MOF men. Moreover, young career officials on temporary secondment from the MOF are positioned strategically throughout the National Tax Agency to ensure that the fine detail of tax enforcement is conducted in line with MOF objectives.

The Japanese have good reason to be wary of selective enforcement of tax law. One prominent Japanese businessman recently described the National Tax Agency only half jokingly as "Japan's KGB." Meanwhile the management consultant Kenichi Ohmae recently reported that if corporations flout the MOF's guidance, tax officials "can come in and ransack every single page of their books." The truth is that throughout East Asia, officials use selective enforcement of tax law to ensure that businesspeople not only comply with, for instance, the unwritten rules of East Asian trade, but are even careful to cover up the truth from the foreign press.

In some cases, people face retrospective enforcement for tax violations they may not have known they were incurring. As a result, most of Japan's prominent citizens find themselves on the wrong side of the law in one way or another. Sometimes the rules, written by the civil servants under "blank check" legislation voted by parliament, are so tight that even the most scrupulous citizens are in technical breach.

In a different context, selective enforcement of electoral rules has long provided the civil servants with a useful edge of power over the politicians. Japan's rules on election campaigning, for instance, are so unrealistic that they are, in the words of the *Economist,* "an invitation to disobedience." An example cited by the magazine gives the flavor: the rules have long limited each candidate to using just a single campaign car, a restriction that is widely ignored in practice. The truth is that to observe the electoral rules strictly is a recipe for defeat. Thus diet members have had constantly to skate on thin legal ice, not only in flouting limits on the size and nature of the financial contributions they are officially permitted to accept but also in ignoring the prohibition on door-to-door canvassing.

The public prosecutors, who in Japan are key members of the bureaucracy, regularly launch selective crackdowns targeting particular politicians, and even more often, but less visibly, the politicians' local grass-roots organizers. In such activities, the public prosecutors have long displayed partisan behavior in attacking politicians who have tried to encroach on the Japanese bureaucracy's economic policymaking prerogatives. The partisanship of the prosecutors has been a constant thread in Japanese administration going back to the 1910s if not earlier. Will the electoral rules be relaxed or abolished as part of Japan's latest attempt to reform its political system? At present the answer is unclear. What is clear is that past efforts at electoral reform have often enhanced the bureaucrats' opportunities for selective enforcement.

Often regulations in Japan are effectively secret or are so numerous that no one person can keep track of them: even top Japanese lawyers have difficulty understanding regulatory nuances. As the *Wall Street Journal* pointed out in 1991, when faced with point-blank questions about what exactly the rules are, MOF officials often go to extraordinary lengths not to answer. Foreign securities firms that want to introduce new financial instruments, for instance, find the MOF refuses to give an opinion on the legality of the proposal. Instead MOF officials often direct the foreigners to a cartel organization such as the Japan Securities Dealers Association, whose opinion the MOF can walk away from if expediency later requires it.

The veteran American MOF-watcher Leon Hollerman has given perhaps the best account of the MOF's customary Sphinx-like pose in parrying queries from bankers and other clients:

Sometimes the Ministry of Finance gives its guidance in clear language. Its officials may say, "We do not approve." Sometimes they are Delphian, saying, "This matter does not interest us." Translated, this could mean "not approved." Equally, however, it could mean nothing at all. The use of ambiguous language by the Ministry of Finance, as well as by MITI, may be a deliberate strategy to induce their clients to be consistently cautious. It also shifts the responsibility for restrictive action to the client by inducing "self-restraint" or the adoption of "self-imposed guidelines."

The clearest case of selective enforcement in recent years was the MOF's ouster in June 1991 of Nomura Securities' strongman chief executive Yoshihisa Tabuchi. The MOF's main allegation — that Nomura compensated big clients for losses sustained in the securities markets — was a non-charge: not only had the MOF's own securities bureau known about Nomura's compensation payments for years, the practice was widespread in the industry and had been explicitly condoned by the MOF. The MOF made matter-of-fact references to the practice in its annual report every year between 1984 and 1989. Compensation payments are typical of a plethora of Rube Goldberg devices used by the Tokyo financial community to fine-tune the financial side of industrial policy.

The MOF's motive in moving against Nomura seems to have been to cut Nomura down to size and to humiliate Tabuchi, who had been one of the most strong-willed personalities in Japanese business. It had been well known for several years that the MOF was concerned particularly about Nomura's links to prominent politicians. As reported in *Euromoney* magazine in 1988, there had been rumors for years that the MOF was embarrassed by Nomura's growing power and was considering using antitrust law to diminish the firm's power.

The Recruit scandal, which discomfited many top politicians in 1988 and 1989, was another case of selective enforcement. The politicians were accused of making aggregate profits totaling more than $20 million thanks to advance allocations of "sure thing" stock in the Recruit Cosmos company. Such stock manipulations are commonplace in Japan and are accepted as a method by which the financial establishment helps politicians find the campaign funds necessary to stay in power. What was unusual, however, in the Recruit case was that detailed information of the Recruit trades somehow reached one of Japan's major newspapers. Foreign correspondents in Tokyo assumed the newspaper had dug up the information for itself by studying public filings. That, however, was not the case, because such filings are not open to the general public in Japan. In other words, the information — involving exact figures for dozens of transactions — had to have been leaked. The question is, by whom? There were only three possible sources — the Recruit organization itself, its underwriter Daiwa Securities, or the Ministry of Finance. All evidence pointed to the ministry.

The MOF's role as protagonist later became explicit when MOF officials launched a tax investigation of the Recruit president, Hiromasa Ezoe. As reported in March 1990, the MOF's tax people ordered Ezoe to pay ¥2 billion (about $16 million) on undeclared capital gains. (Capital gains tax is a field where the MOF's rules are particularly complex.)

The MOF had obvious reasons to hit most of the people involved in the scandal. Hiromasa Ezoe, for instance, had long been persona non grata at the MOF for his superb speculative activities in the stock market. In particular he was rumored to have been an expert in "selling short," a maneuver in which a speculator profits from falling stock prices. As many stocks on the Tokyo stock market are highly volatile, short-sale opportunities abound for those who have a head for figures and a stomach for risk.

Meanwhile, the Recruit scandal's principal political victim, former Prime Minister Yasuhiro Nakasone, is believed to have been singled out because of his private foot-dragging on the MOF's plan to force the highly unpopular consumption tax through the diet. The consumption tax, which was to be levied at 3 percent on most consumer items, was a rare case where almost the entire diet tried to stand up to the MOF. While Nakasone paid lip service to the MOF's plan, he kept it on the legislative back burner right up to 1987, when he stepped down as premier. His successor, Noboru Takeshita, however, bit the bullet and forced the diet to vote the tax into law.

Although diet representatives have talked frequently since about abolishing the tax, the tax remains on the statute books. Thus, even on probably the most unpopular political issue of modern times in Japan, the MOF got its way, albeit after a delay of a decade from the time when it first proposed the tax in the late 1970s. All the evidence is that the diet was subjected to intense pressure to approve the MOF's plan.

A similar case of selective enforcement triggered the downfall of one-time LDP strongman Shin Kanemaru in the spring of 1993. As recounted in an investigative article in the *Sandee Mainichi* weekly, Kanemaru, a member of the outsiders' *tojin-ha,* had reportedly incurred the wrath of the bureaucrats' kanryo-ha after he was caught plotting to break the kanryo-ha's domination of the LDP. The upshot was that he was accused of tax and banking irregularities and promptly arrested. His chief accusers reportedly included then Prime Minister Kiichi Miyazawa, Justice Minister Masaharu Gotoda, and Finance Minister Yoshiro Hayashi, who are all Tokyo University–educated former career civil servants. Kanemaru's supporters — notably the finance minister Tsutomu Hata and LDP Secretary General Ichiro Ozawa — faded away. The *Sandee Mainichi* reported that anyone who spoke up for Kanemaru risked "incurring the wrath of the prosecutors." An isolated Kanemaru was thus promptly eliminated as a political force.

The MOF's power over politicians is reinforced by the way it uses its tax rulings to help politicians it favors. The MOF's treatment of charitable trusts provides an example. Generally such trusts qualify for tax exemption but only after case-by-case examination by the MOF on criteria which are not spelled out. In practice, the recognized way for a wealthy Japanese to get a tax exemption for his charitable foundation is to make a suitably large campaign contribution to a politician who is in favor at the MOF. Meanwhile, corporations that support industry's coordinated efforts to fund approved politicians can expect a return on their money in the form of special consideration in borderline tax assessments.

Thus the MOF has been able to perpetuate a system of power in which it can play favorites by varying tax-law enforcement. Of course, Japan is not the only country where political intervention can moderate a tax assessment. But whereas in other countries such intervention is conducted on an ad hoc basis, in Japan the process has been fashioned into a tool of power for the country's top administrators.

The lever of selective enforcement is augmented by several other unique tools of Japanese power. One such tool is best described as limited monopoly. The civil servants regulate almost every aspect of business life in Japan and are endowed with case-by-case powers to restrict entry into almost every field of important industrial and financial activity. By allowing only a certain number of enterprises into a field, the bureaucrats enjoy special leverage over them. The beneficiaries feel grateful for their limited monopoly. They are then beholden to the bureaucrats who can withdraw or, at least, restrict the privileges more or less by fiat. Just how widespread limited monopoly is is evident in the fact that anyone who wants to go into a business as inconsequential as trading secondhand goods is supposed to get an official permit (under the Antique Trading Law). Such licensing can be fine-tuned to give the authorities detailed control. An example is the meat distribution industry. When the civil servants liberalized the rules on imported beef some years ago, they simultaneously allowed only 3,600 stores of Japan's more than 500,000 food retailers to sell the imports. Businessmen favored by this arrangement can probably be counted on to cooperate with government guidance in other aspects of their business not specifically covered by regulation.

The MOF is a skilled exponent of limited monopoly. In its hands, limited monopoly generally does double duty as both a tool of power and a device to generate economic efficiency (via the Good Cartel, which is the ultimate form of limited monopoly). The MOF has even used the concept of limited monopoly to control the advances of foreign securities firms in Japan. Only a few specified foreign financial organizations are allowed to participate in the various subsectors of the Japanese financial services industry. With other applicants shut out on an arbitrary basis, those who are on the inside enjoy monopolistic pricing opportunities. But because their right to participate is by grace and favor, they must be careful to remain on the right side of the MOF.

In the early days of the Economic Miracle, the Ministry of Finance and the MITI exercised massive nonstatutory power via their case-by-case control over foreign exchange and bank credit. If companies wanted to get permission to import vital machinery or borrow from the bank, they had to conform to the officials' general program for national economic development.

In recent years, the officials' ability to leverage their statutory powers in this way has been curtailed, but it is still quite significant. Officials enjoy considerable power to influence the membership of new research cartels, for instance. This is because such cartels are usually supported by government grants and so the government can indirectly but effectively specify the membership of these cartels.

The MOF's selective enforcement weapon towers over all others as the key to Japanese power. Its magic is that it is invisible. Officially it does not exist and in Japanese conditions is invulnerable to challenge in the courts. This means that no amount of popular pressure for reform in Japan is likely to be very successful in blunting the MOF's power. No agency in world administration is better positioned to protect — and to enhance — its power.

Overlord of industrial policy

Although the MOF tries to maintain as low a profile as possible at all times, its fingerprints are all over Japanese industrial policy. In particular, the MOF is the mainspring of Japanese mercantilism. Ever since the MOF invented the concept of nontariff barriers in the 1870s, mercantilism has been a cornerstone of MOF policy.

Even in the 1990s, the MOF's mercantilist philosophy has occasionally been made publicly explicit. The MOF was, for instance, the protagonist in an effort by Japan to persuade the Bush administration to accept Japanese current account surpluses of 2 percent of GNP indefinitely. The initiative came from the MOF's international affairs vice minister Makoto Utsumi. His proposal became known as the *kuroji yuyo ron,* "the theory that the surpluses are useful." Utsumi argued that the American government needed Japan to run trade surpluses so that Japan in turn could have the money to finance America's budget deficits. The Bush administration's trade representative called on Japan to retract the proposal. In the end the Japanese government apologized, though the apology came not from the MOF but from the Ministry of Foreign Affairs (whose power to influence Japan's economic policy is minimal).

A telling insight into the depth of the MOF's commitment to mercantilism is afforded by its regulation of the Japan Tobacco Corporation. The company is a state monopoly owned by the MOF. Not coincidentally, Japan Tobacco has a record of exceptionally trenchant resistance to efforts by American cigarette makers to open the Japanese market. Up to the mid-1980s, Japan Tobacco controlled the distribution of virtually all cigarettes sold in Japan. It used its position to curtail supplies of American cigarettes and to keep them out of the customer's line of sight in retail displays. It reportedly sent out its people to pull down the promotional material for American cigarettes, and at one point it even registered the names of about fifty foreign cigarette brands as its trademarks. Suddenly Newport, for instance, was claimed as a Japan Tobacco brand name, thus creating a stumbling block for Newport's rightful owner, the Lorillard company of the United States, in exporting to Japan.

It was clear that such tactics came from Japan Tobacco's top management. The registration of American brand names in particular was conducted on the personal orders of the company head. There were no reports that the MOF demurred at these tactics, let alone disciplined any of the executives involved. In fact, when the scandal first broke in the *Wall Street Journal,* the president of Japan Tobacco tendered his resignation, but the MOF refused to accept it.

Foreign cigarette manufacturers were officially directed by the MOF to set retail prices 60 percent higher than those of Japanese cigarettes. This maneuver, a classic ploy of Japanese mercantilism, effectively eliminated the Americans as serious competitors. The Americans did not object much because the arrangement guaranteed them very high profit margins. From the point of view of the American economy, however, the issue was different: thousands of potential American jobs were lost. From the MOF's point of view, the issue was straight mercantilism: allowing the Americans to make large profits on tiny sales ensured far lower imports than if the Americans had been allowed to cut their prices.

Perhaps an even more telling insight into the MOF's mercantilist mindset is its decisive role in protecting the car industry. The MOF used its controls on foreign investment in Japan to block American and European automakers from establishing Japanese manufacturing operations until 1973. It used its taxing powers to levy customs duties on imported vehicles until 1978 and on imported auto parts until 1986. And it even used its powers over the insurance industry to require Japanese motorists to pay three times as much to insure a foreign car as a domestic model. This discrimination was abolished only in 1988.

The MOF's enthusiasm for mercantilism is reinforced by its own private agenda. As an institution, it has been the main beneficiary of Japanese mercantilism because Japan's thwarted purchasing power ends up as savings in MOF-regulated savings institutions.

The MOF is also the mainspring of Japan's cartelization policy thanks to its right to appoint several key executives of Japan's Fair

Trade Commission. The MOF's appointees at the commission, which administers Japan's antitrust laws, naturally turn a blind eye to most cartels — but if a cartel displeases the MOF, the MOF can probably prevail on the commission to launch a selective-enforcement investigation in retaliation. As most major Japanese corporations operate constantly on the wrong side of Japan's antitrust laws, their wish to continue to conduct business as usual clearly requires them to stay on cordial terms with the MOF. Control of the Fair Trade Commission also gives the MOF case-by-case power over mergers and acquisitions. Meanwhile the MOF has direct power to control many retail prices, providing it with another lever over important cartels.

As the financial system's regulator, the MOF sits atop an enormous information pyramid. It can get practically any inside information it needs on industrial activity by calling the big banks or securities firms. Every significant financial organization in Japan maintains one or more executives whose sole job is to help the MOF administer the financial system and the wider economy. These executives, whose activities are known as *mofu-tan* (MOF responsibility), are expected to respond reflexively to MOF queries. When the MOF wanted to know about insider trading laws in the American securities industry a few years ago, for example, Daiwa Securities put a top Wall Street law firm on the case for a week and paid the bill itself. This mofu-tan system has now been extended to American and European financial organizations in Tokyo, which provide information not only about their activities in Japan but increasingly their activities worldwide.

Although the MOF has no direct involvement in the broader aspects of industrial policy, there is little doubt that many of Japan's most important industrial initiatives — targeting, for instance — could not exist without support from MOF-regulated financial institutions.

To say that the MOF sits at the top of a highly organized pyramid of power is not to suggest that it tries to control everything. The analogy is with the chief executive of a large corporation. Realizing he is not all-seeing, he establishes structures which semiautomatically produce the right decisions. Just as a chief executive works through divisions and profit centers in the search for profitable new products, the MOF works through cartels, keiretsus, banks, and bureaucratic agencies to promote economic growth. Its most important work is seeing that the structures' semiautomatic mechanisms for generating economic decisions continue to prioritize the public good. Delegating most things, the MOF reserves the right to reach down occasionally into Japan Inc. to rectify serious dysfunctions and keep the various players on their toes. Just as the executives who report to, say, the chairman of IBM are not always in agreement with each other, the various agencies and power groups that the MOF leads often disagree. But whereas in IBM's case the chairman has traditionally resolved disputes discreetly behind closed doors, in the case of the Japanese bureaucracy, such disputes are often widely publicized. The resulting impression of gridlock provides the MOF and other top agencies with an excuse to do nothing if they do not want to change the status quo. Hence the myth of Japan's ungovernability.

Enjoying immense power virtually unchecked by any Western-style accountability, the MOF is uniquely well equipped to direct Japan's controversial economic strategy.

The world's biggest saver

Japan's budget policies are a model of fiscal rectitude and they are probably the ultimate proof that Japan is driven by a particularly resolute system of centralized power.

Under the MOF's leadership, the Japanese government has been consistently producing budget surpluses for many years, thanks to heavy taxes on corporations and generally low public spending. The MOF deviates from this policy only in years of poor consumer demand when a fiscal stimulus is needed to support the lifetime employment system.

It should be noted that until the Clinton administration focused attention on Japan's budget surpluses in 1993, most foreign observers were under the impression that Japan produced budget *deficits*. The source of the confusion is that Japan operates *two* budgets and its budget accounting is extremely conservative to the point of producing paper deficits where Western accounting would show a surplus.

The fairest way to measure Japan's fiscal prudence is to look at the complete picture as indicated by the OECD's calculation of saving by governments. Generally speaking, a government saves when its current revenues exceed its current expenditures. According to the latest figures available in 1992, the Japanese government was saving 7.8

percent of GNP. By contrast, the Bank of Japan's highly misleading official figures suggested Japan was running a deficit of 1.8 percent. In the OECD league table, the only nation which topped Japan's government savings performance was tiny Luxembourg with a government savings rate of 7.9 percent. Standing just below Japan was Sweden at 6.8 percent, followed by Norway at 4.0 percent, Finland at 3.7 percent, Switzerland at 3.5 percent, and Iceland at 3.4 percent. By comparison, the United States ranked among the lowest in the league table, with a *negative* government savings rate of 2.8 percent.

The MOF has been an avid saver for most of the postwar era. On figures compiled by the Congressional Budget Office, Japan's government savings rate averaged 4.8 percent in the 1970s and 4.6 percent in the 1980s. By contrast, the United States government savings rate fell from 0.4 percent in the 1970s to minus 2.1 percent in the 1980s.

The MOF's policy of maximizing government savings flies directly in the face of repeated efforts by Washington in the last decade to get Japan to increase government spending as a way of reducing America's trade deficits. It also runs counter to the wishes of most diet members. As the *Wall Street Journal* reported in April 1993, the MOF deliberately uses byzantine and archaic accounting methods to obscure the strength of the government's finances, thus bamboozling politicians into voting each year for the MOF's superconservative budgets. MOF officials openly boast about their role in frustrating elected representatives' spending proposals. One MOF official told the *Wall Street Journal,* "In your country [the United States], you at least have politicians in Congress who are fiscal conservatives. But we don't have any. Every politician wants to spend and spend."

What does the MOF do with all its savings? Thanks to the obscurity of the MOF's accounting the answer is not clear, but one guess is that, using nominees' names, the MOF has built up significant shareholdings in important corporations. The MOF's hold over such a large amount of capital in the private sector may thus be an important lever of behind-the-scenes power in guiding the economy. The MOF's support for Japanese corporations' capital-raising efforts in the stock market can in many cases make the difference between success and failure. The MOF also appears to be a major holder of foreign securities, including U.S. Treasury bonds.

One might expect that Japan's business leaders would oppose such tight-fisted fiscal policies, but for the most part they agree that a high governmental savings rate is desirable in the national interest. This was rarely more startlingly apparent than in the spring of 1993, when the Ministry of Finance stonewalled efforts by the diet majority party, the Liberal Democrats, to launch a strong program of public spending. LDP leaders wanted to stimulate the economy not only to please President Clinton but to boost the party's sagging reelection chances. But many in big business sided with the MOF against the LDP. Kazuo Nukazawa, a top official of the powerful Keidanren federation of Japanese business, publicly argued against the LDP spending plan, saying that the nation should be building for posterity rather than indulging in short-term economic palliatives.

Perhaps the best way to get a sense of the power the MOF derives from its savings is to use absolute money numbers: measured by Western accounting methods, the Japanese government's savings in 1991 alone totaled more than $300 billion, more than two times the aggregate net savings of the entire American economy. In effect, the MOF is the world's biggest saver.

Home of the samurai spirit

Can MOF men be trusted to use their immense power solely in the national interest?

After the greed-is-good decade of the 1980s, many in the West will doubt it. But the idea of trusting people with tremendous power is less strange than it first appears. More than half a century ago, John Maynard Keynes proposed that government should empower a dedicated elite to control an economy's program of industrial investment. On the issue of corruption and inefficiency, he felt that industrial planning "will be safe if those carrying it out are rightly oriented in their own minds and hearts to the moral issue."

Keynes was no starry-eyed idealist; he knew what he was talking about because he had served many years in government as Britain's equivalent of an MOF man. And the MOF today is living proof that top officials can be "rightly oriented in their own minds and hearts." In a nation of selfless workaholics, MOF men are rarely outdone in the standards of work performance and loyalty they set for themselves. In fact, according to MOF-watcher Takao Kitagawa, MOF men inflict so much pressure on themselves that they suffer particularly high rates of stress, depression, divorce, and suicide.

The suicides reflect a unique sense of responsibility. Kitagawa explains: "The high suicide rate is not attributable to an unbearably heavy workload. Rather it is because MOF officials are the ultra-elite and are regarded by everyone in society as such. So they feel enormous pressure to excel in their work and to win in the promotion race. The more they are regarded as the ultra-elite, the larger the stress. Thus they feel greater despair than others when they fail in the promotion race or begin to feel they are losing the battle. This sometimes triggers a nervous breakdown and in the worst cases suicide."

What keeps MOF men honest? One factor is that like everyone else in Japanese society, they necessarily live life in a fishbowl. Those who come under suspicion have nowhere to hide. Authority is less inhibited in intruding on people's privacy in Japan than in most Western countries. MOF men work in vast open-plan offices like everyone else in Japan and thus are subject to informal monitoring by their fellow associates. In common with general Japanese practice, MOF men must get their decisions endorsed by several of their colleagues. On the surface, this appears to be a meaningless ritual because officials are so engrossed in their own work that they rarely try to second-guess their colleagues. This trust can disappear fast, however, if they have the slightest suspicion about a colleague's character or personal circumstances. This system of collective responsibility is a latter-day manifestation of the goningumi system by which neighbors in ancient Japan were required to monitor each other, and it encourages colleagues to trespass on each other's privacy in a way that would be considered unacceptable in the West.

On the positive side, MOF men are motivated by a strong sense of idealism. During the greed-is-good years of the Reagan-Thatcher experiment, it became fashionable in the West to sneer at idealism but history down through the ages has shown that idealism is often a more efficient motivator than money. The MOF man's idealism bears comparison with that which has made the Vatican the world's oldest continuously functioning organization. But perhaps an even closer parallel is with the ethos of a well-trained army. Recently the military historian John Keegan itemized the values that inspired the professional soldiers of the Roman Empire. These were pride in a distinctive (and distinctively masculine) way of life, a concern to earn the good opinion of comrades, satisfaction in the largely symbolic tokens of professional success, hope of promotion, and expectation of a comfortable and honorable retirement. Clearly little has changed in two thousand years, for these exact values drive Japan's bureaucrats and particularly the top men at the MOF.

The fact that most MOF men spring from Tokyo University's law faculty serves to buttress their idealism. It provides a common bond that enforces a don't-let-the-side-down ethos. Their greatest reward is the high opinion of their immediate colleagues and superiors and the chance to rise to the very top.

Thus men who rise to the top at the MOF have by definition survived thirty years of intense scrutiny by those best able to pass judgment — their colleagues. But that alone is not enough. Generally, to make the final cut a MOF man has to show in marked degree not only grit and technical brilliance but an uncommon common sense in reading people and their needs.

By definition, the winner in this promotion system is one of the most capable people of his generation. And the prize is worth all the sacrifice. Given Japan's position in the global economy today, the MOF jimu jikan packs more economic power than the president of the United States. This is apparent when one considers that just one of the MOF's many prerogatives is to control the flow of Japan's money abroad. Without Japanese money, the American financial system would be thrown into crisis. The MOF knows this. So does the White House. The MOF's administrative vice minister enjoys the power to veto the American president's economic policies.

5

Supporting Cast

We have seen that Japanese society works on the principle of concentrating as much power as possible in the hands of a few bureaucrats at the MOF. Yet on paper, Japan is a pluralist society equipped with Western-style checks and balances to curb arbitrary government power. How, therefore, do we reconcile the MOF's concentrated power with the standard presentation of Japan as a Western-style pluralist society?

The truth is that secondary organs of power such as the Japanese diet and the press are coopted directly and indirectly by the MOF. They are given a stake in the system in return for showing "self-restraint" in the use of their prerogatives. Thus, although secondary organs of power often make a public show of ritual dissent, below the surface they are remarkably supportive of national policies and strategies as laid down by the top bureaucratic agencies. Here we look at how the diet, the press, and the judiciary fit into Japan's bureaucrat-led power system.

Containing populism

Japan's recent political upheavals constitute a grass-roots revolt against the bureaucrats' power — or so Western observers keep saying. Actually, the idea that ordinary Japanese voters are beginning to assert popular control over the nation's destiny is a recurring theme in Japanology. It first emerged in the 1890s, only to reappear in the late 1910s, the late 1940s, the mid-1950s, and once more in the early 1970s.

Will the latest apparent move by the Japanese people to shape the nation's destiny have more lasting consequences than previous ones? Probably not. Certainly the bureaucrats are better positioned to parry any attack on their prerogatives today than at any time since World War II. But to understand the strength of their position, we must study the history of their relationship with elected representatives.

From the start the bureaucrats have held the upper hand by dint of the fact that they created Japan's electoral system in the first place. The system emerged from a carefully calibrated process of trial and error, which the civil servants launched in 1890 as part of an effort to "Westernize" Japan's traditional decision-making processes. At the outset, the civil servants dipped their toes in the waters of democracy gingerly. In the first election in 1890, only a handful of wealthy men were given the vote. To make doubly sure that "safe" representatives would be elected, the bureaucrats specified that the ballot would not be secret. In later elections these rules were gradually liberalized, but at all times the civil servants retained their power to slow or even roll back the process if it began to challenge their power.

In 1919 Japan began a brief experiment in a more open British-style system of democracy, but abandoned it in the mid-1920s as the mood among the Tokyo bureaucrats and military leaders swung decisively toward ultranationalism. In 1925, the Japanese House of Representatives adopted a highly unusual constituency system that considerably weakened popular representation and ensured a docile reception for Japan's military buildup before World War II. After World War II, MacArthur gave women the vote but otherwise left the prewar rules virtually unchanged. Thus, with the exception of one election immediately after the war, the 1925 constituency system prevailed, down to the election of 1993. As future elections in Japan are likely to be run on significantly different rules, the following account of that system as it has worked up through 1993 is necessarily written in the past tense.

The essence of the 1925 system was that each constituency elected several representatives, but each voter had only one vote. In the language of psephology, this was a multiple-seat, single-vote system. Multiple-seat constituencies are common in Europe, but, in contrast with Japan's single-vote system, they are generally used in combination with a multiple-vote ballot paper enabling each voter to support a slate of candidates. Thus Japan's combination of single votes and multiple-seat constituencies was highly distinctive among the world's voting systems. Just how distinctive can be judged from the fact that its closest parallel in the West was the Cortés electoral system in Franco's Spain.

To American eyes, the multiple-seat, single-vote system seems merely cumbersome, but in fact it has hidden consequences that crucially affect the tone of Japan's democracy. As operated in Japan, the system required each constituency to elect typically three to five members to the House of Representatives. This fostered the development of many fragmented political parties and factions that had great difficulty working with each other in creating a coherent counterweight to civil service power. This fragmentation was particularly evident before World War II and in the early elections after 1947. Superficially the picture changed in 1955, when a political merger created the Liberal Democratic Party.

The LDP went on to enjoy enough representation to control the House of Representatives for the next thirty-eight years. But the merger served merely to disguise rather than to quell the fission inherent in the system. Just below the surface, the LDP remained deeply divided because the original parties that formed the merger never lost — and indeed could not lose — their separate identity. Instead they continued to exist as semiautonomous miniparties within the LDP. Competition among these miniparties rendered the LDP weak and fragile throughout its years of majority in the diet. In particular, the LDP was constantly prey to divide-and-rule tactics on the part of the civil servants and big business. Essentially the LDP was highly dependent on financial support from Japan's big business organizations. Because big business was beholden to the civil servants for various privileges such as the right to operate cartels, the civil servants ultimately pulled the strings on major policies.

The LDP's continuing internal fragmentation after 1955 was a predictable consequence of the electoral system's multiple-seat feature. In order to win a majority in parliament, a party had to run several candidates in each constituency. Thus the LDP's candidates in any particular constituency always had to campaign mainly against each other and, as each voter had just one vote, there was no incentive for LDP candidates to work with each other to get voters to the polls. The most logical way for the LDP to handle the system's various complexities was to allow the miniparties to operate as competing entities in each constituency. This in turn perpetuated a system in which the miniparties not only successfully maintained separate staffs and separate constituency support groups but separate fundraising operations as well.

The electoral system constituted a near-insurmountable barrier to any of the other Japanese parties ever winning a parliamentary majority because it was generally difficult for them to run more than one candidate in each constituency. Without large electoral funding, which most of the smaller parties lacked, running two candidates in a constituency usually fatally split the vote.

The rules on election campaigning were written so strictly that efficient ways for electoral candidates to communicate with the electorate were forbidden. Thus parties had to adopt extremely expensive and often illegal stratagems to build constituency support. One of the oddest rules was that door-to-door canvassing was illegal. Moreover, campaigning was strictly limited to short bursts in the few weeks before elections.

In practice, as an observation group from Harvard University discovered in the 1992 House of Councillors election, electioneering in Japan was reduced almost to pantomime. The only significant form of legal campaigning used in Japan was to hail the public from moving trucks equipped with earsplitting loudspeakers. In 1993, a *Wall Street Journal* reporter aptly described election campaigns in Japan as "a time to plug your ears, tape your windows, and chain the dog."

Riding the loudspeaker trucks, candidates merely repeated their names over and over again. Commenting on the 1992 campaign, one member of the Harvard team told a Japanese newspaper: "So many Japanese were cringing at the loudness of the sound trucks. An election in Japan is viewed as something people have to put up with. It is viewed as silly."

The Harvard group never saw the most effective side of Japanese electioneering. Because there were so few legitimate outlets for campaign money, most campaigning was done via an extraordinary semi-underground network of local support organizations, which in many cases literally bought individual votes: the going rate in 1992 was ¥10,000 — typically delivered cellophane-wrapped in a lunchbox.

With so many supporters to pay off in his constituency, a typical Japanese House of Representatives member in the early 1990s had somehow to meet expenses of as much as ¥200 million ($1.6 million) in an ordinary year. In an election year the bill ran three times as much — up to $5 million in some cases.

A question arises: Given that the 1925 system had created a political vacuum in the 1930s, why did MacArthur not resist its restoration after World War II? In an interview with this author a few years ago, Charles Kades, one of the occupation officials concerned with the decision, explained that General Douglas MacArthur believed the United States had no right to prescribe the fine detail of Japanese political organization. MacArthur apparently felt that because the United States itself was "not perfect" in the details of its own democracy, it should not try to fine-tune Japan's arrangements. Another possible explanation is that because MacArthur had rashly excluded experts on Japan from his team of top advisers, he simply had not understood the strange dynamics of the 1925 system and had raised no objections when the Tokyo elite proposed to restore it in 1947.

MacArthur probably took comfort from the fact that the civil servants' proposal had to be formally ratified by the diet. As it happened, the effort to reinstate the old prewar electoral system aroused considerable disquiet in the first postwar diet. But the civil servants were able to muster enough support from militarist-era holdovers to get the 1925 rules ratified just ahead of an election in April 1947.

A remarkable feature of postwar Japanese politics was the sudden emergence of ex–civil servants as pivotal figures in the diet. Ex–civil servants accounted for fully 9 percent of successful candidates in the 1949 election, up from less than 2 percent in the 1937 election (the last before the Pacific war).

In fact, soon after the war ended, a seat in the diet came to be considered an appropriate second career for retired elite-track civil servants (who generally retire by their early fifties). Typically, about 15 percent of diet members have been retired civil servants in the 1950s and 1960s and they have continued to be an important element in the diet down to the 1990s. Their influence has been important in persuading the diet to hand over much of its power to the civil service in the form of blank check legislation.

It is natural for such retirees to think of their role in parliament as an extension of their previous work, running the country in a rational, nonpartisan way. In the language of Japanese politics they are known collectively as the *kanryoha* — the bureaucrats' faction —

and a key factor in their psychology is their pride in their status in Japanese society by virtue of being former top civil servants.

Most former civil servants who go into politics win election with the help of financial backing from business friends of their former ministry. A notable case in point is the large contingent of ex-MOF men in the diet. They are generally backed by banking and investment cartels responsive to the MOF's guidance. The insurance cartel, for instance, has often fielded thousands of insurance salespeople to campaign for ex-MOF men.

The MOF holds its retirees to a high standard of loyalty. They must toe the MOF line in parliamentary voting. If they do not, vengeance can be swift, as MOF-man-turned-diet-member Masahiro Okashida discovered a few years ago. He came out against the unpopular consumption tax the MOF was seeking to shepherd through the diet. The MOF retaliated in the next election. Okashida found himself opposed by two strong LDP candidates, both of them former MOF men who were heavily funded by financial institutions. Meanwhile, Okashida's funding was reduced to a trickle. He duly went down to defeat.

The kanryoha has been notably successful over the years in winning cabinet office. In fact, in the immediate postwar period, the cabinet was dominated by former civil servants. In particular Prime Minister Shigeru Yoshida, who led Japanese politics in the crucial era of change during the occupation, was a former bureaucrat and as such generally steered American policymaking in directions favored by the bureaucracy. As of 1993, the kanryoha had accounted for no less than twelve of Japan's postwar prime ministers, versus ten prime ministers who had sprung from other backgrounds.

Viewed from a vantage point in the mid-1990s, the important point about the long years of LDP domination is that a weak diet handed over most of its economic management prerogatives to the bureaucrats. Typically this was done via "blank check" legislation that gave the bureaucrats enormous power to write and rewrite Japan's regulations free of oversight by elected representatives.

The significance of these powers is hard to overestimate. Many of Japan's most important policies are driven by the civil servants' use of blank check powers, although the civil servants imply that they have no choice but to follow laws laid down by the diet. A case in point is Japan's famous "not-a-grain" ban on imports of foreign rice. Although the ban has always been presented as having been imposed by elected representatives, the civil servants have always had the power to permit rice imports virtually at will.

The civil servants' ability to vary their regulations at will is part of the secret of their extraordinary informal power to guide every aspect of the economy. Big corporations and banks, for instance, know that if they do not cooperate with an important new civil service policy, the rules may be changed selectively against them as a mark of the civil servants' displeasure.

Clearly, if Japanese politicians are to achieve the freedom to operate independently of the civil servants, the diet must first repeal scores if not hundreds of blank check laws. What are the chances of today's reformist politicians achieving this? It is time to look at Japan's political revolution of 1993.

The revolution of 1993

Japan's diet election of 1993 was widely hailed abroad as a historic break with the past. Western newspapers presented the story as a spontaneous rebellion by the Japanese electorate against Japan's age-old system of money politics. Disgusted voters had supposedly rejected the Liberal Democratic Party and voted into office a radical new coalition headed by a popular young prime minister. All in all, if you believed the press, the 1993 election was convincing evidence that a true Western-style democratic spirit was abroad in Japan.

The truth, however, was different. Consider the idea that the Japanese people had, in the words of the *Wall Street Journal,* decided to "throw out the bums." This was hard to reconcile with the fact that almost every incumbent politician who stood for election in 1993 was reelected. The reason the LDP lost its parliamentary majority was not because its candidates were defeated but because just before the election many of its own candidates had withdrawn from the party to establish two new parties — the Shinseito and the Sakigake. These relabeled LDP representatives retained their traditional local support machinery and used it to win reelection under their new party labels. After the election they joined hands with several of Japan's long-time opposition parties to form a government.

The *New Republic* talked of "widespread public sentiment in favor of cleaner politics." Again, this heroically misrepresented reality. Not one of the major LDP representatives who had been tarnished with scandal in the early 1990s lost his seat in 1993. In fact, some of the most discredited of the LDP's money politics operatives joined the Shinseito to assume the semifarcical role of leading Japan's reform movement.

Even Walter Mondale, America's newly appointed ambassador in Tokyo, was badly taken in. Soon after the new coalition government took office, he commented, "I think there is change going on here. Things have happened . . . More than they are given credit for, the prime minister and the people at the political level rattled a lot of cages around here and declared new principles." Within less than a year, Mondale was to conclude that this assessment was badly misguided.

Perhaps the most hyperbolic comment came from President Clinton. He congratulated the coalition, led by Morihiro Hosokawa, on its "enormous mandate for change." Even by Washington standards, this was a notable case of the triumph of hope over experience. In reality, Hosokawa's Japan New Party had won just thirty-five seats, less than 7 percent of the diet. The Japan New Party had such disappointing results at the polls that it had to combine with no less than six other parties to muster a parliamentary majority. From the outset it was obvious that these other parties had such different interests and agendas that the coalition's life would be measured in months at best. Moreover, Hosokawa's personal influence had been compromised by allegations of financial misconduct that had appeared in the Japanese press even before he had come to office.

As Hosokawa headed for his inevitable downfall, the American press tried to pretend it was not so. In February 1994, for instance, the editors of the *Wall Street Journal* described him as "sublimely popular." Eight weeks later, the truth was apparent for even the *Journal* to see: Hosokawa was ejected from office in one of the most unceremonious exits a Japanese prime minister has suffered in recent years. The Hosokawa coalition was succeeded by the short-lived Hata coalition, which came to office in April and collapsed in June.

Then came the Murayama coalition, Japan's fourth government within a year. Its most notable feature was that, in contrast with earlier coalitions, it was supported by the now truncated LDP. Thus, less than a year after the LDP had supposedly been "overthrown," it was back in control of a majority of cabinet positions. So much for the *Economist*'s suggestion in 1993 that the LDP's ouster had been an event comparable to the fall of the Berlin Wall in 1989.

The most peculiar aspect of the various recent coalitions is the pivotal role played by the Social Democratic Party. The SDP, Japan's long-time major opposition party, participated in the Hosokawa coalition, then helped form the Hata coalition, and finally turned its back on the reformists to make common cause with the LDP in forming the Murayama coalition.

The SDP's role as the catalyst for the 1993 reformist movement was sharply at odds with its known record. It had long operated as a pseudo-party that combined extreme leftist positions on remote foreign policy issues with an appetite for Tokyo's money politics game that made even the LDP look ascetic. Perhaps even more damaging to its credibility, the SDP was covertly funded by the LDP, the party it was supposed to be opposing in parliament.

Evidently as a quid pro quo for LDP money, it had rarely offered effective opposition to LDP policy positions. Whenever the chips were down and the SDP's support was really needed in parliament, the SDP could be counted on to renege on its previous position and cooperate with the LDP. When its support was not needed, it often adopted wildly unrealistic positions: in particular, in most of the post–World War II era, a large section of the party had offered extravagant verbal support for various extremist Third World governments, notably the Albanian Communist junta and the dictatorship of the late Kim Il Sung.

Perhaps the most obvious evidence of the SDP's paper tiger role in Japanese politics was that though its diet candidates hotly disagreed with each other on such foreign policy matters as relations with Albania, they maintained near perfect unity in supporting Japan's trade policies. They even supported Japan's controversial rice import ban. Yet because many SDP candidates ran in densely populated urban constituencies and drew their support from low-paid factory workers oppressed by Japan's high food prices, electoral arithmetic should have led them to oppose the ban. By the time the SDP joined with the LDP to form the Murayama government in 1993, it had virtually eliminated all significant differences with the LDP on domestic policies.

All in all, despite its newly found position at the center of Japanese politics, the SDP richly deserves the label once conferred on it by the prominent Japanese spokesman Tetsuya Kataoka: he called it the "laughing stock of the country."

Other parties in the reform movement also raised some eyebrows in Tokyo. A notable example was the Komeito, the Clean Government Party. As its name suggests, the Komeito, which was founded in 1964, got its start in a self-professed effort to clean out the Augean stables of the diet's money politics. Yet if the prominent political analyst Hirotatsu Fujiwara is to be believed, the party's name is something of an Orwellian joke. In 1985, Fujiwara told of his difficulties in publishing a book on the party's alleged neofascist tendencies. The party allegedly pressured Prime Minister Kakuei Tanaka to suppress the book. Tanaka apparently prevailed on the Japanese newspapers' editorial and advertising departments to boycott the book. Publishing executives handling the book were warned to "watch out for traffic accidents." Perhaps more significantly, the party's religious wing apparently issued thinly veiled death threats against Fujiwara, telling him that its opponents "die young."

Looking back on 1993 and 1994, the only significant reform the various coalitions achieved was to abandon the multiple-seat, single-vote electoral system in favor of a new system that promises to shift Japan permanently away from one-party rule. In the future, Japan will have a two-party system similar to one it enjoyed after the electoral reform of 1919. But a two-party system alone will go only about one-quarter of the way to establishing a true Western system of representation: it will have little power unless it brings the bureaucrats under control, and that means repealing a decades-long accumulation of blank check laws. Will any future Japanese government achieve such power? Given the MOF's demonstrated power over individual elected representatives, the chances are not large.

In any case, the job of electoral reform remains only half completed. The reformists seem to have done nothing to clear away the myriad restrictions on electioneering, in particular the ban on door-to-door canvassing, which makes it difficult for voters to get to know the candidates. A major question is whether the parties can break loose from dependence on corporate donations. There is also the question of whether future prime ministers can achieve more than the present token control over appointments. Historically, Japanese prime ministers have had at their disposal only twenty-three appointments, and these are merely semiceremonial cabinet positions. By contrast, an American president makes eight hundred top-level appointments and two thousand lower-level appointments.

How much has Japan really changed? Listen to Lee Kuan Yew, the semiretired former leader of Singapore, who has been dealing with Japanese officials since Japan occupied Singapore in the early 1940s. Commenting on American hopes that the new coalition government might mark the beginning of an era of pluralism in Japan, he said of the Japanese people:

> I do not see them becoming a fractious, contentious society like America, always debating and knocking each other down. That is not in their culture. They want growth and they want to get on with life. They are not interested in ideology as such or in the theory of good government.
>
> Americans believe that out of contention, out of the clash of different ideas and ideals, you get good government. That view is not shared in Asia.

The key to Lee's insight is that he understands Japanese history. He knows that Japanese society's conformism has not arisen autonomously but rather was imposed from above by virtue of the Japanese leadership's careful structuring of such institutions as the press. In essence, as we will now see, the Japanese public lacks the first essential for true political pluralism, a free press.

A Confucian press

The great bane of industrial policy is individualism. If individuals oppose major programs merely because they cannot agree on all the minor nuances in the fine print, the result is gridlock.

For the MOF and the other agents of Japanese industrial policy, a prime objective is to deflect public attention from the more divisive aspects of national economic programs. In many cases, policies are presented very differently to different interest groups, creating the impression that everyone comes out a winner even though somebody's ox is almost inevitably going to be gored. This, of course, is the politics of illusion, and probably no organization is as adept at it as the MOF.

In the West, the degree to which government can get away with illusion is limited by an important independent power center: the press. The press's role in exposing the contradictions in government statements and the inequities in policies is so much a part of Western life that it is difficult for Westerners to imagine a society in which such countervailing power hardly exists.

Japan is such a society. Far from challenging major economic policies, the Japanese press functions essentially as the establishment's highly efficient public relations department. To call Japanese journalists "coopted" is to belittle the fusion of identity between them and the civil servants. Like the civil servants, the journalists are good Confucians who believe the state has the right to withhold information from the public. Confucius said, "The common people can be made to follow a path but not to understand it."

Where important national economic strategies are concerned, the work of journalists is not so much to inform as to persuade, even to the point sometimes of consciously printing misinformation. A key to the Japanese journalist's mentality is the strong patriotism of the typical Japanese: Japanese journalists bring to their work much the same patriotic fervor that inspires American journalists only in time of war.

The Japanese press is organized in various cartels, and, as elsewhere in Japanese society, this serves to facilitate governmental control. Not only does the government generally turn a blind eye to the newspapers' collusion in business activities, but it actively promotes the cartels by giving them exclusive access to news. Almost all government and private organizations in Japan admit only members of approved press cartels to press conferences and briefings. Even reporting of the Japanese courts is cartelized in this way, and nonaccredited news organizations (such as foreign ones) are legally barred from taking notes. If this were a Western society, these barriers to public information would have long ago fallen, if only because top journalists would have led the charge. But in a Confucian society, top journalists are philosophically insiders helping other insiders to maintain harmony. Japanese journalists go along with a system in which most news reports are written by pools of reporters. Individual journalists add little if anything to the pool reports, which are printed almost verbatim in different newspapers and carry no bylines. The pool system, familiar in the West as a tool of military censors in wartime, serves in practice to blunt any tendency that Japanese journalists might otherwise have to challenge their sources.

The extraordinary lengths to which the press goes in serving the civil service's public relations agenda have long been understood by informed Japan watchers. Writing in *Foreign Affairs* in 1993, Karel van Wolferen put it this way: "Senior Japanese newspaper editors view themselves as public guardians, entrusted to help maintain a disciplined society with a maximum of order and a minimum of conflict." The Japan-watcher David Benjamin is even more blunt: Japanese reporters, he says, are "puppets of government propaganda and bureaucratic blackmail."

One of the Japanese press's most important functions is to promote the country's strategy in foreign policy. The press's highly partisan role in U.S.-Japan trade disputes is a case in point. The press often builds up support for the Japanese side in trade disputes by suppressing or misrepresenting the American side's case. In the process, it seems at times to fan anti-American feelings to dangerous levels. In 1994, for instance, the Japanese press's coverage of a trade complaint by Motorola so inflamed one group of Japanese ultranationalists that they spray-painted Motorola's Tokyo offices with protest slogans. One such slogan read: "Crush the product-pushing U.S. imperialists."

At other times, the Japanese press functions deliberately to create goodwill toward certain countries. A notable example is its coverage of Chinese politics. With a few token pro-Taiwanese exceptions, Japanese newspapers have generally functioned as cheerleaders for the Chinese Communist Party's leadership. In the 1960s, for instance, they offered constant verbal support for Mao Tse-tung's infamous Cultural Revolution, which claimed the lives of tens of millions of Chinese. As with much else that is printed in the Japanese press, the newspapers' pro-Mao reports have always been hard to explain: but clearly by flattering Mao, the newspapers did not hurt Japanese industry's chances of increasing exports to China.

One of the press's most important functions is to make sure that the *tojin-ha,* the outsiders' faction among diet members, is supportive of the civil servants' agenda. In this effort, the press functions as an enforcement arm of the government, readily conducting media lynchings of the civil servants' enemies. This is the real significance of the constant stream of "scandals" discrediting certain elected representatives and businessmen who have incurred the bureaucrats' wrath.

This pattern goes back to the nineteenth century. Major press campaigns to discredit powerful politicians have recurred at intervals of about five to ten years ever since. Although most of these affairs have been little reported outside Japan, many of them have assumed Watergate-style proportions in the Japanese media. A few such scandals focus on sexual misconduct but mostly the central issue is money. In virtually every case, the leaks consist largely of information that could only have come from the MOF — information, for instance, about tax evasion, securities manipulation, sweetheart bank loans, and the rigging of government contracts.

A notable early example of Japan's political scandal genre was the Siemens bribery scandal of 1914. The ostensible issue then was that top navy officials had taken bribes from a supplier, the Siemens company of Germany. But there was a key issue of domestic policy below the surface: the navy had been persistently overrunning MOF-set spending limits. Then in 1932 came the Meito Tax Evasion Case, and in 1940 the Bank of Japan Scandal, both of which seem to have been classic MOF-instigated moves to discredit opponents. Other famous financial scandals include the Yawata steelworks case of 1918 and the South Manchuria Railway scandal of the early 1920s. The Teijin case of 1934, involving shares in the Teijin textile company, brought down the entire cabinet of Prime Minister Makoto Saito.

One of the biggest and most significant such scandals occurred just before World War II. Ichizo Kobayashi, a prominent tycoon, had been appointed Commerce and Industry minister in 1940 as part of an explicit deal in which he was to represent the zaibatsus' interests in a cabinet otherwise dominated by militarists. In that capacity, he strongly and successfully opposed the New Bureaucrats' ambitions to expropriate the zaibatsu families (as expressed in the Economic New Structure manifesto). But Nobusuke Kishi, a prominent New Bureaucrat who would later be convicted by the Americans as a Class A war criminal, got even by investigating Kobayashi's past and presenting allegations of tax evasion and sexual misconduct. Kobayashi resigned in disgrace in April 1941 and, in an important victory for the militarists, was replaced by an admiral.

The first big postwar scandal concerned the Showa Denko aluminum smelting company: no less than sixty-four people were accused in 1948 of various irregularities surrounding low-interest loans from the MOF's Reconstruction Finance Bank. After years of sensational headlines and the ruining of dozens of careers, only two of the accused were found guilty. And in 1954, the so-called Shipbuilding Kickbacks case filled the headlines for months. The main issue was irregular payments of subsidies to the shipbuilding industry. Those indicted included two of the most important politicians of the postwar era, Eisaku Sato and Hayato Ikeda.

Perhaps the person who suffered most from MOF-instigated media lynchings was Prime Minister Kakuei Tanaka. Tanaka was the strongest tojin-ha prime minister in the postwar era and was probably the most formidable individual opponent the MOF has ever faced. An outspoken advocate of a consumer society, he campaigned for easier fiscal policies, spacious and cheap housing, lower taxes, and several other measures that, if he had been successful, would have undermined the MOF's Forced Saving program. Tanaka was the target of two separate bribery scandals in the 1970s and was apparently blackmailed by a rival political party, the Komeito. The bribery charges were eventually dropped but only because he was arraigned instead on charges that he had breached the MOF's exchange control regulations by maintaining a bank account abroad — a heinous offense in the eyes of the MOF, which was always on the alert to ward off the danger of capital flight.

Then came the Recruit scandal of the late 1980s, which centered on breaches of the MOF's securities laws. The Recruit scandal was the first that most Westerners became aware of, though the history of Japan's scandals is virtually the history of party politics in Japan. The extraordinary nature of these scandals is apparent only to those who live through them in Japan. The Japanese press sends dozens of reporters to cover every minor nuance and, in a country where names are often withheld in reports of other types of news, the press seems to go out of its way to create maximum humiliation for victims of political scandals. It is routine, for instance, for the main television channels to interrupt their normal programs to provide lengthy live coverage of the arrests of minor political operatives caught up in these scandals. The pattern is always the same. This is how it was described by the journalist John Roberts in 1974:

When a big scandal breaks, the public is suddenly immersed in a torrent of revelations that gushes forth from the newspapers, magazines, and broadcasting stations day after day, week after week, until the scandal itself seems to be the whole political process, unique and unrelated to anything else in the past. Scandal after scandal erupts and subsides, yet no political lessons are learned and no real reform is achieved.

In a commentary on the election of the reformist Hosokawa government in 1993, Karel van Wolferen wrote that fear of being accused in the constant "scandals" was a prime reason why even the strongest politicians in the new coalition government were likely to behave timidly in the face of the bureaucratic will. This proved prophetic less than a year later when Hosokawa was ousted amid charges of financial misconduct. By contrast, the press almost never targets top MOF bureaucrats for media lynchings. In van Wolferen's words, the press "protects" the bureaucrats. Not only can the bureaucrats avoid scrutiny of their personal peccadillos but they are rarely if ever held personally accountable for specific controversial or unsuccessful policies.

The Japanese press at times consciously functions as the establishment's voice in bolstering the Japanese work ethic. Japanese journalists, for instance, often seem to endorse the propaganda efforts of big business to moderate wage increases. A memorable example was the press's treatment of *Japan at the Brink,* an absurd book written in the 1970s by Konosuke Matsushita of the Matsushita Electric Corporation. Matsushita robustly argued that overpaid Japanese workers were pricing themselves out of world markets. In his view, hunger and starvation were "bearing down on us [the Japanese people] at this very moment." Buoyed by favorable reviews in the Japanese press (the *Asahi Shimbun* praised the book's "far-reaching vision"), the book quickly became a bestseller.

Journalists enthusiastically suppress information that might undermine the national consensus. For decades after World War II, Japanese journalists exercised "self-control" in withholding from the public the fact that the cost of many consumer goods was much higher in Japan than in other countries. The media's self-control on this issue has now been relaxed, but only since Japan passed the United States in per capita income in the mid-1980s. A Japanese journalist explained: "We were doing what was in the best interests of Japan. Every society has things it does not tell the public. Even in America during the Vietnam War, the *Washington Post* and the *New York Times* did not tell all they knew." The press's "self-control" was particularly noticeable in the matter of keeping word of Japan's trade barriers from the public.

Perhaps the most startling example of the press's role in spreading misinformation concerns Japan's perennial shortage of housing space. As we will see in detail in Chapter Six, the housing space shortage is a policy designed to stimulate savings. The press has constantly shied away from scrutinizing the housing policy, particularly the zoning rules that are the government's principal tool in constricting the Japanese people's living space.

In the late 1980s, the press cooperated with a MOF policy of artificially constricting Japan's already very tight supply of land. Among other things, the MOF in 1987 imposed a ban on sales of nearly 300,000 acres of unused government land, much of it in Japan's major cities. The press's cooperation was vital to the policy. Instead of pointing out frankly that the MOF's measures would drive up land prices, the press portrayed these measures as an attempt by the MOF to *reduce* land prices! This spin on the news was most vociferously presented by the "liberal" *Asahi Shimbun*. For years previously the *Asahi* had argued that government land sales were supposedly the main factor causing land prices to rise! In any other sophisticated country, a respectable newspaper would be embarrassed to publish such transparent nonsense. But in Japan, newspapers are not embarrassed to do so because they know most readers will not see the nonsense and certainly no one will draw attention to it.

Piquantly, members of Japan's media cartel seem to have been among the biggest beneficiaries of the bureaucrats' land policy. In particular, the *Asahi* is known to have received a large tract of government-owned land in central Tokyo. The *Nihon Keizai Shimbun,* which has been described by van Wolferen as a "megaphone attached to the Ministry of Finance," has also acquired prime government-owned land in this way. Did the newspaper companies benefit from special below-market prices? As with other aspects of Japanese government, outsiders can never be sure. What is clear, however, is that the MOF routinely allows sales of land at submarket prices and, as the monthly *Bungeishunju* has recorded, such transactions are often channeled via politicians.

Why does all of this matter? Because Japan will never develop a Western-style democracy while its press continues to operate as a Confucian cartel.

A test of pluralism

How deeply committed are Japan's reformist politicians to Western-style constitutional democracy? Few areas of policy provide a more striking test than Japan's defense policy.

Defense is interesting because the Peace Clause of the 1947 Constitution forbids Japan from maintaining any kind of defense force. Yet Japan has long maintained a well-equipped army, and its defense budget — at about $40 billion a year — is now second in the world only to America's.

For decades almost everyone in the Tokyo elite seemed comfortable with this monumental anomaly. Essentially the various concerned parties — government officials, judges, intellectuals, media commentators, and politicians — all agreed to behave as if there was no elephant in the room. This remarkable situation is perhaps the best demonstration of a point that American legal scholars have long made about Japan: it is "a nation governed by men, not laws." This is a delicate way of saying that Japanese officials are essentially accountable to no one and nothing, and they have the power to overrule the law or even the Constitution whenever expediency dictates.

Measured by East Asian tradition, Japanese officials are fully within their rights in wielding arbitrary power. But if Japan is supposed to be on track toward a Western idea of democracy, then the anomalous position of the army should long ago have been addressed by political leaders: essentially the army should be disbanded or, more realistically, the government should hold a referendum to change the Peace Clause.

Before looking at how the new reformist governments of the mid-1990s have coped with this contradiction, let's be clear about the Constitution's wording:

> Aspiring sincerely to an international peace based on justice and order, the Japanese people forever renounce war as a sovereign right of the nation and the threat or use of force as a means of settling international disputes.
>
> In order to accomplish the aim of the preceding paragraph, land, sea, and air forces, as well as other war potential, will never be maintained.

Some observers have maintained that the phrase "In order to accomplish the aim of the preceding paragraph" is a loophole that provides enough ambiguity to legitimize a self-defense force; but, as the French Japan-watcher Robert Guillain pointed out in the 1960s, this is an "unconvincing sophism" that would be laughed out of any Western court. In any case, we know the exact intentions of the original framers of the Constitution. At the time the new constitution was promulgated in 1946, Prime Minister Shigeru Yoshida explicitly stated that the Peace Clause ruled out even self-defense forces. Even the early postwar military chief, Keikichi Masuhara, went on record as saying that "all concerned" with the founding of the postwar defense forces intended to make an appropriate amendment to the Constitution within five years.

The anomaly originated in the unreal world of occupation-era politics. The Peace Clause seems to have been adopted by MacArthur on the suggestion of Yoshida's predecessor, Kijuro Shidehara, at a meeting on January 24, 1946. It appears originally to have been conceived as a spur-of-the-moment political expedient aimed at help-ing MacArthur head off strong public pressure in the United States, Britain, the Netherlands, and Australia for the execution of Emperor Hirohito. MacArthur feared that unrest would break out in Japan if Hirohito was executed.

The clause was an embarrassment to everyone concerned almost from the start. After war broke out in Korea in 1950, MacArthur tacitly admitted that he had made a mistake. Fearing that the Soviets might attack Japan, he personally presided over the founding of the modern Japanese army. A few years later, U.S. Vice President Richard Nixon explicitly admitted that the Peace Clause was a mistake. As he pointed out, every nation should have the right to defend itself.

Yet today, nearly half a century later, the anomaly has still not been rectified. The most amazing aspect of this story is the behavior of the Social Democratic Party. For many years the SDP had been practically alone in acknowledging publicly that Japan's army was unconstitu-tional. Thus when the SDP finally came to power in 1993 as the largest group within Morihiro Hosokawa's coalition government, one would have expected that measures to address the anomaly would at last have been put on Tokyo's agenda. In the event, the SDP chose in 1993 to renounce its previous position. A year later the party excelled itself when SDP head Tomiichi Murayama became prime minister and thus titular commander of the Japanese forces. In a previous life, Murayama had outspokenly exposed the unconstitutionality of the Japanese army.

After becoming prime minister, Murayama moved with remarkable speed to distance himself from his previous position. Within a month, he publicly proclaimed that he no longer felt Japan's self-defense forces were unconstitutional and, in one of several reversals of hallowed SDP positions, vowed to maintain Tokyo's security treaty with the United States.

It was a scene worthy of *The Mikado*, but it came as no surprise to students of Japanese power. In reality, the SDP was bowing to the consensus among the Tokyo elite, which evidently sees advantages in retaining the anomaly as long as possible. In essence the anomaly allows Japanese bureaucrats to have it both ways. They have an army — yet, by citing the Constitution, they can elegantly duck out of the thankless task of playing junior partner to Uncle Sam in global policing duties in such dangerous hot spots as the Middle East.

The betting is that Japan will in the course of its "Westernization" program rectify the anomaly — but only at a time that suits the Tokyo elite. In the meantime, the perpetuation of the anomaly under an SDP prime minister is the clearest possible evidence that the 1993 "revolution" changed little. As ever in Japan, politicians reign and bureaucrats rule.

6

Born to Save

We have seen that the Japanese system of government is designed to help the nation coordinate its energies in pursuing national objectives. Nowhere has this system been more effective than in promoting Japan's national economic growth program. Over the years the government has created many devices that semiautomatically promote growth. These include suppressed consumption, the lifetime employment system, and the lattice-like structure of cartels and keiretsus that dominates Japanese industry. In the next few chapters, we will examine in detail these devices and show how they collectively constitute the Big Logic system that is propelling Japan further and further away from the principles of capitalism. We begin with suppressed consumption.

Western economic commentators have long believed that Japan's savings rate was on the verge of falling, and thus they imagined Japan's years of abnormally high economic growth would soon end. At no time was this prediction made more insistently than in the late 1980s. One leading commentator even described the Japanese as "a nation of pleasure seekers" whose Westernized consumption patterns would reduce Japan's savings rate to Western levels in the 1990s.

Halfway through the 1990s, it is time to do a reality check: as usual, the prophets of Japan's "Westernization" have been confounded. For, far from falling, Japan's savings rate has actually risen. In the four years to 1993, the household savings rate jumped from 14.6 to 16.6 percent. Japan's increased savings rate has been all the more impressive because it has coincided with an economic slowdown that would normally be expected to induce savers to cut their savings.

According to the Paris-based OECD, Japan in 1993 produced $819 billion in net savings, nearly eleven times America's total of just $75 billion. In other words, the Japanese are now saving more than twenty times as much per capita as Americans.

It is a performance that rightly makes Japan the envy of the world. As economists of all stripes agree, a high savings rate is a crucial first objective for a country intent on creating sustainable fast economic growth. Unfortunately, as the world's have-not countries know, a high savings rate is one of the most difficult of all economic objectives to achieve. So why do the Japanese save so much? The answer is one of the great untold stories of Japanese economics.

Why do the Japanese save?

Many Western economists mistakenly believe that the Japanese save for "cultural" reasons. Western economists assume — and assume is the operative word — that the Japanese are frugal people.

This explanation demonstrably does not fit the facts of history. In the late nineteenth century, the Japanese were regarded by Europeans as a nation of spendthrifts. Since then, Japan's savings rate has fluctuated widely. It rose during World War I, fell in the early 1920s, and rose dramatically in the 1930s. In the immediate aftermath of World War II, it plunged and stayed relatively low for a decade. Then, in the mid-1950s, it soared and has remained one of the world's highest ever since.

Some economists maintain that the key to the mystery lies in Japan's unusual salary system, whereby workers receive about one-third of their annual pay in the form of twice yearly bonuses. The theory is that families get used to living within their low monthly salaries and thus save the bonuses. It sounds convincing until you take a closer look. If the salary payment pattern really distorts Japanese consumption, we would expect the Japanese to spend proportionately less than Westerners on daily necessities (where spending power would be constrained by low monthly incomes) and proportionately more on occasional big-ticket purchases such as furniture, carpets, curtains, and vacations (which the Japanese worker should be particularly well placed to finance because of his large twice yearly bonuses). But the pattern we find is precisely the opposite: the Japanese spend heavily on daily necessities and little on big-ticket items.

Another purported explanation is that the Japanese save because they lack an adequate social security system. It is a nice theory, but it is dead wrong. Japan's social security system is one of the most generous in the world, as measured both by the absolute level of benefits and by how those benefits stack up against average incomes.

Once again, as with so many other aspects of Japanese economics, we find that the conventional wisdom explains nothing.

Forced savings

The Japanese save for a very characteristic Japanese reason: the government wants them to. One of the least understood aspects of twentieth-century economics is that a determined government *can* make people save — by the simple expedient of suppressing their consumption.

Suppressed consumption is hardly an unheard-of concept — least of all for Americans. The United States in the early 1940s used a comprehensive policy of suppressed consumption as the cornerstone of a savings policy designed to win World War II. This is how that savings policy looked to one economist who lived through those days, John Kenneth Galbraith:

> Saving . . . rose because money was difficult to spend. Some goods that were wanted were rationed; some, such as gasoline, that were necessary for spending for other things were scarce or also rationed. (It has also been observed that one saves money by staying home.) Some required standing in line. A few customary objects of expenditure, such as new automobiles and new houses, could not be bought. . . .
>
> In 1940, personal savings were 5.1 percent of disposable income. In 1943 and 1944, they were 25 percent.

All this helped the American economy achieve its largest and most rapid expansion ever. Gross national product increased by 50 percent between 1941 and 1945 as output of steel doubled and production of ships and aircraft increased about tenfold.

In a similar plan designed by John Maynard Keynes, the British also used suppressed consumption to win the war. The British government combined tight rationing of consumer goods with a system of compulsory saving. The two policies worked together to provide the vast capital needed to build desperately needed munitions factories.

Even before the Americans and the British adopted these suppressed consumption policies, the concept had already been proven in Japan. As the militarists moved the Japanese economy to a war footing in the 1930s, they had acted comprehensively to suppress consumption. The result was, as we noted earlier, that Japan's savings rate soared in the 1930s. This is how one Tokyo official explained Japan's high savings rate to visiting American journalists before Pearl Harbor: "When there isn't too great an abundance and an unnecessary variety of things to buy, the wage-earner expresses himself by saving his surplus." By 1941, the militarists had cut Japan's consumption to only 42 percent of gross national product. They kept squeezing to the point where consumption bottomed at an almost unbelievably low level of 18.5 percent in 1944.

In the event, although the Japanese lost the war, they had learned an invaluable lesson in real-world economics. It was a lesson they were to apply to dramatic effect in the postwar era. As Japanese production increased in the 1950s, the Tokyo authorities determined to keep a tight lid on consumption. As before, the Japanese wage-earner duly expressed himself by saving his surplus. Since then, almost every government in East Asia has adopted similar suppressed consumption policies, and, lo and behold, they too have achieved almost superhuman savings rates.

It is interesting to note that though American policymaking has been predicated in recent years on the view that East Asia's high savings rates are driven by innate East Asian frugality, a few well-informed observers have understood the true dynamics all along. In particular, the well-connected American Japan scholar Edwin Reischauer predicted in 1955 that "rigid controls on consumption" would be an important feature of future East Asian growth policies. He said: "If there is to be even a partial achievement of the industrialization that most Asian leaders expect, the various governments of Asia will undoubtedly have to play a large part in the process of accumulating capital. While this point is worth emphasizing for Westerners, who are accustomed to the primary role of individual citizens in saving and investment, it is usually taken for granted in Asia."

The many faces of suppressed consumption

The oldest manifestation of the Japanese economic system's suppressed consumption policy is Japan's mercantilist trade policy. The logic is simple: if a nation doesn't import things, it can't consume them. In a policy driven by the MOF, the Japanese economic system has been consciously using tariffs and other trade barriers to stimulate savings since the 1890s. We will take a closer look at Japan's trade policies in Chapter Nine. The focus here is on some of the many other policies that Japan has pursued to suppress consumption.

Before going on, it is important to note that different suppressed consumption policies have different savings effects. Some policies act to increase the household sector's savings. Japan's consumer credit policies are an example. But more often, Tokyo's suppressed consumption policies serve to increase savings not in the household sector but in the business sector. A good example is trade barriers, which raise profit margins for Japanese manufacturers and distributors. If these profits are ploughed back into the business, as they usually are in Japan, they count as business savings.

The important point is that the suppressed consumption policies create savings *somewhere* in the system. Exactly where — whether in the hands of households, corporations, or entrepreneurs — is a secondary consideration. For the pragmatists who run Japan, the overriding point is that the overall level of the nation's savings is as high as possible.

Airport bottlenecks

The Japanese take fewer foreign vacations than almost any other people in the First World. They are only one-quarter as likely to take a foreign vacation as the British, for instance. Yet the Japanese are now nearly twice as wealthy as the British and, even more than the British, they suffer a shortage of vacation facilities at home.

The problem is that, under the government's transportation policy, Japanese cities are denied adequate air links to foreign vacation destinations. At peak vacation times only a small minority can escape the country. Moreover, most employers make it difficult for employees, particularly male employees, to take vacations except at times when the whole nation shuts down briefly for national holidays. The result is that ordinary Japanese have never developed a taste for annual foreign vacations.

The impact on Japan's savings and balance of payments patterns is enormous. If the Japanese were to match the British rate of foreign travel, they would spend an extra $60 billion a year abroad, equal to about half Japan's annual current account surplus.

Japan's shortage of air links is the latest manifestation of a long-running Japanese government policy to minimize foreign vacation travel. Up to 1963, the government actually maintained an outright legal ban on Japanese citizens taking overseas vacations. Since then the government has curbed the number of flights out of the country, with a view in particular to restricting economy-class capacity. Thus although capacity has been allowed to increase each year, it has never been enough to meet the potential peak-season demand.

The shortage of landing rights at Japanese airports underpins a tightly regulated fare system in which Japanese travelers are often charged as much as twice the fares paid by foreigners who buy their tickets outside Japan.

The Japanese government does not, of course, acknowledge the neo-mercantilist logic behind its travel policy. Instead it blames the shortage of air links on bad luck in developing Tokyo's Narita Airport. Opposition by local landowners has ostensibly held up the airport's completion, and as of 1994 the airport was still operating with just one runway. Two additional runways originally scheduled to have opened in 1974 had not yet been completed, ostensibly because the government refused to expropriate just eight local landowners who stood in the way of the project.

Until recently, American observers took the shortage of airport runways as evidence of a surprisingly weak central government. One prominent American Japanologist who studied the Narita saga even wrote a book hailing it as evidence that Japanese society was particularly conscientious in respecting the rights of individuals and small communities. It's a nice picture, but it doesn't check with other things we know about how individuals are treated in Japan. Take, for instance, the government's decision in the 1960s to shrink Japan's then vast coal mining industry. Dozens of communities were turned into ghost towns overnight, but they received precious little sympathy from anyone, least of all the government. Nor was sympathy much in evidence in the case of Minamata disease, a horrific case of mercury poisoning in the city of Minamata in the 1950s. Thousands of victims still have not been compensated in a scandal in which several important elements of Japan Inc. were clearly guilty of negligence and complicity in a cover-up.

Moreover, it is not as if the Japanese authorities are normally reluctant to take a firm line with obstructive land owners. Japan has a record of pushing through the building of nuclear power stations, expressways, and even military airbases with a minimum of sensitivity to local protests.

Even Japan's extensive program of building regional airports has not seemed to suffer from any marked reluctance to expropriate land owners. Perhaps the clearest indication of the government's true mind is that during more than two decades of pandemonium at Narita, the Ministry of Finance has consistently discouraged such regional airports from providing international links. The MOF's attitude has been the more pointed because Prime Minister Kakuei Tanaka in 1972 promised to launch an extensive program of building large international airports. The acute shortage of international air links at regional airports is a major inconvenience for provincial travelers, and it is made much worse by the fact that flights from the provinces to Tokyo do not connect directly with international flights out of Tokyo. Provincial flights are routed to Tokyo's domestic airport, Haneda, which is an exasperating two-hour road connection from the international airport at Narita.

The plight of provincial tourists contrasts markedly with that of Japan's executive set. Most Japanese executives who fly abroad on business are based in Tokyo, and they enjoy an abundance of business-class seats out of Narita. In fact, many Japanese planes are configured exclusively for first-class and business-class passengers. Nor has the Narita bottleneck been a problem for Japan's exporters. Cargo planes are slotted to take off from Narita's single runway even during the busiest hours, and Narita ranks as the world's biggest cargo airport.

Even the American government believes there is something suspicious about Japan's airport bottlenecks. At a travel exhibition a few years ago, the U.S. Travel and Tourism Administration's Japan director Fritz Schmitz accused the Japanese government of deliberately creating a shortage of international flights. Charging Japanese regulators with fixing exorbitant international fares to discourage vacationers, he added: "A picture emerges — let me put this delicately — that the Japanese government may not really be committed to pushing, or should I say allowing, international travel to reach its full potential here."

Money in the bank

The Ministry of Finance uses its regulation of the financial system as a tool to boost the savings rate. Perhaps the Ministry's most important policy in this respect is to restrict the availability of consumer credit, thus directly suppressing consumption.

Until recently virtually the only consumer credit available to ordinary Japanese salarymen was provided by loan sharks, whose interest rates and recovery procedures were so oppressive that credit was an option only for the desperate. As a result, consumer credit as a percentage of gross national product amounted to little more than one-tenth the American rate.

Lately, however, officials have ostensibly liberalized consumer credit but, as with liberalization in many other areas of the Japanese economy, the impact on the real economy has been minimal. Although the banks, for instance, report increases in their consumer lending, much of this has gone to finance purchases of land. And land, of course, cannot be "consumed." Thus in reality much so-called consumer lending in Japan is really investment-related lending.

Meanwhile, the Ministry of Finance maintains hidden restrictions on the availability and use of credit cards. Most credit card holders in Japan are required to pay off their debt in full each month. Such restrictions help to explain why the rate of credit card ownership is only one-third of America's.

The development of a serious consumer credit industry in Japan has also been blocked by a lack of credit checking services. In line with cartel logic, Japanese bankers have a long record of withholding credit information from American and European consumer finance houses trying to establish a beachhead in Japan. The big banks give priority to industry in general and their own keiretsu companies in particular in their lending policies. To make doubly sure consumer credit did not catch on, the MOF long ago advised Japanese banks to withhold yen financing from the Japanese branches of foreign credit organizations.

In the tradition of Japanese public policy, the savings rationale for the credit card restrictions has not been stated explicitly. But Japan's emulators elsewhere in East Asia, notably in Singapore, have frankly acknowledged that their similar policies against credit cards are targeted at boosting the savings rate.

The MOF also spurs Japan's savings rate via its regulation of the insurance industry. All Japan's major life insurance companies are mutuals, which means their profits in theory belong to policyholders. In practice, however, the life insurance companies have long enjoyed the MOF's blessing to minimize their payouts to policyholders, and as a result they have built up vast hidden assets of perhaps as much as $1 trillion. The exact figure is a closely guarded secret because the life insurance companies do not publish meaningful financial statements. What is clear is that the life insurance companies have a vested interest as a cartel in minimizing their payouts as a way of avoiding competition and building their own institutional power.

Adding it all up, financial regulation may account for as much as three percentage points of Japan's savings rate.

Consumer spending: drop before you shop

It is often said that Japan has too many stores. True, Japan has a large number of stores, but their average size is very small. As a result, the Japanese have only about half as much shopping space per capita as Americans.

The structure of retailing in Japan is heavily biased toward tiny outlets specializing in narrow categories of goods such as tofu, fish, and rice cakes. Large supermarkets and general merchandise stores are a rare sight in Japan. Big department stores are located mainly in the centers of Japan's biggest cities, so consumers have to endure a grueling rail commute before they get to the shops. In essence, Japan is a place where you really need to be tough to go shopping.

Various reasons have been offered for Japan's retailing bottlenecks. One problem is said to be a shortage of land; but this is a surmountable problem, as such crowded nations as the Netherlands and Belgium have demonstrated.

Another often-mentioned explanation is that political pressure from Japan's small retailers has been blocking the large store development. This theory, however, greatly exaggerates the small retailers' power. The truth is that the Ministry of International Trade and Industry enjoys wide powers to regulate retailing without reference either to small retailers or their political representatives. Officials seem to operate a nationwide system of tight limits on the aggregate amount of retailing space created each year. Expansion-minded small retailers are, if anything, more disadvantaged by the ministry's rules than large national retailers.

The MITI evidently suppresses retailing as a key part of Japan's industrial policy. Its strategy is supported by other major power centers in Japan, including the mighty Keidanren, Japan's supreme representative organization of industry. The policy is also apparent in the regulation of the postal system: bulk mailing rates are kept artificially high to the point where they discourage most forms of direct-mail selling.

It is not hard to see how Japan's distribution bottlenecks advance the nation's industrial policy. The primary effect is to curb the consumption of luxury goods, particularly imported consumer durables that suffer from a critical shortage of display space in Japanese stores.

The net effect is to depress Japan's consumption by several percentage points and to boost the savings rate by a corresponding amount.

The world's most expensive housing

Much has been said about Japan's real estate collapse of the early 1990s. Overlooked in all the talk was one significant point: housing prices did not collapse. With few exceptions, housing prices between 1989 and 1994 held reasonably steady in yen terms — and rose by around 40 percent in dollar terms.

Even at the time of the real estate market's peak distress in 1992, a typical home in the Tokyo area sold for fully 7.1 times a typical worker's annual income — against a multiple of just 3.4 times in the United States. Given that Japanese houses are on average about half the size of American houses, this means that on a square meter basis the Japanese were paying four times American prices for housing. As of 1994, a typically cramped house one and a half hours from central Tokyo cost more than $600,000.

Perhaps the most compelling evidence of Japan's housing shortage is found in rental properties. Recent figures indicate that the average new privately rented apartment in Tokyo measures only 38.9 square meters. This is about 410 square feet — equivalent to a large bedroom in a middle-class home in America or Europe — and included within this space is a minuscule bathroom and kitchen. Typically such a property is shared by four people.

One thing is clear: Japan's housing shortage powerfully suppresses consumption. Families who spend as much as half their income servicing their mortgage debts hardly have any discretionary spending power left over to buy French wine or American tableware. Japan's cramped housing also physically limits the potential market for American and European furniture and appliances, which are usually too large for Japanese homes. The physical limits on space also depress Japan's energy consumption, which on a per capita basis runs only about one-quarter of America's (and little more than one-third of Britain's).

It is interesting to note that Japan's land prices have not always been remarkably high. They were notably low for many years after World War II, then rose in the mid-1950s. Between 1955 and 1962, housing land prices multiplied sevenfold while salaries hardly doubled. By the mid-1960s house prices in Tokyo were already higher than in New York, although incomes in Tokyo were just one-quarter of those in New York. Rents for expatriate housing in Tokyo were about 150 percent higher than in New York.

Why did Japan's house prices suddenly soar just as the Economic Miracle got under way? As with so many other Japanese economic mysteries, the answer lies in official government policies. The government's zoning policies in particular have been extraordinary. The country has a serious shortage of land yet officials generally refuse to authorize the construction of high-rise buildings except in city centers and along a few main thoroughfares in the suburbs. The populist prime minister Kakuei Tanaka campaigned in the early 1970s to relax the ban on high-rises. He wanted to "verticalize" — his word — the country by raising the average building height to seventeen floors. In a plan that would have taken advantage of new earthquake-proof building techniques, he proposed to transform Japan's congested urban areas into spacious garden cities. In the event, though Tanaka won a mandate at the polls, he seems to have been blocked by the bureaucrats. In most residential areas, there was no appreciable relaxation in the officials' general two-floor height limit. As of the early 1990s, the average building height in the Tokyo region remained at just 1.7 floors.

The official reason for the two-floor height limit is to protect the sunshine rights of neighbors. But this is a transparent excuse: as other countries have shown, equitable methods can be found to compensate neighbors for loss of light. The officials betray their real intentions in new suburbs, where they generally perpetuate the two-floor limit even though there are no sunshine rights to be protected.

The officials have even continued to zone many parts of Japan's urban areas for agriculture. As a result, about one-seventh of the land in the Tokyo area is owned by farmers or is vacant. Ironically, many foreigners have wrongly concluded that the owners of such land are holding out against urbanization. They are actually waiting for their land to be rezoned, at which point they can expect to cash out at prices many times agricultural values.

The officials have also contributed directly to the housing shortage by refusing to sell large tracts of government-owned land in urban areas. In many cases this policy is ultimately traceable to the Ministry of Finance. The Ministry has, for instance, for years been blocking the sale of the Shiodome railroad yard, a huge unused area adjoining Tokyo's ultra-pricey Ginza district.

The Ministry of Finance has been known to use a variety of tax policies to constrict the supply of land. In the late 1980s, the MOF introduced capital gains taxes of up to 96 percent to discourage land from coming on the market. Other tax policies have provided incentives for people to hold their assets in land rather than in securities, providing artificial support for land prices. At various times the MOF has given rollover relief to those who reinvest land gains in further land purchases, creating a balloon effect in a country with an inherent land shortage. MOF policy has also discouraged farmers from trying to get their land rezoned: the MOF's trick here has been to exempt farmers' heirs from Japan's painful inheritance tax only if they keep their land in agricultural use for at least twenty years after inheritance.

Perhaps the clearest evidence that the MOF is intent on keeping

housing prices as high as possible is found in its regulation of mortgage lending. Japanese couples are allowed to take out mortgages of
up to ten times a husband's annual income — about three times the
maximum ratio regulators consider appropriate in the West. With
Japanese home buyers competing for chronically short space and free
to take on huge amounts of debt, they naturally bid up house prices
to sensational levels. As one Tokyo cynic points out, easy money has
been about as benign as the metal spurs that cockfighting enthusiasts
fit on their birds' legs.

The ordinary salaryman's loss is corporate Japan's gain. Repeatedly
evidence has surfaced that Japan Inc. companies have purchased land
ahead of zoning changes. In the early 1970s, the Princeton scholar
Edwin Mills suggested that Japan's big keiretsu trading companies
were colluding to drive up the cost of residential land. Again in the
1980s land boom, the big winners were major Japanese industrial
corporations and banks that benefited from rezoning decisions.

The effect of the land policy on the savings rate is hard to exaggerate. One indicator is a study conducted in the 1980s by the Industrial
Bank of Japan, which found that Japan's land price distortions accounted for fully one-third of the excess of Japan's savings rate over
America's. If anything, the housing policy's contribution to savings
has increased since then.

An official of the European Union once described Japanese housing
as "rabbit hutches." These rabbit hutches are home to a financial
dragon — the Japanese savings rate.

A glut of savings?

It is one thing for a government to force a nation to save — but quite
another to persuade industry to take advantage of the resulting abundance of capital. Industry invests only if it can expect a good return.
In the view of many Western economists, Japan is already saving *too
much*. The former economics editor of the *Economist,* Brian Reading,
for instance, published a book in 1992 arguing that Japan was facing
collapse because it was supposedly running out of ways to invest its
savings.

The Japanese economy's performance in the last three years has
proved such fears groundless. Promised a cartelized market at home,

Japanese corporations encounter little fear in continuing to invest two to three times as much per employee as American corporations. Moreover, as we will now see, Japanese economic leaders have designed a superior system of employment that removes many of the obstacles that discourage the capitalist West from investing in productivity-enhancing new technologies.

7

The Economics of People

Probably no aspect of Japanese economics has been so consistently underestimated in the West as Japan's employment system. Because the system flouts free market principles, Westerners consider it self-evidently incapable of withstanding competition from the "more efficient" hire-and-fire labor system of the United States and Europe. Thus every time the Japanese economy undergoes a temporary slowdown, influential Western publications can be counted on to write the Japanese employment system's obituary. They have been doing this since the 1960s and the argument always is the same: as the world economy "globalizes," Japanese corporations are being drawn into increasingly serious head-to-head competition with Western counterparts and face extinction if they do not adopt the "more efficient" Western system of employment. At no time was this argument presented more insistently than in the recession of the early 1990s. But, as on previous occasions, the Japanese employment system triumphantly confounded its critics by emerging from the recession as strong as ever.

Press commentators have constantly been confounded in their predictions because they view the Japanese labor system in too narrow a focus. They are unduly influenced by one disadvantage of the Japanese system, the fact that Japanese employers cannot cut labor costs as fast as their Western counterparts when demand turns down in a recession. The commentators, however, overlook several long-term advantages of the system for *the Japanese nation as a whole* that are almost invisible to anyone schooled in the short-term, individualistic logic of Western economics.

Unknown to most Westerners, the Japanese employment system is much more complex than it appears and has many hidden but powerful effects that help Japan maximize its output. The system's three main principles — lifetime employment, company unions, and seniority pay — are mutually interdependent and cannot be understood in isolation. They are interlinked in a system that is as well thought out as a Swiss watch. Just as some of the wheels of a watch movement revolve the "wrong way," so some elements of the Japanese employment system seem to defy economic efficiency. But to judge the efficiency of any one part without reference to the larger system is as fatuous as for an engineer to judge the efficiency of a watch's parts individually without reference to the mechanism as whole.

Collectively the three main principles of Japanese labor economics are known to Japanese policymakers as the *sanshu no jingi* — the "three treasures" of Japanese-style management. This designation is well deserved, but before we can understand why, we must discover how these principles emerged in the first place.

The invention of a tradition

The first mistake Westerners make in looking at the Japanese employment system is that they assume its origins lie in Japanese culture. This fundamental misunderstanding goes far to explain the persistent failure of Western theorists to grasp the system's carefully conceived inner logic. As we will see, the system is based on comprehensive labor regulation, and it has been consciously invented as Japan's answer to a Western labor system that Japanese business leaders have long believed is inappropriate for an advanced economy.

The system has existed in its present form only since the end of World War II. By contrast, in the early days of Japan's industrialization in the last century, Japanese employers generally operated by Western hire-and-fire rules, and as a result they suffered many of the same labor relations problems that we think of today as peculiarly Western. It is interesting to note, for instance, that although absenteeism is virtually unknown in Japan today, it has been a major problem in the past. As the economics scholar Robert Ozaki has noted, absenteeism after payday was so common a century ago that employers paid different workers on different days to stagger the disruption of output.

Corporate Japan's earliest efforts to improve on the Western hire-

and-fire model emerged in the textile industry, then one of Japan's most advanced industries. The textile industry pioneered the crucial concept of employment cartels, which restricted competition for labor by requiring rival employers to refrain from hiring from each other. Although such cartels may not seem a significant innovation or even an economically desirable one, we will see that the principle that competing employers do not hire from each other is a vital component of Japan's present employment system. It immediately explains one of the most puzzling aspects of the present system: the Japanese workers' apparent lack of interest in changing jobs. The key reason why workers do not change jobs is not loyalty, as Westerners often imagine, but lack of opportunities.

Apart from a few early experiments with employment cartels, corporate Japan continued to operate a Western-style hire-and-fire system into the 1920s. Things began to change after 1919 when a group of businessmen and bureaucrats founded the Kyocho Kai, a labor economics think tank whose name translates as the Association of Harmonious Cooperation. The late 1910s was a time when harmonious cooperation was in notably short supply in Japanese labor relations. Japan had just suffered a series of bitter strikes in steel, shipbuilding, and mining. Moreover, many employers were troubled by astoundingly high labor turnover rates — as high as 100 percent a year in some industries, according to the labor scholar Mikio Sumiya.

Much of the detail of the Kyocho Kai's work is unclear. What is clear is that the Kyocho Kai's mission had the backing of Japan's supreme economic leaders. One indication of this was that its leading light in its early years was Eiichi Shibusawa. As we saw in Chapter Two, Shibusawa was perhaps the most important of the original nineteenth century architects of Japan's economic growth. He had begun his career at the Ministry of Finance in the 1870s and had gone on to found hundreds of major enterprises including Dai-Ichi Kangyo Bank.

As the Kyocho Kai deliberated during the 1920s and 1930s, Japanese labor relations underwent a sea change. The first noticeable development was that Japanese industry's labor turnover rates suddenly plunged. It seems certain that the Kyocho Kai succeeded in winning general acceptance for the textile industry's principle that rival employers should refrain from hiring from each other.

Many large enterprises adopted a practice of recruiting all new employees in one batch each year, a practice that is now almost universal in corporate Japan. Meanwhile the government imposed controls to restrict the activities of traditional Western-style industry-wide unions. This paved the way for the widespread emergence of company unions in the 1930s.

Then, a few years before Pearl Harbor, the civil servants moved to reduce labor turnover almost to zero in many industries by imposing national regulations governing job mobility. Officials were apparently concerned that competition among employers in a tightening labor market was disrupting Japan's effort to build up war industries. Employers were subject to a general ban on poaching labor from each other, and all exceptions had to be authorized on a case-by-case basis by labor regulators. To be sure of compliance, the regulators also banned individual skilled workers from changing jobs except where their current employer had given explicit approval.

The next milestone came at the end of World War II. The civil servants used the power vacuum left by the demise of the army and the zaibatsus to apply the finishing touches to Japan's labor revolution. One of their boldest and least noticed moves was to narrow the pay gap dramatically between the country's top earners and ordinary workers. This represented a delayed victory for the militant New Bureaucrats, who had argued in the 1930s for tight upper limits on incomes but had been been blocked by the zaibatsu families from implementing the concept.

After the war, officials achieved their egalitarian dream by the simple expedient of tightly controlling salary increases for top earners at a time of rampant inflation. In the tradition of Japanese leadership, the top bureaucrats made the biggest sacrifices. Before the war they had been paid more than seventy times the maximum wage for a police officer. By the 1950s, this multiple had been cut to just five times. Top industrial executives took similar reductions in their real incomes. Since then Japan's top decision-makers have remained remarkably modestly paid and, as we will see, in defiance of Reaganite logic, the fact that total salaries are tightly compressed in Japan is yet another reason for the country's success.

The bureaucrats also made another crucial move toward egalitarianism by promoting a vast expansion in university education.

In the immediate postwar period, the government moved to clamp down on job mobility via the Employment Security Law of 1947. This gave officials case-by-case powers to block employers from advertising for labor and from hiring any worker whose job change necessitated a change of residence.

The comprehensive curbs on job mobility obviously strengthened the hand of employers in resisting demands for wage increases. But they were balanced by regulations making it virtually impossible for employers to fire workers. Here stands revealed the reason why Japanese employers persistently refuse to break with the lifetime employment system: they provide job security not because they want to but because they have to. Again, this principle flouts Western ideas of efficient management. And it is one of the true secrets of Japan's success.

The aftermath of war provided Japanese employers with an opportunity to roll out a pay system in which workers were rewarded for seniority. From the point of view of employers hiring soldiers returning from the war, paying workers bonuses commensurate with length of service was a godsend because it kept a cap on labor costs at a time when money was in very short supply. And workers had no choice but to accept this arrangement because, with six million soldiers and colonists returning from Japan's forfeited overseas empire after the war, there was enormous competition for the available jobs.

The result was that by the early 1950s the full modern Japanese labor system was installed at most major Japanese employers. But why does this strange system work? It is time to look at the system's hidden advantages.

Advantage One: efficient innovation

Japanese corporations have a well-deserved reputation for the speed with which they climb the technology curve. But what is the secret of their success? A big part of the answer is the Japanese labor system.

Consider how valuable the lifetime employment system is in winning worker cooperation for the introduction of productivity-enhancing new technologies. Because Japanese workers enjoy lifetime job guarantees, they see no downside risk in helping their employers improve productivity. In fact, they embrace new technology because they know it will enhance their company's future and their own jobs. When productivity improves, workers can be reassigned to different work, typically making innovative or improved products. Japan's workers and management are thus united in the effort to boost output — and higher output, of course, is otherwise known as economic growth. The American hire-and-fire system sets workers and managers at loggerheads over productivity-improving technology. American workers are naturally suspicious of new technology because they know from experience that American employers often use such technology to cut jobs. Although unions in the United States have long been blamed for slowing America's productivity growth, their obstructionism is entirely rational.

Perhaps the most notable example of how lifetime employment has helped Japanese employers improve productivity is in automation. Whereas in the United States robots are seen as stealing jobs, Japanese workers are delighted for robots to take over dirty, dangerous, and repetitive jobs such as pressing and painting. In Japan, robots are often treated by grateful human workers as part of the corporate family, even to the point where they are named after favorite female singers and movie stars. It is not surprising, therefore, that with only half America's work force, Japan has three times as many robots in operation.

If a corporation is to innovate, it must train its workers to handle ever more sophisticated tasks. Here again the Japanese labor system provides Japanese employers with a vital advantage in that they can undertake expensive training programs confident that they will enjoy a good return on their investment. By contrast, American employers increasingly consider training a dubious investment, because in the American system trained workers are free to take their skills to rival employers. And even if such workers do not leave, they often feel they are entitled to pay raises reflecting their higher skill levels. A recent survey found that American corporations are only one-seventh as likely as their Japanese counterparts to provide new recruits with formal training, and overall they invested only about one-quarter as much as the Japanese in training.

Many Western governments have tried to create a public sector solution to the training problem. They have had little success. For one thing, governments cannot hope to provide the most advanced skills because such skills are commercial secrets known only to certain advanced employers. The result, as Ross Perot has pointed out, is that many government retraining programs merely "teach people to make buggy whips." As far as advanced industries are concerned,

there is no substitute for employers doing their own in-house training.

The Japanese labor system also helps spur innovation by encouraging corporate Japan to invest in research and development. The key
factor here is that thanks to the no-poaching rule, Japanese companies know that their expensively acquired research and development
secrets will not leak to competitors via the job market. Such losses are
a problem for American corporations, particularly in the crucial case
of innovative new production techniques that are hard to patent but
easy for a rival employer to acquire by headhunting a key employee.
American corporations often miss out on vital research and development breakthroughs because their key technologists leave to set up
venture capital operations with the help of secrets acquired before
they left.

Since Japanese corporations can expect to keep more of the rewards from research and development than their American competitors, they naturally do more of it. As of the early 1990s, Japan's
commercial research and development was running at about 3 percent of gross national product versus just 1.6 percent for the United
States.

Another way the Japanese employment system fosters innovation
is by providing an appropriately robust managerial structure that
enables Japanese corporations to undertake the vast investments required to maintain their monopolistic lead in advanced industries. As
we have already noted, Japan's giant electronics corporations now
spend as much as $2 billion to build a single factory — the equivalent
of one-quarter of the yearly sales of Intel Corporation, America's
most successful electronics company. To undertake innovation on this
scale, corporate Japan must be able to count on a high degree of
accountability from its managers and workers — and this is something that, as we will see, comes naturally in Japan's employment
system.

Advantage Two: good management

The high quality of Japanese management is rightly considered to be
a major source of Japan's success. But why is Japanese management
so good? The answer lies mainly in the long-term accountability built

into the lifetime employment system. A Japanese manager knows that the decisions he makes today remain permanently on his record and he may be asked to account for them many years from now. He cannot simply sweep problems under the carpet.

Long-term accountability has never been a more important component of good management than it is today. The complex modern economy provides managers with more temptations than ever to garner short-term profits at the expense of a company's long-term interests. It's easy, for instance, for a production manager to meet profit targets by secretly shaving the quality of inputs. Such tactics do not improve the economy's efficiency, and in the long run they boomerang on any company that uses them. But under the American hire-and-fire system, individual executives can often not only get away with such corner-cutting but actually advance their career by doing so. By the time the problems come to light, most people involved will have moved on, including not only the offender but his counterparts in customer companies.

To try to make sure executives focus on a company's long-term interests, American companies are increasingly having to install elaborate systems to monitor managers. Japanese corporations have no need for such clumsy and costly systems because their managers are largely self-monitoring.

The lifetime employment system also enables Japanese corporations to groom prospective executives for many years. For the chief executive job, for instance, a Japanese corporation generally identifies candidates decades in advance and gives them a thorough grounding in the skills necessary to head the company. In particular, such candidates usually are given substantial hands-on experience in production. By contrast, top American corporate executives are skilled mainly in financial accounting, law, or marketing — qualifications the Japanese consider of little help in promoting the basic agenda of a growth economy, which is to produce more goods each year.

The lifetime employment system creates a unity of interest between individual managers and their companies. Japanese managers know that the path to personal success is to dedicate themselves single-mindedly to the success of their companies. In the West, things are not so simple. Because Western managers face the ever-present danger of losing their jobs in a takeover or a discontinuation of operations, they are unwise if they trust their entire future to their present employer.

Instead they must hedge their bets: they should make themselves visible in the job market by attending industry conferences, speaking at seminars, giving interviews to the media, and networking with headhunters. Often a good strategy is to curry favor with supplier companies in the hope that the compliment will be returned in an hour of need. Executives who are savvy in the art of personal advancement may even find it pays to feed confidential information to management consulting firms working for competitors.

Skeptical Western observers often say that Japanese managers are not ten feet tall. That is, of course, true — but Japanese managers work in an employment system that towers over its Western alternative.

Advantage Three: a spirit of cooperation

Wage negotiation is a notable annual ritual in Japanese industry. Demonstrating workers often fill the sky with red Marxist banners. Labor leaders use language so fiery they would risk arrest in a country like Britain or the United States. Sometimes a mob of slogan-chanting workers will corner a top executive in his office and hold him hostage for hours.

If management still has not gotten the message, the union will have no hesitation in resorting to the ultimate deterrent — the strike weapon. But here things take a distinctly Japanese turn. A Japanese union's idea of a strike is a one-hour work stoppage timed for the lunch break: workers indignantly put down their tools at twelve noon and don't report back for work until one! If the union has planned things right, the "strike" will not have cost the company a single unit of lost production.

This sort of theater of the absurd is one reason Westerners don't take Japan seriously. Underneath the pantomime, however, is a great deal of uncommon common sense. Because the Japanese corporate system has been deliberately arranged to align Japanese workers' interests with their employers, a striking Japanese worker generally feels he's striking against his own long-term future. He knows the company will be left weakened and may not have the capital to stay the course in the technology race. That in turn means lower pay raises and less in the kitty for retirement benefits. In the worst cases, it can bring on the company's collapse, a true disaster for workers in Japan because suitable alternative jobs are hard to find.

Observers unfamiliar with Japanese history assume that the docility of Japanese labor stems from Japanese culture. But in the words of the Japanese-American economics scholar Robert Ozaki, this assumption is "nonsense." As he pointed out in *Human Capitalism,* as recently as the late 1940s Japan's labor relations were notable for widespread confrontation, chaos, and even violence. In fact, labor relations remained tense in many Japanese corporations up to the 1960s.

A key factor in Japan's latter-day labor peace is that by the late 1950s workers began to recognize that capitalism had been abolished in Japan. Not only had it become clear that the zaibatsu families were permanently marginalized, but new entrepreneurs such as Soichiro Honda, founder of Honda Motor, were proclaiming a new gospel of ownerless enterprise in which the founding entrepreneur was merely just another worker. Almost from the start Soichiro Honda's stake in his company was dwarfed by the shareholdings of Japan's great banks and investment institutions acting for the national interest. The pattern was similar at Sony, Matsushita Electric, Toyota Motor, and other supposedly enterpreneurial companies in the forefront of the Japanese Miracle.

Thus the them-and-us divide between management and workers began to disappear. Because the workers had been given lifetime job security, they, more than the shareholders, were the real beneficiaries from an enterprise's existence (after all, wages typically account for about fifty times more than the tiny dividends paid to shareholders in Japan). In all but name, workers became the real owners of most major businesses, a fact that was forthrightly acknowledged in Tetsuo Sakiya's authorized book on the rise of Honda Motor.

That bogey of American labor, the grasping chief executive officer who is "incentivized" by huge stock options, is unknown in Japan. Top Japanese corporate executives are generally salaried employees like everyone else, and they do not have stock options — a fact that probably reflects an informal prohibition imposed by the Finance Ministry. Thus they are under no pressure to make penny-wise, pound-foolish cuts in staffing to manipulate short-term profits. And when they call for pay restraint from the work force, as they do in bad times, they act in the role of the workers' leaders, not the workers' opponents.

Top executives in Japan are modestly compensated by international standards. According to a *Business Week* survey in 1993, chief executives of top Japanese corporations were paid only $870,000 on average versus $3.8 million on average for their American counterparts. On an after-tax basis, a typical chief executive in Japan is paid only about ten times more than the most junior member of staff and just four times the salary of middle-aged workers. In corporate America this latter multiple can be as much as one hundred times, a gap that Fujitsu Chairman Takuma Yamamoto recently characterized as "absurd."

It is sometimes assumed that Japan's low executive compensation is simply a manifestation of the strong egalitarianism that runs through East Asian culture. After all, Confucius said: "In a country well governed, poverty is something to be ashamed of. In a country badly governed, wealth is something to be ashamed of." But, as we have seen, Japan has not always been egalitarian.

The Japanese economic system's policy of keeping a tight lid on top salaries is the linchpin of a highly systematized salary structure in which managerial people are generally paid and promoted according to seniority rather than competence. (Blue-collar workers are streamed separately but are also paid and promoted on a seniority basis.) In the Japanese promotion race, merit becomes a decisive factor only in the case of senior positions that become available toward the end of a manager's career.

The systemization even extends beyond individual corporations. Major corporations in the same industry typically pay nearly identical salary scales. In the auto industry, for instance, the starting salary for graduates recruited in 1993 was ¥194,000 a month at all five of the biggest companies — Toyota, Honda, Nissan, Mitsubishi, and Mazda. Every Japanese corporation discloses its starting pay rate in Japanese financial reference books, providing a signaling system for young graduates sizing up prospective employers.

By systematizing pay and promotion, Japanese corporations save themselves the enormous transaction-cost burden of setting salaries on a person-by-person basis. Given the no-poaching rule of Japanese employment cartels, Japan's egalitarian managerial salary system is easy to maintain because individual managers whose salaries do not fully reward their talents must make the best of it because they generally cannot find alternative jobs elsewhere. Surely such managers become discouraged? Not in the least. All Reaganite wisdom to the contrary, pay is not the only thing people work for, particularly in Japan, where public opinion looks askance at displays of conspicuous consumption. The respect of one's peers and the hope of becoming chief executive are usually much more important incentives for a rising Japanese manager than mere money. (It is interesting to note that those American economists who advocate huge salaries for top managers are themselves usually quite modestly paid: they should know that pay is not the only incentive because in their own case they would rather have a Nobel Prize than the huge compensation packages that they could probably earn on Wall Street.)

The primary rationale of the salary system is to foster teamwork among managers and to eliminate a possible source of friction and jealousy between close colleagues. The system also makes it easy for top management to win workers' cooperation for postings in different departments, a factor that explains not only the remarkable speed with which Japanese corporations can restructure themselves in a crisis but also a generally high level of communication and cooperation between different departments.

The idea that a person should be promoted according to his seniority rather than his competence is to Western eyes one of the strangest aspects of the Japanese employment system. We will look at the Japanese management incentive system later, but for now the point is that a seniority-driven promotions process is a powerful force for cooperation between the generations. Although Westerners argue that competent young people are blocked from realizing their potential in the Japanese employment system, the truth is generally the opposite. Because senior managers are fully protected against being leapfrogged in the promotion race by the younger generation, they are much more likely than senior managers in the West to mentor their staff. In fact, Japan's senior managers improve their own chances of securing one of the ultimate top jobs if they have a reputation for getting the best out of their juniors. Japan's system of open-plan offices and shared responsibility ensures that even incompetent and insecure bosses rarely hinder the flow of ideas from below for long.

In-house cooperation is also fostered by the dynamics of the lifetime employment system. When managers know they are fated to spend the rest of their working lives with each other, they take care not to make enemies. Moreover, an attitude of cooperation with colleagues and with other departments serves to enhance a person's promotion prospects. In any case, individuals working within the lifetime employment system learn quickly that they maximize their own effectiveness by trading favors with colleagues. One example is information-sharing. If, for instance, a Japanese salesman discovers that a particular customer has increased its purchasing budget, he generally has every reason to tell relevant colleagues. He thereby gains their respect, and they will return the favor in due course (because they too want to build a reputation for teamwork). In the West, a salesman is likely to hide such knowledge because healthy reciprocal information-sharing systems cannot strike root in the shifting sands of the hire-and-fire system.

This spirit of cooperation fostered by the lifetime employment system is one reason why Japan's largest corporate organizations generally function more efficiently and purposefully than their Western counterparts.

Maintaining discipline

Perhaps the biggest misconception about Japanese labor economics in the West is that lifetime employment gives workers a free ride for life. Japanese employers supposedly lack any means to discipline work-shy or negligent employees. This could hardly be further from the truth. Employees in the Japanese system are under far more consistent pressure to perform than their counterparts in the West.

In the words of the management consultant William J. Best, Japanese managers are "authoritarian, almost dictatorial." This comment seems to run counter to the image in the West of Japanese managers as consensus seekers. As Best points out, the role of consensus decision-making in Japanese corporations is much exaggerated. Japanese executives consult the lower ranks only on matters where consultation makes sense, such as ways to increase the efficiency of work routines on the factory floor. By contrast, in matters such as work performance targets, executives set a tough pace, and their instructions are not subject to second-guessing from below.

One of the most persuasive disciplinary tools in the Japanese system is early retirement. Generally, the poorer a person's long-run performance is, the more likely it is that he will be asked to take early retirement in his fifties or perhaps even his late forties. This is a much feared penalty because it means that he misses out on the best earning years of his life. Here stands revealed part of the rationale for the seniority pay system: seniority pay is a form of deferred pay, but deferred pay that one receives in full only if one succeeds in staying the course until scheduled retirement age. Officially, early retirees leave voluntarily, but in reality, most do so under threat of coercion. They know that if they resist, their employer has ways of making things uncomfortable. But if they go quietly, they can expect to get a significant termination payment and, more important, vital help in establishing a second career somewhere else. In most cases, large corporations find jobs for their early retirees in closely associated, if less prestigious, companies.

In 1992 and 1993 the Western press began publicizing cases of early retirement at Japanese corporations as if they were something new. Yet early retirement has always been a crucial feature of the employment system. In earlier decades, employers in textiles and ship-building had implemented early retirement programs as large as anything seen in the early 1990s. In the steel industry alone, a total of 114,000 jobs were cut between 1974 and 1987 with the help of attrition and early retirements.

Several other aspects of the Japanese employment system also serve to enforce discipline among workers. A notable dynamic is peer pressure. Workers in a Japanese corporation generally function as part of a clearly identified team, and assignments are given to the team rather than to individuals. As Robert Ozaki noted, workers urge one another on in maintaining the collective pace of work. Japanese society has a sliding scale for punishing people who are not team players, and persistent offenders risk ostracism by their peers. This peer pressure helps explain the apparently irrational behavior of Japanese workers in not claiming their vacation entitlements: an individual worker feels obligated not to claim his rights if this would impair the group's chances of gaining a large salary bonus.

For the worst cases, Japanese corporations find ways to harass an individual shirker into resigning. Typically, offenders are assigned to the *mado giwa zoku* — the tribe by the window. This denotes a special dunce's corner in which Japanese companies place certified pariahs. The term's significance derives from the fact that in Japan's huge open-plan offices, the further away one is from the center of the floor, the less important one's position or section. Members of the mado giwa zoku are immediately recognizable as such, and this alone is generally enough to shame them into resigning. If it isn't, the company can step up the pressure. One window-seat worker in 1993 was reported to have been ordered to write daily essays expressing his "reflections on the day's events." In another case, some unwanted software writers were sent out to the country to chop wood.

In a country where there are few jobs outside for those who cannot hack it within their present corporations, punishments like this get attention.

Hidden checks and balances

The Japanese labor system contains several other hidden checks and balances without which it would not be an effective tool for employers.

Take the supposed rigidity imposed on employers by the general ban on making layoffs. In reality, several safeguards are built into the system to provide considerable flexibility and allow the economy to adjust smoothly to ever-changing conditions. Corporate Japan's system of paying large twice-yearly salary bonuses, for instance, is an important shock absorber. In bad times these bonuses can be cut or even eliminated. This allows corporations to reduce annual pay levels by as much as 40 percent. This margin of flexibility is so wide that few corporations ever need to take full advantage of it.

In 1993 the Japanese auto industry made bonus cuts for the first time in decades, but the cuts were so small that they merely offset increases in basic pay, so that total compensation in 1993 was roughly the same as in 1992. The fact that the automakers could have further reduced pay levels by one-third or more was clearly a factor in the underlying confidence of the industry that it could ride out the world recession and the West's tightening quotas without having to make layoffs.

Another hidden element of flexibility built into the system is that the general legal prohibition on layoffs is subject to an important exception: if a company can convince the authorities that without layoffs its whole future will be jeopardized, it can usually gain exemption from the no-layoff law. Ordinarily this loophole is available only to small employers who are thereby allowed to operate more or less on a hire-and-fire basis. Usually, the lower a company ranks in the keiretsu system, the more closely its labor policies approximate to American-style hire-and-fire. Many of Japan's hire-and-fire employers supply simple subcomponents to companies at higher levels in their keiretsu. The big companies at the top of the keiretsu can thus count on their suppliers' labor flexibility as a swing factor in maintaining the keiretsu's viability in tough times.

Another nuance of the system that provides considerable flexibility is that many corporations maintain a large pool of low-grade workers who are specifically denied employment security under a legal loophole providing for "temporary" employment. Although in practice such workers are rarely fired, the fact that they can be fired affords corporate planners a further insurance policy against bad economic conditions.

These safety valves apart, the system aims to provide stable long-term employment for virtually all higher grade workers in Japan. It is backed by tough laws requiring employers to pay significant compensation to any permanent staff member who is involuntarily terminated. The strength of these laws can be gauged from the fact that some staffers at Japan Air Lines recently were paid as much as $600,000 each to leave.

To help maintain jobs through economic downturns and structural changes, the government operates a system of subsidies for employers. The program pays employers up to $85 per worker for each day that an employee is idle or in a training program. As of May 1993, such payments were being made in the case of 3.7 million workers, most of whom were probably being retrained.

The government also functions as a catalyst in enabling large employers in declining industries to diversify smoothly into more promising activities where they can redeploy surplus workers. In the 1960s and 1970s, for instance, the government helped Japan's once mighty textile companies shift into new industries such as cosmetics, pharmaceuticals, and so-called new materials (by which is meant high-technology materials such as advanced ceramics used in jet engines). The government in effect used its considerable regulatory powers to reserve certain promising niches in these new industries for the textile companies.

The egalitarianism built into the Japanese employment system pays a hidden economic dividend in allowing corporate Japan to pursue tremendous economies of scale in manufacturing. Virtually everyone in Japan counts as middle-class by Western standards; thus manufacturers key their product design and quality single-mindedly to middle-class tastes. This one-size-fits-all ethos of Japan's consumer markets is easy to ridicule but the tremendous economies of scale of Japan's home market are a key reason why the Japanese are generally the world's low-cost producers in any field in which they compete. The significance of this is best seen by comparison with Britain. The British see their ability to make luxury products such as Rolls-Royces and Jaguars as an economic strength, but in Japanese eyes it is symptomatic of economic weakness in that Britain's class structure has left British manufacturers an inadequate home market for the middle-market products on which Japan has built its growth.

Perhaps the most ingenious aspect of Japanese labor economics is the extent to which the main elements of it are mutually reinforcing. The lifetime employment system, for instance, bolsters the company union system. Because employees don't expect to be fired, they have no need for industrywide unions and are content to entrust their negotiating power to company unions.

The employment cartels' requirement for companies not to hire from each other is a hidden support for the lifetime employment system: it protects employers against the loss of their most talented and productive workers. By contrast, in the modern American employment system where aggressive employers are allowed to hire away their rivals' best people, any company that offers career-long employment security finds its payroll gradually silts up with subpar performers. (In fact, the increasing aggressiveness of headhunters in American industry is a key reason why major American corporations have one by one backed away from their former implicit guarantees of job security. Previously a sort of employer etiquette existed in many industries in which it was considered inappropriate to aggressively recruit from competitors.)

A special nuance of Japan's seniority pay system discourages employers from firing people in a time of recession. This nuance stems from an important regulation buried in the fine print of Japanese employment law banning any company that fires permanent workers from hiring any new workers. Because new workers are seriously underpaid under the seniority rules, they are highly profitable employees from an employer's point of view, and therefore employers will take care not to be cut off from this source of profit.

Perhaps the most profound self-reinforcing effect of the Japanese labor system is the way that lifetime employment helps stabilize the Japanese economy in times of recession. To an individual employer, the no-firing rule seems undesirable but, seen from the nation's point of view, the rule pays off in damping the downswing in the business cycle. In the Western system, by contrast, workers fired in a recession necessarily cut back their consumption and this throws other workers out of a job. It also burdens the national social security system. Japanese planners believe, not unreasonably, that workers contribute more to total national output if they are in jobs rather than in dole queues.

In times of economic boom also, the Japanese labor system again proves its superiority because the company union system keeps workers docile and suppresses pressure for inflationary pay increases.

When we add up all the fine print, a picture emerges of a carefully organized and quite self-sustaining system — a system that is the very antithesis of the cultural hangover it has long been portrayed in the West.

The reckoning

We have seen that the Japanese labor system delivers many benefits. But, as Western economists point out, the system also entails various costs arising out of its inflexibilities. Any assessment of the balance between benefits and costs is necessarily intuitive, but most observers who have seen the system firsthand believe Western economists tend to exaggerate the costs.

These economists imagine that Japanese corporations are full of unfirable people with little work to do. In reality, when a Japanese company has underemployed people on its hands, it is forced to find new work for them. It is just common sense: if a board of directors is forbidden by labor regulators from firing workers, it will naturally seek to boost its revenues by putting its workers to work making new products. The natural bias of the Japanese system is therefore toward producing more goods, whereas in the American system it is toward cutting jobs. Each is a valid way to boost the productivity of individual workers. But the Japanese approach is more effective in boosting gross national product.

One critical consequence is that, in sharp contrast to the United States, most new jobs in Japan are created by large corporations. The architects of Japan's labor system take the view that on average a company like Hitachi will be more efficient in creating productive new jobs than, say, a Silicon Valley start-up. Hitachi knows its employees' strengths and weaknesses so it has a fundamental economic advantage in redeploying them into those jobs where they will be most productive. Its workers will hit the ground running as an integrated, well-trained, and well-balanced team.

Hitachi also scores over an entrepreneurial start-up because its financial muscle and its worldwide marketing machine allow it to think big and long-term from the outset. Perhaps most important, Hitachi has generally better information about the world of advanced manufacturing than, say, the small venture capital companies on which America has recently relied to create high-quality new jobs. Using its own intelligence resources and those of other private and public institutions in Japan, Hitachi is well informed on 1) the existing competitors in the new field; 2) the strengths of those competitors; 3) where important components can best be sourced: 4) the progress to date in research and development in relevant technologies; and 5) which technical partners can provide vital know-how.

The lifetime employment system forces Japan's major corporations to keep up a fast pace of new investment, which depresses profits in the short term. From the point of view of the nation as a whole, however, this drawback is more than offset by savings in social security costs thanks to a consistently low rate of unemployment — generally less than half the American rate and less than one-third European rates. As always, the ultimate concern in Japan is GNP: a nation maximizes production by devising ways to maximize the number of people working in productive jobs.

Another disadvantage that is often exaggerated by Western economists is the Japanese system's curbing of individual freedom by limiting workers' opportunities to change jobs. This is less troubling in a Confucian society than it would be in the West, because Confucianism attaches a lower value to individual freedom and a higher value to long-term relationships.

From the point of view of the larger economy, the fact that workers cannot switch employers is not a major problem because most workers in lifetime jobs are employed by major corporations boasting large internal labor markets. The internal labor market in Hitachi is a case in point. A very high proportion of Hitachi's 325,000 jobs are for scientists and engineers. Thus a young scientist or engineer at Hitachi is presented with as exciting a range of possible uses of his skills as an American probably has in, say, the state of Massachusetts. In the case of smaller employers, the internal market in skills is narrower, but such employers belong to a keiretsu and can often contract out their surplus workers to other members of their keiretsu. In fact the flexibility can be stretched even further: competing companies in Japan sometimes lend each other workers on a contractual basis while the workers remain technically on the books of the original employer. (Ironically, this practice has often been interpreted by the Western press as evidence that the entire system is breaking down.)

Another much-criticized aspect of Japanese labor economics is the seniority pay system. Because companies necessarily are bound to pay many older workers more than the "going rate," Western commentators consider seniority pay to be inefficient. But this is to view the matter in too narrow a focus. For both the worker and the employer, the relationship is a long-term one: seniority bonuses are a form of deferred pay and they balance the fact that employees are paid artificially low wages early in their career. It is no more reasonable to suggest that Toyota fire its expensive older workers than it is to suggest General Motors renege on pensions to retirees.

The American press often argues that the seniority pay system penalizes Japanese exporters as a group in competing in international markets. This is an obvious misconception: what matters in international competition is a corporation's *average* cost of labor and the level of the country's currency on foreign exchange markets. Even if Japanese corporations are forced to pay larger seniority bonuses because of the graying of the work force, this is merely a cost of doing business in Japan — one of myriad local factors that exchange rates are supposed to adjust for automatically. (The world currency market is, of course, the most sensitive market of them all.)

Clearly if an employer has a disproportionately large number of highly paid older workers compared to its Japanese competitors, it may have a competitiveness problem. In practice, however, Japanese companies are careful to pace their recruiting over the years to avoid this problem. (Similar employers in Japan usually have similar age profiles: the average age of employees at Toshiba, Hitachi, and Mitsubishi Electric, for instance, were recently 36.8, 37.2, and 38.1 years respectively.)

Westerners also consider the system inefficient because subpar workers cannot easily be fired. But remember that the aim of Japanese industrial policy is to maximize the economy's total output of useful goods and services. Seen from this point of view, to give employers the power to fire subpar performers does no good because these people will probably be subpar no matter where they work.

If the nation is going to maximize its gross national product, such workers necessarily must be employed *somewhere* — thus employers as a group cannot hope that all their employees will be above-average. For each corporation to strive to play the hire-and-fire game in an endless effort to try to improve its staff quality merely generates gratuitous transaction costs. Such costs are often much larger than people realize: in the American aerospace industry, for instance, it was estimated a few years ago to cost about $57,000 to replace a typical junior engineer. In light of labor turnover rates in Silicon Valley that sometimes approach 50 percent a year, the Japanese electronics industry clearly enjoys a sizable advantage in its low labor-market transaction costs.

In assessing the overall merits of the Japanese system, it is useful to remember the group-versus-individual calculus of the bus route example mentioned in Chapter One. A bus route in which the stops are preassigned by the bus company is only a minor inconvenience for passengers as individuals (they cannot stop the bus exactly where it is convenient for them) but it pays off big for the group as a whole (the bus moves faster). The demerits of the Japanese employment system are mainly demerits for individual workers and individual employers. The merits of the system are group merits that accrue mainly to the nation as a whole, most notably easy technological innovation, good management, and a spirit of cooperation.

The Western mind is notoriously blind to the idea of group merits. But for Japan's leaders, looking for group merits is second nature. Group merits do exist and, in the case of the Japanese employment system, corporate Japan reaps great advantages from recognizing and exploiting them.

A system with a future

Most observers who have seen the Japanese labor system firsthand sense it is superior to the West's hire-and-fire system. One such observer is Frank Gibney, who for many years ran a major American subsidiary in Japan. Gibney has argued that lifetime employment makes particularly good business sense in such knowledge-driven industries as semiconductors, where accumulated technological expertise is at a premium.

Another noted expert on the system is the management consultant James Abegglen, a veteran Tokyo resident who invented the term "lifetime employment" in a pioneer account of the system published in 1958. From the start he has believed the system has been an advantage for Japan in global competition. As he points out, if the system were not efficient, the Japanese would long ago have abandoned it.

Perhaps the most interesting comment on the system in recent years has come from the top Beijing-based Japan-watcher Zhu Shaowen. In an interview in 1993, Zhu held up the Japanese employment system as a key reason why Japan, not the United States, will be the model for the new world order. Zhu's comment was the more notable because it coincided with a renewed wave of reports in the Western press erroneously predicting the end of lifetime employment. Why has this myth been propagated with such vigor in recent years? Why indeed.

Reports of the imminent breakdown of the system have been a hardy perennial for so long that they are a standing joke among Japanologists. As the Tokyo-based American businessman T. F. M. Adams recorded as far back as 1969, such reports were already then a cliché of misinformed Western media comment on Japan. In reality, the Japanese labor system has grown visibly stronger in the twenty-five years since Western correspondents started writing its obituary. It's interesting to note that the most counterintuitive aspect of the system, seniority pay, is now more marked than ever: a recent survey of major manufacturing companies found that workers in their fifties are now paid about 2.6 times as much as workers in their twenties, up from 2.2 times in the early 1970s.

The myth of the system's imminent collapse seems to gain currency at times when the United States is suffering particularly badly from unemployment. This seems to be part of a larger pattern in which American journalists assume that anything that is happening in the United States will eventually spread to Japan (the United States is assumed to be running ahead of Japan in social and economic evolution).

Reporting of Japanese labor economics in the early 1990s repeated mistakes propagated during America's large recessions of the mid-1970s and early 1980s. In 1982, for instance, the American Jon Woronoff had stridently predicted the Japanese labor system's imminent collapse. In *Japan's Wasted Workers,* he reported that corporate Japan was searching for "an orderly transition to a new system"; in the meantime, corporations were supposedly slashing recruitment. Although Woronoff's analysis was quickly shown to be wide of the mark, his arguments were repeated almost verbatim by American correspondents in the early 1990s .

Correspondents from some of the most respected publications in the English language even went so far as to suggest in the early 1990s the system had already collapsed — at least at specific corporations such as JVC, Nissan, and NTT, which allegedly had broken with the system by laying off large numbers of workers.

Even by the normal standards of Western press coverage of Japan, however, such reports were remarkable for their outright mistatements of verifiable facts. There were no involuntary layoffs at JVC, Nissan, NTT, or any other significant companies. In fact, no significant employer in Japan broke with the lifetime employment system in the early 1990s.

Why did so many correspondents get it wrong? One factor was corporate Japan's public relations agenda. Corporate Japan has long been reluctant to acknowledge explicitly the strength of workers' job security rights in Japan. One reason is the anomalous status of foreign workers. In recent years, many Americans and Europeans in particular have been hired in a white-collar capacity by major Japanese corporations in Japan. The trend is a gesture of goodwill toward Western talk of "globalization," but corporate Japan would prefer the trend did not go too far. Specifically, it probably does not want foreigners in Japan to claim equality in employment rights with Japanese workers. Corporate Japan would be embarrassed if, for instance, foreign workers pressed job security claims in Japanese courts. Moreover, the Japanese government would hardly be pleased if Washington were to make an issue of the unequal status of American workers in Japan.

Another problem inhibiting full disclosure is that corporate Japan made all-too-real job cuts in the United States and Europe in the early 1990s (including 112,000 in 1993 alone in the United States). If Americans and Europeans had been told the truth that there were no significant forced layoffs in Japan in the early 1990s, corporate Japan might have had a bigger political problem making job cuts overseas.

Then there is the problem of Japan's trade relations with the United States. Japan's employment strategy stands as silent evidence that the Japanese government is not committed to Western-style free trade. To maintain lifetime employment, the Japanese government must make sure that Japan's importing arrangements are structured to shield Japanese employers from the wilder swings of the unstable world trading system.

Under these circumstances, therefore, it is hardly a surprise that in the early 1990s Japan Inc.'s English-language public relations efforts did little to quell Western reporters' speculation about the end of lifetime employment. One think tank, for instance, said that many Japanese employers were saddled with two million "in-house unemployed," workers for whom there was said to be no work. Meanwhile, surveys were published showing that many Japanese workers wanted to change jobs. Some employers even talked tough about the need for restructuring and cost-cutting.

Lacking the language and intent on proving that Japanese economic practices are "dysfunctional," Western publications jumped to the wrong conclusions. Led by the *Wall Street Journal* and the *Economist,* they vied with one another in printing comments from anonymous sources suggesting the lifetime employment system was doomed. It was a classic example of the madness of crowds that often infects the Western press in Tokyo. In the end, even the *New York Times,* which has generally been one of the most reliable American newspapers on Japan over the years, was swept along in the mania.

For long-term residents of Japan, it was déjà vu all over again. They knew that reports of "in-house unemployed" were a hardy perennial of the English-language public relations industry. As far back as 1978, in a previous high-yen "crisis," the Nikkeiren organization had published a survey indicating that the number of "in-house unemployed" in Japan totaled 2.5 million workers. In 1979, there had been a report from the Economic Planning Agency saying that hidden unemployment was rife among married women. As for surveys showing that Japanese workers want to move jobs, they are a constant feature of the news in Tokyo.

To be fair, some correspondents afterwards set the record right, most notably the *Economist*'s Christopher Wood, who in a book in 1994 corrected his 1992 report that Nissan had made layoffs. By contrast, the *Wall Street Journal* continued to compound the confusion. In reporting on Japanese employment in 1992 and 1993, the *Journal* presented two contradictory versions of the facts. In one version, which was presented in most of the *Journal*'s reports, the system was portrayed as a cultural tradition that was now breaking down. But in another version, the *Journal* reported that the system could not break down because it was enforced by government regulation. What was so interesting was that the newspaper went on in each case to predict disastrous consequences for the Japanese economy. Reports that said the system was breaking down went on to predict great unemployment and a long slump. And reports saying the system was holding firm also predicted a long slump, in this case because huge corporations were allegedly heading for bankruptcy as they were hobbled from competing with the West's rapidly downsizing companies.

Perhaps the most significant aspect of recent press coverage was something that was not said: correspondents offered no explanation for why the press has for thirty years been confounded every time it has predicted the employment system's demise. The nearest thing to an acknowledgment of the anomaly has come from the *Economist*. It conceded in 1993 that lifetime employment may have made sense in the Japanese economy's fast-growth phase after World War II (although, of course, its correspondents never said this at the time) but, in a world of downsizing corporations, "the cleverer Japanese firms know that lifetime employment is finished."

The truth is precisely the opposite. Lifetime employment makes more sense now than ever before because it is a key reason why Japan has been the one major industrial country to buck the global trend of ever rising unemployment rates.

The rationale for lifetime employment is also being boosted by the Cost Structure Revolution. In today's most advanced industries, labor costs constitute only a small proportion of total costs, so increasingly when Western corporations lay people off in bad times they are being penny wise and pound foolish. Not only are the cost savings from layoffs minimal, but an employer suffers serious labor quality problems once it starts hiring untrained people when business improves. These new hires inevitably make mistakes, and such mistakes are more costly than ever because workers these days are using equipment that may cost many times their annual salaries.

In this chapter and the previous one, we have seen how Japan develops two fundamental resources of economic success — large amounts of capital plus well-trained and well-motivated workers. These resources cannot be applied to maximum advantage in pursuit of growth without Japan's keiretsus and cartels. It is time to look at the Japanese economics of structure.

8

The Economics of Structure

Many observers in the United States have recently predicted that Japan's keiretsus and cartels will soon break down. They are destined to be proved wrong. The latest predictions, like many similar ones in the past, are based on a mistaken understanding of Japanese industrial policy.

In the case of Japan's cartels, much of the talk of a breakdown has been prompted by a flurry of enforcement activity in 1992 and 1993 by Japanese antitrust regulators. But such activity was merely tokenism, a gesture of goodwill conceived mainly to placate Americans aggrieved by the cartelization of the Japanese economy.

As for the keiretsus, American observers took false encouragement from reports that keiretsu members were selling holdings in each other. In reality, such sales merely represent constant adjustments by corporate Japan to the ever-changing needs of Japan's path-breaking economy. For every block of shares the keiretsus sell off, they invest at least as much in forging new corporate links.

On balance, the keiretsus and cartels made considerable progress in the early 1990s in consolidating their leadership not only in Japan but around the world. As we noted in Chapter Two, the kyosei movement was successful in building many important partnerships between Japanese and American corporations. Such partnerships, based mostly on a division of labor in which the Japanese do the advanced manufacturing and the Americans do the assembly and marketing, constitute a move by Japan's keiretsus and cartels to extend their global reach.

Powerful global monopolistic pressures make such alliances almost inevitable. This was acknowledged in 1993 in *Collaborating to Compete,* a book by partners of the McKinsey consulting firm, who argued that traditional competition among corporations of different countries destroys wealth rather than creates it. Editors Joel Bleeke and David Ernst wrote:

> In businesses as diverse as pharmaceuticals, jet engines, banking, and computers, managers have learned that fighting long, head-to-head battles leaves their companies financially exhausted, intellectually depleted, and vulnerable to the next wave of competition and innovation . . . Managers are beginning to see that many necessary elements of a global business are so costly (like R & D in semiconductors), so generic (like assembly), or so impenetrable (like some of the Asian markets) that it makes no sense to have a traditional competitive stance.

As Bleeke and Ernst went on to point out, the new realities are impelling corporate America to forge alliances with foreign partners who have the "cash, scale, skills, and [market] access" it lacks.

In the case of each item on corporate America's wish list, the Japanese clearly are holding the high cards:

• Cash. Each major Japanese corporation works closely with a huge keiretsu bank, typically a bank with assets of more than three times those of America's largest bank, Citicorp. As these banks are the dominant financial institutions in an economy that now produces half of the world's savings each year, Japanese partners are almost essential in major high-risk investment projects undertaken anywhere in the world.

• Scale. In virtually every area of advanced manufacturing, Japanese corporations long ago passed their American counterparts in the scale of their operations.

• Skills. The Japanese are the acknowledged masters in designing products for global markets and in setting up the necessary global manufacturing systems.

• Market access. In many categories of goods, particularly advanced goods like capital equipment and sophisticated components, the Japanese domestic market is now larger than America's. Thus for American or European corporations to succeed with a global product, they must tie up with Japan's cartels, which are the gatekeepers of Japan's domestic market.

To this list should be added another major Japanese advantage: Japanese corporations are the world experts in the art of "collaborating to compete." Whereas the Americans and to a lesser extent the Europeans have been hobbled by antitrust law, the Japanese have had a century of experience in perfecting corporate alliances as a tool of economic growth.

The making of the keiretsu/cartel matrix

Western observers have long assumed corporate Japan's cartels and keiretsus emerged autonomously from Japanese culture. But in common with most other Japanese economic arrangements, they are actually conscious constructs of official policy.

They were developed as Japan's response to the problems created by the increasing importance of fixed costs in modern industries. These problems first became apparent in the United States. In the wake of the famous railroad price wars in the 1870s, the Yale economist Arthur Twining Hadley published an analysis in 1885 showing that the railroad industry's high fixed-cost ratio threatened economic efficiency by fostering wildly gyrating prices and consequent sharp swings in capacity utilization. Hadley later widened his analysis to show how fixed costs would soon create similar problems for manufacturing industry.

Hadley's work is largely forgotten today, but he put his finger on the basic problem that Japan's zaibatsus were founded to address: how to modify the dynamics of free markets in capital-intensive industries to maximize capacity utilization.

With the concurrence of the Tokyo bureaucracy, the zaibatsu managements began in the early twentieth century to create cartels in most major industries as a way of coordinating the creation of new capacity. Meanwhile each zaibatsu organized its internal affairs to create vertical integration in its manufacturing processes. In the textile industry, for instance, the textile division of each zaibatsu bought its thread from the spinning division; the spinning division bought its cotton from the trading division; and the trading division imported its supplies in the ships of the shipping division.

A law enacted in 1925 provided the bureaucrats with official powers to regulate cartels. Then in the 1930s, officials were given large powers not only to control the cartels' prices and expansion plans, but even to force companies to join cartels. By the late 1930s, the officials had organized Japan's vast munitions industry in particular into cartels.

The rationale behind the officials' cartelization policy was explained in an important book published in 1935 by Shinji Yoshino, the chief civil servant of the Commerce and Industry Ministry. Yoshino argued the case for controls to coordinate industry's production activities in coping with high fixed costs. In explicitly rejecting Adam Smith's case for the invisible hand, he warned of the growing problem of *kato kyoso* — excessive competition. As Yoshino pointed out, if corporations operate on a fragmented, free-for-all basis, they suffer periodic bouts of acute overcapacity, a problem that could be avoided if government takes a lead in pacing the introduction of new capacity.

In criticizing excess competition, Yoshino had the already considerable evidence of Japan's successful experience with zaibatsus to guide him. He was probably also influenced by German experience. By the early 1930s, nearly all Germany's production of raw materials and semifinished goods had been cartelized and fully one-quarter of all manufacturing of finished goods. Cartels proved so effective in boosting German production that Adolf Hitler used cartelization as his central strategy in building Germany's economy for war.

It is notable that from the start, the Tokyo government's high opinion of cartels did not extend to monopolies. Generally, Tokyo has been prepared to countenance monopoly only in the case of state-owned corporations. In virtually every Japanese industry, officials have tried to ensure that there are at least three strong players and usually four or five. This makes it easier for Japanese bureaucrats to control an industry through divide-and-rule. In America, by contrast, in the years before antitrust law was enacted, industry had already gone beyond cartels to monopolies. Such companies as U.S. Steel, Standard Oil, American Tobacco, American Sugar Refining, and United Shoe Machinery had come to secure a share of between 65 percent and 95 percent in their respective markets by the first decade of the twentieth century.

To Japanese leaders such as Yoshino, the American policy of using antitrust law to break up cartels served merely to minimize excessive concentrations of private economic power and was quite counterproductive in promoting efficiency. Yoshino argued that though cartels could become socially disruptive if left indefinitely to their own devices, a little government oversight could minimize the socially disruptive aspects of cartels while preserving certain distinct advantages that American and British economists underestimated.

Yoshino's thinking was reflected in the Economic New Structure manifesto, which in 1940 advocated a permanent break with Western theory on cartels. In December of that year, the Cabinet approved an order giving government-administered cartel associations strong powers over member companies.

The next big milestone came after Japan's surrender in 1945. From the start, one of MacArthur's most important objectives for the occupation was to impose strict American antitrust rules on Japan. But he met considerable resistance from Japanese officials, who in 1949 began to roll back his reforms by persuading him to allow a cartel in the shipping industry. Once the occupation ended, the officials moved quickly to give themselves wide powers to authorize cartels on a case-by-case basis. Writing in 1962, a top MITI official, Yoshihiko Morozumi, sketched out the economic rationale for government-guided cartels as a response to rising fixed costs:

> Free competition provides neither the most suitable scale nor a guarantee of proper prices. Free competition means excessive equipment and low profits. . . . We must conclude that a policy of moderate concentration is a desirable thing which will eliminate excessive competition and promote economies of scale. . . . There is an unstoppable trend taking place here.

Perhaps an even more telling insight into the Japanese bureaucracy's true view of cartels is what schoolchildren in Japan have traditionally been taught about cartels. Because schoolbooks in Japan are subject to comprehensive government regulation, they are a reliable guide to what the government wants the public to know. This is how *Gendai no Shakai* (*Modern Society*), a civics text for junior high school pupils, described cartels in its 1966 edition:

> The good points of cartels are (1) they are able to introduce advanced technologies by using big capital; (2) they are able to produce better quality products at a lower production cost, thus reducing the selling price; (3) they enjoy strength to fight recessions; and (4) they help the country boost its exports.

The textbook also mentioned the usual Western argument against cartels, that they can create inefficiency, but the clear drift of the explication was that cartels are generally a positive force for the economy.

In practice, the Japanese bureaucrats have allowed legal cartels to carry out concerted efforts to exchange or restrict technology, to standardize production, to maximize production runs through product line specialization, to coordinate export efforts, and to organize common distribution facilities. As such commentators as Tetsuo Sakiya have recorded, the Ministry of International Trade and Industry in many cases has even gone beyond its statutory authority in encouraging collusive practices in industry. In particular, it has used various expedients to control entry into industries. In cases such as the auto industry in the 1960s, the officials' administrative advice even required companies to break Japan's antitrust law.

Even the MOF went public in 1970, condemning free competition as "selfish." The full significance of the MOF's view is apparent when you realize that it controls the Fair Trade Commission, Japan's antitrust enforcement authority.

By the mid-1950s, Japanese cartels were visibly working with government to "target" particular industries — to invest so heavily that they quickly established global monopolistic leadership. Japan had realized the importance of such targeting before World War II, and it had already established lucrative global monopolies in the then significant commodities of silk and camphor by the 1920s.

In the postwar era, corporate Japan methodically established global monopolies in a series of increasingly sophisticated products, notably ships, cameras, motorcycles, and watches. Most competitors displaced by these targeting efforts were European rather than American — an important geopolitical point because Japan, still relatively inexperienced in trade lobbying in Washington, could aim aggressively to take over these companies' American sales without rattling any significant cages in corporate America. Other early cases of Japanese targeting involved new products in which American competition hardly existed, notably transistors, transistor radios, and tape recorders.

Western critics of Japan's cartelization program have often pointed out that the program met with resistance from the Japanese auto industry. They tend to assume mistakenly from this that opposition to the program was widespread. True, the auto industry did not accept the MITI's suggestion to merge into three giant companies. But, as far as one can see, few other industries opposed the officials' plans so directly. In any case, even the auto industry has gone much further than Western observers realize in achieving the degree of concentration the MITI originally advocated. It is today dominated by just three giant companies, and most other Japanese auto companies have business and financial ties with this Big Three. And in the case of many parts such as clutches, piston rings, and spark plugs, the industry has slimmed down to the point where Japan has only three significant suppliers.

Not content with restoring the cartel system after World War II, Japanese economic leaders also quickly revived the zaibatsus, albeit in a crucially different form; thus the keiretsu concept was invented. The keiretsus emerged in embryonic form during the last days of the American occupation. The first open move to create the keiretsus seems to have been by the Mitsui group, which in 1950 founded Getsuyokai, an umbrella organization that sponsored regular meetings for top executives of Mitsui companies. Other former zaibatsu companies quickly instituted similar arrangements. These get-togethers were in effect board meetings for the entire keiretsu and, among other things, they provided an opportunity for member companies to strike mutually profitable long-term deals with each other.

In the 1960s, the Ministry of Finance and the Ministry of International Trade and Industry began working with the big banks to foster the growth of interlocking shareholding patterns by which keiretsu companies own stakes in one another. Up to that point, a majority of the shares in former zaibatsu companies was held by the general public. The government altered Article 280 of the Commerce Law to allow companies to increase their capital by assigning new shares to keiretsu affiliates and other associated companies. The Ministry of Finance provided a major up-front incentive for companies to buy one another's shares by allowing the cost of such investments to be deducted against corporate tax. The beauty of it all was that the cost to each company of buying shares in other members of its keiretsu was typically zero: the amount that Company A paid to buy shares in Company B was repaid when Company B bought shares in Company A.

The Ministry of Finance facilitated the keiretsuization process by permitting keiretsu companies to sell special issues of shares at discounted prices to other members of their keiretsu. Existing individual shareholders in the companies concerned seem not to have been given a fair chance to buy these shares. The effect was to further dilute individual ownership in Japanese industry, which resulted in a corresponding boost to keiretsu power and to the power of the ultimate trustees of Japan Inc., the MOF-regulated insurance companies and banks.

Over the years, therefore, Japan has developed an inbred industrial establishment. On one authoritative estimate, about three-quarters of all shares in a typical major Japanese corporation are held by related companies or by a few giant government-guided investment institutions. These shareholders mostly take a long-term view and are indifferent to short-term profits. Due to the structure of the Japanese financial system, these shareholders function virtually as trustees for the nation, and in that capacity they are more concerned with boosting job quality than profits.

The prominent Japanese economist Iwao Nakatani has perhaps put it best: the Japanese financial system is structured to keep shareholders "at bay." Unlike Western corporations, Japanese corporations hardly need to make profits because they can make almost constant issues of new shares to fund their expansion. These issues are heavily bought by Japan's vast MOF-guided financial institutions. As Yutaka Inoue has pointed out, such institutions judge a company not on its profits but on its success in boosting sales (which is another way of saying its success in boosting jobs). By contenting themselves with low profit margins in a world of profit-maximizing Western corporations, Japanese corporations continually increase their global market share. As Iwao Nakatani points out, the evident efficacy of this system poses "far-reaching questions that go to the very heart of capitalism."

All this serves to make the cartelization of the Japanese economy more acceptable to the Japanese public. Whereas in the West cartels are perceived to act against the public interest because their price fixing serves to line the pockets of identifiable tycoons and top corporate executives, Japanese cartels serve to boost the fortunes of the "ownerless" keiretsus. Because it can truly be said that what is good for the keiretsus is good for Japan, the Japanese public is unruffled by the often egregious price-fixing tactics of the cartels.

The lifetime employment system guards against the other major drawback of Western-style cartels, the tendency to featherbed inefficiency. The system forces members of Japanese cartels to minimize costs in an effort to plow back the maximum profits in moving to new technologies that bolster the security of employees' jobs.

Add all the pieces together — the cartels, the keiretsus, the lifetime employment system, and Japan's farsighted financial system (which we will explain in Chapter Ten) — and a picture emerges of a new economic engine that wins by turning conventional Western economic wisdom on its head.

The invisible Good Cartel

The Good Cartel is almost invisible. Although in former times the Japanese media openly discussed the cartelization of the Japanese economy, they have gone quiet on the subject in recent years. This has encouraged the impression abroad that Japan's cartels are in general retreat.

In reality, Japan's cartels have been working to reduce their visibility for fear of angering American antitrust regulators. Not only has the United States generally tightened its antitrust enforcement in the last four decades, but Japan's cartels, by reason of their extraordinary success in conquering global markets, have become a target for American antitrust enforcers (who, much to Japan's chagrin, claim powers to extend their enforcement into the Japanese economy).

In an effort to placate foreign opinion, the Tokyo authorities have even appeared to stiffen antitrust enforcement in the 1990s. Such enforcement efforts have been little more than token concessions to American feelings and, significantly, in no case have Japanese antitrust investigations turned up information that might provide American enforcers with a pretext to bring parallel suits under American law.

The activities of Japan's cartels are heavily underreported in the West because of fear of libel suits. And the press's most promising sources on the cartelization of Japanese industry, American corporate executives, have become notably discreet on the subject out of deference to the feelings of their Japanese counterparts. Consumers in America and Europe rarely see much evidence of cartel pricing in such Japanese consumer export items as computers: in such industries the cartelization is at the component level, invisible to the consumer.

Finance is one of Japan's most visible cartelized industries, but others are readily identifiable. Many of Japan's packaged goods industries are clearly cartelized. Manufacturers of toiletries, for instance, sell in industry-standard packet sizes at industry-standard retail prices. Such areas of the processed food industry as cookies and ice cream are also considered to be cartelized. So is the beer industry. The brewers' habit of raising prices by the same amount on the same day has even been publicly labeled "suspicious" by a former Economic Planning Agency official.

There have been persistent accusations of cartel behavior in capital goods industries — certain Japanese capital equipment makers are alleged to collude to deny American and European customers timely supplies of newly launched machines. This has been particularly notable in the electronics industry, where the pattern has been for new machinery to be available in Japan several months before it is available abroad. This can make a big difference in an industry where some products enjoy a life of only eighteen months before they are made obsolete by subsequent technical advances.

In 1991, a small American company brought suit against Japanese and Korean companies that monopolized the supply of certain components necessary to make videocassette recorders. Writing in 1992, Laura D'Andrea Tyson, President Clinton's soon-to-be chief economic adviser, documented several instances of what she delicately referred to as "cartel-like" behavior in the Japanese semiconductor industry.

In the auto industry, many important inputs are supplied by cartels. Perhaps the most obvious is steel. The steel industry's high fixed costs make cartel-based pricing almost inevitable not only in Japan but in virtually every other major economy. That the Japanese steel industry remains as cartelized as ever was specifically acknowledged in 1993 by Hayao Nakamura, a former Nippon Steel executive who now runs an Italian steel giant. In an interview with the *Wall Street Journal,* he declared: "In Japan, if the [steel] market goes down too much, the big five steelmakers meet, agree on acceptable price levels, and send inspectors to check on each other twenty-four hours a day."

Despite much discussion in the last decade about toughening antitrust enforcement, Japanese regulators have been notably soft on major export-oriented companies. This is less surprising when you realize that antitrust regulators are required to desist from bringing antitrust suits where such suits would would "cause a loss of international competitiveness" at the offending companies. This is a major loophole because virtually every major Japanese manufacturer does at least some exporting. It is a loophole corporate Japan intends to keep.

The uses of the Good Cartel

The Good Cartel is clearly one of the most controversial instruments of Japanese economics, particularly for anyone who upholds the Anglo-American ideal of individual freedom. But this should not blind us to the obvious benefits Japan derives from the cartelization of its economy.

At the risk of repeating some points made earlier, it is worth itemizing here some of these benefits:

• Cartels provide Japanese corporations with high home market prices that fund their heavy programs to upgrade their production technologies. Hence the constantly rising productivity of Japanese workers. High profit margins in the cartelized Japanese auto market help explain why Toyota Motor, for instance, boosted its sales per employee from ¥85 million in 1983 to ¥124 million in 1993 — an increase of 46 percent measured in yen and 227 percent in American dollars.

• Cartels help corporate Japan maximize capacity utilization. In particular, they enable Japanese manufacturers to coordinate their expansion plans. The minimum efficient scale in advanced manufacturing is now so large that when a single new factory is built, it can add considerably to total global capacity. If competitors in the industry compete on an Adam Smith basis, they tend to rush to create new capacity at the same time as demand nears the industry's existing capacity limit. This opens up the possibility of a major capacity glut. The Japanese solution is for cartel members to take turns in adding capacity, thus rationalizing the pace of the industry's expansion.

• Cartels generate efficiencies by reducing transaction costs; cartelization is the main reason for Japan's superior labor productivity in the airline and banking industries, for instance.

• Cartels support the lifetime employment system by discouraging employers from hiring from one another.

• Cartels boost Japan's savings rate by hindering attempts by foreign suppliers to export to Japan.

• Cartels cut the cost of Japan's commodity imports. In many industries, Japanese importers negotiate as a cartel in importing raw materials, driving hard bargains with foreign suppliers. In recent years American officials have become aware of Japanese import cartels involving everything from semiconductor materials to Alaska crabs to wood chips. Japan has long established buying cartels in such basic supplies as coal and iron ore.

• The cartels provide the bureaucrats with a discreet tool for subsidizing targeted industries. As we mentioned in Chapter Two, a good example is the oil industry: the effect whereby high gasoline prices subsidize the auto industry would hardly be possible but for the cartelized pricing structure of both the oil and steel industries in Japan.

• Cartels help Japanese industry achieve efficiencies by standardizing products and components. Standardized components reduce inventories and allow component makers to maximize economies of scale. By establishing consumer standards, the Japanese can define an industry in a way that suits their manufacturing capability. One of the first moves the Japanese made in the 1960s when they targeted the photocopier business, which was then dominated worldwide by Xerox, was to create common standards for components.

• Cartels use standards as a strategic device to eliminate or neutralize foreign competition. In the 1990s Japanese companies were setting global standards in such products of tomorrow as advanced cameras and high-definition laser disk players without significant input from American or European corporations.

• Cartels in finance serve to depress the returns to Japan's savers, thus reducing the cost of finance to Japanese manufacturers.

• Cartels allow corporate Japan to target foreign markets more efficiently. In the smaller national markets of the world, Japanese corporations often seem to avoid competing with each other. The scholar William Davidson noted that this pattern was particularly prevalent in the Asia Pacific region. He cited the Australian computer market, where the Japanese seemed to have divided the business among themselves in a way that allowed each company to dominate a particular market segment: one company took the mainframe business, another the minicomputer business, and a third had the personal computer business. A major advantage to this is that it avoids duplication of marketing and service organizations to support uneconomically small installation bases.

Looking toward the twenty-first century, possibly the most important benefit of the cartel system is in maximizing corporate Japan's returns from its research and development spending. This is worth a closer look.

Efficient research and development

Corporations can achieve great cost efficiencies by cooperating in research and development. They thereby avoid duplicating each other's "dry hole" research.

Economists have only recently become aware of the special importance of research and development in modern economics. Until a few decades ago, research and development was such an insignificant item in industrial costs that attempts to conduct it through industry cartels hardly seemed worth the effort. As recently as 1920, American corporations employed a total of just 9,300 workers on civilian research and development. By the early 1940s, the total was still hardly more than 70,000. It quintupled to 350,000 in the next two decades, and at the last count it was approaching 700,000, a tenfold increase in fifty years. The growth in Japan has been even faster: about 680,000 Japanese workers are now engaged in civilian research and development, up from probably just a few thousand in the early 1940s.

The benefits of organizing research and development more efficiently come into sharp focus when you look at the advanced manufacturing industries Japan is targeting. It has become commonplace in recent years for companies in the semiconductor industry, for instance, to spend as much as 25 percent of their sales on research and development.

Overall corporate Japan is now heavily outspending the United States in research and development. As of the early 1990s, privately funded research and development in Japan at about 3 percent of GNP was nearly twice the American level. Even so, these figures may underestimate Japan's edge. American aerospace corporations that have worked in partnership with Japanese corporations believe the Japanese use conservative accounting definitions that, in American eyes, understate the true level of research and development spending.

Even the published numbers for corporate Japan's research and development spending, understated though they probably are, look impressive. Hitachi, for instance, spends about 6.7 percent of its total group sales revenues on research and development, up from 4.8 percent ten years ago. In dollar terms, Hitachi's budget has jumped from

$1.7 billion to about $6.5 billion in the period. Thus Hitachi is now running level with IBM, whose research and development also totaled $6.5 billion in 1993.

With spending of this size, the case for organizing research and development on an industry-wide basis becomes compelling. By participating in research cartels, corporate Japan can typically get three to four times more bang for its research and development buck than corporate America. In some cases the advantage may be even greater: an NEC official has calculated that Japanese electronics companies developed electron beam technology for about one-fifth what they would have spent had they not cooperated with one another.

Because the Japanese tend to spend at least as large a share of sales revenues on research and development as the Americans, their more efficient organizational approach enables them easily to outpace the Americans in innovation. The result has been that they have in the space of a quarter of a century leapfrogged corporate America in industry after industry, most notably automobiles, electronics, new materials, and robotics.

One outward measure of corporate Japan's success is that in the 1980s it passed corporate America in the number of patents registered per year. Japanese corporations also do a great deal of research on production technology that is never patented. (The Japanese prefer not to patent their ideas if they can avoid it because patents can often be legally circumvented. And patents eventually expire, whereas trade secrets can be kept forever.)

The success of the Japanese in minimizing impurities in steel provides a good example of Japanese-style research at work. Steelmakers have cooperated as a group to develop techniques that cut the sulfur content to as little as 0.001 percent, one-tenth of the lowest level achievable two decades ago. The net effect is stronger steel — and that has cleared the way for major weight reductions in Japanese cars. Perhaps the ultimate example of Japan's successful use of research cartels has been in the computer industry. Japan's computer industry was a negligible also-ran when it first started using research cartels extensively in the 1960s. The progress since then has been extraordinary. Fujitsu's sales, for instance, had shot from just one-fiftieth of IBM's twenty years ago to more than 50 percent of IBM's sales in 1993.

In the long run, if the Americans cannot match the Japanese

in organizing research and development, it is difficult to see how they can hope to continue to play an independent role in global innovation.

The keiretsus

Keiretsus are groups of corporations that have close trading and financial links with each other. Mitsubishi is perhaps the best-known keiretsu; other notable ones include Sumitomo, Mitsui, Fuyo, Sanwa, and Ikkan. Together they constitute Japan's Big Six keiretsus.

Although keiretsus differ greatly, the Mitsubishi group is regarded by many as perhaps the finest example of the genre. Broadly defined, the Mitsubishi group includes hundreds of large companies and thousands of smaller companies that have ties to one or more of the large companies. Most large Mitsubishi companies operate under the Mitsubishi name and display the group's three diamonds trademark (*mitsu bishi* is Japanese for "three diamonds"). A few Mitsubishi companies that have established a strong name in their own right do not use the Mitsubishi name: these include the Nikon camera company, the Kirin beer company, the Asahi glass company, and NYK, the world's largest shipping company.

Each of the Big Six keiretsus is headed by a huge commercial bank and also contains several other financial institutions. At the Mitsubishi group, for instance, the head bank is Mitsubishi Bank. The group also contains Mitsubishi Trust & Banking (an investment management organization), Meiji Life (a mutual life insurance company), and the Tokio Marine and Fire property and casualty insurer. Although these institutions are little known outside Japan, each ranks as one of the largest companies in its field worldwide.

The trading links within keiretsus come in two forms — horizontal and vertical. Horizontal trading links are illustrated in the way that Mitsubishi Motors, for instance, buys steel from Mitsubishi Steel and semiconductors from Mitsubishi Electric. Each company is very large and deals with the others on a footing of rough equality.

By contrast, a vertical keiretsu is shaped as a pyramid with a strong chain of command emanating from the top. The Toyota group, headed by Toyota Motor, is perhaps the definitive example of a vertical keiretsu. The group is organized in four tiers, and Toyota Motor enjoys great power over the other major companies in the group —

companies such as the Nippondenso car air-conditioner maker, the Futaba Industrial muffler maker, and the world's largest manufacturer of headlamps, Koito Manufacturing. These companies in turn control other smaller companies. The total number of suppliers in the Toyota group runs to more than twenty thousand.

The Japanese Fair Trade Commission has calculated that nearly 90 percent of all domestic business transactions in Japan take place among parties "involved in a long-standing relationship of some sort." Most such relationships follow keiretsu lines.

The keiretsus as an information-age tool

Members of Japan's keiretsu behave in much the way people do when they are with their families. Just as family members don't charge by the minute for helping a relative in need, in corporate Japan keiretsu members are equally prepared to deal with each other in a similarly farsighted spirit of give-and-take. The keiretsu banks, for instance, provide their keiretsu partners with a great deal of free information and advice that in the West would be provided by management consultants or investment bankers on a fee basis. Because the keiretsu banks are bound to their corporate customers in permanent relationships, they take a very long view in advising these customers. Thus their advice is much less likely to be marred by hidden conflicts of interest that often influence the advice dispensed by American management consultants and investment banks.

Whereas fee-hungry American investment banks often try to persuade American corporations to make unwise acquisitions, for instance, Japanese banks have no need of such questionable income because they earn their profits in other ways: usually they pay a subpar interest rate on the often large deposits left with them by keiretsu members.

By working on a relationship basis rather than a transactional basis, corporate Japan minimizes transaction costs. In the long run each partner gets back at least as much as it gives, and certainly on average the system works for the benefit of the keiretsu as a whole. Typically the help that company A gives to company B costs company A very little and is a big benefit to company B.

This dynamic reflects in part the Cost Structure Revolution: the marginal cost of providing a keiretsu partner with a good sales lead is almost nothing, yet if such information leads to a multimillion dollar order, most of the extra revenue will go to Company B's bottom line. If companies tried to determine a market rate for passing such information back and forth, the result would be a lot of haggling and very little communication. The problem is that economically significant information cannot always be traded efficiently in a free market economy because the value of information is known to the buyer only after the information has been imparted. And at this point the seller is hardly in an optimal position to bargain for an appropriate fee.

Another information-age problem that the keiretsus help solve concerns so-called asymmetries in technical knowledge between buyers and sellers. As the economist Iwao Nakatani has pointed out, in the case of sophisticated products, the seller typically knows far more about the product's strengths and weaknesses than the buyer. Thus the seller can easily take advantage of the situation. Many consumers who have shopped for personal computers in the United States in recent years have seen knowledge asymmetries firsthand: even after studying the computer market, they often end up being sold too much equipment, or even the wrong equipment entirely. By contrast, the keiretsu system ensures that Japanese firms are well informed when they buy components and machines from each other: because most such transactions take place within a long-term relationship, suppliers are under strong pressure to look out for the buyer's best long-term interests.

It is interesting to look at the way information asymmetries work in the auto industry. This is an industry where component manufacturers can easily boost their profit margins by cutting quality in ways that are hard for auto factory purchasing managers to spot. Later, in the customer's hands, the quality shortfall may become all too obvious. In Detroit, the free market system of sourcing parts through a series of short-term transactions results in a proliferation of suppliers: each automaker has to try to keep track of as many as three thousand suppliers who bid on supply contracts. By contrast, Honda Motor uses a "family" approach to reduce its direct suppliers to just three hundred. Each supplier is an honored member of the Honda family. But if it betrays Honda's trust by skimping on quality, it risks being banished permanently from the hearth. This deterrent galvanizes suppliers to monitor themselves, relieving Honda of the need to conduct constant quality checks on components.

This knowledge-asymmetry problem is now apparent throughout advanced manufacturing — so much so that it is undermining the whole textbook case for free markets. As the texts point out, free markets only deliver their full advertised efficiency if buyers and sellers have "perfect knowledge" — they should know all relevant information for making a rational decision on how to price a transaction.

An effort to deal with this information-asymmetry problem seems to be a key reason why Western corporations have recently been trying to emulate the keiretsu system. The Big Three Detroit automakers, for instance, have switched from a short-term bidding basis in sourcing parts to long-term contracts of typically four years. Meanwhile, in Europe, makers such as Peugeot and Fiat have been creating Japanese-style pyramidal hierarchies of suppliers and are sourcing components on a long-term basis. Such structures, however, are not likely to be as effective as Japanese keiretsus because Western legal contracts tend to encourage both sides to withhold vital information in the interests of propping up their respective bargaining positions. Moreover, legal contracts are increasingly risky in a world of fast-changing technology, and they foster much unproductive jockeying over loopholes.

The truth is that experts who understand the full significance of the keiretsu system believe it provides the Japanese with a key advantage that American and European competitors can never match. As Iwao Nakatani has pointed out, this is particularly clear in the case of research and development.

Writing in a Japanese-language magazine in 1992, he cited the Japanese auto industry as an example:

> Japanese automakers conduct extensive joint research and development activities with the suppliers of their main parts. Joint development enables them to acquire the most up-to-date technical information in many industries on a daily basis and to make full use of that information in new cars.
>
> Yet this joint research system which has become commonplace in Japan cannot easily spread to corporate America. There are two reasons. American companies cannot jointly plan the development of a new car to be sold five years from now with companies with whom they are not sure they will be doing business next year. Long-term joint development requires extended and close relations among firms. The open spirit of American capitalism (the practice of striking deals whenever the quality and price are right) becomes a great barrier in building

a joint development system which can systematically absorb technical information from many industries.

Another major problem is insider trading. When companies do joint research they necessarily must swap confidential information. . . . As is well known, society's sanctions on insider trading are very heavy in the United States. For this reason American executives are far more wary of major joint research projects than Japanese people can imagine. Even if Americans know that without doing joint research they will not win the race [with Japan], they cannot easily do so.

Nakatani's message is clear: this is the age of the keiretsus, and only the Japanese can play the keiretsu game.

Keeping the wheels turning

One of the big benefits of the keiretsu system is that it helps companies maximize their capacity utilization. Keiretsu members buy from one another, providing one another with an important baseload of steady demand. The keiretsus sometimes organize special trading structures that automatically foster reciprocal business: one such structure is a type of buyers' club in which members pay for their purchases partly in a large up-front fee levied annually and partly in a per item charge for everything actually bought. The per item charge is generally low. Thus once a company pays the up-front fee, it has every incentive to channel its purchases exclusively to the designated keiretsu supplier. Under the influence of such arrangements, keiretsu companies are, according to some scholarly studies, about three times more likely to do business with other members of their keiretsu than with outsiders.

Many keiretsus also control retail outlets, which they use as a captive market for their products. The electronics industry provides a good example. The Matsushita Electric company, for instance, controls about 25,000 electrical stores in Japan. Other major Japanese electronics companies such as Toshiba, Hitachi, Sanyo, Mitsubishi, and Sony control a further 40,000 to 50,000 stores. These stores source virtually their entire stock from within their keiretsu and they maintain uniformly high prices. In return the manufacturers protect each retailer's franchise by refusing to license new retailers within the designated territory of an existing one. In Matsushita's case, these captive stores account for fully one-half of its domestic sales.

With such manufacturer-to-consumer links bolted into place, competition from foreign manufacturers is automatically excluded, thus guaranteeing the Japanese manufacturers a steady demand in the home market. Perhaps more important, the practice of maintaining recommended retail prices serves to buttress continued cartel behavior. Sustained by high profits in the home market, Japanese manufacturers can cut prices in export markets and keep American and European rivals permanently off-balance. Such manufacturer-to-consumer keiretsu arrangements are also well established in the oil, automotive, photography, pharmaceuticals, newspaper publishing, processed foods, and cosmetic fields.

In these days of high fixed costs in manufacturing, the keiretsu system's promise of a high level of guaranteed business for members is more attractive than ever before.

Holistic money

Finance is the lifeblood of the keiretsu system. The principal function of each keiretsu's banks and savings institutions is to pump as much of Japan's savings as possible into the big keiretsu manufacturing companies.

The keiretsu financial organizations are renowned for their patience in funding long-term projects and in nursing sick companies through to recovery. In part this long-term mentality stems from the way Japanese financial institutions are regulated, but much of it is inherent in the keiretsu system.

The best way to highlight the strengths of keiretsu finance is to look first at some hidden weaknesses of Western finance. A group of Western financiers trying to support a troubled company are often divided against each other because of conflicting incentives. The higher the interest rate bankers extract for new loans to a troubled company, for instance, the more pain a company's shareholders suffer. Often the banks may have less to gain from keeping a troubled company alive than the shareholders. If, for instance, the banks have secured their lending on real estate assets, they may well see putting the company prematurely into bankruptcy as the best way to save their own hides. In this way they can be sure to come out whole whereas lending the company more money would carry a serious risk of further loss.

Sometimes companies collapse or are seriously damaged by financial accidents. Western financiers are prone to irrational panics and do not always wait to assess a troubled company's true position. By contrast, when a company in Japan has trouble, the keiretsu financial institutions are induced by their long-term ties with one another to find the best solution for all concerned. In essence, they take a balanced view of the problem. If a company truly has no future, Japanese financiers will be quite as ruthless as Western financiers in closing it down. In the recent real estate slump in Tokyo, for instance, the bankers showed little compunction in shutting down bankrupt real estate investment companies. But with industrial companies, the long-term prospects may often justify patience, particularly where a redundant work force might find difficulty securing good jobs elsewhere and thus become a burden on Japanese society as a whole.

The last major keiretsu rescue was of Mazda Motor in the mid-1970s. The story is worth recounting because it vividly illustrates the advantages of the keiretsus' approach to corporate bankruptcy. Mazda hit difficulties because it had bet its future on the so-called Wankel engine. This was a radically new engineering concept that delivered an especially smooth and quiet ride. The engine was, however, a gas guzzler, and after oil prices soared in the mid-1970s, its market prospects dimmed to almost nothing.

If Mazda had been a Western company, it would probably have gone the way of a Packard or a DeLorean. The MOF, however, saw Mazda's plight through the prism of *GNP-shugi,* the policy of maximizing Japan's GNP. It reasoned that the troubles were an unfortunate accident that did not speak to the company's managerial competence. Seen in terms of Japan's effort to maximize its GNP, Mazda as an *organization* was clearly an asset to the nation, even if Mazda as a *company* was bankrupt. The Mazda organization was a large and carefully arranged set of people who worked well together — a major resource of human capital that would take decades to duplicate if one were starting from scratch. Given a chance to recover from the Wankel accident, these workers could once again be fully competitive in the world car market. The alternative of throwing them out of work would severely depress the entire city of Hiroshima, where Mazda's main factories were located.

Luckily, Mazda was a member of the prosperous Sumitomo group. The MOF prevailed on Sumitomo Bank to lead an elaborate rescue effort in which many Sumitomo corporations participated. The result was that thousands of workers found a continuing future for their skills. Today Mazda is one of the ten largest exporters in Japan, with exports of around $13 billion; not bad by comparison even with Boeing, America's biggest manufacturing exporter, whose exports totaled $16 billion in 1993. Moreover, Mazda provides well-paid jobs for nearly 30,000 people.

Crises of Mazda proportions are rare in Japan, but the keiretsu system also serves to provide similarly intelligent solutions in less extreme cases. The keiretsu banks are prepared to look so far ahead in supporting troubled businesses that their lending policies seem almost suicidal to American securities analysts. These banks notably did not lose their nerve in the mid-1980s when, on an estimate by the U.S. General Accounting Office, the Japanese semiconductor industry lost $4 billion in the space of three years. Because the banks remained supportive, the industry came through the tremendous crunch caused by the rising yen without making any layoffs and it went on to stage an impressive recovery.

Far from being suicidal, therefore, such behavior on the part of the keiretsu banks is entirely rational. Part of the secret is that Japanese financial institutions enjoy a much better information flow than their American counterparts and can therefore be much bolder in backing a farsighted company. By contrast, under the West's concept of "transactional banking," American banks are often working in the dark because their customers withhold vital financial information. Such customers have to do so because a bank or institutional investor can quickly turn from a supportive friend to a predatory or litigious enemy. In any case, sharing of important information is inhibited in the United States by insider trading laws. The alternative course, of providing full disclosure on promising new technologies to the general public, is usually barred because to do so would most likely tip a corporation's hand to competitors and undermine its bargaining position with customers and suppliers.

These information blockages are made all the more serious by the fact that advanced corporations these days require large continuing capital infusions if they are to stay at the leading edge. Because the world economy is increasingly operating by Japanese rules, profit margins in advanced industries have been pared to the bone, and any company wanting to stay in the game must do what Japanese corporations do: raise new capital every few years, rather than rely on retained profits, the traditional source of expansion capital for corporate America.

One reason Japanese financiers can afford to be so bold in pumping fresh capital into Japanese industry is that the keiretsu system minimizes financial risks. If, for instance, a Toyota group company such as Nippondenso invests in a major new venture to supply state-of-the-art air conditioners to Toyota Motor, the Toyota group's banks can fund the project with reasonable assurance that Toyota Motor will buy the resulting products. In fact Toyota Motor will have approved the project in the first place and will be committed to supporting it through thick and thin — even to the point of refusing to purchase lower priced air conditioners from a rival American supplier.

The effect of the keiretsu system is to align the financiers' interests firmly with the long-term growth of Japanese industry.

In praise of corporation man

From a conventional economist's point of view, one of the most puzzling aspects of the Japanese economic system is the lowly status it assigns to entrepreneurs. In outright contradiction of Anglo-American economic wisdom, Japan's economic leaders treat entrepreneurial behavior as a disruptive force that often gets in the way of the national effort to build economic strength. Hence, not only are entrepreneurs generally excluded from high-level policymaking, but they are systematically banished to the industrial little leagues.

The Japanese system is littered with obstacles to the growth of small companies. Small companies are, for instance, required to pay as much as 50 percent more for bank financing than large corporations. As the scholars Richard E. Caves and Masu Uekusa have noted, discrimination on such a scale cannot be justified on grounds of the banks' costs. Meanwhile Japan's corporate tax rules contain quirky zones of very high marginal rates that small entrepreneurial companies must pass through if they are to become large. In an effort to avoid these high taxes, successful entrepreneurs often dissipate their profits and energies in establishing many new small companies rather than building a single large one.

At the other end of the corporate scale, the regulators have ways of promoting the continued dominance of the conformist megacorporations. For one thing, government officials administer industrial policy so that entry to many of the most attractive new growth industries is reserved for the megacorporations.

At any event, very few new entrepreneurial companies have broken through to corporate Japan's big league in recent decades. Significantly, the two most notable examples, Sony and Honda Motor, got their start in the occupation era when, as a result of American efforts to foster capitalism, the sun briefly shone on entrepreneurial saplings.

This is not to say that Japan lacks for corporate new blood. In fact, in probably no country in the world are there so many new corporate names emerging all the time in the growth industries of the future. With few exceptions, however, such newcomers start out as divisions of existing megacorporations and are then spun off to become members of their parent companies' keiretsus. Thus the keiretsu system constitutes Japan's answer to the entrepreneurialism the West relies on for economic renewal.

Just how powerful the spinoff concept can be is apparent from the history of the Furukawa group of companies. The group was founded in 1875 when Ichibei Furukawa, the son-in-law of a powerful merchant, bought an old copper mine from the government on favorable terms. Then in 1896, the Furukawa family founded the electric cable maker Furukawa Electric to use the output from the mining company. In 1923, Furukawa Electric in turn founded the Fuji Electric heavy-equipment maker. In 1935, Fuji Electric launched the Fujitsu computer company. In the 1970s and 1980s Fujitsu went on to generate dozens of spinoffs of its own, most notably the Fanuc factory automation company. The Furukawa/Fujitsu/Fanuc group now includes a profusion of other major spinoffs that have stock market listings of their own in Japan.

All these companies are typical keiretsu entities in that there is no significant individual investor participation in any of them (the Furukawa family lost control of the group during the occupation). Even so, the group has not lacked for a spirit of enterprise: many Furukawa group companies are at the leading edge in their markets. Fanuc, for instance, is the world's dominant robot maker. Fujitsu is closing in fast on IBM to become the world's largest computer company. Furukawa Electric is the world's leader in shape memory alloys, a vital commodity in the electronics industry. Fuji Electric is a world leader in transformers and solar cells.

Clearly, success stories on this scale are a powerful testament to the keiretsu system's ability to make the most of technological opportunities.

By contrast, entrepreneurs are seen as a serious cause of malfunction in the Japanese system. Part of the problem is that they are inherently incompatible with the logic of the Good Cartel. Entrepreneurs are more likely to cheat on cartel agreements and to try to renege on important commitments such as paying seniority bonuses to older workers. Few of them have the deep pockets of the keiretsu companies to survive the expensive early stages of targeting an industry. Finally, the idea of cartels helping to enrich identifiable individual entrepreneurs is clearly hard to reconcile with Japan's ideas of social harmony and Confucian fairness.

Another point is that entrepreneurs do not live forever. When they pass from the scene they are succeeded by children who, by the law of averages, will be of unexceptional ability. Trusting large pieces of the nation's wealth to such unreliable hands is not conducive to the nation's long-term good health. Even where wealthy controlling families do not actively destroy wealth by indulging their whims in ill-fated ventures, they constitute a challenge to civil service power. In particular their private worries and aspirations throw sand in the wheels of the nation's industrial policy.

In any case, Japanese economic leaders believe that the entrepreneur's wealth-creating role is much exaggerated in the excessively individualistic societies of the Anglo-American world. In essence they believe that individuals are dispensable. They would argue that America's auto industry, for instance, would have developed along the lines it did even if Henry Ford had never left his Dearborn farm. In other words, Henry Ford and other giants of American corporate success are regarded less as geniuses than as people who happened to be standing in the right place at the right time. In a word, they are the lucky beneficiaries of the increasing returns syndrome as identified by Brian Arthur.

As strange as all this seems to economists of the Anglo-American school, the Japanese are hardly alone in their thinking. The Swiss, the Germans, the Austrians, and the Swedes also have built successful economies with the help of Japanese-style industrial policies.

Where the buck stops

At first sight Japan's top business leaders seem to be accountable to no one. In Japan, after all, shareholders have virtually no powers over management. They are deprived even of the right to sell out to a takeover raider because a majority of each corporation's shares is in the "safe" hands of its keiretsu affiliates. Nonetheless, despite all the collusion implicit in the keiretsu/cartel matrix, Japanese corporate executives are clearly accountable to someone. Otherwise, how can we explain why Japan's top executives pay themselves extremely modest compensation packages by American or British standards?

To whom are Japanese executives accountable? In the first instance, to one another. The keiretsu system provides a strong framework of accountability in which member firms watch each other. If one of a keiretsu's members is weak, this will be a matter of major concern to other members, who will be pressured in good time by the MOF and the MITI into bailing out the weakling in a crisis. In many cases, the keiretsu bank, equipped as it is with both analytical tools and financial power, will take the lead in addressing problems in good time by forcing incompetent or dishonest executives to retire.

In this sense the bankers are a latter-day replacement for the strong proprietors who ran American industry efficiently in the days before professional managers took control of large American corporations.

Western economists see frightening possibilities for conflict of interest in vesting so much power in keiretsu banks. But bank executives are themselves lifetime employees subject to the accountability built into the lifetime employment system, not to mention the stern guidance of the Finance Ministry and the Bank of Japan.

The civil servants perform an important function in ensuring that the cartels are run in the national interest; in fact, the two are locked in a symbiotic relationship. The civil servants grant members of the big cartels special privileges to enter promising new industrial fields, and the cartels return the compliment by being attentive to the civil servants' general policies for the economy.

Because the officials can withdraw or curtail the cartels' pricing privileges at any time, the cartels find it wise to listen attentively to the officials' administrative guidance on other matters. Officials also enjoy a powerful hidden weapon in their ability to set standards for

Japanese industry. Although standard-setting is nominally a matter for corporations, any corporation wanting its products to qualify for government procurement must comply with standards that are at least approved by, if not set by, the government.

Just how powerful the government's standard-setting role is was apparent in 1990 when the Ministry of International Trade and Industry announced what may well be the biggest standard-setting project in history. The project concerns the so-called Factory of the Future and involves a global effort to set standards for hundreds of types of high precision factory robots and other automatic production machines that will work together in the workerless factories of the future. Hitherto, computer-aided manufacturing equipment and computer-aided design equipment have been plagued with standardization problems that have slowed progress toward full-scale automation.

Officials also play a catalytic role in organizing Japan's research cartels. Without a strong government agency watching to ensure fair play, the participants in these cartels might be tempted to take a free ride by, for instance, withholding their best findings from the common pool for their own private use later. As the U.S. Office of Technology Assessment has pointed out, American attempts to copy the research cartel idea have been stymied by a reluctance on the part of participants to lend their best people to industrywide joint ventures.

Government-supervised research and development in Japan is monitored by three main agencies, the Science and Technology Agency, the MITI, and the Ministry of Education. Meanwhile, various advisory councils facilitate a national consensus on government research policies, allocating resources and legitimizing initiatives developed in the private sector by publicly endorsing them. Commenting in 1989, the U.S. Congress's Office of Technology Assessment said: "Japan's track record of successful R & D provides a strong vote of confidence for the top-down approach to planning."

The fact that Japanese bureaucrats can be both powerful and disinterested at the same time is the catalyst that keeps Japanese corporations from becoming the dysfunctional dinosaurs of Western economic theory.

9

Managed Trade, Managed Reality

The Uruguay round of world trade talks in 1993 will probably be remembered as America's last chance to achieve a real breakthough in trade with Japan. It was a moment when the Europeans were as exasperated as the Americans with East Asian mercantilism. If Washington had been adroit, therefore, it could have enlisted considerable international support for a determined effort to change Japan's trade practices. Because this was a world trade agreement, not just a bilateral U.S.-Japan agreement such as the one the Americans negotiated with Japan in 1994, Washington could have piled on the pressure by portraying Japanese intransigence as risking the entire world trade system.

So as the Uruguay round reached its climax in 1993, the Clinton administration's negotiators stood in the spotlight of history. But what began as a *High Noon* confrontation ended in the bathos of yet another American climbdown. Urged on by the *Wall Street Journal* and other media organizations that wanted an agreement at any price, America gave ground to Japan, particularly in the key areas of anti-dumping and financial regulation. In other areas, America and Japan agreed to make matching tariff reductions on each other's goods. Ostensibly this was fair, but America was getting the short end of the bargain because the tariff reductions covered goods like construction equipment and steel, of which Japan is a far bigger exporter than the United States.

Largely ignoring the trade complaints of American high-technology companies, Washington concentrated almost entirely on pressing Tokyo to relax Japan's famed ban on rice imports. Tokyo duly gave ground but only a little. It agreed to import 8 percent of its rice needs by the year 2000, which will probably generate at best about $500 million in sales a year for American farmers. This is a drop in the ocean compared to a recent conservative estimate that Japan's trade policies exclude about $13 billion of imports from the Japanese market.

The gentle art of negotiation

How did rice come to crowd out more economically significant items on America's trade agenda? The answer lies with decisions made in Tokyo, not in Washington. American officials allowed themselves to be outmaneuvered by an elaborate public relations initiative launched by the Japanese well ahead of the talks. Tokyo's strategy always is to focus American press attention as much as possible on certain trade barriers that Japan secretly intends to relax in the forthcoming talks. These barriers invariably are of little significance to Japan's industrial strategy, but, for the benefit of the American press, Tokyo portrays them as "politically sensitive" or "sacred" ones whose relaxation will entail almost unbearable costs within Japan. Although Tokyo's public relations agenda is easy for long-term residents to see through, most foreign correspondents have lived at best only a few years in Japan — too short a period for even the most astute of them to acquire a sense of the seriousness with which Tokyo strategizes ahead of trade negotiations. Tokyo is therefore consistently successful in persuading the press to focus on decoy issues in much the way a matador persuades a bull to charge a red cape. This pays off because, as Tokyo has proven time and again, Washington is driven not by reality but by public perceptions as shaped by the American media.

By contrast, in the case of more important trade barriers against America's high-technology products, Japanese negotiators work to minimize American press coverage. In particular, they prevail on aggrieved American high-technology corporations to keep quiet and negotiate strictly behind closed doors.

One of the most notable uses of the decoy technique was in the mid-1980s, when Tokyo encouraged the American press to portray Japan's quotas on imports of beef and oranges as America's most significant trade grievances. The Reagan administration duly took the hint and squandered much of its negotiating leverage on opening the Japanese market in these minor commodities.

Rice provided the perfect decoy for the Uruguay round. It had great symbolic value: the American press saw something satisfyingly "global" about American farmers supplying the Japanese with the age-old East Asian staff of life. Thus Tokyo launched a massive English-language public relations campaign portraying the rice policy as America's key trade grievance. Meanwhile, it set about exaggerating the degree of domestic opposition to reforming the policy. In particular, it portrayed Japan's supposedly all-powerful farm lobby as an implacable foe of even the slightest liberalization. In reality, however, the farm lobby, in common with Japan's company unions, is noted for the fact that its bark is a lot worse than its bite.

The Tokyo authorities even succeeded in presenting Japanese consumers as vehement opponents of cheap rice imports. Consumers had been unsettled by widespread reports in the Japanese media portraying American rice as a possible health hazard — reports that the Japanese press later blandly retracted after Tokyo agreed to relax the import ban.

This storm in a teacup reached its climax in 1990 when American rice marketers brought a few token samples of American rice to a trade fair in Tokyo. Instead of turning a blind eye or discreetly negotiating behind closed doors, grim-faced Japanese officials confiscated the "contraband" rice in front of the world's television cameras. Thus in the space of a few seconds, Tokyo established the indelible image of the "sacredness" of Japan's rice import ban.

That all this was pantomime is apparent when you realize that Japan has no absolute ban on rice imports and never has had: the 1942 law under which the Japanese rice market is regulated gives the government case-by-case control over rice imports, and in some years in the 1950s, when rice productivity was lower than it is today, bureaucrats permitted imported rice to take as much as 16 percent of the Japanese market. Moreover, as early as 1990 Japanese trade negotiators had indicated privately to Washington that they would, if pushed, make "considerable concessions" on rice in the Uruguay round. As recounted by the former U.S. trade negotiator Glen Fukushima, Japanese officials made clear that they would delay making their concessions until after other countries had made their concessions to secure a Uruguay round agreement. Ever the perfect negotiators, the Japanese dragged the talks out right up to the Americans' self-imposed deadline in December 1993, thus ensuring that the Clinton administration never got a chance to press Tokyo on any much more important trade issues.

The result could hardly have been more satisfactory for Tokyo. All Japan's public relations stressing the "sacredness" of the rice issue made the extremely modest 8 percent opening of the market look like a triumph for the Americans. The impression that the Americans had achieved a famous victory was in no way mitigated when politicians in Japan immediately denounced Japan's trade negotiators as "incompetents." Such denunciations are a standard part of Tokyo's negotiating script: for decades Japan's trade victories had been portrayed at home as defeats in which Japanese negotiators allowed themselves to be "bullied" by the Americans.

To cap it all, the American press's reaction also followed Tokyo's public relations script. The *Wall Street Journal* said the agreement was a "landmark step" toward opening the Japanese market and a "major concession" by Japan. The Associated Press dubbed Japan's rice decision "historic." Historic it was, but not in the way the Associated Press meant. In 1993, after 140 years of U.S.-Japan trade negotiations, the relationship had finally turned full circle. The once anachronistic hermit kingdom on the edge of the world had relegated its former would-be colonizer to the status of an eager supplier of simple commodities.

The emergence of scientific mercantilism

Westerners constantly underestimate how committed Japanese economic leaders are to mercantilism. The truth is that mercantilism is not only one of Japan's oldest economic policies (it has existed in various guises since the early 1600s) but in its modern form it has visibly proved a key tool of economic growth.

Japan's modern mercantilism — what we will call scientific mercantilism — began to take shape in the 1870s after the Finance Ministry official Norikazu Wakayama published a paper on the economic advantages of tariffs. At the time, Japan was barred from levying significant tariffs on imports under the terms of the Unequal Treaties. Finance Minister Shigenobu Okuma quickly found a way around this problem, however, by inventing the concept of nontariff barriers. In a policy statement entitled Fundamental Principles of Public Finance, Okuma in 1875 announced three policies to compensate for Japan's inability to levy significant tariffs against imports:

• The government was to control imports by allocating exclusive import licenses to certain Japanese traders. These traders would have to pay large fees for their licenses.

• The government was to impose various "internal taxes" on certain products. The theory of these taxes was that they would be levied on home-produced and imported goods alike, but in practice the government would confine the taxes to categories of goods that were supplied largely or wholly by foreign producers. Thus the taxes would have a strong de facto mercantilist effect in suppressing consumption.

• The government would grant subsidies to certain home industries to compete with imports.

The most important immediate result of Okuma's plan was that it gave birth to Japan's international trading houses, organizations that today are known by names like Mitsubishi Corporation, Nichimen, and Kanematsu Gosho. The new trading houses' main function was to operate officially-approved cartels to control the country's imports on behalf of the government.

In launching their policy of scientific mercantilism, Wakayama and other Japanese economic leaders were much impressed by the fact that the most successful Western nations were already strongly protectionist. In particular, the United States levied tariffs of typically more than 30 percent in those days. The Germans at this time were also highly protectionist. Not coincidentally, both the United States and Germany enjoyed extraordinarily strong growth at precisely the time when their tariffs were high. Their economies were avowedly driven by the protectionist ideas of Henry Charles Carey and Friedrich List, economists who were famous in their day but are now all but forgotten. Neither is even mentioned in the *Economist*'s Dictionary of Economics, for instance. They have not been forgotten in Japan, however, where their ideas have constituted the subject of examination paper questions for generations of would-be entrants to the higher civil service.

With the dawn of the twentieth century, protectionism began to fall into disrepute in the West, particularly in the United States where expansionist corporations began to chafe at Europe's barriers to American goods. In Japan, by contrast, industrial and economic leaders became more convinced than ever of the virtues of mercantilism. The Japanese perspective was authoritatively explained in 1935 in *Nihon Kogyo Seisaku,* an economic paper, by the top bureaucrat Shinji Yoshino. He held that free markets led to "confusion" that often left modern large-scale manufacturers with serious problems of overcapacity. Thus, entry into capital-intensive industries should be regulated and trade barriers imposed to ensure that foreign suppliers did not reduce domestic producers' capacity utilization rates. In effect Yoshino was addressing the already emerging problems caused by the Cost Structure Revolution.

From a Japanese point of view, an added advantage of a protectionist trade policy was that it served to increase domestic manufacturers' profits, thus bolstering Japan's aggregate savings rate and providing industry with large amounts of capital for expansion.

Even after Japan's defeat in World War II, Japan remained doggedly mercantilist. With the blessing of the American Occupation, Japanese officials established a comprehensive regimen of quotas and tariffs which made foreign consumer goods prohibitively expensive, thereby powerfully suppressing consumption. Meanwhile large sectors of the economy were organized to target export markets.

These policies helped to produce some of the highest savings rates and fastest growth rates in world economic history. But by the early 1960s, the West had begun to press for the opening of Japan's markets. Thus, for the second time in its modern history, Japan was being asked by the West to divest itself of the means to control the workings of its domestic economy. Japan had no compunction in resisting this outside interference. It promptly revived and extended the system of nontariff barriers it had invented in the late nineteenth century.

Mercantilism today

Under pressure from rising anti-protectionist feeling abroad, Japan moved in the 1970s and 1980s to eliminate some of its most notorious nontariff barriers. As a result, many sectors of the Japanese market are today relatively open — particularly textiles, clothing, running shoes, and household wares. This does little for the American trade balance, however, because the Japanese import such goods mainly from countries like China, South Korea, Thailand, Taiwan, and India, which have a big cost advantage over the United States. Moreover, in the case of some sophisticated consumer products, the Americans are stymied in Japan not because of trade barriers but because they have trouble meeting the quality standards set by Japan's domestic manufacturers.

That said, in other product categories significant barriers still exist. Japanese officials see good reasons to persist in mercantilism. First there is the contribution that mercantilism makes toward boosting the nation's savings rate. As Japan strives to consolidate its global leadership in advanced manufacturing, it needs savings more than ever. And, with the continuing swing toward fixed costs in industry, the need for stability in Japan's main markets is stronger than ever.

As we have already seen, Japan's savings these days spring mainly from its neomercantilist system of suppressing consumption. Meanwhile, corporate Japan overcomes the problems caused by high fixed costs with the help of cartels and keiretsus. These serve to discourage imports but, more important and more legitimately, they act as a buffer protecting Japanese producers from extreme price fluctuations in world markets.

The cartel system's role in closing the Japanese market to outsiders is notably evident in glass. Glass making is a classic example of an industry where high fixed costs serve to create powerful pressures toward cartelization in most of the world's markets. Japan is no exception: its three big producers have held their market shares more or less constant at around 50 percent, 30 percent, and 20 percent for most of the postwar period. After years of trying to export to Japan, American makers have gone public with allegations that their Japanese competitors are restricting imports by threatening to boycott Japanese distributors who handle American glass. The upshot is that American companies have only 1 percent of the Japanese market. By comparison one Japanese producer alone now has 25 percent of the American market (where strict antitrust law makes sure that American manufacturers cannot use cartel techniques to keep foreign producers out).

In other protected industries, the Japanese bureaucracy functions as the primary instrument of protection, albeit less overtly than in the heyday of Japanese mercantilism in the 1950s and 1960s. The bureaucrats' efforts these days are concentrated on certain targeted industries, notably high-technology ones. A good example is the helicopter industry. Before foreign helicopters can be imported into Japan, they have to be taken apart and their electronic systems individually bench-tested in Japanese laboratories at great expense to the foreign manufacturers.

The bureaucrats have also been noticeably active in protecting the Japanese pharmaceutical industry. Here foreign suppliers are confronted by a classic Japanese nontariff barrier, a lack of accurate information on how to comply with Japanese regulations. An example of what is involved is the experience a few years ago of one American health care company, which checked with twenty-six different Japanese official and semiofficial agencies on labeling rules before launching a new product in the Japanese market. After no objections were raised, the company went ahead with the product introduction, but six months later it had to abort the effort and recall all supplies of the product. The problem was, as a Health and Welfare Ministry official pointed out, the company was in breach of Japanese regulations because the label carried the name of the American parent corporation, not that of the Japanese operating company.

Few Westerners enjoy a better vantage point from which to assess the real significance of Japan's trade "liberalization" programs than the management consultant C. Tait Ratcliffe. In a critique of Japanese trade policy recently, Ratcliffe talked of "an endless series of Catch-22s" standing in the way of the West's would-be exporters. He highlighted a recent practice by the Japanese authorities to form committees of Japanese and foreign business representatives to "investigate" alleged trade barriers. The foreign committee members are required to take time off from their managerial duties to research Japanese law and provide detailed case studies, yet in the end things rarely change.

Ratcliffe commented: "Anyone involved in this process who fails to experience discouragement from time to time must either be insensitive to his surroundings or enjoy punishment. An objective analysis of what is happening here suggests that the requirement to generate information in fact is being used as a means to slow the pace of change. . . . After a time, one finally realizes that the point is the bureaucracy is not motivated to make changes unless it absolutely has to, and that the politicians, who do most of the talking to foreign interests, are not in a position to require the bureaucracy to do their bidding without a special effort."

Japan's true policy is that it upholds the principle of free trade — except in the almost infinite number of instances where that principle is deemed to be hurting the Japanese economy. In a word, all denials to the contrary, Japan believes in managed trade.

Buying American

One reason why the United States has taken so long to get focused on Japanese trade barriers is that Japanese officials have consistently structured Japan's trade with the United States to make their mercantilism as unobtrusive as possible in American eyes.

In particular, as the management writer Peter Drucker has illustrated, Tokyo has long pursued a policy of favoring American suppliers when buying food and other commodities, thereby minimizing the bilateral surplus with the United States at the expense of suppliers elsewhere in the world. One recent manifestation of this policy was a decision in 1993 to increase Japan's imports of American coal via a new terminal in Los Angeles that is being funded by the Japanese government. The policy was also apparent in 1994 when Japan opened its market to American apples, while continuing to exclude European apples.

Such buy-American policies sound like a favor to the United States, but their significance is almost entirely cosmetic. In actuality, the fortunes of producers in the United States are determined by world commodity prices rather than the purchasing preferences of any particular importer.

At times of extreme trade friction, Tokyo has gone so far as to encourage explicit stockpiling of various imported commodities as a way to reduce the Japanese account surplus. In 1972, for instance, it launched an official policy to stockpile imported agricultural products. The government also facilitated an "emergency purchase" of $320 million worth of commercial aircraft and $320 million of enriched uranium.

A similar concern to smooth over trade difficulties with the United States was apparent in Japan's relatively large-scale importing of American cars in the 1970s. American cars outsold European cars in

Japan by a large margin, yet at that time the European makers enjoyed a large edge over the Americans not only in quality but in value for money. Clearly something other than market forces was at work. Japanese economic leaders were evidently managing Japan's trade to favor the Americans as a public relations gesture to Washington at a time when the Japanese auto industry was making huge increases in its exports to the United States.

Managed trade is still apparent in the auto industry in the 1990s, albeit in a slightly different form. These days, Japan's big auto makers are increasingly importing cars into Japan from their overseas assembly plants. The significant thing is that virtually all these so-called reverse imports are sourced from only one country, the United States. Yet Japan has assembly plants in many countries, and in most of these countries labor is much cheaper than in the United States. Superior American quality is not the explanation because the Japanese get similarly high quality in plants in other countries. A reasonable explanation is that the Japanese auto industry is making a gesture toward soothing American trade friction.

In the late 1980s, the Ministry of Finance helped cut the current account surpluses by offering large tax incentives to wealthy Japanese individuals to import American and European works of art and other collectibles. The most visible such imports were Impressionist paintings, but Japan was also making heavy purchases in virtually every other category of serious collectibles, including vintage cars, old cameras, first editions, coins, diamonds, and gold bullion.

Although Japanese officials have tried to suggest that the Clinton administration's effort to manage American trade is inadvisable, they clearly believe in micro-managing Japan's end of the trade equation.

Jujitsu pricing

One of the Japanese economic system's most important protectionist strategies over the years has been to induce Western companies to price high in selling their products in the Japanese market. This satisfies the Western companies' quest for profits. It is also congruent with Japan's mercantilism, because high-priced goods naturally sell only in disproportionately small quantities.

In many cases, when Western corporations have priced high in

Japan they have been conforming to explicitly stated Japanese government guidance. Sometimes the government has prescribed prices as high as three times those of competing Japanese products.

The price-high strategy has also been reinforced by the way that imports are distributed in Japan. Strange though it may seem, many would-be American exporters to Japan ask a Japanese manufacturer in the same line of business to handle their distribution. The line of least resistance for all concerned is for the Japanese manufacturer to position the imported products at the top of the market, minimizing the competition for its own nearly identical products.

Many American and European corporations have reaped large profits from this strategy for many years but at the expense of depriving their home countries of potential jobs. Meanwhile, because the Japanese producers retain the volume end of the Japanese market for themselves, they are afforded a strong base in which to perfect their manufacturing skills and amortize their fixed costs. This provides them with the springboard eventually to export in volume into the Western competitors' home markets, with decidedly negative implications for Western jobs.

America's biggest export: jobs

Japan's American lobbyists have often argued that those American corporations that "make an effort" in Japan have little difficulty selling there. Major corporations often cited as having succeeded after making such an "effort" are Xerox, Honeywell, NCR, Hewlett-Packard, Texas Instruments, IBM, Du Pont, and Caterpillar.

The implication usually drawn is that these companies are big exporters to Japan. This could hardly be further from the truth. In most cases, these "make-an-effort" corporations are — however unwittingly — agents of Japanese mercantilism. Generally they have secured access to the Japanese market only by agreeing to site many of their most sophisticated manufacturing operations on Japanese soil. Not only is virtually everything they sell in Japan made there, but in many cases they export back to the United States. Thus America's make-an-effort corporations create high-quality jobs for Japanese workers and lucrative sales opportunities for Japanese suppliers of components and equipment. As a net contributor to Japan's trade surplus with the United States, they are therefore part of America's problem, not part of the solution.

The former U.S. Treasury economist Stephen D. Cohen has noted that American corporations' subsidiaries in Japan import remarkably little from the United States compared with similar American subsidiaries in Europe and Canada. Typically the only thing the American economy gets out of its Japanese investments is a tiny stream of dividends and perhaps some royalties for patents, and even these flows are sometimes more than offset by the periodic dispatches of fresh capital going out of America to pay for state-of-the-art Japanese-made manufacturing equipment to keep the Japanese operation at the leading edge.

In these days of trade friction with the United States, Japanese officials are less explicit than they once were about the guidance they give to American corporations setting up in Japan. Until well into the 1970s, however, such corporations were openly required by the Ministry of Finance to comply with a long list of written rules of Japanese industrial policy. Foreign corporations were required 1) to develop Japan's technological resources; 2) to promote Japanese exports; 3) to "cooperate" with Japanese competitors to avoid "excessive competition"; and 4) to safeguard the jobs of their Japanese employees.

The foreigners were also required to uphold Japan's tradition of "industrial harmony," a catchall stipulation that could be stretched to cover almost any afterthought the Finance Ministry might want to append. Also, foreign investors were told that they were more likely to get necessary official permits if they formed a joint venture with a Japanese competitor, a stipulation that almost automatically ensured the joint venture would buy Japanese for most of its parts and equipment.

Under pressure from the United States, Japan no longer puts these rules on paper, but their spirit lives on in the advice American corporations get from management consultants and lawyers in Japan. As a general rule, the more technology an American corporation transfers to Japan, the smoother its path in Japanese society. Many American subsidiaries in Japan are in fact highly profitable. As of the early 1990s, foreign ventures in Japan were enjoying margins about twice the Japanese norm.

In almost every case those American corporations that do well in Japan cooperate closely with Japanese industrial policy. Such corporations are generally accepted as junior members of the Japanese cartels. They also often get to participate in *dango,* the collusive bidding system that Japanese cartels use in tendering for public sector contracts. Even when American corporations succeed in selling made-in-America products in Japan, they usually do so only after they have agreed to make extensive use of Japanese parts and equipment. America's personal computer makers, for instance, are relatively successful in Japan these days, but their success came only after they began sourcing parts heavily from Japan.

In short, the Americans are being co-opted. Marcus Noland, a Japan specialist at the Washington-based Institute for International Economics, has pointed out that Tokyo consciously tries to co-opt American corporations that invest in Japan. These corporations then find they are making better profit margins in Japan than anywhere else, and they actively lobby the American government to desist from trying to open the Japanese market to other American companies. Noland has suggested that American semiconductor makers and American construction companies in particular have been co-opted in this way.

A ratchet effect is at work: the jobs that an American corporation creates in Japan tend to be permanent. In fact, an American corporation may increasingly find itself forced to build its global strategy around preserving and enriching the jobs of its Japanese work force. Hence a notable pattern in the world economic malaise of the 1990s was that American corporations which fired workers in the United States spared their work forces in Japan or even continued hiring there.

Often when an American corporation is moving to a higher level of technology, its Japanese executives lobby to get the new factory for Japan. Their behavior is governed by Japan's unique definition of a corporation. As we have already noted, the *kaisha* — the Japanese-style corporation — exists primarily for the sake of its employees, not its shareholders. Following this logic, local Japanese executives feel they owe their loyalty not to the American top management, let alone the ultimate shareholders in the United States, but to their own work force in Japan and, more generally, to the Japanese economy.

One of the most often cited American success stories in Japan is that of Xerox, whose Japanese joint venture Fuji Xerox employs more than 15,000 people. Yet Fuji Xerox illustrates all the problems entailed in the make-an-effort syndrome. Fuji Xerox imports little from the United States. Moreover, it has effectively hollowed out the American parent company through its exports from Japan and, however unwittingly, has served as something of a Trojan horse by indirectly helping Xerox's many Japanese competitors get started. These competitors were helped by the fact that, in line with the Japanese bureaucrats' requirements, Fuji Xerox sourced many of its components in Japan and thus built up a pool of sophisticated local suppliers of copier components.

For Americans, perhaps an even more troubling example of the make-an-effort syndrome has been the story of IBM's Tokyo subsidiary IBM Japan. When it built its first postwar plant in Japan, for instance, IBM made elaborate efforts to use only Japanese materials and machines, and since then it has been the Japanese bureaucracy's idea of a model Japanese corporate citizen. Almost all IBM equipment sold in Japan is made there, generally using Japanese production machines and components. Meanwhile IBM's Japanese factories export about 25 percent of their output.

In the circumstances, it is hardly surprising that IBM's Japanese work force has been sheltered from the corporation's massive worldwide "downsizing" of recent years. Although IBM cut its worldwide work force from 405,000 to 252,000 between 1985 and 1994, the company actually *increased* its work force in Japan from 17,000 to 23,000. This is despite the fact that thanks to the booming yen, the dollar cost of employing people in Japan has considerably more than doubled since 1985.

Just how faithful IBM Japan is to local norms became clear in the early 1980s after IBM in the United States had caught Hitachi red-handed stealing IBM technology. The case presented IBM Japan with an acute dilemma because the Japanese press portrayed IBM, not Hitachi, as the guilty party. This was because IBM had used entrapment methods to lead Hitachi on, and such methods are considered unfair in Japan. IBM Japan executives sided with the Japanese press and, in an in-your-face rebuke to the IBM parent company in Armonk, New York, they semipublicly apologized for IBM's entrapment of Hitachi.

For Americans, perhaps the most depressing aspect of the make-an-effort syndrome is that in the long run most American-owned businesses in Japan end up being taken over by Japanese competitors.

The pattern usually is that once the Americans have transferred all their important technology to Japan, Japanese government officials and bankers no longer coddle the Japanese subsidiary. In effect, the venture loses its "affirmative action" status and is left to fend for itself in what is for American corporate managements one of the toughest and most baffling business environments in the world.

A few years of low returns and unpleasant surprises and most American managements are amenable to being bought out. The Japanese employees are usually only too eager for such an outcome because in Japan working for a foreign company generally carries a social stigma.

After being taken over by a major Japanese concern, the company's fortunes generally begin to improve again. In fact, some of Japan's greatest corporations started as offshoots of American and European corporations. Among the dozens of companies that could be cited, the most prominent are the giant NEC corporation (started by Western Electric) and JVC (started by RCA). Meanwhile Matsushita Electronics was started as an affiliate of Philips Electronic and Mitsubishi Motors as a partner of Chrysler.

In addition to those Western corporations that have set up factories in Japan, many more have licensed their technology and brand names to Japanese competitors. Again they did so under duress: generally such licensing was initiated at a time when it was impossible for Western corporations to sell their products in Japan. To earn some money from their technology, they felt they had no choice but to enter into such licensing ventures, even if the royalties involved were little more than a pittance. This explains the impressive proliferation of familiar Western brand names in Japan. But the fact that these brand names are owned in Japan by Japanese companies actually precludes the original Western companies who sold the rights from selling in Japan. To add insult to injury, many writers of op-ed articles in the American press have portrayed the proliferation of Western brand names in Japan as evidence of the openness of the Japanese market. The *Wall Street Journal* in particular has often printed such articles.

The bottom line on American corporations' attempts to exploit their technology in the Japanese market is that, as calculated by Senator Jay Rockefeller, American corporations transferred technology worth $500 billion to Japan in the last quarter of a century alone, and Japan paid about $9 billion for it.

Perhaps the unkindest cut for American workers is that the Japanese foreign minister Kabun Muto recently publicly criticized corporate America for establishing subsidiaries overseas. In an attempt in 1993 to quell American anger over trade, he laid the blame for America's deficits firmly at the door of American corporations that had transferred jobs to Japan and other foreign countries.

Blinded by capitalism

Clearly America's trade relations with Japan in the last two decades have been a fiasco. Where does the blame lie?

It is shared by many members of the American establishment, which for years has been remarkably complacent about the hollowing out of the American job base. The McKinsey management consulting firm, for instance, has fostered this complacency by portraying the drain of America's high-technology jobs to Japan as reassuring evidence of American strength. In particular Kenichi Ohmae, speaking in his capacity as a top McKinsey partner, gave the McKinsey imprimatur to this erroneous view. He argued that the trend was proof of corporate America's special expertise in managing overseas operations. McKinsey has also argued that the massive American account deficits are nothing to worry about because America's exports were supposedly dramatically understated in the official trade figures. His view is that the trade figures should be adjusted to count any products made in corporate America's Japanese subsidiaries as an American "export." The adjusted figures would, of course, show a trade "surplus" for the United States. Using this logic, McKinsey maintained that America had no trade deficit with Japan!

The profitability of corporate America's manufacturing Japanese operations has been widely presented by the American elite as if it were evidence of the openness of the Japanese market. This argument was notably made by Robert Christopher, the secretary of the Pulitzer Prize Board, in a 1986 book on American-owned manufacturing ventures in Japan. Even Mike Mansfield, America's ambassador to Japan in the crucial years of the 1980s, has made a similarly misleading argument in an essay sponsored by corporate Japan.

Few people bear more responsibility for the fiasco of American trade policies than Western economists. They have constantly misled

Americans into believing that Japan "shoots itself in the foot" when it practices mercantilism. This point has been used to great advantage by Japan's Washington lobbyists to quell American anxiety over East Asian protectionism. In particular, the lobbyists have fostered vain hopes that once East Asia discovers it is "impoverishing" itself with mercantilism, it will see the "universal wisdom" of American-style open trade.

The error in American thinking has come from the top of the intellectual establishment. The Nobel laureate Milton Friedman must bear a disproportionate share of the blame. Friedman has led the American establishment in adopting a "pacifist" stance toward East Asian mercantilism. Writing with his wife, Rose, he condemned the argument that the United States is foolish to maintain open markets when other countries protect their markets. He said, "This argument has no validity either in principle or in practice. Other countries that impose restrictions on international trade do hurt us. But they also hurt themselves. If we impose restrictions in turn, we add to the harm to ourselves and harm them as well."

Friedman's stance is a typical case of a tendency, noted many years ago by the Stanford economist Tibor de Scitovszky, for economists to overstate the free trade argument out of populist motives. As de Scitovszky authoritatively pointed out, the truth is countries that close their markets to foreign goods often profit from doing so. He wrote, "Free trade can be shown to be beneficial to the universe as a whole but has never been proved to be the best policy also for a single country." He added that intelligent protectionism allows a country to gain at the expense of others not only by maximizing employment in the short term but maximizing economic growth in the long term.

As we have seen, the most important effect of mercantilism is to raise a nation's savings rate. It is time to look at how Japan manages its torrential savings flows.

10

Money at Work

In Chapter Six we saw how Japan has developed powerful techniques to stimulate the flow of savings. For these flows to generate maximum economic growth they must be channeled into the right industries — which primarily means those industries where corporate Japan has the best chance of establishing important global monopolies.

Overseeing this channeling process is a crucial function of the MOF. And although there has been much talk in the Western press in the last two decades that the MOF is liberalizing the Japanese financial system, it still has an impressively tight grip on Japan's savings flows.

One of the frankest descriptions of the latter-day "liberalized" Japanese financial system has come from Akio Mikuni, president of a Japanese credit rating agency. Writing in the *New York Times* in 1993, he said Americans could not understand the Japanese economy without understanding the MOF's extraordinary powers. The MOF, he pointed out, runs the Japanese economy on a "wartime" basis. Mikuni, a Tokyo University–educated former securities industry executive, explained:

> The ministry can shape and control the economy through the informal right to intervene in any and all transactions. It can control which corporations receive bank credit and which do not. It determines interest rates and controls the prices of stocks, real estate and other investments.
>
> It need not explain its actions to the diet, the prime minister, or anyone else. It controls the critical financial information necessary for

an open discussion on economic policy and even for an accurate analysis of individual corporations.

Working behind closed doors, the MOF interacts so smoothly with the Keidanren, the cartels, and the keiretsus that its influence on Japanese corporate finance is virtually invisible to the casual foreign observer. As a writer in the *Nihon Keizai Shimbun* described it in 1993, communication between the bureaucrats and the private sector has so matured that the spoken word is less and less necessary. Communication has reached the level of *aun no kokyu,* a mystical concept from Buddhism denoting a state of empathy in which people silently complete each other's thoughts.

If the MOF's actions in financial policy are generally almost undetectable, the effects of those actions have always been apparent in the singular structure of the Japanese economy. In the early days of the economic miracle, for instance, the MOF induced the bank cartel to channel vast amounts of capital to expand Japan's steel, shipping, electric power, and shipbuilding industries. By contrast, as the banks openly acknowledged, consumption-oriented industries were intentionally starved for funds.

More recently, the Japanese financial system has visibly prioritized investment in such export industries as electronics, new materials, machine tools, and cars. But, because of the MOF's continuing bias against financing domestic consumption, Japan suffers from a shortage of all sorts of leisure facilities, from golf courses and yacht marinas to cinemas and tennis courts.

In essence, the MOF would like to control the ultimate destination of every last yen of Japan's savings. That is an impossible dream, of course. But, as we will see, the ministry has come surprisingly close to achieving its ambition.

The cork in the bottle

Western economists believe we live in a global economy in which money is free to flow to wherever the financial returns look most promising. Thus, American and European corporations can now supposedly compete on equal terms with Japanese corporations to tap Japan's savings torrent.

This analysis ignores a key factor: the Ministry of Finance. The first order of business for the MOF in regulating the financial system is to keep Japanese savings dammed up inside the country. Ordinary Japanese savers are effectively blocked from direct access to foreign financial markets. Conversely, foreign corporations are almost entirely blocked from raising finance in Japan.

The MOF closes the loop by guiding the foreign investment activities of Japan's various financial institutions. The result is that the Japanese financial system is almost completely insulated from the rest of the world. And, as even the *Economist* acknowledged in 1994, after decades of much-publicized deregulation, the Japanese saver is still a captive who by and large has no alternative but to put up with whatever meager return the Japanese financial cartels are prepared to offer him or her. This in essence explains why the Japanese financial system continues to provide Japanese corporations with some of the cheapest capital in the world.

In a word, the impression in the West that Japan has now largely deregulated its foreign capital flows is little more than a figment of the imagination of Western economists. True, in the last fifteen years the MOF has dismantled its once draconian exchange controls, which were introduced in the 1930s to prevent capital flight. But the MOF now has other ways of maintaining its grip. In particular it has prevailed on the American financial services industry to respect the cartelization of Japanese finance. Take mutual funds. Not only are most American mutual fund houses forbidden by the MOF to send direct mail into Japan, but if a saver in Japan phones New York or Boston for the forms to open a mutual fund account, he will be refused. Japanese savers encounter similar problems setting up American brokerage accounts. Of course, the MOF has no formal legal power to tell anyone what to do within American borders. But it is a very powerful organization in international finance and the major institutions of American finance seem prepared to accept its guidance on such matters.

In a few exceptional cases American mutual fund organizations are allowed to market in Japan, but only if they first receive official authorization from the MOF. This sounds easy, but in practice it's a Catch-22. To get such authorization, mutual fund management firms have to set up special bizarrely structured funds solely for use in Japan that are expensive to run and unattractive to investors. And such funds generally have to be marketed through Japanese brokerage houses, which are firmly under the MOF's control.

One reason the American business press has assumed that Japan was serious about deregulating its capital controls was that the MOF in the 1980s allowed many American corporations to list their stocks on the Tokyo Stock Exchange. This action ostensibly meant that Japanese savers could now invest directly in corporate America. The results have been disappointing. The market rules for foreign listings have been designed to ensure that trading in foreign stocks in Tokyo generally fizzles out within a few months of initial listing. Again, the story is of byzantine restrictions and cartel dynamics. Trading has been so low that many American corporations have canceled their Tokyo listings in the last few years, and many more would do so but for the fear of losing face in the eyes of Japanese customers and employees.

It is impossible here to do justice to the full story. However, the degree to which Japan's capital market is insulated from the rest of the world can be summed up in one statistic: as of mid-1994, Japanese stocks paid on average a dividend yield of just 0.7 percent — less than one-quarter the American average. Although a financial analyst would point out that there are many adjustments that need to be made to get an exact comparison, the general message is indisputable: corporate Japan's capital costs are only a fraction of corporate America's.

Banking on the banks

Japan's big banks are the cornerstone of the Japanese financial system. By virtue of their size and their leadership position in the keiretsus, they are much more powerful institutions than America's so-called money center banks.

Japan's top bankers, who spring from the same educational background as top MOF bureaucrats, collaborate closely with the MOF. Thus the big banks remain the MOF's most important instruments for guiding the economy. As with so much of Japanese economics, the closeness of the MOF's relationship with the big banks was in part a spinoff from World War II. Before World War II, the MOF had begun liberalizing the financial system, but in the early 1940s it introduced a tight system of controls on bank lending. The extraordinary new regulatory ethos was summed up in a remark by Kiichiro Sato, a former chairman of Mitsui Bank: "During and after the war . . . the Japanese economy was so controlled that it has become second nature with us to uphold a planned, controlled economy."

After the war, the Ministry of Finance perfected a system of detailed planning in which it promoted economic growth in partnership with the MITI, the Keidanren federation of big business, the big financial cartels, and the emerging keiretsus. This helped the MOF maintain careful case-by-case control over the flows of capital to industry. Not coincidentally, Japan quickly went on to enjoy the fastest growth in its history.

The MOF forced companies to rely mainly on loan capital by putting various restrictions on the availability of equity finance, thus in effect putting the corporations under the banks' thumb. Because the banks in turn were under the MOF's thumb, the MOF enjoyed great control over the investment plans of individual corporations. The pressure for corporations to eschew equity finance was a masterpiece of MOF minimalism: the MOF simply ruled that issues of new shares should be priced at "par," or face value, rather than at the prevailing market price. Given that the MOF also required companies to maintain their dividends, the effective cost of equity finance was far higher than bank loans.

Many of the MOF's most overt controls over the banks have now ostensibly been abolished. Because the MOF works mainly behind closed doors, the evidence that it still enjoys extraordinary regulatory control surfaces only occasionally. The American real estate market has recently provided such an insight. As reported by Mitchell Pacelle of the *Wall Street Journal,* Japanese banks require permission from the MOF before they can foreclose on troubled real estate development companies in the United States, giving the MOF direct influence over real estate markets in major American cities.

The secret of the MOF's continuing influence over the banks' lending is that it has retained a great many indirect controls; an example is its control over the banks' branch expansion programs. Other things being equal, a bank's size in the cartelized Japanese banking system is closely related to the number and location of its branches. In response to American pressure for financial liberalization, the MOF in 1993 finally said it would relax its controls over bank branching

— but only "partially." Few who have observed the pace of Japanese financial regulation over the years are holding their breath.

The de facto cartelization of finance also gives the MOF considerable power. The banks enjoy great benefits from the cartel system — to take just one example, fees for many bank services in Japan are very high. The MOF obligingly turns a blind eye but in return expects the banks to cooperate with its guidance.

As the leading Japanese finance expert Masasuke Ide commented a few years ago, the Ministry of Finance and the major banks "are like father and children." The father protects the children — but demands obedience in return.

The Tokyo stock market as national lottery

In recent years, the securities industry has come to rival the banks as a conduit of savings to industry. This new role has followed the relaxation of MOF restrictions that previously made equity finance unattractive to corporate Japan. Beginning in the 1980s, Japanese corporations have raised huge amounts of capital via issues of new shares and other securities, notably convertible bonds that provide holders with the right to buy shares on preferential terms.

Officially, the right to raise capital in the Tokyo stock market is determined by a cartel of major stockbroking firms, but these firms are subject to strict guidance from the MOF. Virtually without exception, corporations approved to issue bonds or stocks in Tokyo are in targeted industries or are otherwise favored under Japanese industrial policy.

Not content with restricting access to stock market funds, the MOF also controls the source of these funds — the big insurance companies and other major investment houses. Japan's major life insurance companies are mutuals that are tightly controlled by the Ministry of Finance. The MOF is believed to specify overall targets for the insurance companies' investment allocations in various categories of investment, whether it be Japanese stocks and bonds or overseas stocks and bonds.

Viewed from a Western standpoint, the Japanese stock market seems highly dysfunctional. Stocks constantly yo-yo in defiance of financial gravity. Much of the action is directed by the big securities firms, which often act in concert to control stock prices. The victims are small-time speculators, who are openly regarded by the Japanese securities industry as sheep to be sheared.

The Japanese approach to running a stock market looks alarming to foreigners. But from the MOF's point of view, things look quite satisfactory. A dangerous stock market helps the MOF in its primary objective of controlling Japan's savings flows. Savers are scared into avoiding stocks, so they put their money instead in banks, insurance companies, mutual funds, and trust companies, whose stock investment activities are subject to the MOF's guidance. The result is that personal investors are a dying breed in Japan. At last count they owned just 24 percent of all shares outstanding, down from more than 40 percent in 1970 and from as much as 70 percent in the early 1950s.

To say that the MOF actively condones the securities industry's fleecing of small investors is a surprising statement. Where is the evidence? Since the occupation, the MOF has opposed measures that would make the stock market fairer for small investors. In particular, it opposed and eventually killed off an independent stock market watchdog organization established by MacArthur as Japan's equivalent of America's tough SEC. The MOF sometimes blames the Tokyo Stock Exchange for the lack of adequate safeguards for small investors. In practice, however, this is tantamount to blaming itself, because the Tokyo Stock Exchange is a de facto department of the Ministry and for many years its top personnel have been retired top MOF bureaucrats.

The MOF systematically restricts the availability of new financial instruments such as options and futures, which in the West have served as powerful tools to frustrate the activities of market manipulators. A recent study by a committee of foreign financial institutions in Tokyo found that of twenty-five financial instruments readily available to participants in American and European financial markets, only twelve are available in Japan, and of these only seven can be freely accessed.

Compared to regulatory agencies in the West, the MOF enjoys a unique advantage in curbing the growth of new financial instruments because the basic philosophy of regulation in Japan is radically different: as the Tokyo University economist Kazuo Ueda has pointed out, whereas in the West everything is permitted unless expressly prohibited, in Japan everything is prohibited unless expressly permitted.

If a stock market is to work fairly, investors must have equal access to detailed information on a timely basis. Virtually everything about the way the stock market is administered in Japan violates this principle: its financial disclosure rules are full of loopholes that allow Japanese corporations to withhold vital information from small investors (Japan's big investors are a different matter because, via the keiretsu grapevine, they often are privy to a corporation's deepest secrets). Yet on the surface Japan's financial disclosure rules appear in most respects to be almost identical to American rules.

The inadequacy of Japanese disclosure was laid startlingly bare in 1993 when Showa Shell Sekiyu, a Tokyo-listed oil company partly owned by the Royal Dutch/Shell oil group, disclosed more than $1 billion of losses incurred in foreign exchange speculation. This was a new world record for a foreign exchange loss by an industrial company — a truly extraordinary distinction for a relative minnow of a company that employs only two thousand workers. In fact, when Shell executives in Europe first received a message from Showa admitting the loss, they kept wiring back for a correction: Shell's European directors were sure that the number had been mistakenly overstated by a factor of ten. In their experience it was beyond belief that a company of Showa's size could incur such losses. What they didn't know was the loss had been accumulating not for six months, as they had assumed, but for fully three years. In that period Showa had been gambling increasingly wildly on the value of the dollar without a word of disclosure to its shareholders. Contrary to standard Western accounting practice, the MOF's accounting rules allowed Showa Shell's management to hide the worsening losses in several sets of misleading public financial statements.

As described by Yoko Shibata of *Global Finance* magazine, the MOF specifically allowed Showa executives to "roll over" foreign exchange positions in an artificial maneuver that hid the losses. By the time Showa came clean, its risk exposure had ballooned to $7.4 billion, thirty-seven times the maximum $200 million exposure Showa executives were allowed under the company's guidelines. Showa Shell's announcement of the loss was greeted with panic on the Tokyo Stock Exchange, where its shares fell by nearly half within a week.

While there is no evidence that members of the public were deliberately bilked in this case, the general pattern of misleading accounting practices fosters stock manipulation and other shady practices.

Clearly the Tokyo stock market is a place where the unwary lose heavily. But who gains? American observers wrongly assume that the main beneficiaries are unethical insiders such as Japanese securities industry executives. Such executives, however, are closely monitored by the MOF. Not only are they not allowed to benefit personally from the manipulations they conduct on behalf of their firms, but they typically earn less than one-tenth of the compensation of their Wall Street counterparts.

The most visible beneficiaries from Tokyo's rigged stock market are politicians, who have long been rumored to acquire much of the money used in Japanese politics from stock manipulation schemes. But in the larger scheme of things, the politicians' take is relatively minor. Politicians apart, few individuals benefit personally from the systematic rigging of stock prices.

The real winner is the Japanese nation. Japan's big securities firms and investment institutions are in effect proxies for the nation and the profits they make in the stock market are applied to finance Japanese industry. In effect, the stock market is a lottery run for the benefit of Japan's industrial policy.

A yen for exports

One of the most powerful influences on the Japanese economy is exchange rates. For large Japanese exporters, movements in the yen's overseas value is a much more significant influence on profits than fluctuations in Japan's domestic interest rates. For that reason, Japan's industrial planners generally want to keep the yen as low as possible.

In recent years, conservative economists have believed that a government cannot successfully manipulate the value of a nation's currency. Thus, the idea that Japan has purposefully used a cheap currency to undercut foreign competitors is considered by many Western economists to be a feeble and discredited excuse for American industry's poor showing against Japanese competition.

Japan's industrial planners know better. They know that a financial system can be designed specifically to undervalue a nation's currency. In practice, thanks to their enormous regulatory control of the financial system, they have generally kept the yen about 10 to 30 percent below its true value for decades. The result has been to equip Japanese exporters with a unique selling proposition: every new wave of Japanese goods to hit Western markets always offers superb value for money. Therefore Japanese corporations have been able to move with amazing speed to sign up key distributors for new product lines even where they are going up against entrenched Western competition.

Let us be clear about one thing: a cheap yen is not a cost-free policy for Japan. It means that Japan has to pay more yen for its imports and it gets less value when it invests abroad. Yet these sacrifices have been worth making because, thanks to the monopolistic nature of the modern global economy, Japanese cartels can hope in the long run to earn a superb return for the nation once they establish global price leadership.

An undervalued yen has been a recurring motif in the MOF's economic strategy for more than sixty years, and indeed Japan has made its most remarkable advances during periods when the yen was visibly undervalued. In 1931, for instance, the Ministry of Finance unilaterally devalued the yen by a massive 40 percent to help Japanese exporters prosper in the teeth of a global depression. With a cheap yen, Japan's exports of cotton goods and other textiles to the United States soon recovered, and Japanese manufacturers quickly conquered major markets in East Asia that had previously been dominated by the Americans and Europeans.

After World War II, the MOF bargained fiercely with the Americans to keep the yen as cheap as possible. The crucial negotiations that fixed the yen's postwar value took place in 1949. The Americans wanted to set an exchange rate of ¥300 to the dollar, which they reckoned would allow Japanese exporters to prosper. But the MOF dug its heels in, and the Americans were persuaded to peg the dollar 20 percent higher, at ¥360. This created a cycle of prosperity for Japanese exporters, who suddenly found exporting highly profitable. They reinvested their profits in state-of-the-art machinery and overwhelmed overseas markets before competitors woke up.

The MOF's cheap yen has been more difficult to maintain since President Richard Nixon ushered in the era of floating exchange rates in the early 1970s. Nonetheless, the yen has generally been substantially undervalued since then. Even as it hit unheard-of records in the early 1990s, it was still probably quite undervalued. Although this may seem surprising, it really is not. The Japanese were typically working with two to three times as much capital equipment as their

American counterparts. As in the past, in the early 1990s the yen rose only *after* Japanese exporters had securely moved to higher levels of productivity. This refutes the argument often put by the American press that a high yen somehow forces Japanese manufacturers to become more efficient — all historical evidence indicates that an over-valued currency is a major problem for a country, and certainly most American economists now admit that America's high dollar in the early 1980s was a disaster for American industry. Moreover, Japan made its fastest productivity advances in the late 1950s and early 1960s, when the yen was clearly very dramatically undervalued.

Conventional commentators lately have held that the sheer volume of transactions in today's foreign exchange markets makes it impos-sible for governments to control exchange rates. Thus there is suppos-edly little reason to believe that the yen has been undervalued in recent years. This argument overlooks several long-term structural factors that have tended variously to prop up the dollar or depress the yen. For one thing, as we have already seen, American and European observers have consistently underestimated the productivity of the Japanese economy. Consequently foreign exchange speculators have not been prepared to push the yen to a level that would fully reflect Japan's efficiency in making internationally traded goods.

Successive administrations in Washington have created a psycho-logical climate that has tended to deflect attention away from Amer-ica's root problem, its growing lack of competitiveness in interna-tionally traded goods. The spin coming out of Washington has almost always served to prop up the dollar. President John F. Kennedy once lumped dollar devaluation together with nuclear war as the two things that frightened him the most. President Lyndon Johnson pres-sured Tokyo to "defend the dollar" during the Vietnam War. In 1978, President Jimmy Carter unveiled a vastly expensive program to prop up the dollar using, among other things, a buying program on foreign exchange markets. In the early 1980s, President Ronald Reagan ex-empted most foreign buyers of U.S. Treasury bonds from American taxes, a move that suddenly increased the attractiveness of holding dollars to Japanese and European investors. Most recently, President Clinton's administration has been engaged in talking up the dollar.

Meanwhile, on the Japanese side, several structural factors have worked to depress the yen. For one thing, the MOF has pursued monetary policies that have made the yen an unattractive currency for foreign investors to hold. Not only has the MOF generally kept yen interest rates much lower than dollar interest rates, but it has maintained regulatory barriers that make it inconvenient for foreign corporations to keep their cash in yen. The effect has been to minimize the yen's role as an international currency. Moreover, as Prime Minister Yasuhiro Nakasone's former confidant Kenichi Ohmae has noted, the MOF has also artificially boosted the demand for dollar-denominated assets by pressuring Japan's financial institutions into buying American securities against their better judgment.

Ohmae's account of a top-level buy-the-dollar policy in Japan is consonant with a disclosure by Nomura Securities that the Ministry of Finance gave the major financial institutions monthly targets for investing in foreign securities in the early 1980s. Japan's giant insurance companies and trust banks in particular were induced to make vast investments in foreign bonds, particularly U.S. Treasuries.

Perhaps the most telling evidence of Tokyo's cheap-yen policy is something Japanese institutions have not done: required Washington to borrow in yen. Instead, they have allowed Washington to continue to pile up debts denominated in dollars. To Americans it seems only natural that Washington should borrow in dollars — but all historical precedent says this is quite unique given how dependent the American government now is on constant infusions of foreign money to finance its budget. In the past, countries that dominated the world financial system in the way Japan does today have always insisted on lending in their own currency — because they understandably had more faith in their own currency than the typically less reliable currency of the debtor nation. In the great days of British finance in the nineteenth century, for instance, British institutions that loaned to the big debtor nations of those days, Tsarist Russia, China, and the Ottoman Empire, insisted that the loans should be denominated in sterling (or in gold, which amounted to the same thing). By the same token, when American finance took over the lead from British finance in the 1940s and 1950s, American institutions naturally insisted that debtor nations should borrow in dollars. Since the mid-1980s, Japanese financial institutions have enjoyed the same global financial clout that the Americans did in the 1950s, but — hitherto at least — they have shown little interest in forcing Washington to borrow in yen. The Japanese institutions' attitude seems less mysterious, however, if you are aware that the MOF, in pursuit of a cheap-yen policy, tries to keep the yen's profile as low as possible in the world monetary system.

Given these structural factors, the MOF has rarely had to intervene directly in international currency markets in support of the dollar. But there is strong evidence that the MOF does not hesitate to do so when necessary — and it appears to have done so consistently in the early 1980s, when the dollar was not only overvalued but was widely seen to be overvalued. Despite the belief among Western economic theorists that such intervention is futile, the MOF kept the dollar at levels that provided a powerful advantage for Japanese exporters.

The truth is that the MOF's expertise in rigging markets is legendary in Tokyo. In a famous experiment in the early 1980s, for instance, the MOF "froze" the big banks' stock prices and kept their fluctuations within a few percentage points for two calendar years.

Western theorists assume that intervention has a minimal effect because it is supposedly cancelled out by the vast amount of speculative trading in currency markets these days. This overlooks a crucial qualitative difference between intervention buying and speculative buying.

Speculative traders generally structure their trading to minimize the impact on currency rates. They set their buy limits close to the market rate and thus avoid running up the rate against themselves. If speculative buying puts upward pressure on the rate, speculators typically hold off from further buying until the rate drops back down again. Intervention buying is driven by the opposite principle because it deliberately keeps continued pressure on the rate even as the rate rises. So as to be effective, such intervention is usually conducted secretly or against a backdrop of misleading rumors about the intervention's true purpose.

If the MOF wants to keep the yen undervalued, all it has to do is quietly organize a few minutes of extremely intense buying of the dollar occasionally, timed to coincide with some good news about the American economy. Once a higher level for the dollar has been established, speculators regard this as the "correct" level, and the price will take some weeks to drift down to its previous low level. The process is analogous to a ride in a thermal balloon. Every so often the balloon drifts too low and the pilot applies another blast of intense heat, which propels it sharply higher. As the balloon gradually loses heat, it slowly drops and another blast is needed. In relation to the flying time involved, the heat needed to maintain a high altitude is modest.

Top practitioners in international finance have long known that certain countries consistently intervene to keep their currencies low. The most widely noted examples are Taiwan and China. South Korea, Switzerland, and Germany have also at times clearly acted successfully to depress their currencies. Not coincidentally these countries have rapidly strengthened industrial competitiveness vis-à-vis the United States in the era of floating currencies.

Of course, when the yen soared in 1994, many commentators rushed to proclaim it was overvalued. This was unlikely because the MOF had the power to avoid overvaluation and would not have hesitated to use this power. The principal significance of the currency story is that it provides the MOF with an extra reason to resist American requests for the deregulation of Japanese finance. Such deregulation would remove from the MOF's hands the tools it needs to keep the yen from rising too high on foreign currency markets.

The foreign exchange diplomacy of the last quarter of a century has been a classic example of the wonderful congruency between Washington's short-term mindset and Tokyo's long-term one. Washington, constantly focusing on short-term electoral politics, has generally fought to avoid the apparent rebuke that a falling dollar would represent in the eyes of the American electorate. Meanwhile, Japanese economic policymakers, intent on establishing leadership in as many of the world's major industries as possible, have always been happy to rein in the yen's strength.

Financial efficiency — and high-tech wheelbarrows

American observers often characterize Japanese finance as "inefficient." As we saw in Chapter Two, however, Japanese finance cannot be considered inefficient by any normal measures because worker productivity in Japanese finance is exceptionally high. Japanese banks in particular are massively more efficient than their American counterparts as measured by assets per employee.

It turns out that critics of the Japanese financial system's efficiency employ a highly controversial definition of efficiency. In their view, the fact that Japanese regulators ban many new financial instruments used in the United States in itself constitutes financial inefficiency.

Why do Japanese regulators ban many popular American financial instruments? Part of the reason should already be apparent: the proliferation of American-style financial instruments in Japan would cramp the style of Japanese leaders in channeling the maximum amount of funds to Monopolistic Supergrowth industries.

Tokyo looks askance at American financial instruments for another important reason: in common with continental Europeans, the Japanese believe such instruments detonate an unwarranted explosion in transaction costs. Although in theory many American financial instruments such as futures and options serve to help corporations minimize financial risks, in practice such instruments often serve merely to enable Wall Street firms to make large profits by exploiting the gullibility, ignorance, and carelessness of their customers. Of course, these transactions create much well-paid employment on Wall Street, but anyone who thinks that every new job in financial services is good for the economy should remember that about 15 percent of the population of the Weimar Republic was engaged in moving wheelbarrows of money around.

Perhaps the clearest example of the worthlessness of new financial instruments is in investment management. America's thousands of investment management firms are eager users of new financial instruments. But do such instruments help improve investment returns? In the aggregate the answer is a clear no. For all the increasingly frenetic trading on Wall Street, the investment returns of about three-quarters of American investment management firms have underperformed those of the Standard and Poor's index in the last decade.

The Tokyo crash as industrial policy

At first sight the Tokyo stock market crash of 1990 to 1992 lent support to the idea that Japan's financial markets were now so liberalized that the Ministry of Finance could no longer control them. In reality, the MOF never lost its grip on the markets: it engineered the crash as a counterintuitive piece of industrial policy to effect the transfer of wealth from rich private citizens to corporate Japan.

Japan has a long history of financial crises: there have been five major stock market collapses since World War II, and in most cases the crises were triggered consciously by the MOF. The most bewildering crisis occurred between 1949 and 1950, when in the space of just fourteen months, the stock market fell by 66 percent. By comparison the crash of 1990 to 1992, which took the market down 62 percent in thirty-two months, was a good deal less frightening. As the Japan scholar Edward Barry Keehn has pointed out, this most recent bursting bubble resembled previous *obaron* — overloan — crises that the MOF engineered in the banking industry in the 1950s and 1960s to force vital changes in the structure of the Japanese economy.

Of course, to casual observers, the crash looked like a classic financial accident of the sort that has punctuated world economic history ever since the famous tulip speculative mania of seventeenth-century Holland. In reality it was the end result of a deliberate policy by the MOF to pump up the financial markets in the so-called bubble years, which began in the mid-1980s and continued through 1989.

As C. Tait Ratcliffe pointed out, the MOF's key decision that started the process was to increase Japan's money supply rapidly in the latter half of the 1980s. This helped induce a fall in interest rates, cutting borrowing costs for industry. The easy money also served to trigger a boom in real estate, as bankers financed speculators in making ever larger real estate purchases. The resulting high real estate prices provided further relief for manufacturing corporations, which typically own large amounts of real estate and could now use the enhanced value of their real estate holdings as extra collateral in borrowing safely from the banks, thus buying time in adjusting to the high-yen era that followed the Plaza Accord of 1985. Meanwhile stock prices also soared, again in large part as a result of buying by speculators financing their purchases with easy money. For Japanese corporate managements, the bloated stock market represented a unique window of opportunity to sell large amounts of new securities at peak prices.

In appraising reports of Japan's troubled financial sector, it is useful to distinguish between two quite separate forms of losses:

• *Real-economy losses.* A real-economy loss arises when, for instance, an overly optimistic corporation invests in an expensive new factory that later turns out to be unneeded and has to be scrapped. Mistakes and misappropriations by corporate managements are a serious problem for society in that they render the whole nation poorer.

• *Symbol-economy losses.* The symbol economy is a term sometimes used in reference to the stock market. A symbol-economy loss is a loss caused by a financial transaction — it arises when a speculator buys a company's stock at a high price and later is forced to sell at a much lower price. Such a loss does not necessarily mean a loss to society, for the share price may have fallen not because of any underlying corporate mismanagement but rather because the investor paid a foolishly high price for the shares in the first place.

Most of the Japanese financial disasters the Western press reported in the early 1990s were merely symbol-economy losses that had few if any negative implications for the real economy. The truth behind the bubble story was that mainline corporations profited handsomely by selling vast amounts of securities at inflated prices to ill-informed speculators in the boom of the late 1980s. These securities' prices subsequently collapsed, but this did not hurt the issuing corporations. The victims were the buyers of the expensive shares, typically rich private citizens or small entrepreneurial companies. From the point of view of Japan's economic leaders, all this was in a good cause: the government has no brief to reward greedy speculators. Quite the reverse. By squeezing the rich, the crash leveled out inequalities of personal wealth and thus bolstered the egalitarianism on which Japan's social contract rests. Money was transferred from the hands of the rich to Japan's great industrial corporations, whose prosperity is synonymous with the prosperity of the nation.

Perhaps the best example of the counterintuitive effects of the bubble's bursting was provided by a boom in warrant issues in the late 1980s. Warrants are investment instruments that entitle an investor to buy a corporation's shares several years down the road at a price established at the outset. If the stock price subsequently rises, the warrant's value also increases. By the same token, if the stock price falls, the warrant's value falls. The warrant is worth little or nothing if the market price of the stock falls decisively below the buying price agreed at the outset in the warrant contract. In the case of most Japanese warrants issued in the 1980s, the market price of the stock fell way below the agreed price, so the warrants duly became virtually worthless. As calculated by the economic analyst Kenneth Courtis in 1992, this represented a loss of about $150 billion for the buyers of the warrants. It amounted to a gain of about $150 billion for the issuers, however — a select group of key Japanese corporations. They received the warrant money, yet, for the most part, were spared the need to dilute their share capital by issuing new shares to the warrant holders.

What this means is that, as many observers (including this writer) pointed out at the time, the MOF in the late 1980s engineered a brief and unrepeatable period of essentially costless capital for Japanese industry that would inevitably have to be followed by a market crash. The subsequent bear market was a crisis only for those people who imagined the stock market boom would go on forever (they are the same people who think money grows on trees).

Japan's much-publicized real estate collapse followed a similar pattern. Large corporations made huge profits by selling real estate at peak prices. The unfortunate buyers were mainly small entrepreneurs and wealthy private individuals.

Some commentators suggested that the bursting bubble had propelled the banking system to the brink of collapse. But on analysis the evidence proffered turned out to be merely hearsay. Typically, sweeping generalizations were drawn from a few anecdotes often attributed to unnamed sources.

Many press reports on the banks' foolhardiness were based on a lack of knowledge of the quirks of Japanese banking. One such quirk is the Japanese banking cartel's system of so-called compensating balances. When Japanese bankers ostensibly lend, say, $100 million, they typically require the borrower to place $20 million of this on deposit with their bank. Thus the effective amount lent is only $80 million. This quirk, which has its roots in Japanese bank regulation, can be very misleading for uninitiated foreign observers, who repeatedly recounted how during the bubble years the banks had loaned more than 100 percent of the value of collateral — a practice that even a junior bank clerk knows is a fundamental breach of banking prudence. In actuality, when the banks' lending was adjusted for compensating balances, it was seen to be fully secured.

Perhaps the clearest illustration of how much myth was mixed in with the facts was an extraordinary report in the *Economist* concerning Prime Minister Kiichi Miyazawa's house in Harajuku. The property had been worth $22 million in the late 1980s but, according to the *Economist,* had been accepted as collateral for bank loans totaling more than $100 million. This implied such lax banking controls that the obvious inference was that the *Economist*'s information was wrong or incomplete. But the *Economist* routinely assumes that top Tokyo bankers are less sophisticated than the average London bank clerk and so, without checking, it presented the Harajuku loan as evidence that Japanese banks had more or less taken leave of their senses during the bubble era. In reality, the *Economist* overlooked a crucial fact: the prime minister's house was not the sole security for the loan. Far from it. The loan had been secured on several properties of which his house was not even the most important. In the aggregate these properties afforded the bank adequate security, and the bank's apparent madness was a figment of the *Economist*'s imagination.

By discarding the rumors about Japanese banks' real estate loans and looking merely at facts, one discovers a less distressing picture. For a start, the banks' total exposure was a lot lower than it appeared at first. Much of what was described as real estate lending was actually lending to manufacturing corporations secured by real estate. Assuming that manufacturing remained generally healthy, the matter of the collateral's value was insignificant. In fact, virtually without exception industrial corporations had little difficulty servicing their debts. As of 1993, the Japanese banks' problem loans — loans on which interest payments were in arrears — represented only 3.5 percent of total assets. This was little more than half the ratio found at a typical major American bank. This helps explain why, even in 1992 at the height of the panic in the West about Japanese banking stability, the Standard & Poor's credit rating agency accorded the major Japanese banks higher ratings than their American counterparts.

One problem for American reporters in Tokyo in the early 1990s was that the Japanese banks' spokesmen were unconvincingly vague in denying rumors of catastrophically large problem loans. Meanwhile Tokyo's English-language public relations magazines seemed to go out of their way to spread alarm. *Japan Update* predicted a financial "panic" in which major banks could collapse. It cited specific banks that supposedly had loan losses of up to four times the publicly admitted figures. Even the Japanese banking industry itself did little to scotch these wild rumors. This reticence seemed irrational, but was in fact quite rational. The banks were under regulatory pressure at the time to conduct a ruthless purge of small-time real estate speculators who could not pay their interest bills. Rendering relative innocents penniless is a distressing process for everyone involved, and the bankers found their jobs easier if they could plead that the banks' own backs were against the wall.

Many Western analysts assumed that falling stock prices and real estate values would induce a 1930s-style Great Depression in Japan. In this they were making assumptions that do not apply in Japan. In particular they surmised that Japanese employers would be scared into making large layoffs. As we saw in Chapter Seven, Japan's employment regulation made sure this did not happen and so the entire train of Western logic — the idea that collapsing employment would trigger collapses in consumption, savings, and industrial investment — was nothing but a red herring that deflected attention from Japan's fundamental strengths.

Of course, the Japanese economy did slow down in the early 1990s. But the assumption of most Western observers that the financial crash precipitated the economic slowdown is not supported by the evidence. Japan's economy continued to boom for nearly eighteen months after the stock market crash began. When the economy slowed down in 1991, it had enjoyed five years of expansion, Japan's longest economic boom since World War II. A pause was therefore overdue. In view of depressed demand in Japanese exporters' major Western markets, the surprising thing was that the pause had not come earlier.

Given that the financial turmoil did not cut Japan's savings rate, the only other significant way it might have hurt the real economy was by misallocating savings flows. Did the abundance of finance in the bubble years encourage corporations to waste money on boondoggles? Tellingly, the business press reported few cases of egregious corporate boondoggles in Japan. Christopher Wood has suggested that some corporations were guilty of extravagance in using capital raised in the bubble to upgrade company dormitories (in which young Japanese executives live until they marry). This hardly looks like reckless overconsumption, given that the residents of these dormitories are often Japan's brightest — people who in New York would have a starting salary of $90,000 a year, drive a Porsche, and fly to the Virgin Islands for weekends. Remember Japan's per capita incomes are nearly 40 percent higher than America's.

A few much-exaggerated scandals excepted, most of Japan's savings went into industrial investment and other approved uses. In real estate, for instance, real-economy losses were trivial because, unlike in the United States, Japan has no large-scale problem of overbuilt office space. In fact, Japan is still badly in need of more office space, as anyone who has ever seen a typical Japanese office realizes. Space is at such a premium that Japanese executives typically work at desks that take up less than half the room of an ordinary American desk. This fundamental shortage was apparent in the early 1990s in rents, which stood about twice New York levels. Some tenants even faced substantial rent increases. One major American aerospace company whose Tokyo office rent had been raised in 1990 was amazed to be presented with a demand for a further increase in 1992. Despite the strain in real estate finance, building work continued wherever it had been initiated so there was no expensive dislocation in the form of half-built buildings going to waste.

Christopher Wood and several other Western commentators have suggested that Japanese industry overinvested in new manufacturing capacity in the bubble years. But they offered no convincing evidence of specific cases of overinvestment. The evidence of history is that Japanese industry has repeatedly created vast amounts of new capacity and then confounded foreign pundits by finding vast new markets for the resulting output. At home Japanese corporations can generally charge healthy profit margins; overseas they cut prices ruthlessly if necessary and regard the losses as a market development cost in establishing leadership in future growth areas such as Indonesia and China. The effect of Japan's capacity additions is to scare foreign manufacturers into cutting back their investment plans, thus hastening the day when Japan establishes a Monopolistic Supergrowth grip on the industry.

By 1994, it was apparent that Japan was girding itself for a new leap forward with the help of powerful Keynesian economic stimulation via increased public spending. Keynesianism has, of course, been out of fashion in the West for decades, where its side effects such as inflation, increased government borrowing, and a rise in imports are deemed intolerable. These side effects have hardly been a concern in Japan, where wage increases are tightly contained, the national budget is in surplus most years, and various natural and artificial barriers to imports ensure that the benefits of budgetary stimulation do not leak abroad.

In short, while American observers continued to dwell on the illusory gloom of the past few years, the Japanese were focusing on a bright future. Just how bright this future is we will now see.

11

Monopolistic Supergrowth

Japan needs three things principally to continue to grow:

- New technologies
- Capital
- Access to world markets

On all these fronts, Japan has never been better positioned than it is today.

First, new technologies are being invented at a rate never seen before. Most such technologies are emerging in industries where corporate Japan has already established leadership.

Second, capital, the critical factor needed to exploit these new technologies, is clearly now more abundant than ever in Japan.

Third, despite everything the Western press says, access to world markets is now easier for Japan than ever before. The United States in particular is fast losing all ability to bargain with Japan on trade because Washington is now critically dependent on Japanese finance to fund the federal deficit. And because corporate Japan has already developed so many world monopolies, no advanced Western country can now raise barriers against Japanese goods without causing industrial dislocation in their domestic economies. In short, just when it has become possible for one country to establish an abiding lead over all others, Japan finds itself running clear of the pack.

Technology: Horn of Plenty

Many commentators in the early 1990s argued that Japan's growth had ground to a halt because Japan was supposedly running out of new investment opportunities. The argument was put most insistently by Brian Reading in a 1992 book entitled *Japan: The Coming Collapse.* Reading, a former economics editor at the *Economist,* was exemplifying a peculiar lack of vision that has hampered British economic thinking ever since Britain started losing its leadership position more than a century ago.

The British have constantly underestimated the economic prospects for new technologies. Victorian England failed to see the economic potential of such an obvious winner as the telephone. Testifying before Parliament, a top British post office executive said: "The Americans have need of the telephone but we do not. We have plenty of messenger boys."

This anecdote has long been a source of amusement for Americans who like to contrast the can-do spirit of American enterprise with the penny-pinching negativism of a declining Britain. But these days Americans have little to laugh about. Since the mid-twentieth century they have been almost as unimaginative as the British. When in 1948 Bell Laboratories invented the transistor, for instance, the Americans imagined the only major consumer market for the new device was in hearing aids! They considered it merely a miniaturized successor to the vacuum tube and told Sony Chairman Akio Morita that miniaturization held little promise because Americans liked their electrical gadgets to be big and solid. But, imbued with the true spirit of economic growth, Morita saw things differently. He realized that miniaturization afforded not only the obvious possibility of shrinking appliance dimensions but also of packing more functions and capability into full-size appliances. Seen in this way, the new technology's possibilities were endless.

In the mid-1990s, the opportunities opened up by technology have never been greater. For a start, existing technologies have nowhere nearly been exploited fully. Many consumer goods that have hitherto been confined to the First World are now destined for explosive growth in the Second World, thanks to the abundance of important high-tech materials, such as silicon. In the past, consumer goods were always too costly in terms of scarce materials such as copper and zinc to be affordable in the Second World. There were only enough such materials for the one-tenth of the world's population which inhabited the First World. Now technology allows manufacturers to make more and more with less and less. Using such technology, the vast emerging nations of East Asia are beginning to provide their peoples with the basics of a Western-style consumer society.

For Japan, these emerging economies present huge opportunities to sell manufacturing equipment. Making manufacturing equipment is a classic fixed-cost game: as Japanese industry produces more such equipment, it spreads its large fixed costs and thus can afford to make substantial cuts in its prices. Then as these nations prosper they become major markets for a whole host of other Japanese exports.

Looking toward new technologies, Japan's opportunities are unlimited. The energy field alone offers a cornucopia of opportunities for economic growth. As countries such as China, Indonesia, Malaysia, and perhaps Brazil begin to catch up with Western living standards early in the next century, they will start drawing heavily on the world's traditional energy sources. To make way for this new source of demand, the world will be forced to find means not only to achieve greater energy efficiency but to develop entirely new sources of energy. Thus the energy crunch will spawn huge new energy-related industries. Japan is well positioned to lead most of these industries.

Japan is in the vanguard, for instance, in superconductivity, which has many potentially important energy-saving applications, notably in allowing the world's electric utilities to make dramatic efficiency gains with superconductivity-based storage techniques. Japan has also established leadership in solar energy. Corporations like Kyocera, Sharp, and Sanyo Electric have been commercializing the technology for limited use in pocket calculators, air conditioners, and street lights. These companies have been cutting costs by between 10 and 15 percent a year in a pattern similar to that previously seen in the semiconductor industry. The cost of a household system has fallen in the last twenty-five years from $500,000 to $60,000. Japanese engineers expect to get the cost of a household system down to $10,000 by the end of this decade. At this point, demand is expected to explode, and the technology will accelerate economic growth in such sunny, and populous, regions as India, Indonesia, and southern China. As of 1994, the MOF had established a subsidy program to pay for half the installation cost of household solar energy systems, a move intended to crank up the industry for a global export effort later in the decade.

Japan leads in the development of many new energy-efficient transportation technologies. One exciting example is the magnetic levitation ("maglev") train, which is expected within twenty years to become a competitive alternative to transcontinental plane travel. The new technology uses magnetic forces to enable a train to hover over the track, virtually eliminating mechanical friction and allowing trains to travel at up to 300 miles an hour. Such trains will be much more energy efficient than planes because their carrying capacity in relation to wind resistance is much greater.

Japan is also working on similarly spectacular technology for sea travel. A new superconductive magnetic propulsion system developed by Mitsubishi Heavy Industries and Toshiba Corporation will enable ships to skim across the ocean at up to 110 miles per hour. It is a technology that promises to revolutionize not only cargo transport but naval warfare. The new ships' attractions for military chiefs include not only speed but practically silent operation.

Then there is Japan's new automated city cargo delivery system. This revolutionary concept will be pioneered in Tokyo and then cloned elsewhere. The idea is for urban cargo deliveries to be conducted by a vast system of underground driverless trains. The Tokyo system, which will cost $99 billion, will cut the energy consumption of cargo deliveries by 80 percent and will free up 76,000 truck drivers for other work. And by virtually eliminating trucks on the roads, it will dramatically cut pollution and increase traffic speeds.

Health care is another major growth industry in which Japan is well positioned to establish leadership. Here again the prospects are almost limitless. Japan's Science and Technology Agency has published an impressive list of product development targets for the year 2015:

• Artificial organs that will overcome the body's rejection system
• New treatments that will roll back cancer by converting cancer cells individually into healthy ones
• Robots to nurse the elderly and the handicapped
• Commercial production of new medicines in outer space (by manufacturing in space, Japan will be able to create many new materials that are impossible to make on earth because of distortions created by the earth's gravity)

• Superconductor-based diagnostic equipment which will supersede today's $1.5 million magnetic resonance imaging (MRI) equipment at a fraction of the cost

Another industry where Japan can look forward to almost unlimited growth prospects is electronics. According to Robert L. Kearns, a fellow of the Economic Strategy Institute in Washington, high-definition television alone is expected to create a worldwide market worth conservatively $40 billion a year by 2010.

Besides being an entertainment medium, high-definition television will have many specialist applications in areas such as medical technology. Already hospitals in Japan are using three-dimensional high-definition television to teach brain surgery to medical students. Nissho Iwai, a Japanese trading corporation with interests in medical technology, estimates that high-definition television could double the size of Japan's domestic medical technology market by the end of the century.

The technology will spawn dozens of applications in aviation and defense. High-definition radar displays are expected to enable air traffic controllers to supervise increasingly crowded skies more safely. High-definition television promises to be an important military tool; it will allow quicker friend-or-foe identifications. Another important application will be in creating visual databases that will store images for architects, engineers, and magazine art editors. In the future, movies will be made in high-definition format and distributed to movie theaters by satellite.

In recent years, the American press has suggested that Japan has stumbled badly in high-definition television because the Japanese standard has been superseded by a new and better American standard. In reality, Japan's system can be upgraded to the American standard by the addition of a simple converter. In any case, it would be surprising if the American system was not better than the Japanese system because the American design has come a decade after Japan's. As yet, no one in America can mass-produce the new American high-definition system. The manufacturing capability to make the American system does not reside in the United States but rather in Japan, which could begin manufacturing American-standard equipment almost overnight.

Other products in the Japanese electronics industry's pipeline include flat television and videophones. Both will probably take off in the late 1990s, and they could prove almost as big as high-definition television in the global marketplace. Although American commentators sometimes predict an American comeback in such electronic products, the prospects for American participation are generally limited to design and software. The key parts will be made in Japan, in accordance with Japan's central objective of being the manufacturing workshop of the world.

Japan is also moving to the fore in space technology. As America cuts its space budget, Japan is functioning increasingly as America's partner in projects such as the space shuttle. Characteristically, the Japanese are focusing on possible commercial applications of space technology: they are aiming to build factories in space, where weightlessness will allow the manufacture of new materials which are impossible to make on earth.

In the very long run, Japan would appear to have an important advantage in space transportation in that it reportedly leads the world in developing nuclear propulsion systems, a necessary requirement to bring Mars within easy reach of the earth. Eventually, this technology would cut the duration of a one-way trip to Mars to only 90 days, from 250 days at present.

Japanese industry also sees huge growth prospects in computers. Supercomputers now being designed in Japan may operate as much as ten times faster than today's American supercomputers with the help of Josephson junction devices. These devices, named for the concept's inventor, Brian Josephson of Cambridge University, are in effect superconducting transistors. They promise to be a Japanese monopoly because IBM, which did much of the early work on them, dropped out of the highly expensive race to commercialize the technology more than a decade ago.

The Japanese are also making rapid progress in other areas of the computer industry. Hitachi, for instance, announced in 1993 that it had made an important breakthrough in developing new memory chips which could hold 40 million pages of information on a one-square-inch sliver of silicon. This capacity is about five hundred times that of the most sophisticated present-day memory devices, and it opens up unheard-of new economic growth opportunities in everything from aerospace to entertainment.

Corporate Japan is expected to build large new revenue sources merely by adapting existing technologies to create attractive new products. The auto industry offers numerous possibilities. Take electronic car navigation devices that are now catching on in Japan — these devices not only display road maps showing a driver his exact location but provide detailed information about traffic jams and weather conditions. The Japanese electronics industry launched the devices in 1990, and as of 1993 they were selling at a rate of 120,000 units a year. The industry expects to cut prices by about two-thirds, to $700, by 2000, powering a fortyfold increase in unit sales. Car navigation devices are basically an application of Japan's prowess in flat panels, CD-ROMs, and plastic optical cables. Largely on the strength of the car navigation boom, sales of optical cables alone are expected to increase one hundredfold between 1993 and 2000.

The Japanese auto industry is also expected soon to launch intelligent car lighting systems, which will automatically adjust to road conditions, and antisleep systems, which will prevent drivers from dozing off at the wheel. And the industry seems to have a potential winner in new technology to suppress mechanical noise. Already in use in some Japanese air conditioners and refrigerators, the concept is now being commercialized in cars by Nissan Motor.

Even in such mature products as cameras, the Japanese keep coming up with lucrative new features such as Canon's new "antishake" lens. Such gadgetry creates constant product obsolescence, ensuring strong sales even in such mature markets as the United States and Japan.

As we approach the twenty-first century, technology is now more than ever a Horn of Plenty — and it is bestowing its biggest favors on Japan.

Capital: the rich get richer

Can Japan maintain its tremendous savings flows indefinitely? The answer depends mainly on whether Japanese leaders can maintain their highly effective suppressed consumption policy.

We have already seen that this policy served to maintain a high savings rate in the early 1990s. Despite predictions in the United States to the contrary, the chances are slim that recent political upheavals in Japan will herald a true American-style consumer society in which savings rates will fall to American levels. In reality, because the suppressed consumption policy was created by bureaucrats rather than elected representatives, elected representatives have little power to change it. Moreover, Japanese consumers are hardly pressing for real change. Quite the reverse. Because they are now among the world's richest consumers, they can more easily bear the suppressed consumption policy today than ever before.

Officials are under no pressure to make real changes because their allies in the Japanese press continue to withhold from the public all knowledge of how official consumption suppression policies work. Moreover, at higher levels in Japanese society, everyone recognizes that the suppressed consumption policy has been a cornerstone of Japan's success. In Japan, more than in other countries, if something is not perceived to be broke, no one sees any need to fix it. Reports in the West that the Japanese are becoming a nation of consumers are invariably based on flimsy evidence. Much has been made, for instance, of the fact that the Toys 'R' Us chain has opened operations in Japan and has been well received. But such successes are tokenism as is evident in the fact that the press mentions only the same very limited list of successes in every report on Japan's consumer revolution. (Toys 'R' Us, incidentally, does little to puncture East Asian mercantilism because most of its merchandise is made in Japan or elsewhere in East Asia.)

Abroad, the chances of a serious American challenge to the suppressed consumption policy have dwindled almost to zero. When Washington in the late 1980s feebly tried to get Tokyo to relax the policy, the result was a memorable American diplomatic fiasco. The effort, which centered on changing Japan's land zoning policies, came as part of the Bush administration's so-called Structural Impediments Initiatives. Washington failed to set any effective targets for Japanese performance in zoning. Thus, as with all such previous Tokyo-Washington agreements, this one was so misconceived that it became an embarrassment to Washington almost as soon as it was signed.

The reality is that it is far harder for Washington to get substantive changes in the suppressed consumption policy than even in trade policy. The opportunities for Tokyo to evade and procrastinate are just too large. More important, Japan's anticonsumption policies are seen by Tokyo as a matter of Japanese sovereignty, so foreigners have no right to ask for changes.

Clearly, then, there is little question that Japan can maintain its high savings rate. But can it continue to channel these savings into targeted industries? This is a crucial question. Most theoretical economists in the United States assume that the MOF has largely lost its power to control savings flows. They believe that Japan is working toward a true liberalization of its financial system. All corporate borrowers, foreign as well as Japanese, will, therefore, soon supposedly have equal access to Japan's savings flows. In reality, the Japanese financial system remains very far from liberalized, especially in the sense of allowing foreign corporations the same opportunity as their Japanese competitors to tap Japanese savings.

America's negotiating position with Japan has already weakened to the point where the political will in the United States to pressure Japan to liberalize its financial system has now virtually disappeared. When the Clinton administration in late 1993 threatened to curtail Japanese financial institutions' access to the United States if Japan did not implement further liberalization measures, the editors of the *Wall Street Journal* urged American business executives to lobby against the administration saying that the absence of financial liberalization in Japan was not a problem for the United States. As the Ministry of Finance grows ever more powerful, its ability to enforce its Japan-first financial policies continues to strengthen.

The final piece of the capital mosaic is the ability of Japanese industry to earn an appropriate return on capital: this depends on whether the cartels can maintain a good grip on global markets.

Guarding the fortress

As we noted in Chapter One, conventional economists believe the Japanese, the Americans, and the Europeans, are destined to "converge" toward roughly the same standard of living. This argument reckons without the Good Cartel.

The Good Cartel strengthens Japan's grip on global markets by guarding against unauthorized leaks of Japanese technology. Its most obvious contribution is that, in underwriting the lifetime employment system, it constitutes an almost insuperable obstacle to foreign corporations hiring knowledgeable Japanese technicians and engineers. Moreover, the profit dynamics of the cartel system powerfully discourage Japanese corporations from transferring technology abroad.

Michael Borrus, a leading American expert on this subject, says: "The data are pretty clear. The Japanese don't transfer technology, period." Certainly they do so rarely, and then generally only as an inducement to get important foreign corporations to switch to Japanese production equipment or components. As the American Congress's Office of Technology Assessment has pointed out, Japan is particularly loath to sell advanced technology "no matter how lucrative the financial rewards might be."

Viewed by Westerners unfamiliar with the dynamics of cartels, this seems irrational. Japanese corporations know, however, that by sticking together in refusing to transfer technology, they will speed the day when they will have the entire field to themselves, unchallenged by Western competitors. Then they can enjoy the luxury of shaping the global market on their terms. It is a prize worth winning. By contrast, if the technology is sold to an outsider, only one member benefits from the sale but all members suffer from the new competition. The damage to the group will generally be much more than the benefit to the individual, so in accordance with normal Japanese logic the individual will willingly forego the immediate benefit for the sake of the group's welfare.

Japanese corporations control diffusion of their technology so carefully that they are notably reluctant to establish high-technology factories abroad. Again, this pattern clearly stems from cartel logic. If a Japanese cartel allowed its members to do leading-edge manufacturing abroad, this would inevitably involve transfers of know-how that foreign competitors could acquire simply by hiring some of the Japanese corporations' foreign employees.

Moreover a policy of saving the best technology for the domestic economy serves to boost Japanese workers' incomes — and thus the fortunes of the Japanese economy. As the Japanese people get richer, they save more. The banks have more money to lend. Corporations can buy more equipment. Japanese workers achieve ever higher levels of output. In the end everyone wins. The Good Cartel's future is a bright one.

Access to world markets: an open door

Japan needs continuing access to world markets if it is to keep growing. The conventional wisdom is that this access is now being constrained by trade friction. The truth is the opposite: the West's markets are now more open to Japanese goods than ever.

The West first began claiming it could not import any more Japanese goods as far back as the 1930s. And in its postwar form, the argument has been with us since the early 1970s. Yet in the last twenty-five years, Japan has multiplied its exports to the United States ten times and to Europe fifteen times.

If the West could not moderate Japan's trade policies two decades ago, it enjoys far less power to do so today. Because so many Western corporations now depend on Japanese-made components, large pressure groups now exist in Western business circles which side automatically with Tokyo in trade disputes. In any case, Japan's very success has given it the money to buy the best lobbyists in the world's capitals.

Moreover, those new industries Japan is now targeting have never existed in the West. The West therefore simply cannot complain about the economic policies driving the production of goods that Western corporations have never made and are incapable of making. By definition there are no entrenched Western competitors whose lobbying activities might create problems for Japan's exports. Protectionist feeling in the United States has been remarkably less focused in the case of video cassette recorders, for instance, than cars.

As Japan extends its technological lead in new industries like superconductivity, advanced materials, and optronics, Western governments are coming under increasing pressure to bury the hatchet and switch to courting Tokyo in an effort to attract Japanese direct investment. A leading indicator of this trend is Britain, which once fiercely resented Japan's success but now is delighted to help Japan target the European market for cars and electronic products.

In the United States, industries that once used to fight to open Japanese markets have virtually given up the effort. The American semiconductor industry, for instance, reserves its greatest lobbying efforts these days not to open the Japanese market but merely to try to ensure that it can buy Japanese manufacturing equipment on a timely basis.

Japan's very wealth is now a priceless advantage in world trade because few competitor nations can now make goods that meet the Japanese consumer's high quality standards. The lead economy's immunity to consumer imports has a strong mercantilist effect that was apparent in Britain a century ago and the United States in the 1950s. In the view of some Japanese leaders, this natural immunity alone will soon sweep Japan's trade surpluses to levels that will dwarf even the record surplus Japan enjoyed in 1993. Citing imperial Britain's huge current account surpluses, the influential Japanese economics professor Ryutaro Komiya has noted that between 1905 and 1913, Britain's capital exports averaged more than 7 percent of gross national product — about twice the ratio Japan achieved in 1993.

Freely translated, Komiya's message was this: the West has seen nothing yet.

Master of the East

Washington has long complacently viewed South Korea, Taiwan, mainland China, and other emerging economic powerhouses in East Asia as America's "secret weapon" in responding to the Japanese economic challenge. Washington has labored under the illusion that it can readily play these countries off against Japan, thus supposedly enabling it to retain powerful leverage over Tokyo.

In the 1990s, however, a startled Washington is beginning to realize that Tokyo has turned the tables: now these countries are *Japan's* secret weapon. Increasingly Japan has the ability to play these countries off against the *United States.*

The strategy is clear. Japan sells manufacturing equipment and sophisticated components to other East Asian nations. These countries in turn sell the resulting products in the American market.

The new sense of shared destiny among East Asian nations was made pointedly clear in 1994 when Prime Minister Morihiro Hosokawa received an ostentatiously warm welcome in Beijing just a week after U.S. Secretary of State Warren Christopher had had a notably chilly reception there.

Even South Korea, historically the country most antagonistic to Japan, is now playing the game Japan's way. "We're hooked on Japan, I'm afraid," a top Korean trade official, Lee Sang Yul, told the

New York Times in 1993. "When the Korean economy was just beginning to develop, we had to rely on Japan for technology and parts. Once we had their system, we kept buying." Another Korean economic leader said that Japanese officials "have this model in which they control everything and they are just applying that model to a new area, Asia."

Most of Korea's leading industries such as steel, semiconductors, and cars depend on Japan for parts and technology. About half the value of a typical Korean car, for instance, is accounted for by Japanese inputs. In shipbuilding, South Korea not only depends on Japanese components but openly functions as Japan's junior partner in operating a joint Japan-Korea cartel, which accounts for three-quarters of the world's new ships each year.

It is a similar story in Taiwan, where in 1992 an official of the Information Industry Institute publicly complained that Taiwanese companies had "no bargaining position" in trying to resist price increases in vital Japanese components.

The international trade figures bear out the story: Japan's surplus with East Asia hit $42 billion in 1992, more than double the 1989 figure. Corporate Japan's total investment in the area as of 1992 was $59.9 billion, more than triple 1985 levels. In the process, American producers of manufacturing equipment and components have been virtually eliminated from East Asia, which until the early 1980s had been one of their major markets.

Japan's Asian hegemony is a crucial asset not only because it provides Japan with a rapidly growing and vast market for Japanese goods but because increasingly it is becoming an important public relations tool. Essentially countries accounting for about half of the world's total population have decided to play the economic game by Japan's rules. The question Westerners must now ask themselves is this: can half the world be wrong?

As Japan has advanced into ever higher levels of manufacturing technology, the Japanese economic establishment has been more than willing to help Japan's East Asian economic satellites in less sophisticated manufacturing. But in return these satellites have had to exercise "self-control" in exporting to Japan. In practice this means selling through Japan's cartel of big keiretsu-affiliated import corporations, which function as the Japanese economic system's agents in making sure that imports do not cause "confusion" in the Japanese market.

The satellites are not complaining. This bargain has brought them unprecedented prosperity with economic growth rates of typically seven to ten percent a year. Just how far this process has already progressed is largely overlooked in the West. Few, for instance, noticed that in 1993 Singapore, a tiny island state whose population is mainly Chinese, surpassed Britain in per capita income. Just thirty-five years ago when Singapore won its independence from Britain, its per capita income stood at less than one-third of Britain's.

According to economist Kenneth Courtis, two-thirds of the growth in the world automotive industry in the 1990s will come from East Asia. Echoing this forecast, the Industrial Bank of Japan has calculated that the Japanese car industry's total annual sales in Asia will reach 6.9 million units in the year 2000, more than double the level in 1990.

All this Japanese activity in Asia is part of a comprehensive effort by Japanese economic leaders to map out industrial policy for the entire East Asian region. As the veteran American Japanologist Leon Hollerman has pointed out, the Japanese have been talking about a pan-Asian division of labor since the early 1960s. And in 1970 the influential Japanese economist Kiyoshi Kojima publicly argued the case for nation-by-nation industrial specialization in a paper entitled "An approach to integration: the gains from agreed specialization."

Now Kojima's plan is becoming a reality. Sanwa Bank has disclosed that the MITI's guidance for the automobile industry, for instance, requires Malaysia to make gears and electrical equipment, Indonesia to make truck engines, the Philippines to make transmissions, and Thailand to make diesel engines. Final assembly of vehicles will be done in each of these countries using parts sourced from the others. The strategy not only generates economies of scale but is proof against expropriation by governments of the host countries. Any country that nationalized Japan's local factories would end up with a busted flush — a lot of transmission systems or gearboxes and nowhere to sell them. As of 1993, Toyota had faithfully carried out the officials' plan by siting a steering gear operation in Malaysia, an engine block operation in Indonesia, a transmissions operation in the Philippines, and a diesel engine plant in Thailand. Mitsubishi Motor, Honda, and Nissan were also reportedly pursuing similar plans for "complementary production" in East Asian countries.

Similarly, in consumer electronics, Japanese economic leaders have decided condensers and tuners will be made in Malaysia, motors in Thailand, and batteries in Indonesia. A Japanese government study indicates that Malaysia will specialize in final assembly of fax machines, word processors, and microcomputers (presumably using many parts sourced elsewhere in Southeast Asia as well as advanced components made only in Japan). Malaysia is also a key staging post for Japanese industry in assembling room air conditioners and audiovisual equipment.

As the investment banker Jeffrey E. Garten has reported, Tokyo is backing up this strategy with assistance to East Asian nations to build roads, ports, and other essential infrastructure. Tokyo then steers Japan's multinationals into investing in the areas concerned, it finances comprehensive training programs for local workers, and it provides insured loans to joint ventures. As corporate Japan vacates low-level manufacturing entirely, Tokyo is increasingly prepared to provide Japan-financed East Asian ventures privileged access to the Japanese market.

Meanwhile Japan's East Asian satellites are increasingly hollowing out what remains of America's employment base in medium-tech manufacturing. Most of America's production of hard disk drives, for instance, has migrated to Singapore. Much of America's semiconductor manufacturing has migrated to South Korea. Meanwhile Taiwan supplies many of the simpler components for America's personal computers (with Japan retaining the business of making the more sophisticated ones for itself).

By corralling nearly 100 percent of the East Asian market for many kinds of equipment in the 1980s, the Japanese leapfrogged the Americans to seize dominant global market share positions in hundreds of crucial niches in machine tools, semiconductor manufacturing equipment, process plant, and heavy electrical machinery. Once Japanese output passed that of the United States, Monopolistic Supergrowth forces began to work powerfully in Japan's favor, giving it the edge it needed to take the fight directly to the American companies' home market.

Even so, the experts continued throughout the 1980s to portray the United States as the big winner from East Asia's growth. Why have the experts been confounded? A major reason seems to be Western wishful thinking about the depth of East Asia's commitment to Westernization. Although the satellites have much that divides them from Japan, they are closer psychologically to Japan than to the United States. Traditions which they share with Japan include everything from chopsticks and bamboo to Buddhism and Chinese proverbs.

Perhaps the most important shared tradition is Confucianism, which originated in China and is East Asia's equivalent of the religion-based ethical systems of the West. Confucianism emphasizes respect for superiors and conformity to society's wishes while Christianity urges believers to abide by individual conscience — even at the expense of offending superiors or putting themselves at odds with society. In Confucian eyes, the big flaw of the Christian West is a tendency toward divisiveness and selfishness. In Christian eyes, the flaw of Confucianism is a tendency toward subtle — and sometimes not so subtle — authoritarianism. Thus Confucianism is almost the polar opposite of Christianity and the often undiplomatic efforts by the West to spread Western ideas in the East provide an important source of shared anti-Western feeling throughout the region.

Above all, these nations share a history of struggle against Western colonization. For all the devastation that Japan's militarism wrought on the rest of East Asia in the 1930s and 1940s, there is grudging admiration throughout the region for the leadership role Japan has consistently played over 140 years in overcoming Western economic and political influence.

The Japanese are often accused of condescension toward the rest of East Asia, but there is probably less here than meets the eye. The reality is that the relationship between rich and poor countries is always somewhat strained. Given that the income gap between the Japanese and, for instance, the Chinese is actually wider than that between Americans and, say, Haitians, the Japanese have been surprisingly successful in achieving a meeting of minds with the Chinese in which both sides can work comfortably in economic partnership.

All this means that pan-Asianism — Japan's pre–World War II movement to rally all East Asian peoples in a united front against the West — never really died. Japan's leadership of East Asia is now evolving along lines Tokyo envisaged when it unveiled the Greater East Asia Co-Prosperity Sphere more than half a century ago. Although the Co-Prosperity Sphere has always been derided in the West as a transparent propaganda ploy, the rights and wrongs of Japan's position then and later have always seemed less clear-cut to many

Asians. It is notable, for instance, that the original meeting in Tokyo in 1941 at which the Co-Prosperity concept was launched drew attendance from several freedom fighters from Asian countries then colonized by the Western powers. Even in the aftermath of World War II, there was considerable sympathy for Japan's efforts to repulse Western encroachment. This was perhaps most memorably demonstrated at the Tokyo Tribunal, which tried Japan's leaders on war crimes after the war: the judge who represented India caused a sensation by exonerating all twenty-eight accused military leaders, whom he regarded as operating from "pure patriotic motives."

One thing is clear. East Asians have in recent years been increasingly frank in acknowledging Tokyo's hegemonic position. In both Singapore and Malaysia, government officials have launched "Look East" campaigns that openly reject the Western economic and political model in favor of the Japanese one. Even Thailand, Indonesia, and China are now happy to acknowledge Japan as their teacher. Although the South Koreans continue to criticize Japan, the sincerity of their flattery is evident in the fact that their bureaucrat-driven business system is virtually a carbon copy of Japan's, albeit about thirty years behind Japan in economic evolution.

If you look at what East Asians do as opposed to what they say, their deference to Japan is unmistakable. Take the issue of the so-called comfort women who were forcibly dispatched to the war front to provide sex for the Imperial Army. Although this has been a big issue in the Western press recently, East Asian governments have done less than nothing to plead the victims' cases with Japan. In 1993, President Kim Young-Sam of South Korea went out of his way to shield Japan from victims' claims for compensation. In 1994, both Malaysia and Vietnam publicly indicated they would not press individual claims against Japan. In a pointed dig at the West, Malaysia's pro-Japanese Prime Minister Mahathir Mohamad said he had no more intention of seeking redress from Japan than from Britain, Malaysia's other colonial oppresser. Perhaps most surprisingly of all, even Corazon Aquino, when she was president of the Philippines, turned down a request for an official investigation of the comfort women's case.

East Asian nations have a natural tendency to cooperate with each other much more than uninitiated Westerners assume. Few observers of East Asia have had a better insight into how East Asian nations

truly view one another than Pearl Buck, the Nobel Prize–winning
American author of the 1930s best seller *The Good Earth*. She was
born and educated in China and taught for a time at a university in
Nanking. In a letter to Eleanor Roosevelt in the immediate wake of
the Japanese attack on Pearl Harbor in December 1941, Buck made
an extraordinary prophecy that the Japanese, Chinese, and other East
Asian peoples would form a grand anti-Western alliance after the war
ended. Buck maintained that there was "in all the Oriental peoples a
very deep sense that the white man generally is or may be their
common enemy, and in the final analysis it remains always a possibility that the point may come when these peoples, even such present
enemies as the Chinese and the Japanese, may unite as colored against
white."

Many experienced observers of East Asia believe that Japan and
China are now in the 1990s bearing out Buck's extraordinary prediction. There is also at work here something even more important than
Asian fellow feeling and that is Asian pragmatism. The pragmatic
East Asians want to be on the winning side when the race between
the United States and Japan is over. Most East Asian nations switched
to the Japanese side during the 1980s. They were reacting not out of
love of Japan but dismay at Reaganomics. East Asian leaders understood by the mid-1980s something that many Americans do not seem
to understand even today: that even a power as great as the United
States will not remain great much longer if it must borrow from other
powers to pay its way in the world.

A profitable home base

Japanese planners have long organized the Japanese market as a
profitable home base that enables Japanese industry to maintain an
extraordinarily high level of investment in future technologies. Recently there have been predictions in the West that this advantage will
soon be whittled away. In actuality, Japan now enjoys an almost
unlimited supply of new industrial policy tools to help boost industrial investment. In modern conditions, one such tool, subsidies, can
be designed to have as powerful a mercantilist effect as tariffs and can
be practically impossible to detect. The Japanese government's tendency to pay top dollar in its procurement programs is one important

method of subsidizing industry. Although in theory the Tokyo government's procurement programs are supposed to be increasingly open to foreign suppliers, in conditions of modern complexity, it is easy for Japanese officials to specify criteria that favor Japanese contractors. Moreover, many ostensibly private Japanese corporations — in industries like railways, electricity generation, and telecommunications — tend to channel similar subsidies to industries like electronics and electrical engineering that have been targeted by the bureaucrats.

The Tokyo government also enjoys an extraordinary variety of even less direct tools for boosting targeted industries. Officials have long used their regulatory powers in broadcasting, for instance, to create planned obsolescence in the television industry, thus generating timely demand for new-generation products. They have, for instance, suppressed the development of cable television services in favor of promoting satellite television. From the point of view of Japan's industrial policy, satellite television is a much more intelligent way of increasing television choice than cable. Whereas much of America's investment in cable has gone toward digging up roads, most of Japan's investment in satellite goes toward boosting high-technology jobs in electronics.

This economic benefit to the electronics industry is further enhanced by government standard setting, which maximizes hardware sales. To receive the full range of satellite broadcasts, for instance, a Japanese viewer must pay nearly $2,000 for duplicate tuners, decoders, and satellite dishes.

Japan's lax antitrust policy can also be expected to provide important support for Japanese industry's profits going forward. Because most American corporations conducting manufacturing in Japan are implicitly or explicitly junior members of Japanese cartels, they constitute a vital power block that will make it very difficult for Washington ever to bring effective antitrust actions against Japan. All in all, if corporate America can no longer muster a general consensus to oppose Japan's cartel/keiretsu matrix, Washington cannot be expected to do anything.

Finally, what of anti-dumping rules that in theory make it difficult for corporate Japan to maintain its system of charging lower prices abroad than at home? Here again the news for Japanese industry could hardly be better. Although Japanese industry's practice of pricing its products lower overseas than in the home market constitutes an overt rejection of the rules of capitalism, capitalist nations of the West seem more impotent than ever to change Japanese behavior. The fact that Japan is now moving into product categories that have never existed in the West means that there are no organized lobbies in the West to pressure governments on this issue.

In short, Japan has never been freer to organize its economy on its own terms free of backseat driving from the West.

America's last stronghold

The single significant advanced American industry that continues to enjoy a clear global lead is aerospace. But even here the outline of a Japanese victory is beginning to take shape. Certainly the industry's economics make it vulnerable to Japan's targeting methods. Its cost structure is more heavily biased toward fixed costs than almost any other industry because virtually all of the cost of making aircraft components is in research and tooling. By comparison the incre- mental cost of producing each additional unit is in most cases quite low. Moreover, the industry lends itself to Japan's strategy of acquir- ing leadership by degrees, starting with basic components and moving up the sophistication curve. Perhaps even more troubling for the Americans, no industry makes such huge demands on capital, capital which in one way or another is already coming increasingly from Japan. Finally aerospace is the ultimate monopolistic industry, domi- nance of which would be worth almost any sacrifice to Japan.

There is no lack of evidence that Japan is eyeing this industry with interest. The FSX affair — in which Japanese officials lobbied Washington with great determination a few years ago to transfer key American aerospace technologies to Japan — testifies to that. The U.S. Trade Representative's Office stated in 1994 that aerospace has long been targeted by Japan and Japanese aerospace companies are getting large amounts of help from the Japanese government. Already Japan supplies many crucial components to the American aerospace industry. Every succeeding generation of American passenger jets in- cludes a bigger proportion of Japan-made parts than the previous one.

The pattern is driven by the ever-increasing power of the Japanese government to project its industrial policy onto the United States.

Partly this stems from the control Tokyo officials enjoy over the Japanese airlines' plane purchases. When a company like Boeing is designing a new plane, Tokyo commits Japan early on to buying a large number of such planes in return for Boeing giving major component contracts to Japanese aerospace companies. Tokyo's bargaining power is hard to exaggerate: already the world's three busiest air routes are all domestic Japanese routes and Japan has been Boeing's largest market in recent years. Given the heavy bias toward fixed costs in the aircraft industry, Boeing is more than delighted to be promised so many orders by Japanese airlines. In response to complaints by Boeing's labor unions, the company has publicly said it has no choice but to source more and more parts abroad if it is to maintain overseas sales.

Meanwhile Japan is now the world's main source of aircraft lease financing — a fact that is increasingly giving the Tokyo Finance Ministry and the Japanese banks the ability to influence aircraft purchases by airlines around the world.

In the future as Japan's aerospace ambitions grow, Tokyo can be expected to use its control of landing rights in Japan as a bargaining chip to persuade American and European airlines to buy planes made mainly or substantially with Japanese components. As we have seen, landing rights in Japan are artificially restricted by Japanese transport regulators. As a result the few foreign airlines that have access to Japan enjoy a highly profitable franchise and can be expected to be attentive to the guidance of the Japanese government in the matter of aircraft purchases. Tokyo has had long experience in this sort of bargaining, having pioneered the concept in the shipbuilding industry more than thirty years ago: at that time, it offered American and European oil companies increased access to the Japanese market if they agreed to buy Japanese supertankers.

As it is, Japan's success in aerospace is already considerable. Boeing has contracted out most of the body of the new Boeing 777, for instance, to Japanese aerospace companies. Scheduled for launch in May 1995, the 375-seat 777 will be highly economical to operate and is expected to be Boeing's first big new plane for the twenty-first century.

Officially the 777's Japanese content is put at 21 percent, but this percentage counts only those parts that Japanese contractors supply direct to Boeing. If Japan-made materials, components, and subsystems supplied to Boeing's contractors in the United States, Europe, and Asia were all counted, Japan's share would be much larger, and perhaps would exceed even America's net share.

Several Japanese aerospace companies are making rapid progress in acquiring American aerospace know-how, notably Fuji Heavy Industries, Kawasaki Heavy Industries, Mitsubishi Heavy Industries, Shin Meiwa Industry, and Japan Aircraft Manufacturing. All are major contractors for Boeing's 757 and 767 aircraft; they are also major contractors to McDonnell Douglas.

Tokyo is using a similar strategy in the jet engine business. It has, for instance, been using its airline companies' purchases of jet engines as a bargaining chip to persuade Pratt & Whitney, the aircraft engine division of the United Technologies company, to include Mitsubishi Heavy Industries as a partner in the development of its new generation of passenger jet engines. Pratt & Whitney has recently agreed to transfer production of the engine's combustor, the chamber in which combustion takes place, from Connecticut to Nagoya in central Japan. As of 1993, Pratt & Whitney was under pressure to increase Mitsubishi's participation in return for getting an order for twenty engines from Japan Air Lines.

Meanwhile, Ishikawajima Harima Heavy Industries is in partnership with General Electric in developing jet engines, in particular the GE90 engine. General Electric has agreed to provide Ishikawajima with the manufacturing technology to build the engine for the Japanese air force's new FSX fighter jet. Kawasaki Heavy Industries is participating in a joint project with Britain's Rolls-Royce.

For now, the American aerospace industry executives scoff at talk that they may soon be overtaken by the Japanese. American aerospace executives tell anecdotes of mistakes or apparent mistakes the Japanese have made in the aerospace industry. They argue that airframe systems integration — the task of designing and assembling a plane so that all the parts work together — is a gigantic undertaking from which outsiders, even the Japanese, are likely to remain permanently excluded.

But some well-informed American observers are not convinced by the American aerospace industry's confidence. They see parallels with the overconfidence displayed by the American steel and auto industries in years gone by. American Electronics Association's Tokyo director John Stern, for instance, believes that the Americans underestimate the Japanese industry's capability to break into systems integration. Leon Trilling, a professor of aeronautics at MIT, has publicly suggested that Japan's partnership with Boeing in the 777 project is an attempt by the Japanese to break down the ramparts around the Americans' technological fortress in aerospace systems integration.

Seen in terms of group logic, the outcome seems clear. The American and European airframe makers are required by antitrust law to compete with one another. By contrast, the Japanese aerospace industry functions under no such constraints and can organize itself as a well-coordinated single unit that can split the Western firms and play them off against each other. Given the aerospace industry's high fixed costs, the existing players need the backing of their governments to survive. The odds against the Americans maintaining their independence in the long run seem poor in the absence of a total reappraisal of the laissez-faire thinking that has dominated American aerospace policy in recent years.

Research and development: buying the future

Can Japan achieve a sustainable technological lead in all the industries it is targeting? At first sight this seems doubtful. After all, Japan probably boasts no more than one-fifth of all the world's scientists and engineers. Japan, however, enjoys many hidden advantages that will enable it to harvest a disproportionately large share of all the world's future technological breakthroughs.

For a start, Japanese corporations have a productivity advantage in research because of the Japanese cartels' efforts to minimize research overlaps. Moreover, Japanese leaders focus their research budgets almost entirely on creating new products and production technologies, while the West spends heavily on fundamental research with no immediate economic applications. Although Japanese science is often scorned in the West, in economic terms the Japanese strategy is a clear winner. Japan's research creates immediate economic benefits and, thanks to the penchant of Western scientists to publish their findings, Japanese corporations are usually quicker on the draw in commercializing Western theoretical breakthroughs than Western corporations.

All in all, it is probably not an exaggeration to say that more than thirty percent of all the world's economically significant research is now being conducted in the home islands of Japan.

In addition, Japanese corporations are now beginning to do research abroad. Here again, they enjoy an important efficiency advantage in that their cartels allow them to avoid duplication also in overseas research just as surely as at home. Thus as corporate Japan steps up its overseas research activity, Western corporations are going to be increasingly at a disadvantage. The future choice presented to these corporations will therefore be either to reduce their research or to opt to become junior partners in cartelized research programs directed from Tokyo. A leading indicator of this new trend is that IBM in the 1990s has been cutting back its independent research activities while diverting many of its scientists to work on joint-venture research projects with such Japanese competitors as Toshiba.

Corporate Japan's research activity abroad has taken off only recently and seems to have been spurred mainly by the yen's doubling in value in the mid-1980s, which suddenly meant that it was cheaper for corporate Japan to employ Western researchers than Japanese ones. Already, progress has been impressive. Corporate Japan has established 150 research and development facilities in the United States alone. Corporate Japan's participation in European research is even greater. It now boasts a total of 192 research and development facilities in the European Community.

Japan's links with Russian science are also shaping up as an important advantage. Despite Japan's stance of generally refusing to help Russia economically, Japanese corporations have been tapping into Russian expertise in advanced industries such as aerospace. In 1993, the Society of Japanese Aerospace Companies announced that it had reached agreement to gain access to advanced aircraft engine laboratories in Russia. In addition, Russian experts have been contracted to provide training for Japanese engineers. Mitsubishi Electric disclosed in 1993 that it had bought technology from a Moscow-based institute to help it develop maglev transportation systems. In a program coordinated by the MITI, Japan is also hoping to buy other Russian technologies in such fields as superconducting materials and nuclear fusion.

The Japanese are excited in particular about an innovative sea-surface plane the Russians have been developing. The plane uses special aerodynamic efficiencies of flying just above the surface of the water to achieve extra lift. Japanese experts are talking about building a version that will carry as many as one thousand passengers at a saving over present-day air transport costs of about 50 percent per passenger.

American commentators sometimes suggest that Japanese corporations will have difficulty attracting the West's top scientists to work in Japanese-owned laboratories. Again they exaggerate Japan's problems. In competing to hire the world's best scientists, employers must offer research funds, equipment, and patience. Corporate Japan offers all these in spades. A telling example of how money is helping corporate Japan leapfrog the Americans in research is NEC's new research institute at Princeton, New Jersey. This facility has hired many top researchers from AT&T's nearby Bell Laboratories, and the atmosphere at the NEC laboratory is being compared to that of Bell Labs in its heyday fifty years ago.

Meanwhile Hitachi has located four of its twenty-two laboratories overseas. In the Silicon Valley, for instance, it is studying high-speed chips; in Detroit it is studying car electronics; in Ireland, it is collaborating with university researchers to develop supercomputer software; and finally in Britain, Hitachi is funding major research at the Cavendish Laboratory, a famous Cambridge University institution that has produced more than eighty Nobel Prize winners.

Several Japanese automakers have established research and development operations in the Detroit area. Nissan alone now employs four hundred research workers in its Detroit facility and plans to add one hundred more in the next few years. Among the futuristic projects American scientists are working on for Nissan is the development of technology to reduce the number of road accidents. The project taps American expertise in human sight and cognitive processes.

Japanese corporations enjoy a hidden commercial edge in research competition in that they know far more about American research than American corporations know about Japanese research. Almost by definition, it requires the conjunction of two or more disparate breakthroughs to create a successful new commercial application. Thanks to the U.S.-Japan knowledge imbalance, Japan has often stolen a march on the Americans in developing commercial applications for American technologies whose potential was not fully understood in the United States.

The Sanyo electronics company, for instance, owes its lead in solar energy to just such an edge. Its own breakthrough in manufacturing thin-film amorphous silicon coincided with RCA's discovery that amorphous silicon can generate impressive amounts of electricity from sunlight. Within a few years it had launched solar-energy calculators, the world's first solar-powered consumer goods.

Western corporations can do little to rectify the information imbalance because openness is as distinctive a feature of Western society as closedness is of Japanese society. Japanese researchers in the United States can sometimes quite legally pick up more information in a single conversation in Silicon Valley or Boston than they could discover in a year of laboratory experiments in Japan. Take, for instance, the supercomputer industry, which is now led by Japanese corporations. Japan reportedly raced ahead thanks in part to Japanese researchers' access to American government laboratories such as Lawrence Livermore and NASA's Ames Research Center.

Japan's researchers even learn a great deal from attending American conferences and seminars. Such occasions can be highly revealing because American scientists, living in a society shaped by individualism, maintain a tradition of public disclosure to further their careers and their research programs.

Ironically, corporate Japan's superior ability to keep its technologies under a bushel has long been characterized by the American press as a problem for Japan. As reported by the *Wall Street Journal,* for instance, Japan "lags" behind the United States in the development of publicly accessible databases of scientific research. As the *Journal* has reported, Japanese regulation has severely stunted the growth of public databases on Japanese science. The *Journal*'s conclusion is that this is an unintended effect of regulatory muddle. A more realistic interpretation is that the regulators are quite deliberately and rationally curbing access to Japan's scientific databases to minimize leaks of valuable information to foreigners. Far better to keep Japan's databases private and restrict access to members of the cartels, keiretsus, and other authorized organizations. Thus while Japanese government officials and corporate Japan's researchers have access to confidential information on Japanese research, Americans and Europeans enjoy no similar access. Inevitably this information advantage strengthens the Japanese economic system's bargaining position in forming technological alliances with Western corporations.

It seems clear that Japan will continue to have advantageous access to the West's best university laboratories. The point is that as governments in both the United States and Britain have cut back their subsidies for university education, American and British science faculties have come to rely increasingly on subventions from foreign corporations, particularly the Japanese, to make ends meet.

Partly for this reason, Japanese researchers are specially welcome at many top Western universities, and they are going abroad to study in ever larger numbers. In recent years more than twenty-five thousand Japanese researchers have gone to the United States annually. Most such researchers are on sabbatical leave from Japan's top corporate or government research programs.

Thanks to a law enacted in the United States in 1981, foreign corporations can even acquire patent rights to research conducted in American universities. This has opened the door for corporate Japan to commission America's top universities to take on designated research projects. In return for paying part of the cost, Japanese corporations pick up the commercial rights to the resulting technologies.

As Sheridan Tatsuno has highlighted, the Massachusetts Institute of Technology in particular is becoming increasingly dependent on funding from corporate Japan. As of 1990, Japanese corporations and cartels had endowed thirteen professorial chairs there. MIT has set up an industrial liaison program in which corporate sponsors who pay a fee of about $50,000 a year get access to special briefings and advance knowledge of important research. As of the late 1980s, forty-two Japanese corporations had already joined this project.

Other big American schools that are engaged in similar ventures with the Japanese economic system include the California Institute of Technology, Columbia, Cornell, New York University, Princeton, and Penn State.

Japanese corporations are beginning to extract bankable benefits from links with American and European universities. According to a study a few years ago by the U.S. General Accounting Office, such links have helped Toshiba, for instance, develop new technology for recording images on disks, Toyota to devise new engineering stress sensors, and Asahi Chemical to computerize its manufacturing process.

Meanwhile Hitachi has reported exciting results from the Cavendish Laboratory in Britain. Scientists there have helped develop new technologies that could make possible vastly more powerful computers. They have mapped out a practical way for electrons to be manipulated individually in semiconductor memories, allowing each electron to function as a separate store of information. This in turn makes possible a dramatic reduction in the amount of energy consumed — and heat emitted — by electronic chips, a vital condition for the practical exploitation of ultra-high-capacity memory chips currently being considered.

Just as Japan is moving purposefully to exploit Western scientific brainpower, the United States seems to be in full-scale retreat. One problem for the Americans is that the federal government is finding it increasingly difficult to play its traditional patronage role in American science. The federal government is hampered not only by budget restraints but by the fact that "globalized" American corporations now often function more as an instrument of Japanese and European industrial policy than American industrial policy. Thus if the United States government subsidizes American corporations' research, there is no longer any guarantee that the resulting economic benefits in terms of expanded manufacturing capacity will accrue to the American economy. As the Japanese technology expert Masanori Moritani has pointed out, even if America tried to stop American corporations from selling technology to Japan, the ban would be difficult to implement given corporate America's desire always to maximize its immediate profit opportunities. The conflicts of interest are already acute. They reportedly have undermined, for instance, the Sematech program, in which the United States has been attempting to reestablish itself at the forefront of semiconductor technology. Two of Sematech's major participants, Motorola and Texas Instruments, had already established joint ventures with the Japanese in parallel fields of research. Thus there were understandable fears that technology developed by Sematech would migrate to Japan via these joint ventures.

Adding up all Japan's advantages, it seems certain that the Japanese economic system will establish global hegemony over most areas of research and development within the next fifteen years. It will then be in a stronger position than ever to control the monopolistic technologies on which its manufacturing lead is founded.

The Japanese challenge

It is often suggested that the very pace of technological change will prevent the Japanese getting out too far ahead of the Americans.

According to this argument, even if the Japanese dominate existing technologies, future technological opportunities may be in new areas in which even the Japanese have no special advantage. Thus these new breakthroughs offer a chance for the Americans to get back into the game of leading-edge manufacturing.

There are major problems with this argument. For a start, on the law of averages those companies that spend more and organize their research better are more likely to discover new technologies. Lone geniuses working without corporate support are less and less of a factor in technological progress. Most discoveries come from concerted efforts by corporations and clearly as the Japanese increase their corporate spending on research the chance that they will own the new technologies increases. But let us assume that some American company defies the odds and comes up with a major new technology. This technology alone will not generate income. In modern conditions if a company is to exploit a new manufacturing technology, it typically must have a whole business system in place so it can move rapidly to global leadership. This business system ideally should include a preexisting worldwide marketing network, strong capital resources, a large pool of skilled labor, a roster of trusted suppliers, a first-rate management, and good protection of its intellectual property. (Some might argue that Compaq Computer and Dell Computer achieved great success from scratch, but they are mere assemblers and are not engaged in fundamental manufacturing.)

For lone inventors and small technology boutiques, the only option is to sell their ideas at an early stage to bigger companies. The highest bidders are likely to be the Japanese simply because in most fields the Japanese have the best business systems already in place to exploit the commercial value of a technology very quickly. Those pioneers who refuse to sell out and instead try to commercialize their technologies on their own are likely to face resistance from existing cartels in the field and may have difficulty establishing effective global distribution. In any case, as American pioneers have discovered to their cost in recent decades, Japanese corporations can often successfully reverse-engineer a new American technology or tie up the inventor by flooding the patent office with similar patents that severely limit the inventor's ability to exploit his technology. When it comes down to a legal battle, Japan's cartels nearly always win if only because they have the resources and patience to outlast their opponents.

More than ever before, the future belongs to the strong. The world seems headed for a truly dramatic change in the balance of economic power in the next two or three decades. On the calculations of the Tokyo-based economist Kenneth Courtis, Japan could be outproducing the United States by a factor of three times by the year 2050, assuming unchanged economic policies in the United States. This means the average Japanese will be six times as productive as his American counterpart. Thus within the lifetime of today's generation of high school students Japan could account for nearly half of the world's entire production.

Will the United States prove these calculations wrong? It is time to consider how Americans should respond to the Japanese challenge.

12

Whose New World Order?

In the fifty years since World War II, America's share of world economic output has fallen from about 50 to just 21 percent. By contrast, Japan's share has soared from 1.5 to 16 percent. All the elements are in place for Japan to continue increasing its share as America's gradually declines: Japan's higher level of investment alone would be a sufficient reason to expect superior growth from Japan, even without all the other advantages cited in Chapter Eleven. Meanwhile the United States, now sadly shorn of its lead in major monopolistic industries, is increasingly finding itself competing in world markets against low-wage countries — not just low-wage assembly economies such as South Korea and Taiwan but even emerging Third World nations such as Thailand (in the case of rice) and China (in the case of apparel and textiles).

One prediction is safe: most American economic commentators will continue to be blind to the fundamental facts of America's changed economic relationship with Japan. In the future as in the past, the commentators will seize eagerly on developments that seem to justify their complacency. New American industries will probably emerge that will seem — for a time — to be the magic bullet that will dispose of America's economic problems. America's short-term trade figures or productivity growth rates will seem to improve dramatically. Meanwhile, grass-roots pressure may seem to rise in Japan for an abandonment of Japan's growth policy. The various institutions of Japan's Big Logic economics will undoubtedly continue to evolve and each change will seem to Americans like evidence that the Japanese at last want to move toward Western economic ideas. We may even see Japan's employment situation worsen dramatically as Japanese officials and industrialists experiment with adjustments in the lifetime employment policy. The Japanese bureaucracy's cohesion may undergo some seemingly serious strains. The Tokyo stock market rollercoaster may dip sharply downward yet again. The MOF may let a bank go under.

In reading the news, therefore, Americans should remember that Western commentators constantly fall into the trap of assuming that Japan's growth has been driven by one or two ephemeral advantages whose removal thereby supposedly puts Japan's entire future in jeopardy. They should recall that simplistic predictions of Japan's economic demise were already prevalent as far back as 1912. At that time British commentators regarded the Emperor Meiji as the mainspring of Japan's modernization drive, so his death in 1912 was presented in Britain as a signal that Japan's already phenomenal record of rapid economic development had ended.

The truth is that Japan's culture of intelligence, pragmatism, and loyalty has enabled it to adapt flexibly and surefootedly to a variety of economic conditions over the last 140 years. This culture equips Japan well to make whatever adjustments are needed to keep the Big Logic system in good shape to cope with the unexpected in years to come. Japanese culture has endured for centuries precisely because it has built-in mechanisms for reacting promptly and effectively to societal problems and challenges.

In the 550 years since Westerners first tried to persuade the Japanese of the advantages of Western ways, the Japanese have seen no less than six Western empires come and go — Portugal, Spain, the Netherlands, France, Britain, and the Soviet Union. Under the circumstances, it would be surprising if Tokyo ever shared Washington's assumption that the American hegemony would last forever.

We are today seeing the final fulfillment of a famous prediction made by the shogun's chief bureaucrat, Masayoshi Hotta, in the 1850s. He said that by staking everything on building foreign trade, Japan would bring "the blessings of perfect tranquillity" to foreigners, and Japan's hegemony would come in time to be acknowledged by all the world's nations. Assuming there is no major disruption in world trade, the stage is set for Japan to surpass the United States to become the world's largest economy by the year 2000. It is a prospect Americans are singularly unprepared for.

America's need for action

Americans palpably yearn to restore America's lost preeminence in the world economy. But what can they do to achieve that goal?

One thing is clear: they should stop trying to remake Japan on American principles. Such attempts infringe Japanese sovereignty and are therefore an open invitation to the Japanese to take evasive action. The Bush administration's Structural Impediments Initiatives, a program aimed at increasing Japan's consumption rate, was an object lesson in the inadvisability of trying to interfere in Japan's internal affairs. Not only did the changes President Bush prescribed fail to get Japan to increase its consumption (a failure that Japan experts such as Clyde Prestowitz had predicted at the time), but Bush established a troubling precedent that one country can meddle in the fine detail of another country's internal economic policies. If Japan at some future date turns the tables and attempts to prescribe the details of American economic policies on, say, housing and retailing, Americans will understand how far President Bush went in overstepping the boundaries of prudent diplomacy.

Although America should not attempt to dictate detailed policies to Japan, it can and should influence Japan indirectly by exercising American sovereignty. If national sovereignty means anything, America has a fundamental right in natural justice to decide what it imports and from whom. By presenting Japanese exporters with the possibility of less favorable access to the American market, Washington can concentrate Tokyo's mind on seeking ways to improve America's side of the U.S.-Japan trade bargain.

The obvious course is for Japan to set numerical targets for its imports. Japanese officials will, of course, protest and, as true professionals in the art of trade bargaining, they will make full use of the Washington lobbying system to portray numerical targets as inimical to America's long-term interests. But they know perfectly well that America, in attempting to exercise its sovereignty, would be adopting a course that Japan has always regarded as the inalienable right of every nation. The Clinton administration has been trying to persuade Tokyo to accept numerical targets but, as of this writing, it has had little success. The fault lies not with the administration's policy but rather with the Washington trade lobby and its allies in the press, who not for the first time have hopelessly undermined America's negotiating credibility. Until the American establishment can achieve a reasonable unity of purpose in its international economic strategy, Japan and other strong exporting nations will continue to stonewall American presidents with impunity.

A move to numerical targets is, of course, incompatible with the utopian version of free trade that America has championed for decades. Abandoning the dream of utopian free trade may seem regrettable, particularly as Americans have been proud of their country's role in underwriting the world trading system in the last five decades. But to pragmatists it is obvious that, with the booming East Asian region operating on mercantilist principles, the days of utopian free trade are clearly over. Managed trade, if carried out intelligently, is a wealth creator. East Asia, which has been running on managed trade for decades, can testify to that.

In any case, trade is not the central problem for America. America's real problem is how to raise its output, particularly in advanced industries that it formerly dominated. Better access to foreign markets would certainly help achieve this objective, but there are many other difficulties holding America back. In order of importance these include undersaving, the proliferation of useless service activity in both the private and public sectors, inadequate investment in research, a growing shortage of manufacturing skills, and an obsession in the business press and the securities industry with quarterly earnings trends. As well-informed economists such as Lester Thurow have argued, for the most part these difficulties can be addressed only by an effective industrial policy.

The problem for Washington is that America at present does not have the organizational resources needed to administer an ambitious industrial policy. In particular it lacks the strong government agencies of East Asia. Worse, Americans refuse to give their government agencies strong powers to get things done. They blame America's ills largely on a bloated bureaucracy. But this is a misdiagnosis. The primary blame lies not with America's bureaucrats but with the system within which the bureaucrats must operate. Because American lawmakers saddle the various arms of government with conflicting and ever-changing mandates, the result is a vast proliferation of competing bureaucratic agencies whose only visible achievement seems to be to burden industry with increasingly heavy paperwork.

With the single exception of defense policy, the United States lacks the logical, hierarchical structures necessary to ensure good government. Worse, in the light of the extreme separation of powers in the American Constitution, it lacks the ability to create such structures. In truth, the United States is, unbeknownst to itself, in the throes of a constitutional crisis.

Although the Constitution was an admirable document in its time, it is now showing its age. It bears responsibility for much of the fractiousness of America's political culture. It has slowed America's adjustment to modern conditions, and as a result the American system has changed less in the last two centuries than the supposedly hidebound systems of Europe and East Asia.

The Constitution's weaknesses are apparent in everything from gun control to education, from trade policy to the federal budget. Thanks to the extreme degree to which power is dispersed in the United States, few in government have a clear mandate to get anything done — or at least done well. Moreover, the very process of seeking political power in the United States subjects aspiring American leaders to exceptionally large temptations to accept support from powerful lobbies that will later undercut their authority and freedom to act in the national interest.

The budget deficit alone is sufficient evidence that the Constitution is in need of a radical overhaul. Why are other countries more responsible in their fiscal arrangements than the United States? The answer in part is that in most other countries, responsibility for the budget process is vested mainly in one bureaucratic agency. This agency's officials have real power, and their performance is judged not on their soundbites but on their long-term record of prudence and self-control. By contrast, as Japanese officials point out, budget-writing in the United States is a case of too many cooks. Apart from the White House and the Congress, the participants include the Office of Management and Budget, the Treasury, the Internal Revenue Service, and the president's Council of Economic Advisers. As if all this weren't enough, interest group lobbies have in recent decades acquired enormous power without accountability. The result is literally anarchy.

The more one looks at America's economic difficulties, the more clearly one sees that the basic issue is excessive individualism. In modern conditions, every society needs to set judicious limits to individualism if it is to break the natural gridlock that hinders the acceptance of badly needed new policies.

A malleable America

Americans see government intervention as a recipe for muddle and waste. But their doctrinaire rejection of industrial policy is misguided. As Clyde Prestowitz has pointed out, if Washington does not come up with an effective American industrial policy, Japan's industrial policy will prevail in America by default. Tokyo is already projecting its global industrial policy into America, and this process is bound to gather strength as Japan lengthens its lead in advanced industries. The Japanese economic system's investments in the United States, for instance, clearly have the effect of hastening the American economy's shift out of advanced manufacturing and into software, design, and final assembly. Some Americans may welcome this shift, but the fact is that the division of labor on American soil is being reshaped by decisions taken in Tokyo that are not even disclosed to Americans, let alone shaped by American democratic processes.

America's position contrasts sharply with that of other advanced nations. Most such nations have well-developed industrial policies of their own and therefore enjoy some ability to recognize and moderate the impact of Japanese influence on their economies. Member countries of the European Union, for instance, are much more successful in requiring Japanese transplant factories to buy locally made components. American officials also impose local-content requirements, but in the American case, such requirements are riddled with loopholes. America's weakness in the face of Japanese industrial policy is partly a function of America's extreme individualism. Because power is so diffused in America and because various American power centers — at federal, state, and local levels — are locked in perpetual turf battles with one another, it's easy for well-organized foreigners to play divide and rule in influencing American economic policies.

The most egregious manifestation of America's excess individualism is the lobbying system. Americans often excuse this system by claiming that similar influence-buying drives other advanced nations, but that is simply not true. The *Japan Economic Journal* has put it most pointedly: "Influence in Washington is just like in Indonesia. It's for sale." Even the *Economist,* an admirer of most manifestations of America's extreme commitment to laissez faire, has made a similar point: "America has the most advanced influence-peddling industry in the world. Washington's culture of influence-for-hire is uniquely open to all buyers, foreign and domestic . . . its lawful ways of corrupting public policy remain unrivaled."

The whole history of Japan's trade relations with America testifies to how powerfully the lobbying system has worked to Japan's advantage. With the help of friendly editors and scholars, the lobbyists have found it a simple matter to prevent the U.S. Congress from taking tough action on trade through two decades of severe trade tensions.

Thus, in Japanese eyes, America is a uniquely malleable nation that can be counted on to give way almost automatically to pressures from abroad. Although the author Pat Choate and the former presidential challenger Ross Perot have made a start on exposing the pervasiveness of lobbying in the United States, there is undoubtedly much that still has not come to light. Merely what is already in the public domain, however, indicates a shocking acceptance of money politics in the United States. Even the presidency has been touched by the lobbying scandal, as these examples testify:

• President Jimmy Carter drew much of his support for his presidential library from a famously shady Japanese billionaire, a man who was convicted as a Class A war criminal during the occupation. Well known in Japan for his connections to organized crime, Carter's benefactor was heard as recently as the 1970s describing himself as the "world's wealthiest fascist." Carter consented to have his connection to this controversial benefactor widely publicized in Japan.

• President Ronald Reagan in 1988 accepted a fee of $2 million plus other benefits totaling $5 million to give a few speeches in Tokyo. The fees were paid by a Japanese media tycoon and were astronomically larger than Reagan could have expected for a similar visit to Paris or London. They are best seen as a thank-you from the Japanese economic system for Reagan's services in helping Japanese corporations get off the hook on dumping charges in the 1980s.

• President George Bush's brother, Prescott, accepted a $250,000-a-year consulting contract in 1989 from a company controlled by Japan's most prominent organized crime leader.

The critical factor in these scandals is how they are seen in Japan: they support a widespread impression in elite Japanese circles that prominent Americans will do almost anything for money.

Few Americans realize there are ominous precedents for this sort of globalization. America's governing elite is behaving much as Chinese rulers did in the final decades of the Chinese empire.

Just how close the parallel is can be gauged from some of the rhetoric doing the rounds in Tokyo recently. The Japanese are beginning to talk about America the way the British and French used to talk about China. One noted Japanese partner of McKinsey & Co., for instance, suggested in a 1989 book that the Japanese economic system should stop regarding the United States as a united entity and should make a policy of bypassing Washington in conducting hard-headed diplomacy with individual American states. He even advocated that Japan should discipline America's elected representatives by imposing sanctions on any state whose elected representatives opposed Japanese objectives. He suggested in particular that Tokyo should organize embargos on Japanese investment in such states. It is easy to dismiss such thinking as an isolated aberration but the author of these proposals is in fact one of Tokyo's most visible policy advisers, a key political fixer and erstwhile prime ministerial confidant.

This thinking echoes the sort of divide-and-rule strategies which Europeans adopted in forcing the Chinese empire to "globalize" itself in the nineteenth century. When the so-called Last Emperor Henry P'u Yi was ousted in 1912, China's imperial tradition was almost four thousand years old. It was finished off by just seventy years of injudicious "globalization."

At this stage the American establishment is about twenty years into its cycle of misconceived "globalization." Can it change course? Clearly the need for action is urgent.

Toward an American renaissance

Societies don't easily reform themselves from within. Resistance to change is almost automatic because a society's leaders naturally tend to see little wrong with the system that propelled them to power.

Nonetheless, history has many examples of societies that renewed themselves when faced by a foreign challenge. At times of national stress, idealistic leaders somehow emerge to help guide society to fairer and more effective political and economic institutions. As we saw in Chapter Three, Japan was an object lesson in this sort of societal renewal in the mid-nineteenth century.

But where is the American elite today? Top Americans in business, finance, law, the media, and academic life are in material terms some of the most privileged people in history. Yet, many of them continue to hide behind Adam Smith's dictum that they do best for society when they do best for themselves. They tiptoe away — albeit increasingly guiltily — from any evidence that casts doubt on this self-serving philosophy.

It is clear that American politicians are increasingly powerless to change American society. They need help from elsewhere in the American establishment. But most members of the American establishment see strong reasons to shirk their responsibilities to society. American business executives seem to be focused mainly on their stock options and in trying to maximize corporate America's short-term profits through downsizing since they have become increasingly dependent on Japanese cartels. America's top investment banks enjoy notably cosy relations with the Tokyo financial community and earn large fees and profits from selling American financial assets to foreign institutions and governments. Top American law firms make a fine living doing quasi-lobbying in Washington and handling the legal side of America's asset sales. Management consultants make a profitable business of selling information on corporate America to corporate Japan and doing public relations work for Japan's globalizing cartels.

American media organizations cannot be counted on to provide guidance in the future. They are increasingly subjecting themselves to the same sort of self-censorship that has always ruled in Japanese journalism. It is, for instance, well known in the publishing industry that when American magazines write major articles on powerful foreign countries, they are in some cases required to provide advance notice to advertisers from the country concerned. Those advertisers then generally withdraw their advertising from that issue. Given the ferocity of profit pressures in the American media, this functions very effectively to reduce coverage of Japan — and particularly the sort of lengthy articles that are needed to give real insights into the changing power balance between the United States and Japan.

Americans cannot hope for much from their scholars either. Virtually every American who studies Japanese economics depends on Tokyo for funding. Such funding is not supposed to compromise academic freedom, but in reality self-censorship is evident even in America's most prestigious universities. After fifty years of intense

study of Japan by American scholars, huge areas of Japanese economic life such as employment regulation and the suppressed consumption policy remain dark continents to American scholarship. It
is safe to say that in the competition for funds, a proposed study of
say sumo wrestling or medieval Japanese love poetry is likely to win
more funding from Tokyo than an analysis of Japanese cartels. When
the *Harvard Business Review* a few years ago began publishing some
well-informed articles on Japanese economics, it was reputedly pressured by Harvard professors to back off. The professors were worried
that Harvard's funding from Japan might be reduced.

Where, therefore, can Americans look for real leadership to guide
them in these critical years. By a process of elimination, only one
promising source of help remains: America's most successful entrepreneurs. Specifically, people who have already made so much money
that they can remove themselves from the self-enrichment rat race to
focus on loftier goals. Ross Perot has already spoken out but there are
others who can probably be more persuasive in winning over establishment thinking in the United States. What should these entrepreneurs do? They should fund a far-reaching political process designed
to catalyze constitutional and societal change that will build a fairer,
stronger America. This process must include constitutional reform
and the creation of new economic institutions vested with real power
to lead America in pursuit of long-term economic growth. Bearing in
mind Benjamin Franklin's wisdom on the importance of hanging together, they should undertake their Rebuild America program as a
group: individual action is likely to be ineffective and even counterproductive. Although few of these leading entrepreneurs will want to
run for political office themselves, they can perform a historic role in
establishing a foundation to support a new breed of elected representatives who are independent of the present anarchic lobbying system. Above all, this Rebuild America program should be based on a
search for the truth — a disinterested, nonpartisan effort to analyze
the mistakes of America's past and the true reasons for East Asia's
success. An early objective would be to establish a truly independent
school of East Asian studies at one of America's top universities. That
no such school exists today is a devastating comment on the quality
of intellectual leadership America has had in recent decades. Such
an organization is desperately needed to provide a counterweight to
the self-censoring university departments and finlandized Washington

think tanks that dominate the American intellectual marketplace to-day.

Perot's experience in being savaged by the press will scare away many potential leaders of a Rebuild America movement. But there is a solution to this problem: the proprietors of America's top media organizations should be invited to join the effort. (It is a remarkable fact that, thanks to a sort of honor-among-thieves ethic in publishing, such proprietors are among the few prominent Americans whose private lives are a no-go area for the press: this principle can be extended to include their friends and allies.)

Cynics will find a Rebuild America movement unrealistic — or even un-American. But it is hardly either. The American Revolution provides the precedent. After all, who were George Washington and Thomas Jefferson but intelligent men of means who saw more to life than merely enriching themselves? The difference this time is what is needed is less a revolution, more a renaissance. What's in it for the leaders of this renaissance? Not much, perhaps — except the respect and gratitude of their grandchildren. Certainly without some such renaissance, today's young Americans will have many years ahead of them to reflect on the self-absorption that has — so far, at least — characterized their elders at this pivotal moment in American history.

Global leadership: a historic vacuum

In 1924 the British philosopher Bertrand Russell postulated that, given man's age-old capacity for collective rivalry and hatred, the march of science would eventually threaten the destruction of civilization. He thought that to avoid extinction, the human race had no alternative but to band together under the leadership of a single superpower. And that superpower should, he argued, be the United States. Given that Russell was noted for far-left views, his choice of America for ultimate leadership was a surprising one, but he evidently was so convinced of the dangers ahead that even an American-dominated world seemed greatly preferable to an anarchic one.

Clearly seventy years later, Russell's prescient case for superpower-dom is stronger than ever: at the end of the twentieth century, the world has never been more desperately in need of firm, consistent, wise leadership. For the first time in history everyone on the planet is everyone else's neighbor. Nuclear weapons, pollution, exploding population growth, and the looming possibility of mass migrations from the Third to the First World are contributing to a historic crisis which cries out for firm global leadership.

Now that the cold war is over, the way is at last clear for the United States to secure a mandate from the world's major nations to take on the role Russell advocated for it. In one of the great ironies of history, however, America's capacity to assume permanent unipolar hegemony is weaker today than at any time since Russell made his comment. A world superpower has only two choices in exercising leadership — the carrot or the stick. America's ability to use the carrot, in the form of economic aid, is now increasingly seriously curtailed by the federal budget crisis. So America is left with the stick, military superiority. But the stick is an unattractive persuader in the best of times and is clearly a highly dangerous one in an era of nuclear weapons.

Moreover, in the long term, there is even a question mark about America's ability to retain military superiority. If America continues to lose position economically, all bets are off. Already America's military position is less comprehensive than many realize. As we have already noted, America relies heavily on Japanese manufacturers for fundamental materials and components used in American weapons.

Moreover America is increasingly dependent on Japanese funding to maintain a global military establishment. America's bases in Japan, which are the last remaining major American fortresses in Asia, are paid for almost entirely by the Japanese taxpayer. As the *Mainichi Daily News* pointed out in 1994, even America's military intelligence operations in East Asia are now conducted and funded largely by Tokyo. In particular, Tokyo pays for a top secret American intelligence center in Japan that is Washington's most important window on military developments throughout East Asia. The center is largely operated by former Japanese army personnel who analyze satellite photographs and other highly classified materials on behalf of the U.S. Department of Defense. The Defense Department's dependence on Japanese funding began in 1978 and has been increasing rapidly as the yen has risen and American budget problems have worsened. The Defense Department seems to think that it is quite natural for America to get its information on, for instance, North Korean weapons deployments via Tokyo. From a Japanese point of view, however, the arrangement is extraordinary. Perhaps the best way to understand this is to imagine what Americans would have thought if, in the early 1900s, a weakening British empire asked the United States to fund British military installations and espionage operations in the Americas. To say the least, Americans wouldn't have had much confidence in Britain's long-term future as a superpower. The final absurdity is that the proximate cause of America's deficits is that Washington has dramatically cut the taxes of America's rich — which hardly seems like the act of a well-governed superpower in the eyes of Japan's heavily taxed elite.

Without an advanced manufacturing base, America has largely lost the economic prowess that was once its main tool in providing effective peacetime leadership to the world. America no longer has the ability to stand up economically to even tyrannical regimes (this was the subtext of President Clinton's refusal to use trade sanctions against China in 1994 — the sanctions would have hurt America more than China because China had plenty of other advanced trading partners who were prepared to take America's place). America is less well placed than Japan to court the Third World by offering valuable basic technologies: because Japan, unlike America, has withdrawn almost entirely from low-grade activities such as coal mining and textile spinning, it can cheerfully offer technologies in these fields to the Third World without undermining its own domestic economy.

Does the European Union have the necessary tools to lead a world in crisis? Tokyo hardly thinks so. Although the American economist Lester Thurow has portrayed a united Europe as the natural successor to America in leading the world, Europe appears to the Japanese to be a crazy quilt of linguistic, ethnic, and religious differences. Thus Brussels will probably be permanently denied the necessary degree of centralized power to act decisively on the world stage. As the Japanese officials understand very well, Brussels enjoys only token powers to tax the European public and without taxation powers it will remain a paper tiger in geopolitics.

China has also been talked about as a future hegemony — but it is clearly not ready for such a role. Quite apart from its other difficulties, China boasts an economy only one-seventh the size of Japan's.

In the meantime, the world's problems must be addressed. Whether Japanese leaders like it or not, the time has come for them to make their move.

Can Japan lead?

American observers insist that Japan lacks the skills to lead the world. Jeffrey E. Garten has commented that the United States is far superior to Japan in leadership capability because "it has ideological appeal, an international outlook, and a willingness to propose initiatives and muster global support for them."

It is worth considering this assertion carefully. Does Japan lack ideological appeal? The Japanese system may not on balance seem like an attractive model for people brought up in the individualistic societies of the West. But Westerners account for only one-tenth of the world's population. Japan is already the role model for most of East Asia, a fact openly acknowledged in Singapore, Malaysia, Indonesia, Thailand, Taiwan, South Korea, and increasingly in India and China. These countries together account for close to half the world's population — and, economically speaking, the faster growing half.

As we have noted, Americans tend to exaggerate the width of the psychological divide between the Japanese and other East Asians. For all the supposed unresolved bitterness over World War II, South Korean leaders, for instance, are at least as comfortable with the Japanese as with Americans. It could hardly be otherwise because the South Korean economic system has amazingly close ties to the Japanese system. The Korean system was founded by Park Chung Hee, a Korean soldier who like many of his compatriots served with the Japanese Imperial Army in Manchuria in the 1930s. When in 1961 he became Korea's president after leading a military coup, he applied the Manchurian system to Korea, and in many ways he remained more faithful to the original model than postwar Japanese leaders.

Garten echoes a prevalent view in the American policymaking establishment when he says Japan lacks an international outlook. Again this does not stand up to close scrutiny. Japan monitors other countries on a highly organized basis. Japan's foreign policy experts not only speak the relevant languages but spend a lifetime building up relationships with key foreign power brokers and information sources. When the Japanese need to exert economic influence over a country, they always seem to know far better than the Americans which buttons to press.

The reason American observers like Garten imagine Japan is weak in international policymaking is that Japan's real policymaking takes place almost entirely behind closed doors. Because policymaking is almost never discussed publicly in Japan, Americans assume such discussion is not taking place. Japan's behind-closed-doors diplomacy has enormous pragmatic advantages. Japanese policymakers can mull various options among themselves without giving undue offense to those foreigners potentially on the receiving end. In particular, Japan can evolve policy without alerting potential opposition ahead of time and can try to present its considered decisions in ways that save face for foreign nations.

By contrast, America's public foreign policy process can be a distinct public relations disadvantage. Foreign countries rarely enjoy being talked about in Washington as if they were pawns at America's disposal. Japan itself knows well how much offense America's open policy discussions can create because Japan has often been the subject of such clumsy American discussion. In the first decades after World War II, for instance, American think tanks, scholars, press commentators, and government officials noisily applied themselves to the question, "What shall we do with Japan?" Many of the more naive participants implied that Japan was a vassal state that would remain permanently at America's disposal.

Tokyo is clear-sighted in arranging its diplomatic priorities, and hitherto it has shrewdly regarded maintaining maximum trade access to Western markets, particularly the United States, as much more important than any other diplomatic objective. In practice, this priority rules out high-profile diplomacy in the Middle East and other world flashpoints. If Tokyo took an overtly different line on such flashpoints, American public opinion could well swing strongly against Japan — with serious consequences for Japanese industry's access to the American market. This is no empty fear. America's body language implies that Japan's role should be merely to rubber-stamp American foreign policy initiatives. The *Washington Post* columnist Jim Hoagland said this explicitly in 1993: "Imagine Japan, content to play little brother to America for half a century, deciding to go its own way politically and militarily now that the cold war is over. This is thinking the unthinkable."

It is worth seeing Japan's diplomacy problem from a Japanese point of view. First, Tokyo knows all too well that having different views from Washington's is "unthinkable." Second, Tokyo realizes that American foreign policy is subject to frequent 180-degree turns at short notice: the Bush administration's switch from arming Saddam Hussein to declaring him a new Hitler is only one of the more recent examples. In the circumstances, it is hardly surprising that Japan's foreign policy pronouncements tend to be few and strangulated in tone, and unwelcome foreign policy requests from Washington evoke a pantomime of evasion and procrastination in Tokyo.

Tokyo knows something about U.S.-Japan cooperation that even such sophisticated American observers as Jeffrey Garten seem to find hard to understand: Japanese and American thought processes are as different as oil and water. Long experience has shown that the Japanese and Americans are simply incapable of working together amicably as equal partners, either in business or in government organizations: the conceptual and practical obstacles inherent in U.S.-Japan relations make truly equal partnerships a utopian dream. In virtually all U.S.-Japan corporate joint ventures, for instance, the Japanese partner quickly takes charge. For the purpose of saving the Americans' face, major decisions are generally presented as if both sides participated equally but, behind the boardroom door, the Americans are often given little choice but to rubber stamp the Japanese side's strategies.

As Chalmers Johnson has pointed out, Japan's real views on, for instance, how the International Monetary Fund and the World Bank should be run are sharply at odds with the laissez faire policies Washington currently prescribes for these institutions. Thus, in being self-effacing Tokyo is merely heeding the Japanese proverb *Sendo oku shite fune yama ni noboru:* too many boatmen drive the ship into a mountain. Tokyo consoles itself that its time will come. In the meantime, while Washington still is strong enough to veto Tokyo's ideas, Tokyo can achieve nothing by wrestling Washington for the tiller.

The truth is that the idea the Japanese cannot lead comes from the same misinformed observers who a few years ago said the Japanese lacked creativity, and before that they said the Japanese could not make high-quality products — in other words, the American media.

A will to lead

Every society tends to think of its own customs and culture as superior to those of other societies. It is a view found even among newly discovered Stone Age tribes in the Amazon jungle. It would be surprising, therefore, if Japan — surely one of the most carefully organized of societies — had any lack of confidence in the benefits of a prospective Pax Nipponica.

The truth is, as the Harvard Japan scholar Ezra Vogel has pointed out, the Japanese have been privately discussing their plans for Pax Nipponica for years. In Vogel's view, the Japanese, like earlier generations of Westerners, take their economic success as evidence of superior moral worth.

Certainly Japan's dramatic 140-year ascent from feudal autarky is evidence of unique organizational competence. Japan has, within the confines of its own borders, tackled and overcome many of the problems facing our planet. No other government can match Japan's record in providing a large population with a life of prosperity, safety, and satisfaction in a cramped and virtually resourceless country. Tokyo has, for instance, achieved a stunning victory in population control. Thanks to various policies that have to this day remained largely unpublicized in the West, Tokyo cut the Japanese birth rate from one of the world's highest in the 1930s to one of the world's lowest in the 1970s. Moreover, Tokyo has made startling progress in improving the Japanese environment. Within a decade of the first oil shock in the 1970s, Japan had transformed itself into one of the cleanest, most energy-efficient nations. Previously it had been one of the worst environmental offenders.

Viewing the world from a Japanese standpoint, Japan is probably the nation that has come closest to achieving Jeremy Bentham's idea of the greatest happiness for the greatest number of people. Americans argue that Japan is no paradise for women. And in Western terms that is clearly so — but there is little evidence that Japanese women want real change. Despite five decades of Western reports of awakening feminism in Japan, Japanese women have, as mothers, pointedly perpetuated traditional sex roles in raising their children. In any case, among Japan's East Asian satellites, Japan's social conservatism is hardly a disqualification for leadership.

By anyone's standards, Japan has to be considered a triumph of social planning — a country with virtually no narcotics, vandalism, unemployment, hunger, guns, homelessness, or juvenile delinquents. The institution of the family is probably stronger in Japan than in any other major country. Japan's abortion rate is only one-third of America's, yet illegitimate births account for only 1 percent of births in

Japan versus 23 percent in the United States. Divorce in Japan runs only about one-third the American rate and about half the rates of Britain and Germany. Crime is so rare that parents let seven-year-olds ride the Tokyo subway unaccompanied. Only a minuscule 0.2 percent of Japanese adults are illiterate — the lowest rate in the world.

Many of the sensational stories about Japanese society's alleged drawbacks are notorious media myths. Japan's supposedly high rate of suicide among teenagers, for instance, is a myth: the suicide rate among American teenagers is actually about 15 percent higher. Japan's supposedly sensational rate of death from overwork (which is known in Japanese as *karoshi*) is also a myth.

The secret of Japan's famed internal order is a degree of subtle coercion absent in Western societies. The police employ none-too-gentle tactics to get miscreants to inform on each other. People's privacy is deliberately minimized at every level in Japanese society — from the open-plan offices in which everyone works to the *koseki* family register system, in which a family's deviations from societal norms are semi-publicly recorded. Even in Japan's show business industry, employers are under societal pressure to boycott entertainers whose lifestyles fall short of appropriate standards. Despite Japan's image abroad as one large boot camp, remarkably few of the inmates want to escape. Most Japanese executives dislike being posted to the West, even if they would never say so to a Westerner. When the Japanese in the United States apply for permanent American residence, they almost invariably do so at the behest of their companies and do not want it for themselves. When they return to Japan, they are unwilling to work for foreign firms, even for large increases in pay.

The truth is that they regard their country as little short of an earthly paradise and they accept societal pressure as a matter of commonsense, wondering how any advanced society can function any other way. In short, if the Japanese are called upon to create a New World Order, they know what is needed: Japan writ large.

Blindside

Is the United States the victim of a Japanese economic conspiracy? We raised the question in Chapter One, and now it is time to answer it.

Yes, there is a conspiracy — but it is an American conspiracy, not a Japanese one. High-minded Americans in the economics profession and in the media have been consistently trying to keep the world safe for utopian free trade, and in that endeavor they have constantly blindsided the American public about the reality of East Asian economics.

One critical truth in particular has been comprehensively suppressed: that East Asian mercantilism is a highly effective policy in boosting East Asia's all-important savings flows. American economists and economic commentators have always understood the connection between trade barriers and savings rates, so ostensibly their guilt is great. But they have an alibi: with virtually no exceptions, they have not lived in East Asia. They have depended for their understanding of the facts on a few crucial business publications.

Unfortunately, the business press's coverage of Japan has been a story of negligence evidently born of a concern not to look too closely at Japan's trade policies. With few exceptions, business publications have utterly failed to provide their correspondents with the solid cultural and linguistic training needed to begin to unravel the true story of Tokyo's economic strategy. Their excuse has been that effective language training would be too expensive. And true, total fluency in reading Japanese is almost beyond the reach of Americans who come to the Japanese language in adult years. But the point is that with as little as two years' study, a reporter can acquire enough of the language to scan the headlines, use standard reference books, and read advertisements and signs. The American press has not contemplated even this modest investment. As a result, American press correspondents in Tokyo have always existed in a state of intellectual weightlessness with no fixed reference points to guide them. As the reporting of the early 1990s Japanese "slump" amply demonstrates, they have been uncommonly susceptible to that quintessential journalist's disease, the madness of crowds. One thing is clear: if the position were reversed and Japanese correspondents in America were constantly in disarray because they could not read English, the American press would hardly be sympathetic. In the world's most literate society, the champions of American freedom of expression have been functional illiterates. This has not prevented them from constantly attributing America's poor exports to Japan to the alleged failure of American exporters "to try hard enough." The irony is that no organizations have been more remiss in not trying hard enough than the deep-pocketed institutions of the American press.

The editors of the *Wall Street Journal* bear disproportionate responsibility: if twenty years ago, they had highlighted the comprehensive nature of East Asian mercantilism and pointed out mercantilism's extraordinary effect in boosting East Asian savings rates, American public opinion would have followed a very different path. Instead, the *Journal* has consistently misrepresented the facts of Japan; it has systematically suppressed articles from contributors who understood Japanese economics; and it has powerfully fostered vain hopes in America that Japan would soon converge toward American social and economic values.

The *Journal* has led the American financial press in turning a blind eye to the power that Japan now enjoys by virtue of the fact that more than half the world's new savings each year originates in a financial system tightly controlled by MOF bureaucrats. If a single individual such as John D. Rockefeller or even a cartel of, say, nationalized French banks enjoyed as much financial power as the MOF, even the *Journal*'s editors, besotted as they are with their simplistic free-market rhetoric, would long since have got the message. That they have not yet done so will be remembered as the Japanese economic system's single most extraordinary public relations victory.

A special irony of the *Journal*'s position is that its parent company, Dow Jones, is probably America's most profitable unregulated monopoly; yet *Journal* editors unblushingly advocate that American manufacturers can be made "more efficient" through exposure to such extreme forms of destructive competition as dumping by foreign manufacturers operating from the sanctuary of protected home markets.

Part of the problem with the American press is that, as David Halberstam has pointed out, American business coverage is left largely to journalists who would not shine in other branches of the journalistic profession. Many American business journalists notoriously break the first rule of journalism by indulging in "thesis journalism." This leads to widespread misreporting not only in their coverage of East Asia but of most of Europe, and it blinds the American public to how rapidly the world beyond American shores is changing. In Europe, for instance, per capita income at current exchange rates now exceeds American levels in eight economies: Switzerland, Finland, Sweden, Norway, Denmark, Luxembourg, Iceland, and the former West Germany: many of these economies openly reject American free market theories that are treated as self-evident truths in the United States, particularly in matters such as cartels, social policy, and government intervention in the economy.

But even America's mainstream journalists and editors are clearly gripped by an extraordinary lapse of professional curiosity. In essence they refuse to look directly at Japan. Nowhere is this pattern more obvious than in how books on Japan are reviewed in the American press. Books written by the few informed, independent writers in the field are generally reviewed by lobbyists, trade lawyers, and scholars inordinately intent on currying favor with Tokyo-based foundations. Such reviewers often indulge in ad hominem attacks, speculating darkly about the author's motives and even implying that writers are driven by racist motives. They may systematically comb through a book in search of the tiniest inaccuracies on immaterial side issues — a towering irony given that their reviews are being printed in newspapers that have for decades been persistently wrong on major issues such as lifetime employment. The essential point is that the American press will resort to almost any pretext to avoid discussing the central point that America is being consistently outperformed by East Asia's radically different form of economics.

As for a conspiracy on the Japanese side, it clearly does not exist. Essentially the Japanese people have little understanding of the aggregate results of their actions. Only a tiny group of oligarchs knows how all the myriad pieces of the Japanese economic jigsaw fit together. Even quite senior Japanese decision-makers see clearly only one or two pieces. They do not try to see the overall picture, because in the Japanese scheme of things, they would be guilty of rising above their station if they did so. When the subject turns to international economics, most Japanese merely echo what they read in Japan's often highly misleading newspapers.

Westerners have failed to understand Japan because they have lacked the shrewdness to adjust for the peculiarities of Japanese patterns of communication. As a matter of Japanese group logic, when Japanese organizations refer to their internal workings in the presence of outsiders they often present a fanciful "consensus" version of reality. Because this fanciful reality is presented to foreigners and uninvolved Japanese alike, Westerners can hardly complain that they have been singled out for hoodwinking. This fanciful reality is notably apparent in how the Japanese talk about their economy: their consensus version is that it is a true American-style market economy.

Most Japanese, of course, know something of Japan's trade barriers and cartels but, using East Asian logic, they naturally assume that there are similar deviations from market perfection in the United States that are overlooked in America's "consensus version" of American economics.

Perhaps the most startling feature of the Japanese people's interaction with foreigners is their persistent tendency to downplay Japan's strengths. Japanese executives are coached in formulaic English-language answers to questions commonly raised by foreigners, and their answers err heavily on the side of self-deprecation. In the mid-1980s, for instance, one textbook on business English taught Japanese executives to say that the Japanese auto industry was expected to be driven out of business by Korean competition within a decade.

It is important to realize that for the ordinary Japanese salaryman chivalry rather than deception is the motive for talking self-deprecatingly about Japan's economic strengths. Not only do the Japanese hate to sound boastful but, because they are acutely aware of how much better they have been doing than Americans in the economic growth race in the last four decades, they affect to an extreme degree the demeanor of a modest winner trying hard not to tread on the loser's toes. Their true mind is that they feel sorry for America, something which, in a terrible moment of truth, Prime Minister Kiichi Miyazawa actually blurted out to his great embarrassment at a press conference in Washington in 1992. What the ordinary salaryman says in a situation where he stands in no defined relationship to his listener is often highly arbitrary, and the listener is expected to note the emotional content of what is said (in this case, the modest winner) rather than the literal meaning. Most Japanese would be startled to realize that the West's lamentably unacclimatized diplomats and press correspondents take such talk literally.

But what of the mindset of those at the top of the Japanese system who know only too well that Americans are under vast illusions about Japanese economics? Surely here there is some sort of conspiracy? Well actually no. Japan's leaders undoubtedly justify their strategy in their own minds by thinking of it as legitimate public relations. Unfortunately for Westerners, Japan's public relations, like many other aspects of Japanese life, follows a directly opposite line of logic to Western logic and therefore leaves uninitiated Westerners badly misled. Whereas Westerners often find it profitable to overstate their personal virtues and those of their products, Japanese leaders feel justified in seeking advantage by applying the opposite logic of downplaying themselves and their institutions. Corporate Japan has often used this logic to acquire, for instance, transfers of American technology by downplaying Japan's ability to compete in the area concerned — but is this more morally reprehensible than for Wall Street investment bankers to exaggerate their ability to make money for their clients?

The tendency toward understatement and less-than-full disclosure should be seen in the larger context of Japan's Confucianism. Although Confucius counseled rulers to act benevolently at all times, he saw no reason why they should disclose information that made the task of governing more difficult. He had little faith in the wisdom of ordinary people who he thought often did not know what was good for them. Clearly if Japan's rulers feel, as they do, that they have a duty to withhold information from the Japanese people or to mislead them with confusing or disingenuous body language, a fortiori they feel under no obligation to level with foreigners.

In Japanese eyes, Westerners forfeit their right to be brought fully into Japan's confidence because they chronically refuse to accept Japan for what it is. In pressing constantly for reform of Japan's internal institutions, Westerners are seen by Japanese leaders as condescending or overbearing or both. To understand how fiercely East Asians resent Western criticism, one need merely look at Singapore, whose leaders have openly punished Western publications that criticize Singapore's political system. The resentment is also strong in Japan but is expressed more subtly: in the characteristic Japanese fashion of "bending like a reed" before foreigners, Japanese leaders appear to accept the validity of Western criticisms. Westerners will continue to be misled by such behavior for as long as they pass judgment publicly on Japan's internal affairs.

Once one understands Japan's concern to keep the West out of its internal affairs, Japan becomes much easier to gauge because one is then on notice to read between every line. And the truth is that Japanese leaders often drop subtle hints that their words should not be taken literally. Sometimes the hints are hard to mistake, even for a Japan neophyte: in the English-language version of his autobiography, the great Japanese industrialist Takuma Yamamoto, for instance, warned foreign readers not to take his book too literally.

Yamamoto, the principal architect of Fujitsu's extraordinary success in the last two decades, pointed out that corporate Japan's decision-making processes are confidential and he suggested that the reader "will find it fun to use his imagination" in reading between the lines.

Westerners could do worse than take lessons from the Chinese. The Chinese automatically read between the lines in listening to the Japanese (and, of course, the Japanese do the same in listening to the Chinese). By contrast, by expecting East Asians to be open in talking to the outside world, the West is implicitly asking East Asia to accept Western cultural norms. From an East Asian viewpoint, Westerners invited themselves into East Asia in the first place so the onus is on them to adjust to East Asian rules, not the other way around.

Clearly the Japanese oligarchs' ultimate aim is for Japan to supersede the United States as the world's dominant society. It is an idea that Americans have difficulty dealing with rationally and they consider such an aspiration a "conspiracy" against the United States. In fact, any Westerner who suggests that Japanese leaders have aspirations to supersede the United States risks being branded a "conspiracy theorist." This view is founded on an extraordinary unstated assumption that the Japanese somehow see their values as inferior to those of the United States and thus less acceptable to the world. In truth it is, of course, natural for the Japanese to believe that Japanese values are a better guide for the world than American values. That the Americans simply assume that all right-thinking Japanese automatically must support American values is an understandable misconception, given the uncomprehending way Japan is reported in the American press, but a misconception just the same.

Although Japanese leaders disguise it well, they feel much more reserved and detached than their American counterparts about the U.S.-Japan relationship. This is almost inevitable given the history of the relationship. In the official American version, Japan and the United States became fast friends within months of the beginning of the occupation. For Japanese leaders the experience was a lot more complicated. Their attitude is best understood by imagining how Americans would feel if their country were ever occupied by a foreign power. Suppose that Vietnam was a great power that occupied America after dropping atom bombs on Chicago and San Francisco. The Vietnamese would, of course, want to "Vietnamize" American institutions to give the Americans the benefit of Vietnam's superior values and make sure the Americans never again undertook misguided military adventures. If Americans were very wise and very well led, they might respond to this historic crisis by making a few symbolic changes to indulge the Vietnamese press's expectations, while secretly preserving for posterity a deep hope that American culture and institutions would triumph in the end. They might even remain calm as President Johnson and General Westmoreland went bravely to their death on the scaffold. But they would still remain Americans and would certainly relish challenging the Vietnamese in economic competition after the occupation ended.

In essence, nations are highly resistant to foreign attempts to reform them, and this is particularly true of old nations such as Japan. This point should not come as a surprise: it was widely made at the time of MacArthur's occupation of Japan but MacArthur unwisely brushed it aside. The result was a predictable fiasco that was scathingly denounced in 1948 by the West's great Japan scholar of that time, Sir George Sansom. Referring to "more than average incompetence" among American occupation officials, he commented: "With great ideological fervor and a conspicuous lack of wisdom, they proclaimed intentions that were quite incompatible one with another and, as a whole, impossible of realization."

Unfortunately for the American public's understanding of the modern world, the American press believed MacArthur's version of the occupation, not Sansom's. As a result, the U.S.-Japan relationship has rested on false foundations ever since. The exigencies of the cold war led Americans not only to perpetuate the myth of an Americanized Japan but to embellish it. Whether Japan liked it or not, it had to submit to being presented to the world as living proof that American values were universal norms. If Japan wanted to continue to enjoy favorable access to the American market it had little choice but to play along.

The misunderstanding has been perpetuated also by the peculiarly emotional way in which Japan's economic differences with the United States are viewed in America. Many Americans see economics in quasi-religious terms. So instead of accepting Japan's nonmarket mechanisms as legitimate options and adjusting American economic policy to cope with them, Americans see them as heresies. From a Japanese point of view, however, this is highly unreasonable: the Japanese feel that if Japan's new system makes two blades of grass grow where one grew before, it is self-evidently a boon to mankind. Americans might reply that the Japanese system has succeeded only because it has been free-riding on the open world trading system, but this interpretation is undoubtedly wrong. Although Japan has clearly benefited greatly from operating mercantilism in an open world trading system, the Japanese system would still probably be considerably more effective in creating prosperity than capitalism even in a world in which America and Europe operated fully by the precepts of managed trade.

America's semi-religious view of economics has powerfully induced Japanese leaders in recent years to disguise the extent to which their system contradicts the precepts of free market capitalism. They have not always been so disingenuous. Back in the 1960s, Japanese leaders often frankly tried to persuade Americans of the wealth-creating possibilities of Japan's new ideas. Matsushita Electric founder Konosuke Matsushita once outlined for an American business executives' conference the economic virtues of Japan's cartel system. He was scornfully dismissed as a misguided greenhorn who had not fully understood the occupation's lessons in capitalism. Rejections of this sort have clearly not improved U.S.-Japan communications.

Sometimes it seems as if Americans see Washington as the Vatican of world capitalism and Tokyo as merely another diocese, albeit an important one. Any attempt by Tokyo to challenge the rules as laid down by Washington is automatically considered schism. For the Japanese, a more appropriate metaphor is the secular one of corporate competition. Tokyo is playing Microsoft to Washington's IBM. Microsoft defers to IBM while it is the weaker party but if it judges that the balance of power has swung its way, there is no law of the universe to stop it from challenging IBM. Just as IBM has no universal right to lead the world computer industry in perpetuity, Washington has no universal right to lead the world indefinitely. In the end, the most successful economy will lead the world.

This is cold comfort for ordinary Americans who have seen their country first feed Japan, then prop it up, and finally transfer to it many of America's most valuable technological assets. But Japan's leaders probably do not feel overly guilty about their ingratitude: they know, far more clearly than ordinary Americans, that American society in the last thirty years has been poorly served by its politicians, its media, its scholars, and its business elite.

Virtually every American who has mediated U.S.-Japan relations in the last fifty years has had a vested interest in treating Japan like a little brother fated always to trail a half step behind the United States in national maturity. Meanwhile Japanese leaders, with their capacity for living on several levels at once, simultaneously have detested American condescension and have used it, jujitsu style, to extract trade and technological favors.

The American establishment's tendency to condescend to Japan is hardly a crime against humanity. But then, the Japanese establishment's tendency to encourage such condescension hardly is either. Rather than feeling deceived by Japan's counterintuitive behavior, Americans should remember George Washington's words: "No nation is to be trusted further than it is bound by its interests."

With few exceptions, America's Japan-watchers have never tried to see the world from a Japanese point of view. Had they done so, they would have stopped condescending to Japan long ago. In failing to do so, they have blindsided themselves.

A Confucian New World Order?

Despite the evident avidity with which Japan has sought to surpass the United States in recent decades, we should not exaggerate the speed with which the world power structure will change in the years ahead. Japan is not a crusading nation intent on winning over the hearts and minds of the world's masses to a new ideology. Rather it is a highly pragmatic nation that is concerned first and foremost with its own security and well-being. The means toward those objectives are a matter for infinite flexibility.

In fact, assuming the Tokyo-Washington relationship is not completely ruptured by recent disputes, Tokyo may long be happy for Washington to continue to reign supreme as the world's ostensible remaining superpower. Behind the scenes the relationship would gradually change as Tokyo assumed the role of the senior partner, but for public consumption the partnership's decisions might be accepted more readily in certain quarters, particularly in Europe and Latin America, if they were presented as coming from Washington. The structure would therefore resemble many successful business partnerships: Tokyo would play the powerful if unobtrusive Mr. Inside while

Washington played the gregarious Mr. Outside. This sort of ambivalent power structure does not sit well with the West's traditional concern for transparent political processes and for full disclosure but it is highly characteristic of how power works at every level in Japan.

Ultimately, however, the true locus of power will not be in doubt. As American economic power dwindles, Japan will have little hesitation in accepting supreme responsibility. In the eyes of Japan's own elite, Confucianism is a key advantage that equips Japan admirably to lead the world. Not only does Confucianism give Japan a strong bond with many of the world's most populous nations but it is a made-to-measure creed for Japan's idea of the New World Order. Many of the world's problems boil down to requiring today's generation to make sacrifices to ensure a more secure future for later generations. That's a tough choice for a Western democracy, but it is one that Confucianism instinctly approaches with the right mindset.

For one thing, Confucianism legitimizes efforts by a leader to conceal — and even misrepresent — what he is doing (so long as he feels he is motivated by a concern for the general good). More important, Confucianism legitimizes hierarchy not only among individuals but among nations. In fact until the eighteenth century, the entire Confucian world was a hierarchy with China acknowledged as the Celestial Empire by tribute nations from Vietnam to Japan. A frankly stated proposition that some nations are more equal than others circumvents some of the conundrums implied in American rhetoric on global problems. Pax Americana urges, for instance, Third World nations to adopt democracy yet Washington often gives scant weight to the opinions of such populous countries as India and China in setting the world agenda.

By openly viewing the world in hierarchical terms, Japan suffers no similar embarrassment. With just 2 percent of the world's population, it will purposefully set its own global agenda, oblivious of the squabbling that will no doubt continue to characterize the deliberations of the other 98 percent.

Notes

Chapter one

page
1   "Japan will never again become a world power": Quoted in *Nikkei Weekly*, August 22, 1992.
2   "knickknacks": Michael Schaller, *The American Occupation of Japan: The Origins of the Cold War* (Oxford: Oxford University Press, 1985), p. 224.
2   this would eliminate Japan's trade surpluses: Emmott's conclusion read: "Japan's economy is passing through a phase of imbalance with the world that will soon be righted."
4   Economic New Structure: Chalmers Johnson, *MITI and the Japanese Miracle: The Growth of Industrial Policy, 1925–1975* (Tokyo: Charles E. Tuttle, 1986), p. 150.
5   facts that the American press's prophets of doom overlooked: Several of the examples which follow are based on conversion of Japanese yen numbers at then ruling exchange rates of between ¥112 and ¥143 to the dollar. At the time of writing in September 1994, the rate stood at ¥98 to the dollar, which made Japan's numbers look even larger in dollar terms. Some observers in Tokyo, however, believed in September 1994 that the dollar would soon stage a significant rally, which if it were large enough might somewhat reduce Japan's advantage in 1995 comparisons.
5   the world's largest manufacturing economy: Kenneth Courtis as quoted in Eamonn Fingleton, "Don't Let Up on Japan," *New York Times*, April 9, 1994.
5   Hitachi: Although Hitachi and IBM differ in their product mix in many ways, they are broadly comparable in their technological sophistication. Hitachi's interests extend to such areas as pollution

page   control and nuclear power station equipment. IBM is increasingly an assembler rather than a manufacturer and in fact gets many of its parts from Hitachi.

5   68 percent the size of America's: The comparison is based on gross national product. GNP includes gross domestic product plus net accruals from foreign investment (the latter are a positive for Japan and a negative for the United States).

5   The bottom line on the 1990s: *Kokusai Hikaku Tokei* (Tokyo: Bank of Japan, 1994).

6   reputed goal of passing the United States by the year 2000: This goal has never been explicitly stated but, in a 1970 book that clearly drew on confidential sources in the Japanese bureaucracy, Herman Kahn said Japan's economic goal was to surpass the West and went on to predict that the Japanese economy would surpass America's in size by the year 2000.

8   In 1950, Japan was only 3 percent: Kenneth Courtis, "A new policy paradigm for Japan," Deutsche Bank, September 1, 1994.

9   Japan's tax rates are higher than America's: A comparison by M. Homma in *Zeminaru Gendai Zaisei Nyumon* (Tokyo: Nihon Kei-zaisha, 1990) found that, after adjusting for write-offs and loopholes, the real corporate tax burden in Japan was 50 percent, versus 31 percent for the United States. For wealthy individuals, income tax rates and inheritance taxes are much higher in Japan than in the United States but capital gains tax rates are ostensibly much lower. The low capital gains tax rates for individuals, however, are beside the point because Japanese individuals avoid direct investment in stocks and instead invest most of their money via financial institutions. They are therefore subject indirectly to an institutional capital gains tax rate of about 50 percent, which is much higher than the rate on most capital gains in the United States (interview with Hideo Sakamaki, chief executive, Nomura Securities, August 1, 1994).

9   rising from 10.2 to 18.2 percent: Gardner Ackley and Hiromitsu Ishi in Hugh Patrick and Henry Rosovsky, *Asia's New Giant: How the Japanese Economy Works* (Washington, D.C.: Brookings Institution, 1976), p. 173.

10   Nobel Prize–winner Milton Friedman attributed Japan's success: Milton and Rose Friedman, *Free to Choose* (New York: Avon Books, 1981), p. 53.

10   The *Wall Street Journal* is still scratching its head: See Karen Elliott House, *Wall Street Journal*, February 24, 1994. She said Japanese banks had run up big debts backing corporate Japan in a decade-long policy of "export at all costs." In other words, the

page Japanese were conducting a nationally organized dumping campaign.

13 As the Berkeley economist Paul Romer: *Economist,* September 11–17, 1993.

13 Richard Baldwin: *Business Week,* May 16, 1994.

13 Fixed costs are the up-front costs: It should be noted that fixed costs come in various degrees of "fixity." Some costs are fixed in the short term but can vary in the longer term. Machinery is a good example: a factory's depreciation costs for machinery are fixed so long as no additional machines are bought. But if a factory doubles its capacity, its machinery depreciation costs will double. By contrast, research and development costs are absolutely fixed in the sense that no matter how much a company increases production of a certain product, the up-front research and development costs will generally not increase. Note that up-front costs of this sort are normally termed "sunk" costs in the language of conventional economics.

13 The swing to fixed costs has been particularly marked: Charles Corbett and Luk Van Wassenhove, *California Management Review,* Summer 1993, p. 116.

13 strong manufacturers to grow ever stronger: Entry costs are soaring in advanced industries. As Laura D'Andrea Tyson has recorded, to achieve minimum efficient scale in a semiconductor foundry required an investment of $500 million in 1991, up from $150 million just six years previously.

14 By contrast, the simple tools in the famous pin "manufactory": Much of the equipment used two hundred years ago was in need of constant repair but repairs, of course, are variable costs that are generally incurred in proportion to the amount of use involved.

15 the Japanese have consistently achieved superb capacity: Even measured by conservative Japanese standards, Japan's capacity utilization was the highest among the Group of Seven nations in 1993, the worst year for the Japanese economy in two decades. See *Kokusai Hikaku Tokei,* Tokyo: Bank of Japan, 1994.

15 In 1978, for instance, *Time* magazine reported: "From go-go to go-slow," *Time,* June 26, 1978.

16 Judging by independent evidence: The figure of 85 percent for Japan is a conservative estimate derived from Yoshikazu Kano's conclusion that the breakeven point in Japanese industry was 85 percent in fiscal 1991. The figure of 70 percent for the world comes from Lester Thurow, *Asian Wall Street Journal,* September 20, 1993.

18 about 90 percent of all research and development: *Making Things*

page *Better* (Washington, D.C.: Office of Technology Assessment, 1990), p. 222.

20   These screens can cost as much as $1,200 each: *Asian Wall Street Journal*, July 23, 1993.

21   "positive feedbacks": Writing in *Scientific American* in February 1990, W. Brian Arthur explained: "The parts of the economy that are knowledge-based . . . are largely subject to increasing returns. Products such as computers, pharmaceuticals, missiles, aircraft, automobiles, software, telecommunications equipment and fiber optics are complicated to design and to manufacture. They require large initial investments in research, development and tooling, but once sales begin, incremental production is relatively cheap."

21   Arthur was rebuffed repeatedly: The economics profession is terrified of increasing returns. As John R. Hicks pointed out in 1939, in the event of a proliferation of increasing returns in industry, "the threatened wreckage is that of the greater part of economic theory."

21   America's telecommunications imports from Japan: Interview with John Stern, American Electronics Association, Tokyo, March 9, 1994.

22   Even AT&T has publicly admitted: Pat Choate, *Agents of Influence: How Japan's Lobbyists in the United States Manipulate America's Political and Economic System* (New York: Alfred A. Knopf, 1990), p. 8.

27   competitive communism: See Douglas Moore Kenrick, *Where Communism Works: The Success of Competitive Communism in Japan* (Tokyo: Charles E. Tuttle, 1990). As Kenrick points out (p. 9), even those few chief executives in Japan who own large shareholdings in their companies generally set an ostentatiously frugal example. Toyota Motor's chief executive, Soichiro Toyoda, for instance, gets his shoes repaired until they completely wear out and his wife dresses in ready-made clothes. When the company organized a three-day conference for its directors, they were housed in a company dormitory in the same conditions as the company's new recruits.

27   rejects the central capitalist idea that individuals: See T. A. Bisson, *Japan's War Economy* (New York: Institute of Pacific Relations, 1945), p. 50.

31   unofficial conferences of shifting little groups: Carl Randau and Leane Zugsmith, *The Setting Sun of Japan* (New York: Random House, 1942), p. 82.

31   In its epic scale and stopwatch coordination: As recounted by the

page historian Malcolm Kennedy, within hours of the Pearl Harbor attack, the Japanese hit the Philippines, Thailand, Malaya, Singapore, Hong Kong, Borneo, Guam, Wake Island, Shanghai, and Tientsin. The view that the Japanese were leaderless was a classic example of the Western mind's eagerness to underestimate Japanese society. The army ran Japan in those days and, although all through the 1930s military leaders repeatedly claimed they had little control over troops in the field in China and militant junior officers at home, this often was no more than a transparent excuse to give themselves deniability in pursuing controversial policies.

35 For an industry to be targeted: The criteria for targeting are drawn from, among other sources, Johnson's *MITI and the Japanese Miracle.*

36 Thus the Japanese economic system has focused single-mindedly on developing its manufacturing prowess: Japanese leaders' wisdom in targeting manufacturing industries is paralleled in Germany, where a government-bank system of industrial planning has ensured that 32 percent of all jobs are in manufacturing. The corresponding figure for the United States is just 17.5 percent.

45 Where exchange rate appreciation: *Highlights of the Analysis of the Main Developments in Japan's International Trade in 1993* (Tokyo: Ministry of International Trade and Industry, 1993), p. 16.

45 Perhaps the most startling fact of the early 1990s: It is interesting to note the success of just one Japanese company, Citizen Watch, in making products that top American companies evidently could not make for themselves. According to Nomura Securities, as of November 1992, Citizen Watch was supplying Compaq with computers, Motorola with mobile telephones, and Hewlett-Packard with ultra-miniature hard disk drives.

45 with Japan's labor costs now as much as 50 percent: Yutaka Wada, *Asian Wall Street Journal,* July 14, 1994.

47 Japanese officials frankly acknowledged: See Hiroshi Nakamae, *Nikkei Weekly,* April 25, 1994.

47 The central objective of the new administration's policy: U.S. White House official Bowman Cutter as quoted in *Mainichi Daily News,* July 11, 1993.

Chapter two

page

50 Between 1980 and 1993 . . . 14 percent: Tadashi Nakamae, *Nikkei Weekly*, July 26, 1993.

50 from sea to shining sea: Kevin Kelly, "Besting Japan," *Business Week*, June 7, 1993.

50 murdering: *Business Week*, October 18, 1993.

51 Japan probably extended its lead: Certainly 1993 was another year of increasing market share for the Japanese electronics industry generally. As measured by just its top 75 companies, the industry produced sales of $405 billion in 1993. The American industry, *as measured by the top 200 companies,* produced just $416 billion. *Electronic Business Asia,* September 1994.

52 in some Boeing planes: *Economist*, November 11, 1989.

56 less than one-tenth of America's proportion of accountants: Frank Gibney, *Miracle by Design: The Real Reasons Behind Japan's Economic Success* (New York: Times Books, 1982), p. 212.

57 Many foreigners mistakenly believe Japan wastes: most of the statistics that follow on retailing are drawn from *Encyclopaedia Britannica's 1993 Book of the Year.*

60 The industry's productivity was described: The description of the Japanese tobacco industry as "very weak" comes from *Service Sector Productivity* (Washington: McKinsey Global Institute, 1992), p. 9; "particularly weak" comes from Daniel Strickberger, *Asian Wall Street Journal*, March 21, 1994.

60 a direct comparison of output volumes: Although extra-long cigarettes are believed to be somewhat more prevalent in the United States than in Japan, the average lengths in the two countries are probably similar. In any case, the implications for labor productivity of length differences are negligible. No statistics have been published on the size of cigarettes in the two countries.

60 Japan Tobacco needed just 19,100 workers: interview with Japan Tobacco, June 8, 1994. McKinsey blamed Japan's allegedly low overall level of manufacturing productivity on industries that do not compete internationally and, by way of explanation, added: "For example, there is very weak productivity in the Japanese food products, beverages, tobacco, apparel and leather industries."

60 By comparison, American tobacco manufacturers: American Tobacco Institute.

61 The American press routinely: Subsequent comments are based on William Lewis, *Asian Wall Street Journal*, April 8, 1993, and Karl

page Zinsmeister, *Asian Wall Street Journal*, March 11, 1993. Zinsmeister described Japanese banks as being in "an inefficent backwater state."

64 Japan passed the United States in the quality of infant health care: Paul Kennedy, *Preparing for the Twenty-First Century* (London: HarperCollins, 1993), p. 220.

64 The incomes of the top one-fifth: Taichi Sakaiya, *What Is Japan?: Contradictions and Transformations* (New York: Kodansha, 1993), p. 7.

67 Certainly research by Salomon Brothers: *Forbes,* November 13, 1989.

68 at least 50 percent of the global market: It should be noted that many economists consider that a company dominates a market with a market share of as little as 25 percent. See entry on monopoly in the *Economist*'s *Dictionary of Economics*.

68 "chokepoints": Perhaps the most striking statement has come from an unnamed IBM executive, as summarized in 1994 by the British management commentator Robert Heller: "The Japanese, by virtue of the technological fortresses they have built along almost every highway, have a power analogous to that of John D. Rockefeller. His Standard Oil Trust didn't own all the oil, but through the railroads and the pipelines it controlled all the access to markets."

68 Flat panel displays: Corporate Japan has recently announced plans to manufacture flat panels in the United States but it is investing so little that the factories concerned are evidently involved merely in the less sophisticated parts of the manufacturing process.

69 Notebook computers: Some notebook computers ostensibly are made outside Japan — but virtually all the sophisticated manufacturing needed to make them is conducted in Japan.

69 Semiconductor materials and equipment: The source for most of this paragraph is an official in the United States government.

70 Cellular phones and pagers: Interview with a former Motorola executive.

70 Ferrite: David P. Hamilton, *Asian Wall Street Journal*, August 30, 1993.

71 "sweating bullets": Stuart Auerbach, *Washington Post*, March 25, 1991.

72 Auto parts: Interview with an executive of a major American auto company.

72 the Neon . . . is made using Japanese presses: Hajime Karatsu, professor of Tokai University, *Nikkei Weekly*, June 9, 1994.

73 Just how strong: James Fallows, *Looking at the Sun: The Rise of*

page *the New East Asian Economic and Political System* (New York: Pantheon, 1994), p. 423.

74 Between 70 and 80 percent: Tom Forester, *Silicon Samurai* (Oxford: Blackwell, 1993), p. 129.

75 Carbon fiber: *Holding the Edge* (Washington, D.C.: U.S. Government Printing Office, 1989), p. 167.

75 Most construction equipment: Fred R. Bleakley, *Asian Wall Street Journal*, June 28, 1993.

76 Brookings Institution: Philip H. Trezise of the Brookings Institution has argued that America should accept dependence on Japan for military technology in the same matter of fact spirit as it has come to accept dependence on the Middle East for oil. See Philip H. Trezise, *Brookings Review,* Winter 1989/90, p. 12.

77 one of the most humiliating episodes in American business history: Choate, *Agents of Influence,* p. 8.

77 The true significance of these arrangements: A small minority of U.S.-Japan partnerships might be called reverse kyosei deals in that they involve Japan buying manufactured goods from America. But there is usually less to such deals than meets the eye. Hitachi, for instance, has agreed to buy mainframe processor chip sets from IBM. Such chip sets are made in volumes of only a few thousand and are design-intensive rather than manufacturing intensive. Thus Hitachi, in its strategy of concentrating its resources single-mindedly in ultra-high volume manufacturing, is as happy to leave this niche business to IBM as Toyota Motor is to leave the Silver Shadow market to the Rolls-Royce company. In another important reverse kyosei deal, Mitsubishi Electric agreed to buy computers from IBM. In this case the computers will be made by IBM's Japanese subsidiary; the high-paying jobs involved will go to Japanese rather than American workers.

78 Ford Motor: Mazda later announced plans to buy some European-made Fords for sale as Mazdas in Europe — but only because it was European quotas that prohibited it from selling Japan-made Mazdas.

78 Harley-Davidson motorcycles: Peter Bellamy, auto writer, Tokyo.

79 IBM has entered a $2 billion joint venture: *Japan Scope,* Spring 1993.

79 Sanford Kane: cited in *Making Things Better* (Washington, D.C.: Office of Technology Assessment, 1990), p. 205.

80 Seven years later IBM is singing a different song: Robert Keatley, *Asian Wall Street Journal*, July 4, 1994. He reported that IBM was opposing efforts in the United States to tighten America's anti-

page dumping regulations. The efforts were being supported by the American steel industry, American ball-bearing makers, and semiconductor-making companies such as Intel. IBM's stated reason for its stand was it is a "big exporter" and "increasingly suffers from antidumping measures in other countries."

80 Most American scholars and authors who study Japan: Glen Fukushima, former U.S. trade negotiator, as cited by Choate, *Agents of Influence*, p. 172.

81 the many privileges: See Ichiro Kawasaki, *Japan Unmasked* (Tokyo: Charles E. Tuttle, 1969), pp. 72–74.

83 Nomura Securities' English-language magazine: *Japan Scope,* Summer 1993.

85 Japanese leaders quite openly advise their subordinates: Joel Kotkin and Yoriko Kishimoto, *The Third Century: America's Resurgence in the Asian Era* (New York: Crown, 1988), p. 199.

85 bending the facts about Japan to head off protectionist tendencies: A notable example was a *Wall Street Journal* article in 1992 by the Hudson Institute's Alan Reynolds, portraying Japan as so "depressed" that America should set aside differences on trade and help "the Japanese economy get back on its feet." Reynolds omitted to mention that the unemployment rate in "depressed" Japan was just one-third of America's.

85 virtually all the *Journal*'s influential editorial page articles: In 1993, the *Journal* was the subject of a round-robin letter that described the *Journal*'s editorial page articles on Japanese economics as "persistently slanted and misinformed." The letter, drafted by the present writer, was signed by thirty-three Japan observers, including several scholars who are regarded as leaders in the field. A truncated version of the letter was published in the *Asian Wall Street Journal* on May 25, 1993, and the full version appeared in *American Prospect*'s summer 1993 issue.

86 the best solution for the [American] trade deficit would be to stop reporting it: *Asian Wall Street Journal,* February 28, 1994.

86 In a bizarre comment: George Melloan, *Asian Wall Street Journal,* March 1, 1994.

86 a powerful "bad news" spin in Japanese public relations: A good example of this spin was apparent in Prime Minister Kiichi Miyazawa's address at the opening of the diet in January 1993. Although he was just months away from a crucial general election, he could see only bad economic news: Japan's economic position, he said, was now "very grim." As it happened, the trade surplus for 1992 was announced the same day Miyazawa spoke — and it

page was the highest any country had recorded in history. In fact, Japan's competitiveness was so strong that the yen was destined to rise by 19 percent in the twelve months after Miyazawa spoke, without noticeable ill effects on Japanese employment.

86 Japanese business leaders deliberately exaggerate their problems: C. Tait Ratcliffe, *Mainichi Daily News,* October 1, 1992.

86 "Poor little me" complex: Keyes Beech, *Not Without the Americans* (Garden City, N.Y.: Doubleday, 1971), p. 151.

86 allay Western unease at Japan's growing power: A concern to allay Western unease may help explain a 1989 survey in which Japanese scientific leaders said that Japan was ahead in only two of forty-seven key technologies. These findings were promptly derided as false modesty by American experts, who believed that Japan was ahead in a majority of the categories concerned. The reaction of the former IBM chief scientist Lewis Branscomb was typical. "Come on, my friends, you are better than that and you know it," he said. "I don't think they really believe that America is ahead."

86 "very disturbing": Anthony Sampson, *The Midas Touch: Understanding the Dynamic New Money Societies Around Us* (New York: Dutton, 1990), p. 82.

87 "disaster": Kennedy, *Preparing for the Twenty-First Century,* p. 295.

88 "a silly book": *New York Times* review, as reprinted in the *Japan Times,* December 4, 1970.

88 conditions approaching anarchy: As cited in "Fine, thank you," *Atlantic Monthly,* May 1993.

Chapter three

91 These are the best people so far discovered . . . : Sir George Sansom, *The Western World and Japan: A Study in the Interaction of European and Asiatic Cultures* (Tokyo: Charles E. Tuttle, 1977), p. 115.

91 In 1609, they ordered: Masakazu Iwata, *Okubo Toshimichi: The Bismarck of Japan* (Berkeley: University of California Press, 1964), p. 10.

92 like wild birds . . . : Francis Hawks as quoted by Pat Barr, *The Coming of the Barbarians: A Story of Western Settlement in Japan 1853–1870* (London: Penguin Books, 1988), p. 20.

92 The following morning the Americans were amazed: Ibid., p. 21.

93 in a witty — but ultimately unsuccessful — attempt: Ibid., p. 32.

page

93 The Perry mission left the Japanese with an abiding: Ivan Hall, *The National Interest*, Summer 1992.

93 A telling indication of Perry's aggressive mindset: Pat Barr, *The Coming of the Barbarians,. p. 21.*

93 he used the threat of force: Entry on William Perry, *Encyclopaedia Britannica*, 1970 edition.

94 leading British historian Sir George Sansom: Sir George Sansom, *The Western World and Japan.* p. 277.

96 "semibarbarous" nation: Matthew C. Perry, *Correspondence Relative to the Naval Expedition to Japan* (U.S. Congress, 1855).

97 What Japan admired was not Western culture: Robert Guillain, *The Japanese Challenge* (London: Hamish Hamilton, 1970), p. 36.

97 Japan in the year 2040: See Daniel B. Ramsdell, *The Japanese Diet* (Lanham, Md.: University Press of America, 1992).

98 Such workers were generally professional engineers: Ronald Seth, *Secret Servants: A History of Japanese Espionage* (New York: Farrar, Straus, 1957), p. 140.

98 within weeks of first sighting: Ezra Vogel, *Comeback: Case by Case: Building the Resurgence of American Business* (Tokyo: Charles E. Tuttle, 1985), p. 32.

98 imitate perfectly our manufactures: Jeffrey E. Garten, *A Cold Peace: America, Japan, Germany, and the Struggle for Supremacy* (New York: Times Books, 1992), p. 63.

99 By 1876, some 400 foreign experts were working: William W. Lockwood, *The Economic Development of Japan: Growth and Structural Change* (Princeton: Princeton University Press, 1970), p. 328.

100 The earliest Western influence: Tessa Morris-Suzuki, *History of Japanese Economic Thought* (London: Routledge, 1989), p. 50.

101 the Meiji Ishin: Traditionally this term has been translated as the Meiji Restoration, but in fact a more appropriate translation is the Meiji Revolution.

102 One of the first samurais to take the plunge: John G. Roberts, *Mitsui: Three Centuries of Japanese Business* (New York: Weatherhill, 1973), p. 119.

104 Charles LeGendre: Joyce C. Lebra, *Okuma Shigenobu: Statesman of Meiji Japan* (Canberra: Australian National University Press, 1973), p. 24.

104 perhaps as many as one million Filipinos: Mark Twain, *Atlantic Monthly*, April 1992.

104 As early as 1908: Garten, *A Cold Peace*, p. 66.

page

104 keep the Chinese in their place: *China: A Short History* (New York: W. W. Norton, 1944), pp. 150 and 163.

105 The United States ... actually helped Japan: According to a letter in *Time*'s issue of May 29, 1939, from L. R. Severinghaus, the United States was at that time supplying Japan with about 50 percent of the war materials to conduct the Japanese war in China.

105 Japan began running large budget deficits: Johnson, *MITI*, p. 119.

105 Thus in the five years to 1935: Ibid., p. 121.

106 After the battle of Tarawa: John Keegan, *A History of Warfare* (New York: Alfred A. Knopf, 1993), p. 377.

106 130,000 British troops surrendered in Malaya alone: John Toland, *The Rising Sun: The Decline and Fall of the Japanese Empire* (New York: Bantam Books, 1971), p. 316.

108 Official posters displayed everywhere: Willard Price, *The Japanese Miracle and Peril*, pp. 333–334.

109 According to the top Japanese banker Hiroshi Takeuchi: as quoted by Marie Anchordoguy, *Computers Inc.: Japan's Challenge to IBM* (Cambridge: Council on East Asian Studies, 1989), p. 21.

109 too far: *Asian Wall Street Journal*, June 15, 1993.

110 A spiritual revolution ensued almost overnight ... world.: *Nippon Times* as quoted by Robert B. Textor, *Failure in Japan* (New York: John Day, 1951), p. 33.

111 Peace and Happy: *Mainichi Daily News*, November 2, 1993.

113 "Dumbness has been bred into these people.": *Philadelphia Bulletin* as quoted by Walt Sheldon in *The Honorable Conquerors: The Occupation of Japan 1945–1952* (New York: Macmillan, 1965), p. 75.

113 This "situational" aspect: Clyde Kluckhohn as quoted in Textor, *Failure*, p. 41.

114 "go anywhere they are aimed.": Keyes Beech, *Not Without the Americans* (Garden City, N.Y.: Doubleday, 1971), p. 149.

116 the permanent elimination of capitalist control: Koji Matsumoto as quoted by Chalmers Johnson in December 1992.

117 Measured by the standards ... forty-five years. Quoted by Noam Chomsky, *Deterring Democracy* (London: Vintage, 1991), p. 338.

117 MacArthur exacerbated the occupation's blind spots: Hans Baerwald, *Japan's Parliament: An Introduction* (New York: Cambridge University Press), p. 7.

117 According to a report in the *New York Herald Tribune*: Cited in T. A. Bisson, *Prospects for Democracy in Japan* (New York: Macmillan, 1949), p. 126.

page

117 Chiune Sugihara: Articles in the *Mainichi Daily News* on July 7, 1993, August 18, 1993, and May 18, 1994.

118 no sign to the world of dissension: See Baerwald, *Japan's Parliament,* p. 12, and Michael Schaller, *The American Occupation of Japan: The Origins of the Cold War* (Oxford: Oxford University Press, 1985), p. 47.

118 "anesthetizing": Textor, *Failure,* pp. 34–35.

120 not permitted to talk: Interview with an interpreter who served in the occupation.

120 Some American officials seem to have profited: This paragraph and the following one are drawn from Roberts, *Mitsui,* p. 383.

121 one prominent Washington official: Ibid., p. 394.

121 Perhaps the most startling example: Ibid., 392–393.

122 The end result is that: The Allies originally intended to confiscate much of Japan's manufacturing plant and give it to injured nations. In the first months of the occupation, however, the U.S. State Department wisely opposed this scorched-earth reparations strategy on the grounds that it would be highly inefficient in helping injured nations, while wantonly undermining the already impoverished Japanese people's ability to pay their way in the world. The crucial decisions to absolve Japan of responsibility to compensate victims of Japanese militarism were made several years later as a direct result of the Draper-Johnson mission.

As recorded in the *Bank of Tokyo Weekly Review* of May 8, 1961, Japan's reparations totaled $1,012 million. But even this figure, low as it is, seems to be considered an overestimate by some sources. According to the 1970 edition of the *Encyclopaedia Britannica,* Tokyo paid a total of just ¥153 million in reparations out of assets held within Japan up to May 1949, when the Americans halted Japan's reparations program. An unspecified amount of reparations was paid out of Japanese assets held abroad (believed to be assets held largely or entirely in former Japanese colonies).

Many of Japan's former colonies have been among the major beneficiaries of Japan's aid program in recent decades but their aid receipts cannot be considered reparations. Such receipts typically are spent largely or entirely on purchases from major Japanese corporations and form part of Japanese industrial policy. In any case, Japan's aid has never been distributed directly or even indirectly to victims of Japanese military aggression. One thing is clear: as the *Encyclopaedia Britannica* pointed out, Tokyo's reparations payments were dwarfed by what Washington spent

page propping up the Japanese economy in the first years after World
War II.

122 Germany's continuing reparations program: Michael Z. Wise, *Atlantic Monthly,* October 1993.

122 The mission definitively opposed: Calder, *Strategic Capitalism,*
p. 42.

123 a stay of just three weeks in Japan: Roberts, *Mitsui,* p. 394.

124 Japanese men born between 1932 and 1942: *Nikkei Weekly,* September 13, 1993.

126 one-seventh of the world's fishing catch: G. C. Allen, *The Japanese
Economy* (London: Weidenfeld & Nicolson, 1981), p. 84.

126 Japan's roads were the worst in the industrialized world: *This Is
Japan* (Tokyo: Asahi Shimbun, 1963), p. 222.

Chapter four

129 hires only about twenty: *Nikkei Weekly,* March 28, 1994.

137 Meiji oligarchs inherited: Ichiro Kawasaki, *Japan Unmasked* (Tokyo: Charles E. Tuttle, 1969) p. 181.

139 the Home and Finance Ministries had started as one unit: Lebra,
Okuma Shigenobu, p. 19.

139 Finance Ministry officials seem to have acquiesced: Johnson,
MITI, p. 133.

139 The MOF put up the money: Lockwood, *Economic Development
of Japan,* p. 509.

140 The Industrial Bank of Japan: Calder, *Strategic Capitalism,* p. 159.

140 massive statutory powers to monitor and veto: Johnson, *MITI,*
p. 136.

140 the MOF acquired draconian powers: See Calder, *Strategic Capitalism,* pp. 35–36.

141 a meeting between MacArthur and Foreign Minister Mamoru
Shigemitsu: Richard B. Finn, *Winners in Peace: MacArthur,
Yoshida, and Postwar Japan* (Berkeley: University of California
Press, 1992), pp. 17–18.

142 a calamitous 91 percent: Roberts, *Mitsui,* p. 381.

142 By 1949 the yen had lost 95 percent of its August 1945 value:
Finn, *Winners in Peace,* p. 334.

142 This view was expressed publicly: T. A. Bisson, the deputy head
of the occupation's government section, commented that the Japanese government "not only refused to take measures to check inflation but adopted policies that served to increase note inflation."

page

142 Kazuo Tatewaki: Kazuo Tatewaki, *Banking and Finance in Japan* (London: Routledge, 1991), p. 11.

143 ultra-nationalist MOF officials: See Johnston, *MITI*, Ch. 4.

143 "sitdown strike": Bisson, *Japan's War Economy*, p. 203.

144 the MOF managed to emerge from the purge virtually intact: John D. Montgomery, *Forced to Be Free: The Artificial Revolution in Japan and Germany* (Chicago: University of Chicago Press, 1957), p. 86.

146 No less than eighteen of Hong Kong's top law firms: *Asian Wall Street Journal*, August 5, 1993.

146 it gathers together under one roof: Jeffrey E. Garten, *A Cold Peace: America, Japan, Germany, and the Struggle for Supremacy* (New York: Times Books, 1992), p. 110.

146 the diet has no substantive power over the budget: Kanji Haitani, *Comparative Economic Systems: Organizational and Managerial Perspectives* (Englewood Cliffs, N.J.: Prentice-Hall, 1986), p. 89.

147 the MOF promptly embraced the rival organization: Chalmers Johnson, *Japan's Public Policy Corporations* (Washington, D.C.: American Enterprise Institute, 1978), p. 78.

148 every new government policy in Japan is first screened: John Creighton Campbell, *Contemporary Japanese Budget Politics* (Berkeley: University of California Press, 1977), pp. 2–3.

148 The MOF also enjoys considerable direct executive control over the Bank of Japan: Information in this paragraph is drawn from *BZW Japan*, August 1990.

150 In those days hundreds of retired army and naval officers: Bisson, *Japan's War Economy*, pp. 257–261.

150 Even former MOF administrative vice ministers: Nobuyuki Oishi, *Nikkei Weekly*, March 28, 1994.

151 The MOF's high-handedness in disregarding: See *Japan Economic Journal*, August 19, 1989, and December 1, 1990.

151 the MOF decided in the end: *Nikkei Weekly*, January 24, 1994.

151 Shunji Taoka: Shunji Taoka, *Asian Wall Street Journal*, October 22, 1992.

152 Robert M. Orr, Jr.: As quoted by James Fallows in *Looking at the Sun,* p. 270.

154 the MOF succeeded in cutting the Japanese civil service's total staff numbers: *Nikkei Weekly*, September 14, 1991.

155 The concept of using selective enforcement as a tool: This paragraph is drawn from Sakaiya's *What Is Japan?*, pp. 90–92.

156 A classic example of the indirect way: Ibid., p. 37.

page
156 officials use selective enforcement of tax law: As with many other Japanese policies, the tradition of using selective enforcement of tax law to influence the citizenry is more visible to Westerners in South Korea than in Japan because Korean officials are less adroit in covering their tracks. Korea officials have a well-known habit of ordering tax audits of citizens who buy luxury German cars. (Tax audits of foreign car buyers were once the norm also in Japan but Japanese tax officials have eased up on this tactic in recent years.) James Fallows (*Looking at the Sun,* p. 389) has recorded that after a Korean boutique owner handling Gucchi products was quoted in a foreign newspaper criticizing the Korean government's 1989–1990 campaign to suppress consumption of foreign luxury goods, she was targeted by tax agents and ordered to remove luxury goods from her shelves.

157 The partisanship of the prosecutors: Lebra, *Okuma Shigenobu,* p. 124.

157 Sphinx-like pose: Leon Hollerman, *Japan, Disincorporated: The Economic Liberalization Process* (Stanford: Hoover Institution Press, 1988), p. 67.

159 The MOF's role as protagonist later became explicit: *Mainichi Daily News,* March 13, 1990.

160 *Sandee Mainichi*: As quoted in the *Mainichi Daily News,* April 21, 1993.

161 Antique Trading Law: *Mainichi Daily News,* September 21, 1993.

161 When the civil servants liberalized the rules on imported beef: Douglas Frantz and Catherine Collins, *Selling Out: How We Are Letting Japan Buy Our Land, Our Industries, Our Financial Institutions, and Our Future* (Chicago: Contemporary Books, 1989), p. 88.

162 *Kuroji yuyo ron*: See *Press Guide,* July 1990, and the *Asian Wall Street Journal,* June 15–16, 1992.

162 A telling insight: Information on Japan Tobacco's mercantilism comes from David Halberstam, *The Reckoning* (London: Bantam, 1987), p. 703.

163 Foreign cigarette manufacturers were officially directed: Robert Keatley, *America and the World 1982* (New York: Pergamon Press, 1983), p. 704.

163 protecting the car industry: Information in this paragraph is drawn from *News from JAMA,* October 1992.

164 Control of the Fair Trade Commission: See Calder, *Strategic,* p. 93.

164 enormous information pyramid: See the *Asian Wall Street Journal,* December 28, 1990.

page
166 the MOF deliberately uses byzantine: *Asian Wall Street Journal,*
April 19, 1993.
168 John Keegan: John Keegan, *A History of Warfare* (New York:
Alfred A. Knopf, 1993), p. 272.

Chapter five

171 1925: As cited by the political scientist Harold S. Quigley.
173 perpetuated a system : *Mainichi Daily News,* November 30, 1989.
173 a time to plug your ears: *Asian Wall Street Journal,* July 14, 1993.
173 With so many supporters to pay off: The figures in this paragraph
come from Shunji Taoka, *Asian Wall Street Journal,* October 22,
1992.
174 A remarkable feature of postwar Japanese politics: The figures in
this paragraph come from Montgomery, *Forced to Be Free,* p. 47.
175 thousands of insurance salespeople: *Asahi Evening News,* February 9, 1990.
175 The MOF retaliated: *Japan Financial Report,* February 26, 1990.
175 dominated by former civil servants: See Malcolm Kennedy, *A
Short History of Japan* (New York: Mentor Books, 1964), p. 297.
See also Montgomery, *Forced to Be Free,* p. 54.
177 semifarcical role: As the veteran Australian Japan-watcher Gregory Clark pointed out, the Shinseito in particular included in its
ranks "many of the more corrupt members" of the former Takeshita faction of the LDP.
177 enormous mandate for change: NHK television, September 28, 1993.
179 laughing stock of the country: Tetsuya Kataoka, *Waiting for a
Pearl Harbor: Japan Debates Defense* (Stanford: Hoover Institution Press, 1980), p. 36.
179 Hirotatsu Fujiwara: Hirotatsu Fujiwara, *Tanaka Kakuei: Godfather of Japan* (Sapporo: Nihon Shoko Shinkokai, 1985), pp. 38,
78, 90, 112, and 122.
180 Lee Kuan Yew: *Asian Wall Street Journal,* November 9, 1993.
182 puppets of government propaganda and bureaucratic blackmail:
Mainichi Daily News, June 30, 1993.
182 Crush the product-pushing U.S. imperialists: *Asian Wall Street
Journal,* February 22, 1994.
182 cheerleaders: As recorded by Andrew Horvat, the editors of all but
one of Japan's major newspapers provided written guarantees to
the Chinese leadership in the 1960s that they would not criticize
China.

page

183 the leaks consist largely of information that could only have come from the MOF: Hirotatsu Fujiwara has reported that former Prime Minister Kakuei Tanaka used charges of tax evasion to hit back at the Komeito party and its associated religious institution, the Sokagakkai, which had been blackmailing him. Fujiwara, *Tanaka*, p. 122.

183 the navy had been persistently overrunning MOF-set spending limits: Lebra, *Okuma Shigenobu, pp. 115 and 118.*

183 brought down the entire cabinet of Prime Minister Makoto Saito: Sakaiya, *What Is Japan?*, p. 251.

183 one of the biggest and most significant such scandals: Information in this paragraph is drawn from Dan Kurzman, *Kishi and Japan: The Search for the Sun* (New York: Ivan Obolensky, 1960), p. 155.

184 apparently blackmailed by a rival political party: Fujiwara, *Tanaka*, p. 122.

184 John Roberts in 1974: John Roberts as quoted by Karel van Wolferen in *The Enigma of Japanese Power* (New York: Alfred A. Knopf, 1989), p. 95.

185 fear of being accused: van Wolferen, *Foreign Affairs*, September–October, 1993.

185 Konosuke Matsushita: See Konosuke Matsushita, *Japan at the Brink* (Tokyo: Kodansha, 1976), p. 31.

185 The press's "self-control" was particularly noticeable: Heizo Takenaka, *Asian Wall Street Journal*, September 22, 1993.

186 a ban on sales of nearly 300,000 acres: *Mainichi Daily News*, February 20, 1993.

186 members of Japan's media cartel: See Eamonn Fingleton, *Atlantic Monthly*, October 1990.

186 such transactions are often channeled: *Bungeishunju*, May 1993, as quoted in the *Mainichi Daily News*, May 1, 1993.

188 "unconvincing sophism": Guillain, *The Japanese Challenge*, pp. 195 and 196.

188 Shigeru Yoshida explicitly stated: *Mainichi Daily News* staff, *Fifty Years of Light and Dark: The Hirohito Era* (Tokyo: Mainichi Newspapers, 1976), p. 203. For good measure, Yoshida added: "In the past all imperialist wars were justified in the name of self-defense."

188 "all concerned": *Mainichi Daily News* staff, *Fifty Years*, p. 312.

188 a spur-of-the-moment political expedient: Kataoka, *Waiting for a Pearl Harbor*, p. 10.

Chapter six

page

190 a nation of pleasure seekers: See Chapter Three, A Nation of Pleasure Seekers, in Bill Emmott's *Sun Also Sets: Why Japan Will Not Be Number One* (London: Simon & Schuster, 1989).

190 an economic slowdown that would normally be expected to induce savers: See entry on consumption function, *Dictionary of Economics* (London: The Economist Books, 1988), p. 87.

191 the Japanese were regarded by Europeans as a nation of spendthrifts: See Chalmers Johnson, Japan Foundation newsletter, December 1988.

191 fluctuated widely: See Lockwood, *Economic Development of Japan*, p. 264.

191 In the immediate aftermath of World War II: See Peter Drucker, *Wall Street Journal*, January 9, 1990.

192 one of the most generous in the world: Sakaiya, *What is Japan?*, p. 6. As the Tokyo University political scientist Takashi Inoguchi has pointed out, Japan's ratio of pension benefits to wages passed even that of the former West Germany as long ago as 1983. Japan has one of the world's most generous state health care systems.

192 This is how that savings policy looked: J. K. Galbraith, *Money: Whence It Came, Where It Went* (Boston: Houghton Mifflin, 1975), p. 248.

192 All this helped the American economy: John Keegan, *A History of Warfare* (New York: Alfred A. Knopf, 1993), p. 313.

193 This is how one Tokyo official explained: See Carl Randau and Leane Zugsmith, *The Setting Sun of Japan* (New York: Random House, 1942), p. 56.

193 They kept squeezing: Bisson, *Japan's War Economy*, p. 201.

193 Edwin Reischauer predicted: Edwin Reischauer, *Wanted: An Asian Policy* (New York: Alfred A. Knopf), 1955. It is interesting to note that today forced saving is a powerful factor even in Singapore, which is often considered one of the most laissez faire of the East Asian supereconomies. The city state has evolved a savings regimen that the Harvard economics professor Robert Barro has labeled "coercive."

194 The Japanese take fewer foreign vacations: Much of this section is drawn from Eamonn Fingleton, *Atlantic Monthly*, July 1990.

195 $60 billion: This figure is based on the assumption that each extra traveler would match the average spending of existing travelers, who are mainly young females.

page

195   the government actually maintained: An indication of how tightly
      the government controlled spending is that as of 1964, students
      were permitted to take only a minuscule $50 out of the country
      to fund overseas trips. See Joel Kotkin and Yoriko Kishimoto, *The
      Third Century: America's Resurgence in the Asian Era* (New York:
      Crown, 1988), p. 110.

195   Japan's then vast coal mining industry: Yamada City alone lost
      fully half its population in the space of a decade as a result of the
      mine shutdowns. See Kakuei Tanaka, *Building a New Japan: A
      Plan for Remodeling the Japanese Archipelago* (Tokyo: Simul
      Press, 1973), p. 55.

196   Perhaps the clearest indication: According to Susan Moffat of
      Associated Press (*Mainichi Daily News,* December 4, 1989), the
      MOF overruled the Transport Ministry and insisted that Osaka's
      new international airport should have only one runway because
      Japan "can only afford only one." See also the *Asahi Evening
      News,* December 5, 1989.

196   an extensive program of building large international airports:
      Tanaka, *Building a New Japan,* p. 115.

197   the rate of credit card ownership: See *Nippon '92* (Tokyo: Jetro,
      1992), p. 45. It should be noted that the MOF has a history of
      imposing hidden restrictions on the usefulness of credit cards in
      Japan. For many years the banks issued cards which were valid
      only in Japan. Moreover, cards were generally limited only to
      certain narrow categories of people such as top executives. Per-
      haps the biggest restriction was a stipulation requiring most credit
      card holders to pay off their debts in full at the end of each month.
      This rule was ostensibly liberalized in 1993 in response to pressure
      from Washington but the liberalization appears to apply only to
      new accounts.

198   the MOF long ago instructed: See Jack Seward and Howard Van
      Zandt, *Japan: The Hungry Guest* (Tokyo: Yohan Publications,
      1985), p. 69.

198   about half as much shopping space per capita: See Eamonn
      Fingleton, "Eastern Economics," *Atlantic Monthly,* October
      1990.

199   the mighty Keidanren: Yoshihiro Inayama, a former head of Kei-
      danren, is on record as criticizing investment in retailing as a
      hindrance to Japan in the economic growth race. As the *Wall
      Street Journal* reported in December 1990, Inayama called for
      curbs on capital spending by retailing and other service-oriented
      industries.

page

199 Even at the time of the real estate market's peak distress: See Yumiko Ono, *Asian Wall Street Journal*, October 5, 1992.

200 only 38.9 square meters: See Eamonn Fingleton, "Eastern Economics," *Atlantic Monthly*, October 1990. (Statistical note: Just how cramped Japanese housing really is is a revelation to most Western experts on Japan: the statistics often quoted for home size in Japan are actually for *houses* — thus millions of minuscule rental apartments and company dormitories are excluded.)

200 Japan's land prices have not always been remarkably high: Information in this paragraph is drawn from Seiichi Takahata, *Industrial Japan and Industrious Japanese* (Osaka: Nissho, 1968), pp. 413 and 399.

200 "verticalize": Tanaka, *Building a New Japan,* p. 195. Tanaka also advocated tax benefits for high-rise buildings (p. 7). Some observers argue that the Japanese don't want their housing to be "verticalized." But the truth is, the Japanese have never been given a clear choice between tiny, pricey low-rises and spacious, inexpensive high-rises.

201 the officials betray their real intentions in new suburbs: The exact administrative mechanisms by which officials control zoning are unclear. But as the controls seem to be applied uniformly throughout the country it must be assumed that they constitute a national policy decided at top level. In any case central government in Japan generally maintains very tight control over most aspects of local government. According to the policy analyst Kenichi Ohmae, even Japan's largest cities cannot install a single street lamp, for instance, without central government authority.

202 has surfaced that Japan Inc. companies: See Patrick and Rosovsky, *Asia's New Giant,* p. 716.

Chapter seven

205 bsenteeism after payday: Robert Ozaki, *Human Capitalism: The Japanese Enterprise System as World Model* (Tokyo: Kodansha, 1991), p. 82.

205 earliest efforts: The employment cartel system seems to have been invented before the end of the nineteenth century by the Central Federation of Cotton Spinning Companies. A few years later, a similar cartel was recorded as operating among the Nagano area's important silk-reeling companies.

206 As the Kyocho Kai deliberated: As recorded by Jerome B. Cohen,

page the Kyocho Kai made a high-profile effort in 1937 and 1938 to establish suitably harmonious industrial relations as the economy moved to a war footing.

206 labor turnover rates suddenly plunged: In *The Japanese Industrial Relations Reconsidered* (Tokyo: The Japan Institute of Labor, 1990), Mikio Sumiya records that annual labor turnover rates fell from about 100 percent a year in the immediate aftermath of World War I to just 20 percent in the mid-1920s. See pp. 34 and 48.

207 a delayed victory for the militant New Bureaucrats: According to Fujitsu chairman Takuma Yamamoto in *Fujitsu: What Mankind Can Dream Technology Can Achieve* (Tokyo: Toyo Keizai, 1992), the idea of compressing top salaries actually predated World War II and originated with the militarists, who had identified Japan's then yawning wealth gap as a barrier to economic growth.

207 simple expedient: As recorded by Jerome B. Cohen, corporate executives' salaries were rigidly frozen at their levels of June 1945.

208 regulations making it virtually impossible: interview with Thomas Nevins, a Toyko-based employment consultant.

209 their obstructionism is entirely rational: Mikio Sumiya says that resistance by Japanese workers to new technologies introduced after World War I was a key reason why the Japanese establishment set out on a search for a better employment system.

209 a recent survey found that: Survey by the Organization of Economic Cooperation and Development in 1993. See the *Economist,* July 17, 1993.

213 widespread confrontation: Ozaki, *Human Capitalism,* p. 68.

213 a new gospel of ownerless enterprise: See Tetsuo Sakiya, *Honda Motor: The Men, the Management, the Machines* (Tokyo: Kodansha, 1982), pp. 87, 93, 94, and 162. From early in his business career, Honda Motor founder Soichiro Honda promised to retire from the company at retirement age and vowed that his family would have no influence in the company after he retired. He kept his word on both counts. In fact, Soichiro Honda got his big break when he announced his commitment to ownerless enterprise to Mitsubishi Bank in the early 1950s. As Sakiya records, the bankers were extremely impressed and from that time on placed their full trust in the company. It is clear in retrospect that Honda was articulating a new attitude that was required from entrepreneurs if they were to have a chance of growing in a society dominated by the great keiretsu companies and the bureaucrats' industrial policy.

218 "reflections on the day's events": *Tradepia,* Summer issue, 1993.

219 paid as much as $600,000 each to leave: Valerie Reitman and Jathon Sapsford, *Asian Wall Street Journal,* August 10, 1994.

page

219 the government operates a system of subsidies: See Junichi Saiki, *Asian Wall Street Journal,* July 22, 1993. See also Kanji Haitani, *Comparative Economic Systems: Organizational and Managerial Perspectives* (Englewood Cliffs, N.J.: Prentice-Hall, 1986), p. 307.

224 $57,000 to replace each junior engineer: C. Jackson Grayson, Jr., and Carla S. O'Dell, *American Business: A Two-Minute Warning* (New York: Free Press, 1988), p. 174.

225 Gibney has argued: Gibney, *Miracle by Design,* pp. 218–219.

225 Zhu Shaowen: *Nikkei Weekly,* October 15, 1993.

225 T. F. M. Adams: T. F. M. Adams and N. Kobayashi, *The World of Japanese Business: An Authoritative Analysis* (Tokyo: Kodansha, 1969), p. 104.

225 paid about 2.6 times as much: *Sanwa Economic Review,* April 1994.

226 Correspondents from some of the most respected publications: See, for instance, Christopher Wood, "Kerplunk," *New Republic,* November 23, 1992.

227 Why did so many: See, for instance, LeRoy Howard, *Japan Update,* February 1994, p. 7.

227 112,000: *Asian Wall Street Journal,* February 24, 1994. Japanese corporations had 1,695 plants employing an average of 233 workers in 1993, versus 1,724 plants employing an average of 294 workers in 1992.

228 the cleverer Japanese firms know that lifetime employment is finished: *Economist,* September 18, 1993.

Chapter eight

232 In the wake of the famous railroad price wars: F. M. Scherer, *Industrial Market Structure and Economic Performance* (Chicago: Rand McNally, 1970), p. 196.

232 A law enacted in 1925 provided the bureaucrats with: This paragraph is based on Lockwood, *Economic Development of Japan,* pp. 567 and 571.

233 nearly all Germany's production: Fritz Voigt as quoted in Scherer, *Industrial Market Structure,* p. 158.

233 between 65 and 95 percent: Lockwood, *Economic Development of Japan,* p. 223.

234 the Cabinet approved an order: Bisson, *Japan's War Economy,* p. 240.

234 the economic rationale for government-guided cartels: See Yoshi-

page hiko Morozumi, "A Statement Against Free Competition in the
Japanese System," in *Readings on Contemporary Society and Political Economy*, ed. Daniel I. Okimoto and Thomas P. Rohlen
(Stanford: Stanford University Press, 1988), p. 80.

234 *Gendai No Shakai: Gendai No Shakai* (Tokyo: Chukyo Shuppan,
1966), pp. 105–106.

235 the Japanese bureaucrats have allowed legal cartels: Richard E.
Caves and Masu Uekusa in Patrick and Rosovsky, *Asia's New
Giant*, p. 493.

235 beyond its statutory authority: Ibid.

235 the officials' administrative advice even required companies to
break Japan's antitrust law: Sakiya, *Honda Motor*, p. 135.

235 "selfish": *Computers Inc.: Japan's Challenge to IBM* (Cambridge:
Council on East Asian Studies, 1989), p. 81.

235 silk and camphor: These products were listed in 1925 by the U.S.
Commerce Secretary Herbert Hoover as among eight essential
commodities monopolized by foreign nations (Japan's global market share was put at 75 percent in silk and 95 percent in camphor).
See Shuichi Harada, *Labor Conditions in Japan* (New York: Columbia University Press, 1928), pp. 34 and 67.

236 In the 1960s, the Ministry of Finance: See Guillain, *The Japanese
Challenge*, p. 298.

236 a major up-front incentive: *The Structure and Operation of the
Japanese Economy* (Sydney: John Wiley, 1970), p. 117.

237 On one authoritative estimate: Shoichiro Irimajiri, adviser to
Honda Motor.

238 token concessions to American feelings: In one recent case, the
Fair Trade Commission broke up a cartel in wrapping paper. In
another, the commission investigated the Japanese subsidiary of
Apple Computer for alleged breaches of antitrust. This sort of
activity makes headlines but not a new policy.

238 Finance is one of the Japan's most visible cartelized industries:
Even the *Wall Street Journal*, which has a notable record of turning a blind eye to Japan's cartelization policies, agrees. Commenting on Japan's financial services industry on August 25, 1992, the
Journal's editors wrote: "There is an entire canon of licensing
requirements, interest-rate regulations, and trade association
agreements that amount to cartels."

239 "suspicious": Former Economic Planning Agency official Sumiko
Takahara, *Yomiuri Shimbun*, February 21, 1992.

239 "cartel-like": See Laura D'Andrea Tyson, *Who's Bashing Whom:
Trade Conflict in High-Technology Industries* (Washington, D.C.:
Institute for International Economics, 1992), p. 120.

page

239 Hayao Nakamura: *Asian Wall Street Journal*, May 21–22, 1993.

239 antitrust regulators are required to desist from bringing antitrust suits: *Making Things Better* (Washington, D.C.: Office of Technology Assessment, 1990), p. 208.

240 Cartels cut the cost of Japan's commodity imports: This paragraph is based on a commentary by the Washington antitrust lawyer Joseph P. Griffin in the *Nikkei Weekly,* May 2, 1992.

241 One of the first moves: Yotaro Kobayashi, *Fuji Xerox: The First Twenty Years 1962–1982* (Tokyo: Fuji Xerox, 1983), p. 152.

241 one company took the mainframe business: William H. Davidson, *The Amazing Race: Winning the Technorivalry with Japan* (New York: John Wiley, 1984), pp. 253–254.

243 electron beam technology: *Economist*, April 5, 1980.

245 "involved in a long-standing relationship of some sort": Robert L. Cutts, *Harvard Business Review*, July–August 1992.

246 It is interesting to look: This paragraph is drawn from an article by Honda Motor's adviser Shoichiro Irimajiri in *Economic Eye,* Autumn 1992.

247 Iwao Nakatani has pointed out: Iwao Nakatani, *Chuo Koron,* February 1992.

248 about three times more likely: Michael L. Gerlach, *Alliance Capitalism: The Social Organization of Japanese Business* (Berkeley: University of California Press, 1992), p. 144.

248 Many keiretsus also control retail outlets: See Cutts, *Harvard Business Review.*

249 Such manufacturer-to-consumer keiretsu arrangements: Ibid.

256 Although standard-setting: Sakaiya, *What Is Japan?*, pp. 251–252.

256 Factory of the Future: Tom Forester, *Silicon Samurai: How Japan Conquered the World's IT Industry* (Oxford: Blackwell, 1993), p. 143.

256 computer-aided manufacturing equipment: Forester, *Silicon Samurai,* p. 126.

256 American attempts to copy the research cartel: *Making Things Better,* p. 202.

256 Japan's track record . . . planning: Office of Technology Assessment, *Holding the Edge: Maintaining the Defense Technology Base* (Washington, D.C.: U.S. Government Printing Office, 1989), p. 91.

Chapter nine

page
258 $13 billion of imports: Masatoshi Moriyama, *Asian Wall Street Journal*, December 14, 1993.
259 Glen Fukushima: *Mainichi Daily News*, November 19, 1993.
260 "landmark step": *Asian Wall Street Journal*, December 15, 1993.
260 "historic": *Japan Times*, December 16, 1993.
260 Norikazu Wakayama: Wakayama's book, *Hogo Zeisatsu*, drew heavily from the then influential American economist Henry Charles Carey, who was known as the "father of American economics." At that time American economics was synonymous with protectionism. See Tessa Morris-Suzuki, *A History of Japanese Economic Thought* (London: Routledge, 1989), p. 59.
261 three policies to compensate: Junesay Iddittie, *The Life of Marquis Shigenobu Okuma: A Biographical Study in the Rise of Democratic Japan* (Tokyo: Hokuseido, 1956), pp. 169–170.
261 levied tariffs of typically more than 30 percent: Fallows, *Looking at the Sun*, p. 196.
263 its three big producers: *Business Week*, December 13, 1993.
263 one Japanese producer alone: *Mainichi Daily News*, December 18, 1993.
264 one American health care company: See Eamonn Fingleton, *Atlantic Monthly*, October 1990.
265 favoring American suppliers: Peter F. Drucker, *Managing for the Future* (Oxford: Butterworth Heinemann, 1992), p. 53.
265 At times of extreme trade friction: This paragraph is drawn from the *Economist*, August 10, 1974.
267 prices as high as three times: As recounted by James Abegglen and George Stalk, Jr., when it first operated in Japan.
268 a long list of written rules: Adams and Kobayashi, *The World of Japanese Business*, pp. 239–240.
269 Marcus Noland: *Asian Wall Street Journal*, June 7, 1993.
270 generally using Japanese production machines and components: Less than 20 percent of IBM's Japanese sales represents parts and products sourced from the United States: other estimates put the figure below 10 percent. See the *Nikkei Weekly*, November 23, 1992.
271 Kabun Muto: *Mainichi Daily News*, April 19, 1993.
272 In particular Kenichi Ohmae: Kenichi Ohmae, *Beyond National Borders: Reflections on Japan and the World* (Tokyo: Kodansha, 1987), pp. 24–39.
272 Robert Christopher: Robert C. Christopher, *Second to None:*

page *American Companies in Japan* (New York: Fawcett Columbine, 1986). Christopher's book was described by the *Wall Street Journal* as "Important . . . Convincing . . . Fascinating." *Time* magazine said it "presents an argument for pragmatic optimism: many U.S. companies are competing on their opponents' home ground more effectively than most Americans realize."

273 Tibor de Scitovsky: Tibor de Scitovsky, *Readings in the Theory International Trade* (London: George Allen and Unwin, 1950), p. 358.

Chapter ten

275 *aun no kokyu: Nihon Keizai Shimbun*, February 1, 1993.

275 In the early days of the economic miracle: Calder, *Strategic Capitalism*, p. 156.

276 keep Japanese savings dammed up inside the country: The U.S. Treasury has been pressing Japan for years to dismantle the rules blocking Japanese citizens from opening bank accounts abroad and requiring Western corporations to get the MOF's permission before raising capital in Japan. See, for instance, *Mainichi Daily News*, November 6, 1991.

277 The market rules for foreign listings: When companies list on the Tokyo stock exchange, they are required to "place" — sell — a tranche of stock to investors in Japan. This tranche then becomes the basis for trading in Tokyo. The problem has been that sellers and buyers are rarely evenly matched. At times when sellers predominate, the Tokyo shares are sold back to the home stock market — generally New York in the case of American companies. But once the shares go back to New York they rarely return to Tokyo because the rules allow Japanese brokers to levy a special expensive surcharge on purchases of shares from New York. In practice, intelligent investors will not want to pay this surcharge. Thus the flow is one-way — back to the home market — and eventually there are so few shares left in Tokyo that virtually no trading takes place there.

278 Kiichiro Sato: Johnson, *MITI*, p. 71.

278 the MOF also required companies to maintain their dividends: See Sakiya, *Honda Motor*, p. 178. See also Peter Drucker in *Inside the Japanese System: Readings on Contemporary Society and Political Economy*, ed. Daniel I. Okimoto and Thomas P. Rohlen (Stanford: Stanford University Press, 1988), p. 109.

278 Mitchell Pacelle: Mitchell Pacelle, *Asian Wall Street Journal*, May 11, 1993.

279 "partially": *Nikkei Fax*, May 21, 1993.

280 sheep to be sheared: According to Robert Carroll, in *Tokyo Journal*, ordinary investors are known within the Japanese securities industry as *dobu* — "the gutter." He quoted one former brokerage salesman, saying: "We were told not to waste telephone time on the small investor, just say anything to make the sale and get out." When securities firms recommend that big institutions buy a stock that is expected to go up, they simultaneously recommend small investors to sell.

280 they owned just 24 percent: *Nikkei Weekly*, May 10, 1993.

280 only twelve are available: Kazuo Ueda, *Asian Wall Street Journal*, May 17, 1993.

280 Kazuo Ueda: Kazuo Ueda, *Asian Wall Street Journal*, May 17, 1993.

281 The inadequacy of Japanese disclosure: Yoko Shibata, *Global Finance*, February 1993.

287 certain countries consistently intervene: The Japanese commentators Yoshisuke Iinuma and Takatoshi Ito in 1994 named South Korea and Taiwan as countries with a notable reputation for manipulating their currencies' dollar value.

288 rich private citizens: Corporations also bought overpriced stocks in the late 1980s but usually they did so on a reciprocal basis thus for each corporation the effect was a wash: Company A gained by selling high-priced stock to Company B but lost by having to buy Company B's high-priced stock.

291 they are the same people who think money grows on trees: Even in the last wild weeks of the great bubble market in late 1989, several prestigious publications argued that Japanese stocks were good investments that would head higher in 1990. By contrast, informed long-term foreign residents of Japan had been convinced for some time that the market was in a bubble phase that would soon end with disastrous consequences for investors. This writer's view was recorded in *Euromoney* in February 1989 ("Making Hay"), in which he predicted the stock market would peak later in the year and would be followed by a "prolonged bear market."

292 one discovers a less distressing picture: Commentators who predicted that bad real estate loans would bring down the Japanese banking industry overlooked a pivotal point that proved them wrong: rents remained high and provided entirely adequate sup-

page port for almost all real estate loans. As surveyed by *Fortune* in 1994, a typical Tokyo office rent was $144.98 per square foot — more than four times the equivalent figure for New York, $31.25.

293   A pause was therefore overdue: Apart from natural cyclical slowdown, the Japanese economy was also strained by the rising yen. Even Japanese industry, strong as it is, can hardly be expected to adjust to a 40 percent currency appreciation in the space of four years without some strain.

Chapter eleven

295   despite everything the press says: In April 1992, Dow Jones vice president Karen Elliott House, for instance, approvingly quoted the analyst Akio Mikuni, saying: "We can't export our way out of this downturn." The facts proved them both wrong: in the next two years, Japan increased its exports by $47 billion — an amount equal to the entire GNP of Singapore.

297   the MOF had established a subsidy program: *Nikkei Weekly,* April 18, 1994. Also see the *Nikkei Weekly,* December 28, 1992.

304   Michael Borrus: Quoted by Tom Forester in *Silicon Samurai: How Japan Conquered the World's IT Industry* (Oxford: Blackwell, 1993), p. 214.

304   Particularly loath to sell: See Office of Technology Assessment, *Arming Our Allies: Cooperation and Competition in Defense Technology* (Washington, D.C.: U.S. Government Printing Office, 1990). It is interesting to note that both South Korea and Taiwan also complain vociferously about corporate Japan's refusal to transfer advanced technology. See Fallows, *Looking at the Sun,* pp. 385 and 397.

306   Ryutaro Komiya: *Economic Eye*, Winter 1993.

306   The new sense . . . was made pointedly clear: *Asian Wall Street Journal*, March 21, 1994.

306   "We're hooked on Japan, I'm afraid": Lee Sang Yul as quoted by James Sterngold, in the *New York Times,* April 13, 1993.

307   About half the value of a typical Korean car: See Kenneth Courtis, *World Link,* September–October 1992.

307   countries accounting for about half: According to the University of British Columbia scholar W. Mark Fruin, Japan's economic methods are consciously being emulated in Taiwan, South Korea, India, Singapore, Hong Kong, the Philippines, Malaysia, Indone-

page sia, and China. See W. Mark Fruin, *The Japanese Enterprise System: Competitive Strategies and Cooperative Structures* (Oxford: Clarendon Press, 1992), p. 10.

308 6.9 million units: *Nikkei Weekly,* August 23, 1993.

308 Kiyoshi Kojima: Quoted by Hollerman, *Japan, Disincorporated,* p. 137.

308 Toyota had faithfully carried out: *Japan Scope,* Spring 1993.

308 map out industrial policy for the entire East Asian region: See Edward J. Lincoln, as quoted by Fallows in *Looking at the Sun,* p. 486, n. 50.

311 exonerating all twenty-eight accused military leaders: Arnold C. Brackman, *The Other Nuremberg: The Untold Story of the Tokyo War Crimes Trials* (New York: William Morrow, 1987), p. 392.

311 President Kim Young-Sam: *Nikkei Weekly,* August 15, 1993.

311 Prime Minister Mahathir Mohamad: *Mainichi Daily News,* August 28, 1994.

311 even Corazon Aquino: *Aera,* November 1, 1993.

311 Few observers of East Asia have had a better insight: Pearl Buck as quoted by Toland in *The Rising Sun,* p. 511.

313 many ostensibly private Japanese corporations: Ira C. Magaziner and Mark Patinkin have reported that Japan's phone company for a long time bought optical fiber from Japanese companies at three times the world market price — yet these same Japanese suppliers were allegedly selling abroad at below-market prices. See *The Silent War: Inside the Global Business Battles Shaping America's Future* (New York: Random House, 1989), p. 296.

314 long been targeted by Japan: See 1994 National Trade Estimate Report on Foreign Trade Barriers, released March 31, 1994.

315 already the world's three busiest air routes: *Nikkei Weekly,* April 19, 1993.

315 In response to complaints by Boeing's labor unions: *Mainichi Daily News,* August 10, 1994.

315 Officially the 777's Japanese content: *Nikkei Weekly,* April 19, 1993.

316 bargaining chip: *Nikkei Weekly,* May 17, 1993.

317 Leon Trilling: *Technology Review,* May–June, 1993.

317 one-fifth of all the world's scientists and engineers: Definitional problems make it difficult to estimate Japan's share of the world's technological personnel. But few doubt that Japan is disproportionately strong in this area. According to one source, per 1,000 of population, Japan boasts 317 scientists and technicians versus just 55 in the United States. See Andrew L. Shapiro, *We're Number One: Where America Stands — and Falls — in the New World Order* (New York: Vintage Books, 1992), p. 67.

page

318 150 research and development facilities: Stephen Budiansky, *U.S. News & World Report*, March 22, 1993.

318 192 research and development facilities: Jetro as quoted in the *Mainichi Daily News*, May 9, 1993.

318 Japan's links with Russian science: Information in this paragraph is drawn from the *Mainichi Daily News*, May 29, 1993 and June 1, 1993.

318 sea-surface plane: *Nikkei Weekly*, March 28, 1994.

319 the atmosphere at the NEC laboratory: Stephen Budiansky, *U.S. News & World Report*, March 22, 1993.

319 just such an edge: See Magaziner and Patinkin, *The Silent War*, p. 216.

320 thanks in part to Japanese researchers' access: Forester, *Silicon Samurai*, p. 103.

321 patent rights to research conducted in American universities: See Elliott Negin, *Atlantic Monthly*, March 1993.

321 such links have helped Toshiba: Ibid.

Chapter twelve

325 shorn of its lead: The machine tools industry provides a classic example of America's loss of monopolistic leadership. According to Edward Faltermeyer of *Fortune,* America once dominated the industry but now ranks a poor fourth in the world, behind Japan, Germany, and Italy.

332 One noted Japanese partner of McKinsey & Co.: See Kenichi Ohmae, *Heisei Ishin, Zero-Based Organization and Constitution — World View Through GNP* (Tokyo: Kodansha, 1989), pp. 125–126.

335 Bertrand Russell: Bertrand Russell, *Icarus,* 1924, as cited in Dennis Gabor, *Inventing the Future* (London: Penguin Books, 1964), p. 158.

336 even America's military intelligence operations: *Mainichi Daily News*, August 25, 1994.

338 Jeffrey E. Garten: Garten, *A Cold Peace,* p. 197.

339 Jim Hoagland: Jim Hoagland, *Mainichi Daily News*, January 27, 1993.

341 Pax Nipponica: Vogel, *Comeback,* p. 16.

342 the suicide rate among American teenagers: See van Wolferen, *The Enigma of Japanese Power*, p. 88. Also see Grayson and O'Dell, *American Business*, p. 275.

342 *karoshi*: Death from overwork is difficult to define. Overwork is a key — sometimes the key — contributory factor in death from heart disease. In a famous study in Massachusetts published in 1972, job troubles, rather than smoking or cholesterol, were identified as the surest predictor of heart disease. See *Fortune*, November 30, 1992. Heart disease is much more prevalent in the United States than in Japan. William T. Ziemba and Sandra L. Schwartz have suggested that a happy work environment in Japan is a key reason for Japan's excellent male life expectancy figures, which are relatively speaking even more remarkable than the figures for Japanese females.

344 David Halberstam: Halberstam, *The Next Century* (New York: Avon, 1992), p. 87.

349 Sir George Sansom: See Foreword by Sir George Sansom in Jerome B. Cohen, *Japan's Economy in War and Reconstruction* (Minneapolis: University of Minnesota Press, 1949), p. viii.

Bibliography

Abegglen, James C. *Management and Worker: The Japanese Solution.* Tokyo: Kodansha, 1973.

American Economics Association. *Readings in the Theory of International Trade.* London: George Allen and Unwin, 1950.

Anchordoguy, Marie. *Computers Inc.: Japan's Challenge to IBM.* Cambridge: Council on East Asian Studies, 1989.

Baerwald, Hans. *Japan's Parliament: An Introduction.* Cambridge: Cambridge University Press, 1974.

Barr, Pat. *The Coming of the Barbarians: A Story of Western Settlement in Japan 1853–1870.* London: Penguin Books, 1988.

Bartlett, Donald L., and James B. Steele. *America: What Went Wrong?* Kansas City: Andrews and McMeel, 1992.

Benedict, Ruth. *The Chrysanthemum and the Sword.* Cambridge: Houghton Mifflin, 1946.

Bergner, Jeffrey T. *The New Superpowers: Germany, Japan, the U.S., and the New World Order.* New York: St. Martin's Press, 1991.

Bisson, T. A. *Japan's War Economy.* New York: Institute of Pacific Relations, 1945.

———. *Prospects for Democracy in Japan.* New York: Macmillan, 1949.

Braddon, Russell. *The Other 100 Years War.* London: Collins, 1983.

Burstein, Daniel. *Yen!: Japan's New Financial Empire and Its Threat to America.* New York: Simon & Schuster, 1988.

Calder, Kent E. *Strategic Capitalism: Private Business and Public Purpose in Japanese Industrial Finance.* Princeton: Princeton University Press, 1993.

The Cambridge Encyclopedia of Japan. Cambridge: Cambridge University Press, 1993.

Choate, Pat. *Agents of Influence: How Japan's Lobbyists in the United*

States Manipulate America's Political and Economic System. New York: Alfred A. Knopf, 1990.

Clark, Colin. *The Conditions of Economic Progress*. London: Macmillan, 1940.

Cohen, Jerome B. *Japan's Economy in War and Reconstruction*. Minneapolis: University of Minnesota Press, 1949.

Cohen, Stephen S., and Zysman, John. *Manufacturing Matters: The Myth of the Post-Industrial Economy*. New York: Basic Books, 1987.

Congressional Budget Office. *Assessing the Decline in the National Saving Rate*. Washington, D.C.: 1993.

Cusumano, Michael A. *Japan's Software Factories: A Challenge to U.S. Management*. New York: Oxford University Press, 1991.

D'Andrea Tyson, Laura. *Who's Bashing Whom: Trade Conflict in High-Technology Industries*. Washington, D.C.: Institute for International Economics, 1992.

Davidson, William H. *The Amazing Race: Winning the Technorivalry with Japan*. New York: John Wiley, 1984.

Dietrich, William S. *In the Shadow of the Rising Sun: The Political Roots of American Economic Decline*. University Park: Pennsylvania State University Press, 1991.

Dollar, David, and Edward N. Wolff. *Competitiveness, Convergence, and Specialization*. Cambridge, Mass.: MIT Press, 1993.

Dore, Ronald. *British Factory, Japanese Factory: The Origins of National Diversity in Industrial Relations*. Berkeley: University of California Press, 1973.

Drucker, Peter F. *Managing for the Future: The 1990s and Beyond*. Oxford: Butterworth-Heinemann, 1992.

The *Economist*, Correspondents of. *Consider Japan*. London: Gerald Duckworth, 1963.

Emmott, Bill. *The Sun Also Sets: Why Japan Will Not Be Number One*. London: Simon & Schuster, 1989.

Encyclopaedia Britannica Book of the Year: 1993.

Fallows, James. *Looking at the Sun: The Rise of the New East Asian Economic and Political System*. New York: Pantheon Books, 1994.

————. *More Like Us: Making America Great Again*. Boston: Houghton Mifflin, 1989.

Finn, Richard B. *Winners in Peace: MacArthur, Yoshida, and Postwar Japan*. Berkeley: University of California Press, 1992.

Forester, Tom. *Silicon Samurai: How Japan Conquered the World's IT Industry*. Oxford: Blackwell, 1993.

Frantz, Douglas, and Catherine Collins. *Selling Out: How We Are Letting Japan Buy Our Land, Our Industries, Our Financial Institutions, and Our Future*. Chicago: Contemporary Books, 1989.

Friedman, Benjamin M. *Day of Reckoning: The Consequences of American Economic Policy Under Reagan and After.* London: Pan Books, 1989.

Fruin, W. Mark. *The Japanese Enterprise System: Competitive Strategies and Cooperative Structures.* Oxford: Clarendon Press, 1992.

Fujiwara, Hirotatsu. *Tanaka Kakuei: Godfather of Japan.* Translated by John Clark. Sapporo: Nihon Shoko Shinkokai, 1985.

Galbraith, John Kenneth. *American Capitalism: The Concept of Countervailing Power.* London: Pelican Books, 1963.

———. *A History of Economics: The Past as the Present.* London: Penguin Books, 1987.

Garten, Jeffrey E. *A Cold Peace: America, Japan, Germany and the Struggle for Supremacy.* New York: Times Books, 1992.

Gerlach, Michael L. *Alliance Capitalism: The Social Organization of Japanese Business.* Berkeley: University of California Press, 1992.

Glickman, Norman J., and Douglas P. Woodward. *The New Competitors: How Foreign Investors Are Changing the U.S. Economy.* New York: Basic Books, 1989.

Grayson, C. Jackson, Jr., and Carla O'Dell. *American Business: A Two-Minute Warning.* New York: Free Press, 1988.

Hadley, Eleanor M. *Antitrust in Japan.* Princeton: Princeton University Press, 1970.

Haitani, Kanji. *Comparative Economic Systems: Organizational and Managerial Perspectives.* Englewood Cliffs, N.J.: Prentice-Hall, 1986.

Halberstam, David. *The Reckoning.* London: Bantam, 1987.

———. *The Next Century.* New York: Avon, 1992.

Harada, Shuichi. *Labor Conditions in Japan.* New York: Columbia University Press, 1928.

Hartog, Joop, and Jules Theeuwes, eds. *Labor Market Conditions and Institutions: A Cross-National Survey.* North Holland: Amsterdam, 1993.

Heller, Robert. *The Fate of IBM.* London: Little, Brown, 1994.

Hollerman, Leon. *Japan, Disincorporated: The Economic Liberalization Process,* Stanford: Hoover Institution Press, 1988.

Holstein, William J. *The Japanese Power Game: What It Means for America.* New York: Charles Scribner's Sons, 1990.

Iddittie, Junesay. *The Life of Marquis Shigenobu Okuma: A Biographical Study in the Rise of Democratic Japan.* Tokyo: Hokuseido, 1956.

Ito, Takatoshi. *The Japanese Economy.* Cambridge: MIT Press, 1992.

Jackson, Tim. *The Next Battleground: Japan, America, and the New European Market.* Boston: Houghton Mifflin, 1993.

Jetro. *Japan's Industrial Structure: A Long Range Vision.* Tokyo: Jetro, 1974.

Johnson, Chalmers. *MITI and the Japanese Miracle: The Growth of Industrial Policy, 1925–1975.* Tokyo: Charles E. Tuttle, 1986.

Kahn, Herman. *The Emerging Japanese Superstate: Challenge and Response.* Englewood Cliffs: Prentice-Hall, 1970.

Kawakita, Takao. *Okurasho: Kanryo Kiko no Choten.* Tokyo: Kodansha, 1989.

Kawasaki, Ichiro, *Japan Unmasked.* Tokyo: Charles E. Tuttle, 1969.

Kearns, Robert L. *Zaibatsu America: How Japanese Firms Are Colonizing Vital U.S. Industries.* New York: Free Press, 1992.

Keegan, John. *A History of Warfare.* New York: Alfred A. Knopf, 1993.

Kennedy, Malcolm. *A Short History of Japan.* New York: Mentor Books, 1964.

Kennedy, Paul. *Preparing for the Twenty-First Century.* London: HarperCollins, 1993.

Kester, W. Carl. *Japanese Takeovers: The Global Contest for Corporate Control.* Boston: Harvard Business School Press, 1991.

Kikuchi, Makoto. *Japanese Electronics: A Worm's Eye View of Its Evolution.* Tokyo: Simul Press, 1983.

Kobayashi, Yotaro. *Fuji Xerox: The First Twenty Years 1962–1982.* Tokyo: Fuji Xerox, 1983.

Kodansha Encyclopedia of Japan. Tokyo: Kodansha, 1983.

Kotkin, Joel, and Yoriko Kishimoto. *The Third Century: America's Resurgence in the Asian Era.* New York: Crown, 1988.

Krugman, Paul. *Trade with Japan: Has the Door Opened Wider?* Chicago: University of Chicago Press, 1991.

Kurzman, Dan. *Kishi and Japan: The Search for the Sun.* New York: Ivan Obolensky, 1960.

Kuttner, Robert. *The End of Laissez-faire.* New York: Alfred A. Knopf, 1991.

Lardner, James. *Fast Forward: Hollywood, the Japanese, and the VCR Wars.* New York: W. W. Norton, 1987.

Lattimore, Owen, and Eleanor Lattimore. *China: A Short History.* New York: W. W. Norton, 1944.

Lebra, Joyce C. *Okuma Shigenobu: Statesman of Meiji Japan.* Canberra: Australian National University Press, 1973.

List, Friedrich. *The National System of Political Economy.* London: Lonmans, Green, 1909.

Lockwood, William W. *The Economic Development of Japan; Growth and Structural Change.* Expanded edition. Princeton: Princeton University Press, 1970.

Magaziner, Ira C., and Mark Patinkin. *The Silent War: Inside the Global Business Battles Shaping America's Future.* New York: Random House, 1989.

Matsumoto, Koji. *The Rise of the Japanese Corporate System: The Inside View of a MITI Official*. London: Kegan Paul, 1991.

Matsushita, Konosuke. *Quest for Prosperity: The Life of a Japanese Industrialist*. Kyoto: PHP Institute, 1988.

Maurette, Fernand. *Social Aspects of Industrial Development in Japan*. Geneva: International Labour Office, 1934.

Montgomery, John D. *Forced to Be Free: The Artificial Revolution in Germany and Japan*. Chicago: University of Chicago Press, 1957.

Moritani, Masanori. *Japanese Technology: Getting the Best for the Least*. Tokyo: Simul Press, 1982.

Morris-Suzuki, Tessa. *A History of Japanese Economic Thought*. London: Routledge, 1989.

Nau, Henry R. *The Myth of America's Decline: Leading the World Economy into the 1990s*. New York: Oxford University Press, 1990.

Nester, William R. *Japanese Industrial Targeting: The Neomercantilist Path to Economic Superpower*. Houndmills: Macmillan, 1991.

Ohmae, Kenichi. *Heisei Ishin: Zero-based Organization and Constitution — World View through GNP*. Tokyo: Kodansha, 1989.

Okimoto, Daniel I., and Thomas P. Rohlen. *Inside the Japanese System: Readings on Contemporary Society and Political Economy*. Stanford: Stanford University Press, 1988.

Patrick, Hugh, ed. *Japan's High Technology Industries: Lessons and Limitations of Industrial Policy*. Seattle and Tokyo: University of Washington Press/University of Tokyo Press, 1986.

Patrick, Hugh, and Henry Rosovsky, eds. *Asia's New Giant: How the Japanese Economy Works*. Washington, D.C.: Brookings Institution, 1976.

Perry, Matthew C. *Correspondence Relative to the Naval Expedition to Japan*. U.S. Congress, 1855.

Perot, Ross. *United We Stand: How We Can Take Our Country Back*. New York: Hyperion, 1992.

Peters, Thomas J. and Robert H. Waterman. *In Search of Excellence: Lessons from America's Best-Run Companies*. New York: Harper & Row, 1982.

Porter, Michael E. *The Competitive Advantage of Nations*. London: Macmillan Press, 1990.

Prestowitz, Clyde V., Jr. *Trading Places: How America Allowed Japan to Take the Lead*. Tokyo: Charles E. Tuttle, 1988.

Price, Willard. *The Japanese Miracle*. London: Heinemann, 1971.

Randau, Carl, and Leane Zugsmith. *The Setting Sun of Japan*. New York: Random House, 1942.

Reading, Brian. *Japan: The Coming Collapse*. London: Weidenfeld & Nicolson, 1992.

Roberts, John G. *Mitsui: Three Centuries of Japanese Business.* New York: Weatherhill, 1973.

Sakaiya, Taichi. *The Knowledge-Value Revolution or a History of the Future.* Tokyo: Kodansha, 1991.

———. *What Is Japan?: Contradictions and Transformations.* New York: Kodansha, 1993.

Sampson, Anthony. *The Midas Touch: Understanding the Dynamic New Money Societies Around Us.* New York: Dutton, 1990.

Samuels, Richard J. *The Business of the Japanese State: Energy Markets in Comparative and Historical Perspective.* Ithaca: Cornell University Press, 1987.

Sansom, Sir George. *The Western World and Japan: A Study in the Interaction of European and Asiatic Cultures.* Tokyo: Charles E. Tuttle, 1977.

Schaller, Michael. *The American Occupation of Japan: The Origins of the Cold War.* Oxford: Oxford University Press, 1985.

Scherer, F. M. *Industrial Market Structure and Economic Performance.* Chicago: Rand McNally, 1970.

Schumpeter, Joseph A. *Capitalism, Socialism, and Democracy.* New York: Harper & Brothers, 1942.

Seth, Ronald. *Secret Servants: A History of Japanese Espionage.* New York: Farrar, Straus and Cudahy, 1957.

Seward, Jack and Howard Van Zandt. *Japan: The Hungry Guest.* Tokyo: Yohan Publications, 1987.

Smith, Adam. *The Wealth of Nations, Books I–III.* London: Penguin Books, 1986.

Takahata, Seiichi. *Industrial Japan and Industrious Japanese.* Osaka: Nissho, 1968.

Tanaka, Kakuei. *Building a New Japan: A Plan for Remodeling the Japanese Archipelago.* Tokyo: Simul Press, 1973.

Tatewaki, Kazuo. *Banking and Finance in Japan.* London: Routledge, 1991.

Temple, Sir William. *Observations upon the United Provinces of the Netherlands.* London: A. Maxwell, 1673.

Textor, Robert B. *Failure in Japan.* New York: John Day, 1951.

Thurow, Lester. *Head to Head: The Coming Economic Battle Among Japan, Europe, and America.* New York: William Morrow, 1992.

Toland, John. *The Rising Sun: The Decline and Fall of the Japanese Empire.* New York: Random House, 1970.

Tolchin, Martin and Susan J. *Selling Our Security: The Erosion of America's Assets.* New York: Penguin Books, 1993.

Toyo Keizai Seikai Kancho Jinjiroku. Tokyo: Toyo Keizai, 1994.

U.S. Congress, Office of Technology Assessment. *Arming Our Allies:*

Cooperation and Competition in Defense Technology. Washington, D.C.: U.S. Government Printing Office, 1990.

————. *Holding the Edge: Maintaining the Defense Technology Base*. Washington, D.C.: U.S. Government Printing Office, 1989.

————. *Redesigning Defense: Planning the Transition to the Future U.S. Defense Industrial Base*. Washington, D.C.: U.S.Government Printing Office, 1991.

Van Wolferen, Karel. *The Enigma of Japanese Power*. New York: Alfred A. Knopf, 1989.

Vogel, Ezra F. *Comeback, Case by Case: Building the Resurgence of American Business*. Tokyo: Charles E. Tuttle, 1985.

————. Japan as Number One: Lessons for America. Tokyo: Charles E. Tuttle, 1980.

Wade, Robert. *Governing the Market: Economic Theory and the Role of Government in East Asian Industrialization*. Princeton: Princeton University Press, 1990.

Waldrop, M. Mitchell. *Complexity: The Emerging Science at the Edge of Order and Chaos*. New York: Simon & Schuster, 1992.

Yamamura, Kozo. *Economic Policy in Postwar Japan: Growth Versus Economic Democracy*. Berkeley: University of California Press, 1967.

Yoshino, Shinji. *Nihon Kogyo Seisaku*. Tokyo: Nihon Hyoron Sha, 1935.

Acknowledgments

In writing this book, I benefited greatly from the generosity of many people. In particular, I am indebted to James Fallows, Washington editor of the *Atlantic Monthly*. It was at his suggestion that I wrote this book, and he recommended several of my articles on Japanese economics for publication in the *Atlantic*. In his own writing, he masterfully demolished the Convergence Theory — the view long prevalent in the West that the Japanese were somehow destined to converge to Western social and economic values — and thus has opened the Western world to informed accounts of the Japanese economy.

I am also greatly indebted to Chalmers Johnson, the dean of American Japanologists, for particularly timely and gracious support. Others who provided vital inspiration and generous practical help included Clyde V. Prestowitz, Jr., and Leon Hollerman.

I am grateful for the insights of Karel van Wolferen, C. Tait Ratcliffe, Marie Anchordoguy, R. Taggart Murphy, John Stern, Rupert Wade, Steven R. Reed, and Ivan Hall. I also acknowledge the help of many people I cannot name, notably a government official in Washington who not only helped me identify the Japanese economic system's areas of monopolistic leadership but did me the great service of introducing the work of W. Brian Arthur.

The New York literary agent Joe Spieler showed great vision and resourcefulness in finding superb publishers for the book.

Houghton Mifflin's editor in chief, John Sterling, lived up to his reputation as one of New York's wisest and most effective editors. The final editing work was overseen smoothly by Rebecca Saikia-Wilson. Jane Manilych's detailed suggestions helped improve the explication. Luise Erdmann and Dorothy Henderson spotted solecisms and patiently handled last-minute amendments.

Paul Marsh, William Miller, and Mary Clemmey were highly professional in arranging for the book to be published in Europe and Japan.

Carol O'Brien of Simon & Schuster in London provided valuable advice that significantly improved the finished manuscript.

Jim Fallows, Clyde Prestowitz, Leon Hollerman, Karel van Wolferen, and Tagg Murphy made valuable comments on various sections of the book. Since Japanese economics is, however, a field noted for the degree to which even long-time observers sometimes differ in their perception of the facts, I alone take responsibility for the finished product.

Last, I must thank my wife, Yasuko Amako. She dug out important sources at the diet library in Tokyo, critiqued my ideas, and read successive drafts of the book. Most important, she coped with fortitude with the unexpected setbacks that await any writer rash enough to undertake to report intelligibly on Japanese finance.

Eamonn Fingleton
Shiba, Tokyo
November 1994

Index